D0445121

Conquering Learning Disabilities *At Any Age:*

How an ADHD/LD Kid
Graduated from Yale and Cambridge,
and Became a Marine Officer,
Military Historian,
Financial Advisor and Caring Father

By: Bryan Mark Rigg, PhD

Foreword by Dr. Edward M. "Ned" Hallowell,
author of *Driven to Distraction* and
Delivered from Distraction

Other Books by Bryan Mark Rigg, PhD:

Hitler's Jewish Soldiers: The Untold Story of Nazi Racial Laws and Men of Jewish Descent in the German Military

Rescued from the Reich: How One of Hitler's Soldiers Saved the Lubavitcher Rebbe

Lives of Hitler's Jewish Soldiers: Untold Tales of Men of Jewish Descent Who Fought for the Third Reich

The Rabbi Saved by Hitler's Soldiers: Rebbe Joseph Isaac Schneersohn and His Astonishing Rescue

Flamethrower: Iwo Jima Medal of Honor Recipient and U.S. Marine Woody Williams and His Controversial Award, Japan's Holocaust and the Pacific War

"What is hateful to you, do not do to others."
Hillel the Elder, a Jewish Sage[1]

"Don't forget to dance with those who brought you to the dance."
Southern Proverb

"It takes a village to raise a child."
Ancient African Proverb

Here I am at the ancient Mayan city of Tulum, Mexico, with my sons, Justin and Ian, and my daughter Sophia. I enjoy spending time with my children in places where they can learn about ancient cultures and participate in active learning and athletic activity. All very good for ADHD-types. March 2016

Marilee Gladys Rigg, née Davidson. This is a picture of my mother when she was 24-years-old in 1961. As a child, she struggled in school probably due to ADD and dyslexia. From her negative experiences in school, being called "stupid" by a school administrator when she was 10 years old, she wanted to help me when I started to also struggle in the classroom. She was a force of nature in finding me help with my ADHD and dyslexia when I was a child during a time when there were not many resources for families like mine in the world.

Dedication

THIS BOOK IS DEDICATED TO my children, Sophia, Justin and Ian. May they always love the genes they have, the zany humor they possess and the unique way they view the world. I love you all dearly and know you have made—and will continue to make—this world a better place.

This book is also dedicated to my mother, Marilee Rigg, who helped me more than anyone to *CONQUER* my LD!

For more information about this title or to order other books
and/or electronic media, contact the publisher:

Fidelis Historia, LLC
Dallas, TX 75254
www.BryanMarkRigg.com

ISBN:
978-1-7345341-7-7 (Hardcover)
978-1-7345341-8-4 (ebook)

Printed in the United States of America

Cover artwork: Dan Swanson and Shannon Christine
Interior design: Darlene Swanson • Van-garde Imagery

Neither the United States Marine Corps nor any
other component of the Department of Defense has
approved, endorsed, or authorized this book.

Disclaimer:
The advice I provide in this book about how one should live with ADHD/Dyslexia/
LD is drawn from my personal experiences and academic research and should not
be considered a substitute for medical advice from a qualified practitioner.

And concerning Learning Disabilities (LD), this book will primarily focus on the
LD categories defined as ADHD, dyslexia and speech impediments although I
know there are many more out there. There is only so much this book can cover
and indeed LD includes many other "afflictions" which I have been unable to
explore in the interest of time and research.

Table of Contents

Advance Praise for
Conquering Learning Disabilities

"I want you to read this book right up to the near finish, where he writes, 'In the end, to overcome LD/ADHD is to realize the greatness within you,' and learn about what he had to overcome and how he says he did it. Read this story and see the greatness unfold, page after page. Learn how so-called disabilities can turn into super-powers, with the right help and guidance, and with a deep connection to the people, ideas, and powers that catalyze greatness."

Dr. Edward M. "Ned" Hallowell, author of *Driven to Distraction* and *Delivered from Distraction* and Harvard University Medical Faculty

"This important, insightful and moving first-hand account of triumph over adversity will inspire and help many. It deserves a prominent place in every school and public library."

Susan Hauser, assistant dean, Yale College, 1973-1999

Bryan Rigg's *Conquering Learning Disabilities* is characteristically well researched, well documented and well written. Uncharacteristically, it is deeply personal as Rigg explores his life, his upbringing, his education, his failures, his successes, his setback, and his triumphs through the lens of his ADHD personality traits. As one who has shared this past quarter century with Bryan, I found his work deeply honest, emotionally powerful and intellectually insightful. He knows himself and shares that knowledge gracefully with others seeking to empower them to view what others perceive as disabilities as a source of strength and fuel for life's many struggles. A man of unique talent, committed to telling honest even if painful truths, he has turned these talents upon himself and the reader will be better informed, better guided and more determined than ever to confront the ways in which they learn and the ways in which they cannot learn. As one who wrestled with Learning Disabilities as did one of my children, I read this work with admiration and, above all, with gratitude.

Michael Berenbaum, Professor of Jewish Studies, American Jewish University. Deputy Director President's Commission on the Holocaust (1979–80), and Project Director (1988–93) and then Research Institute Director (1993-1997) of the U.S. Holocaust Memorial Museum.

Bryan's personal story is a testament to the magic that happens at the Starpoint School. His achievements are a testament to the life skills of caring, perseverance and initiative he learned at this school. He continues to embrace these life skills all throughout his life.

Kimberly Payne, Assistant Director and Teacher at The Starpoint School, Texas Christian University (1979-1981, 1996-Present)

Bryan Rigg's book *Conquering Learning Disabilities at Any Age* is a contribution to the field. Bryan is remarkable in his intellect, perseverance and goal-directed thinking. He found what worked for him as he dealt with his learning differences and has developed the habits that make his performance at his highest level. His accomplishments are outstanding. He shares his journey with the students (and their parents) who are looking for guidance in dealing with their learning differences. Though Bryan was able to use strenuous exercise to focus his attention, I have worked with students who could use this strategy and others though using every type of exercise and dietary plan, needed medication. Each person is unique and will have a different journey in dealing with challenges in learning and attention. Bryan's book is a wealth of strategies that will help all those who struggle with these challenges.

Joyce S. Pickering, SLP/CCC, CALT, QI, LDT, AMS-EC, HUM.D. Executive Director Emerita Shelton School & Evaluation Center, Dallas, TX

First Foreword:
By Dr. Edward M. "Ned" Hallowell
Author of *Driven to Distraction* and
Delivered from Distraction

IN ANSWER TO THE QUESTION "What do Riggs do?" Bryan Rigg taught his two little boys to reply, "Never give up." In answer to the question "What type of girl are you?" Bryan taught his little girl to say, "Strong and smart," which Bryan would follow with, "And what else?" Without missing a beat his daughter would reply, "Beautiful."

In this book you will learn that against enormous odds and obstacles of forbidding menace, Bryan indeed never did give up. You might even be able to discern why, as I believe I did, or you might not, because he gives you so many reasons it's difficult to settle on one or two. You will also learn that he was and is strong and smart, and is in his own masculine way—beautiful. You will read the fabulous story of a man who shot for the moon, and in one piece got there.

I didn't know anything about him until he set his sights on meeting me and didn't let up until we were sitting in my backyard on a sunny September Saturday in 2021. I had suggested we talk on the phone, but that's not Bryan's style, as I would come to understand. He does in person.

He wanted to meet me because I have ADHD and dyslexia, as does Bryan, and I've written some books about those conditions. He also is a graduate of the same high school I graduated from, Phillips Exeter Academy. A lover of slogans and aphorisms, he'd close his every email or text to me with Exeter's motto, *non sibi,* Latin for "*not for self.*"

When I met him at my front door, I was immediately struck by his size. I'd guess 6'4", maybe taller, and a trim, say, 240. Not much body fat, and you could tell that mattered to him. We shook hands, maybe embraced, I can't recall, but within minutes we were sitting at my picnic table under our sun umbrella while I was being regaled with stories from the life of Bryan.

How long does it take to tell a blowhard from a person who truly is larger than life? In person, I'd say seconds. That's why in person matters so much, as Bryan knew. It's too easy to fool someone in writing or over the phone, but it's much more difficult to fool someone, or at least fool me, in person. Within seconds I knew that this Bryan guy was the real deal, a true to life, undiluted, genuinely in love with serving human kind, heroic inspiration and model from whom we all could learn.

I want you to read this book right up to the near finish, where he writes, "In the end, to overcome LD/ADHD is to realize the greatness within you," and learn about what he had to overcome and how he says he did it.

As a child he was both physically and sexually abused. Those alone could finish off a life. The physical abuse took the form of spankings and paddlings, and given the Texas culture were not regarded as abuse. The sexual abuse came from a boy 10 years older than Bryan and did not happen once, but twice. But that's all it takes to cost a kid his innocence. And yet, from my reading of Bryan's story, he did not lose his innocence. He remained a person who always looked for, and usually found, the good in others, even when they mistreated him.

He was lucky in that he had a mother straight from heaven, a devoted, smart, loving mom who knew Bryan was smart, not in the conventional sense but in an even better sense, and did all she could to get him the help he needed.

He was also lucky in that his mom found Starpoint, a school that knew how to educate—in the true sense of that word, to lead out—different learners like Bryan. One of the teachers at that school, Mary Stewart, taught Bryan lessons on how to get on in life that have stayed with him to this day.

He learned not just how to work around what he was not good at, but far more significantly, how to exult in and make use of his unique special powers. This was a boy who became a man who could not let go of an idea once it took up residence in his mind, nor any more go with the flow than grow a tail. He made his own discoveries and didn't rest until he brought them forth to the world.

One of his most remarkable discoveries unfolds in his book *Hitler's Jewish Soldiers*. Although advised by some not to pursue such an unlikely if not disturbing topic, Rigg couldn't let go of it until he'd done his work with it. The resulting book received rave reviews, various honors, and praise from one of the Yale professors who tried to dissuade him from writing it.

The more he learned about ADHD, the more Bryan detected it in people throughout history. While neither historians nor psychiatrists are supposed to diagnose the dead, Bryan finds strong suggestions that Nietzsche may have had ADHD, as well as other figures he provocatively brings up. A true detective, he used his ADHD talents to find a relative he hadn't even known existed.

As you can see, Bryan ranges far and wide. We learn about his life as an officer in the Marines; as a soldier in the Israeli army; as a successful financial advisor; as a man who did his best in marriage, only to his regret see it end in divorce; and as a man who is a devoted father. In fact, I interviewed his son, Justin, for my podcast, *Dr. Hallowell's Wonderful World of Different*. An 11th-grader at Exeter, Justin is an outstanding young man who inherited his dad's ADHD and has learned how to thrive with it. Neither Bryan nor Justin used medication to deal with their ADHD. They succeeded by relying on diet, exercise, structure; finding outlets for their creativity and love of high stimulation; and treasured mentors like Mary Stewart.

Here I am with my friend, world-renowned ADHD-expert Dr. Edward "Ned" Hallowell. During this meeting at his home, we discussed ADHD, what it is and how it can be beneficial to people. Dr. Hallowell is one of my heroes, and through his centers and books, he helps make people aware of what ADHD is and how those with the condition can live productive lives. 11 September 2021.

I will end here, as I do want you to read the book now. But let me pick up one remark I made at the outset. I wrote that I believed I figured out why Bryan never gave up, and never gives up. He attributes his positive attitude and success to his mother, to the schools he attended, to the Marines, to his spiritual leanings, to his diet, to intense physical exercise, and to a work ethic that never lets up.

I'm sure all of those played major roles, but they can all be summed up under the heading of *connection*. Connection, almost always, is the force that drives resilience, and more than resilience, outrageous courage and large-scale daring. Bryan not only found people who wanted to connect with him, but he had a special capacity to connect back deeply, not just with people like his mom or Mary or professors at Yale, but also to connect passionately with ideas and with his own vision of greatness. It was Alfred North Whitehead who said, "There can be no moral education without an habitual vision of greatness."

Bryan Rigg's vision of greatness and his visceral connection to it, to the point of its being habitual, drove him to pursue it with every sinew and corpuscle of his being, with every drop of *Semper Fi* the Marines instilled, with every molecule of *I've-gotta-track-this-down* that investigating *Hitler's Jewish Soldiers* filled him with, with every heartbeat of devotion to his children that led him to teach them sayings on how to be a good and honorable person.

Read this story and see the greatness unfold, page after page. Learn how so-called disabilities can turn into superpowers, with the right help and guidance, and with a deep connection to the people, ideas, and powers that catalyze greatness.

Non sibi. Right back atcha, Bryan. *Non sibi.*

Dr. Edward M. "Ned" Hallowell

Harvard University, 27 December 2021

This picture was taken of me and my mother, Marilee Rigg, at her second wedding in the summer of 1992. The events so described in this book that chronicle my success throughout life could not have happened without this wonderful woman.

Second Foreword:
A Letter from Marilee Rigg, the Mother of Bryan Mark Rigg

Dear Readers,

I am writing to you as a reader of my son Bryan's work. I am so proud of Bryan and his passion to share with you his struggles and the wisdom he gained while *conquering learning disabilities*. While everything he said is true (honesty is one of his strengths), I am humbled by his appreciation for my role in his early success. You could read this and think that I didn't make mistakes while circumventing the perils of raising an ADHD-child (we called him "hyperactive" and "learning disabled" when he was a child). To you parents reading this, rest assured it was trial and error for me. There were days when I felt it was the proverbial one step forward and two back. There were many times when I thought that nothing I was doing was making a difference. What a heart-wrenching situation it is to see your precious child struggle to just be normal (i.e., like being able to read) and to think he possibly would not accomplish much in life. I welcome you into the growing community of parents who are navigating these waters. It's not easy and I assure you that while there are times you may feel at your wits' end, you will be successful in raising your child if you draw on patience, consistency and truly listen to your God-given gift: your ADHD/LD child.

Sincerely,

Mamma Rigg,

Arlington, Texas, April 2021

Mary Stewart and I are pictured at my home in Dallas before we attended a Starpoint School event in the summer of 2001.

Third Foreword:
A Letter from Mary Stewart, the Special Education Teacher of Bryan Mark Rigg

Dear Readers,

Bryan has honored me by asking me to write a few words about our time together when I was his teacher at Starpoint School at Texas Christian University. He has also honored me by continuing to include me in his life and endeavors. He has shared his successes and has spoken of the challenges as a child he had with learning differences (when he was a child, we unfortunately called them Learning Disabilities).

Even as a little boy, Bryan's tenacity was one of his tools. I fondly remember him marching into school each morning (after we had established that this was going to be a friendly and supporting place), and there he would go about his work with incredible energy. He so wanted to accomplish "good." That is perhaps my strongest compliment to any person. He just needed the tools to succeed. Bryan had a very supportive mother, and indeed we learned from her too. She had been trying to find a way to help her child who had so many learning differences. I believe this loving place was the right fit for Bryan. Along with methods and materials, the environment was positive and conducive to encourage children to embrace the "love of learning." This still fits with my way of thinking. Engagement in learning is essential. Active engagement is always seeking the key into the child's way of learning.

The entire environment in which Bryan found himself at Starpoint embraced differences, and was based on respect of those differences. We built on existing strengths, filled in gaps, worked on social skills, and made sure goals were attainable. These skills increased confidence and self-esteem.

Bryan's gaps were immense. He could not read or write at the age of eight, and was of course emotionally bruised by his previous experiences in school. We, my colleagues and I, knew the methods and materials to help such a child. Bryan responded to them well and had a good start. Through the years, he still had other challenges, but he met and overcame them with a lot of great teachers.

I love the enthusiasm of children. The way they think outside the box and are so pure in their thinking and expression. I still love the children who color outside the lines and say, "I am here!," "Watch me go!," and "Please, don't hold me back!" That is our Bryan.

In closing, I must extend a huge thank you to Kansas State Teacher's College and Kansas University for giving me the tools to help children like Bryan. And my wish for you, dear Reader, is that you come away with new tools to help yourself and others embrace their differences and develop new techniques in order to learn.

Sincerely, Mary Stewart

Fredonia, Kansas, August 2021

This Book at a Glance

"The mind is its own place, and in itself can make a Heaven of Hell, a Hell of Heaven."

John Milton, *Paradise Lost* [2]

IRONICALLY, THIS BOOK HAS TAKEN me 20 years to write. I say it's ironic because it explores my struggles to confront and overcome my Attention Deficit Hyperactivity Disorder (ADHD), dyslexia and related Learning Disabilities (LD).[3] As I look back, however, I am glad I took the time I did to write this manuscript because I probably needed those two decades to fully understand how to successfully deal with these "disorders." To help the reader from the outset get a feel for what I have written, I think it is important to outline the book's organization.

The Introduction introduces the concepts of ADHD/LD and why it is important to explore them. It teases the reader with some of my biographical information to give one a feel for why I wrote this book and it foreshadows how I explore LD-issues in later chapters.

Chapters 1 and 2 present a working theory of the history of ADHD/dyslexia/LD. It is important to know where these conditions came from and why we have them. Knowing about our evolutionary background helps us understand ADHD/dyslexia as age-old gene expressions that determined how we processed information and behaved so as to ensure the survival of the bipedal species that eventually became *Homo sapiens*. ADHD/dyslexic-genes are built on millions of years of evolution that helped us survive in the wild and gather our food as Hunters, which allowed us in turn to pass on our DNA. Knowing the historical and scientific background of ADHD/dyslexia will empower people affected by these conditions to think of themselves as unique and not defective.

Chapters 3-5 journals my personal history and struggles with ADHD, dyslexia and a speech impediment.[4] I explore childhood stories illustrating my battles with these conditions to help you understand what it was like for me and my family to deal with my "afflictions." I share an experience of sexual abuse as well, which may have heightened my ADHD-symptoms.

Chapter 6 dissects how a diet that sought to eliminate artificial additives from all meals, called The Feingold Diet, changed my life. Although drugs were prescribed for me, they were the wrong choice for my brain chemistry. In radically changing my *entire* environment feeding me only natural foods, my family—namely, my wonderful mother—helped me gain control over my ADHD and live a healthier life. ADHD-medications can indeed help people with the condition, however, my family did not choose medication for many reasons especially since my mother found that it could affect my physical growth and that it made me behave strangely. Moreover, she wanted to empower me to control my condition naturally without pills if other natural alternatives could be utilized.

Chapter 7 chronicles the school Starpoint that put me on track and helped me learn how to learn. By reviewing Starpoint's pedagogic techniques, I hope to give both families and teachers interesting lessons in teaching ADHD/LD-children.

Chapter 8 examines how my life improved as I mastered new learning techniques and gained confidence at Starpoint. It also reviews how my ADHD actually helped me succeed in school and on the athletic field. It evaluates the learning environments that laid the foundation for my scholastic success; namely, caring teachers and small, individualized classes.

Chapter 9 reviews how active ADHD/LD-children's imaginations are, and consequently, how these children may be harmed when they are raised in a religious environment that focuses on fear, shame and guilt. Just as families fight hard to find the right school for their LD-children, they must also find a religious setting that focuses on positive aspects of God, not hellfire and damnation for sins that many religious denominations stress. The more an ADHD-child can experience freedom to explore who they are, and not worry about the fear of the Almighty sending them to Hell for their sins, the more they can flourish as human beings. In this vein, when a religious environment teaches a child about Hell, Satan and eternal damnation, it is perpetuating a culture of "child abuse."[5] We need to shun institutions that teach such theology, especially when raising our ADHD/LD-children. If God is part of your world, then make sure a child embraces the positive attributes of an Almighty that focuses on love, charity, tolerance and acceptance.

Chapters 10 and 11 explore details in my life that allowed me to analyze my ADHD/LD more accurately. These chapters further investigate how ADHD/LD can help one become unique and strong.

Chapter 12 scrutinizes my ADHD as I confronted divorce. Relationships for ADHD/LD-people are more complicated than for the average person. My journey through marriage, divorce and then recovery will hopefully give people in general, and ADHD-types in particular, some guidelines on how to keep their relationships healthy. I also review suggestions for ADHD-people if divorce becomes inevitable.

Chapter 13 explores how my ADHD helped me as a historian to research and write my three historical books and this memoir. Each one of my historical projects encountered opposition due to my presentation of a truth about an event that debunked established historical claims. And sometimes I faced opposition because I was simply too "truthful." Dr. Edward M. "Ned" Hallowell, a leading expert on ADHD and longtime faculty member at the Harvard Medical School, claims that ADHD-types are often agents of change who see things differently, and quite often, more clearly than others might.[6] I would like to think the groundbreaking research I accomplished about World War II and the Holocaust, and my discussion of living successfully with ADHD in this volume qualify me as an ADHD-agent of change. My ADHD enabled me to consider new angles and threads in my historical research, which in the end *always* revealed unknown facts that were eventually endorsed by leading scholars in the field. I have received feedback, also, from early reviewers of *Conquering Learning Disabilities* that this book presents important facts and new insights supported by my personal experiences about how to handle ADHD/LD-issues. My ADHD-brain helped me navigate these adventures in chaos and ultimately produce valuable works of scholarship.

Chapter 14 analyzes how my ADHD-brain enabled me to hyper-focus on creative ways to adapt and improvise to take care of my family when I lost my job with a large Wall Street firm. I also explore how this experience pushed me to start my business, yet another ADHD-like trait.

Chapter 15 explores an interesting foundation for a case study of an ADHD-person who used his skills for evil. When doing research on Nazi Germany, I met with the world-renowned Yale University psychiatrist Dr. Fritz Redlich who had done a medical study on Adolf Hitler. In the course of his research, he concluded that Hitler had ADHD and that he used it for evil. Of course, Hitler had many mental problems, but the fact that he had ADHD-issues, which apparently did not get dealt with properly, reveals some interesting lessons for one who studies ADHD.

Chapter 16 explores a unique event in my life: While at Yale, I discovered a lost relative. My ADHD's curiosity and ability to see unique patterns in life allowed me to find this person who became one of my closest relatives, my Aunt Mary.

Chapter 17 explores how I was able to use my skills to save a man's life. Although thousands of people worldwide save lives daily, I believe my ADHD allowed me to act quickly and competently in order to rescue this man from death with only minutes to spare.

Chapter 18 reviews the philosophies and success strategies that my battles with ADHD/LD have taught me and that I put into practice every day of my life.

The Conclusion re-examines many issues I have mentioned throughout the book and provides some new analysis. Moreover, this chapter reviews the lessons and support that are vital for ADHD/LD-people to make their lives healthier.

Before I end this introduction, I offer these admissions. Two of my ADHD-symptoms are reflected in the pages of this book. First, in writing this book, I hyper-focus on the inclusion of supportive evidence for claims and conclusions. I wanted not only to provide information that will benefit those interested in ADHD, but I also wanted to provide the academic support behind it. Often, when I read motivational books and/or ADHD-manuscripts, I find them full of trite phraseology, lacking in source material. In contrast, I have tried to give meaningful advice citing credible doctors, philosophers, dieticians, academics and psychiatrists. So, do not let the hundreds of endnotes, bibliographic entries, or numerous citations to authorities overwhelm you. Many will, of course, not feel this way, but for those who do, please just take the time and re-read what is here if something seems to be confusing or too in-depth.

Secondly, my ADHD-symptoms show up when I repeat my conclusions. Sometimes, I do this subconsciously, but other times, I do it consciously to ram home important points. So, please be patient and look for the underlying message throughout the manuscript. And that message is my hope that this book will help ADHD/LD-people feel better about themselves, their potential and their brains, so they can become more successful than they might otherwise have been.

Furthermore, I also want to help those who are teaching, or raising, ADHD/LD-children. It is not easy for teachers, parents or other caregivers to learn new techniques to help the ADHD/LD-people in their lives live more successfully, but I hope this book gives such people new insights into what can be done for the charges in their care. In part, I managed to overcome my ADHD, dyslexia and speech impediment on my own, due to my initiative in responding to the cards I was dealt. But I also benefitted from *proper guidance* that helped me discover new ways to manage my ADHD and dyslexia and to eradicate my speech impediment. If I can benefit from having an ADHD/dyslexic-brain and find ways to control it, anybody can do so, providing they develop the right mindset, nurtured through the education and support they receive. In that process, I believe that those who care for us will benefit just as much from the lessons within this book. In other words, this book is not simply my ADHD/LD-story; it's your story and educators' and caregivers' too! With this in mind, at the conclusion of most chapters, I provide several takeaways you can apply in your life or the lives of those in your care. This will be coupled with suggested action steps you might want to consider in order to help you and others cope with your concerns more effectively from day to day. So, in conclusion, thank you for picking up this book. I hope you find it entertaining and educational.

INTRODUCTION:
Emerging from the Darkness

"Deep into that darkness peering, long I stood there, wondering, fearing, Doubting, dreaming dreams no mortal ever dared to dream before."

— Edgar Allan Poe, "The Raven"[7]

I AM A PhD WITH ADHD, dyslexia and a speech impediment. Odds were greatly stacked against me ever achieving an advanced degree. In fact, statistics would have forecasted the opposite, predicting many like me would drop out of high school. As I get older, I believe that my "learning disabilities," ironically, helped me achieve great things. I share my journey in the hopes of encouraging others to find their way through the darkness of ADHD/dyslexia and build a personal framework for success. I hope my story will inspire people with learning disabilities to embrace their dreams, even if such dreams are ones no "mortal dared to dream before."[8]

A "learning disability" like mine affects about 10% of US citizens (some statistics put it as high as 20%).[9] Experts claim that the majority of the US prison population has ADHD.[10] Renowned ADHD-expert, Dr. Hallowell, writes that our prisons "are full of people with undiagnosed ADHD."[11] It is frequently found "among manic-depressives, sociopaths, violent people, drug abusers, and alcoholics."[12] When I read that, I shake my head. Are they really talking about me? The more I learn about ADHD, the more I wonder how I have gotten to where I am today. Many reasons I am not behind bars stem from the love and training I received as a child. Some experts say that for a child to succeed in life, he needs just one person to believe in him.[13] Well, I was lucky to have more than one, and each in their own ways taught me how to handle my condition. Although this book is part autobiographical, it also is about my supporters, mentors, coaches and teachers, and the enduring lessons about self-confidence and learning they taught that anyone can use, especially ADHD/LD-types.

I had the good fortune of having these people believe in me and only now do I realize the impact of their guidance. I have not been in prison partly because of information my mother read after meeting with an LD-expert, Dr. Stephen Maddox, at the Fort Worth Child Study Center in the 1970s. He warned that criminal activity often tempted boys like me. It didn't help to assuage her worries when he also told her I probably would drop out of school by eighth-grade. However, and ironically, this also gave her a sense of urgency to find me help quickly. My mother, Marilee Rigg, née Davidson, and my grandmother, Edna Davidson, née Barby, worked hard to get me support after hearing such predictions. Perhaps my mother sometimes secretly wished she could have put me in prison, but I have made it safely to the shores of adulthood and graduated not only from junior high, but also high school and beyond.

My mother was, of course, particularly happy when I received my PhD from Cambridge University in 2002. In England, and especially at Cambridge, the graduations are steeped in tradition and pageantry. Dressed in my cap and white tie, I looked like Harry Potter. The leadership of Darwin, my residential college, brought us into the Senate House's large viewing room, built like an ancient Greek temple. It was an intimidating ceremony, but also delightfully exciting because I knew I was following in the footsteps of famous graduates like Isaac Newton, Oliver Cromwell, Alexander Pope, John Milton, Charles Darwin, Maynard

Keynes, Bertrand Russell, J. Robert Oppenheimer, Salman Rushdie, Stephen Hawking and many more. We lined up in different groups while we waited to step up before Vice-Chancellor Sir Alec Broers. He sat in a large chair in the center and the graduates knelt before him and received his blessing. He conducted the whole ceremony in Latin.

University of Cambridge

My PhD graduation at Cambridge University's Senate House, 2 February 2002. Here, I am kneeling before Vice-Chancellor Sir Alex Broers while he declared in Latin that I was now a "Doctor of Philosophy." This ceremony was full of pomp and circumstance. We were told beforehand that we were carrying on a rich legacy of academic excellence, following in the footsteps of Isaac Newton, Charles Darwin, Bertrand Russell, Stephen Hawking, among others. My ADHD helped me perform well at Cambridge, inspiring me to think out of the box about historical issues.

When my turn came, I felt my heart pound. As the vice-chancellor cupped my praying hands, he announced, "In the name of the Father, Son, and Holy Ghost, I declare you a Doctor of Philosophy (*Auctoritate mihi commissa admitto te ad gradum Doctor Philosophiae, in nomine Patris et Filii et Spiritus Sancti*)." I glanced up at my mother in the viewing stands. She wiped her wet eyes with a handkerchief. Later, while walking in the courtyard outside the Senate House on the grass, which as a PhD holder I could now do, I asked, "Mom, why were you crying?" I expected her to reply, "I'm so proud of you." Instead, she said, "I can't believe this is happening. I just hoped you'd get out of junior college."[14] She later explained, "I was so shocked, Son, at your graduation because I just didn't think you were that smart as a child."[15]

I hope that by sharing my journey of struggles and triumphs, some of my ADHD/dyslexic-"cousins" might benefit from it, rather than travel down the road that, according to some experts, leads to destruction for many. Throughout this book, I will often use the analogy of a "Hunter" used by Dr. Thom Hartmann to describe an ADHD-person. Researchers stress that ADHD-people often express the traits of a "Hunter" versus a "Farmer" (non-ADHD-types).[16] Consequently, Dr. Hartmann uses Hunter to describe the behavior and learning abilities of those with ADHD. Because this Hunter/Farmer concept will be explored more later, I wanted to introduce these terms now so you know why I am using them throughout the text.

I have put my story down in print since I have often heard from friends, family and colleagues that it gives hope to parents of children with ADHD/dyslexia, people with learning "disability" (LD)-issues and teachers of children with learning differences. While reading this volume, continually remind yourself that we know little about the brain and its evolution. By the time this book goes to print, I'm sure there will be more breakthroughs in neuroscience, but we still have much more to learn than we have ever discovered. American author Herman Melville, who probably suffered from learning disabilities, wrote about how little we know about things in general, and his observations in 1850 are as true now as they were then:

Methinks we have hugely mistaken this matter of Life and Death. Methinks that what they call my shadow here on earth is my true substance. Methinks that in looking at things spiritual, we are too much like oysters observing the sun through the water, and thinking that thick water the thinnest of air. Methinks my body is but the less of my better being.[17]

And German philosopher Friedrich Nietzsche, another complicated thinker who probably had ADHD himself, echoed Melville when he wrote in 1873:

What, indeed, does man know of himself! Can he even once perceive himself completely, laid out as if in an illuminated glass case? Does not nature keep much the most from him, even about his body, to spellbind and confine him in a proud, deceptive consciousness, far from the coils of the intestines, the quick current fibers?[18]

In other words, we must maintain a humble mind, knowing that the beginning of wisdom is in realizing that we cannot know everything. We can know more than yesterday, but we must also realize that what we know is quite small in relationship to what is yet to be known. In exploring the mind and how we process data, we are still learning how best to learn. We are far from knowing completely how we can increase our capacity to obtain and retain information. Looking at LD currently might really be like looking at the sun as an oyster through the water. We need to be able to see the sun without a refractory medium. We need to learn as much of the truth as we can, embracing both how we can be "spellbound" and able to gain new knowledge concurrently. In other words, by studying about those who struggle the most in learning, we might improve the process of learning for everyone. And in the end, although there are some universal truths about the brain and how we learn, we must also realize, to quote Dr. Hallowell, that "No brain is the same. No brain is the best. Each brain must find its own special way."[19]

In this book, I argue that if I could succeed at some of the best universities in the world, many others also can, with the right mindset, support system and discipline. Of course, for some others, that "right mindset" might not take you necessarily on a journey to excellent universities as it did for me, but hopefully it will take you on a path of more success and fulfillment. Furthermore, most ADHD-people have more potential to succeed than the average person, if only they are not demoralized by the time they reach teenagerhood. Thinking differently than the average person is to be welcomed, because it helps one cogitate about things in unique ways. And thinking differently can be a formidable tool in solving problems, in dealing with people and in learning. Ultimately, I hope every ADHD-person and every parent or teacher of an ADHD-child who reads this book is empowered by it, knowing the unique potential this condition confers. In the end, success or failure all depends on how one looks at oneself. As Michelangelo said, "The greater danger for most of us lies not in setting our aim too high and falling short; but in setting our aim too low, and achieving our mark."[20]

Now, why and when did I start writing this book? Well, from 2002 through 2021, when lecturing about my history books, I started my talks by describing my humble beginnings. As a successful financial advisor and owner of my own firm, a former professor, a Marine officer and a Yale and Cambridge graduate, I felt the need to let people know about my troubled youth to add balance to what seems on the surface a privileged life.

Before my lectures, when the person introducing me mentions my accomplishments, I feel uncomfortable because I know some in the audience must be thinking, "Oh great, we have an arrogant, privileged guy who's going to talk down to us," or "This guy probably comes from a rich family, so what can he possibly tell us about our condition?" Consequently, I then mention that I failed first-grade twice, had learning problems, struggled with school and wasn't expected to graduate high school. Surprised by this beginning, the audience often laughs. They become comfortable with me. I am a human being with faults.

When I discuss these personal issues, many tell me I have touched them. Countless parents and grandparents have explained that I have given them hope for their children or grandchildren. Several have asked me to meet their families and explain the techniques that helped me. And numerous people, whether directly connected to an ADHD/dyslexic-child or not, have encouraged me to write my story to help others. So here it is. I hope this book will help other ADHD/dyslexic-people achieve a better life by learning from my experience and hopefully educate those without these issues not to "react harshly to those with the disorder[s]."[21] Moreover, I also wrote it to give those teachers and parents who focus on kids like me proof that they are healing souls and shaping the next generation, and to show how they may do so more effectively.

I have been on this earth for five decades, and feel I am only now understanding how life works, so I sometimes question whether I can truly offer anyone a good road map. Given the feedback from countless people, my insights have helped those with ADHD. As Henry David Thoreau, the American naturalist and philosopher, wrote, "I should not talk so much about myself if there were anybody else whom I knew as well."[22] I know what helped me achieve my dreams and this book may help others do the same. I suggest answers to frequent questions and options for difficult problems by telling an interesting story, providing some inspiration and giving some examples of what can be done. I do not want this book to mirror other "self-improvement books" that "are narcotics in ink... They obtund with false promise" and are full of "platitudes."[23] I give examples of techniques and tactics of diet, behavior and psychology that helped me succeed. It is certainly not meant to be a panacea for all, but I fervently hope my example will help others.

I am alarmed by the growing number of LD-children in America. Figures are difficult to come by because there is not a universal way to define the conditions that make up LD or a central location for data that is collected on learning disabilities, but at nearly every venue where I have spoken, numerous attendees tell me about their children, grandchildren or friends' children who are LD. It affects many families, like an unknown virus. The number of LD-children in the US ranges between 5 and 20 million, depending on how one defines learning disabled. In 2002, over 6 million children "with disabilities" had received "special education and related services." By 2019, that number had grown to 7.1 million. According to ADHD-expert Dr. Hallowell, between 5% and 10% of Americans have ADHD. Out of a total U.S. population of around 350 million in 2020, 17 to 35 million people could be affected with various forms of ADHD.[24] Yet, some experts have claimed that only around 15% have been diagnosed. As Dr. Hallowell claims, "The relative paucity of professionals who know how to diagnose ADHD...skews the numbers [of those with ADHD]."[25] According to another ADHD-specialist, Dr. Hartmann, around 10% of the world's children have ADHD, and in the U.S., between 10% and 20% of our children are classified as hyperactive.[26]

My three children have LD-issues, indicating a strong genetic component to this condition, especially since my ex-wife, the mother of my children, has a brother and grandmother who are severely dyslexic.[27] All my children have attended a special education school in Dallas, the Shelton School, to help them cope with their unique ways of dealing with the world. During the process of helping my daughter, Sophia, we found many experts willing to say she had LD, but most did not clarify her type of LD. During the process, my daughter felt insecure and confused by the countless counseling sessions and tests she underwent. When she was five years old, as we searched for a school for her, she felt scared by the ordeal. One school told us, "We don't know what your child needs, but we don't have it." It probably did not help that she had crawled under the desk and licked the principal's leg during her interview. Throughout this process of finding a school for her, we drove by the local junior high building one day and my daughter looked at her mother in the rear-view mirror and asked, "Mommy, maybe that school will take me?" My ex-wife broke into tears. Luckily, though, we found Shelton, one of the premier schools in the U.S. for LD, and it helped Sophia a lot, even though we disagreed with their promotion of drugs over a change of lifestyle to deal with learning disabilities. I empathized with my daughter because I also remembered the countless doctors and therapists my mother took me to when trying to ascertain what troubled me. So, I know all too well, both as a person who grew up with LD and as a parent dealing with LD-children, how this condition can affect a family.

In the end, our society must change how we deal with ADHD/dyslexic-people because our communities have not corrected the "problem." James M. Kauffman, a University of Virginia professor of curriculum and special education, wrote the following:

> I am not very happy with most of what I see in our field today [when studying LD/ADHD]. I think we are in a period of considerable upset and danger, and our future could look rather bleak depending on how we respond to current pressures.[28]

The LD-problem of children today is diagnosed more readily than in decades past, but the solutions are inconsistent. From my studies and personal experience, I believe that attitude, diet, exercise and avoiding drugs provide some of the most important keys to solving LD-problems.[29] Many may say, "This is self-evident." Well, if it is, then why are we having so many problems?

Every school, for example, should have a mandatory one hour of recess daily instead of the current three a week for a few minutes (although this varies by school district and by state). Exercise is proven to help hyperactive kids live "normal" lives. I think our society struggles with ADHD/dyslexic-problems because we understand so little about positive mind conditioning, good eating habits and effective physical training. I also believe that taking personal responsibility instead of expecting a school, or doctor, or drug to cure the problem is a major key to living with LD.

I have called this book *Conquering Learning Disabilities* to encourage those with LD to develop the motivation and staying power to conquer their problems. Remember the four *D*'s of life: Dedication, Determination, Discipline and Desire. We know people can get motivated quickly to do things, especially when in danger, but may have trouble when doing so requires incremental and methodical personal changes. This is especially the case with ADHD/dyslexic-people. Psychiatrists are calling ADHD "one of the major causes of school, work and relationship problems in our society."[30] This disorder affects millions who take drugs to "function" in society.[31] Most fail at doing their best to fight their problem and realize their dreams. Many have goals, but few take the steps necessary to achieve them.

I do not want to give false hope that people in general, and those with ADHD/dyslexia in particular, can achieve everything they want. A mature person will realize their limitations. I understand I cannot become a computer programmer or nuclear scientist, because I do not have the abilities, interest or training for those fields—I acknowledge my limitations. One should not desire what is unobtainable or undesirable. The ancient Greeks knew this, and wrote on the portal to the Oracle of Delphi, "Know thyself" (γνῶθι σεαυτόν).[32] Saying it another way, German philosopher Nietzsche said, "He, however, has discovered himself who says, 'This is my good and evil.'"[33] Knowing yourself and capabilities liberates you not by giving you more opportunities, but by giving you a clear indication of what is possible for your life. Nonetheless, the majority of people, especially those with ADHD, live below their potential and that is where motivation comes into play, because only motivation will help you realize your real potential. This is often difficult for ADHD-people since society gives them so much negative feedback and because motivation centers in the brain are affected by ADHD and people with the condition can often feel easily overwhelmed. So learn how best to filter the feedback you get and how you turn on and off your motivation centers in accomplishing daily tasks.

Many have dreams, but most have difficulty realizing them due to poor planning or insurmountable obstacles getting in their way. People rarely say, "I'm living the life of my dreams!," or, "I'm doing my best to accomplish my dreams." The great unknown is motivation, yet I feel that motivation, more than anything else, saved me when struggling with learning difficulties. This is key for an ADHD-person since he or she must be strongly determined to work twice as hard as others at ordinary tasks to master them. It was, and still is, the motivation to accomplish more than is expected of me that drives my soul. And it is my willingness to be motivated by those who deeply care about me that fills my sails with wind.

I did not want to be "learning disabled" (who does?), but I am a much richer person because of it. It motivated me to struggle for everything I attained. As a result, I learned that determination and drive are often what brings intelligence and ability to light. To be correctly motivated, you must first accept your condition and make it your asset instead of your crutch. I tried to instill this in my daughter by often asking her when she was young, "What type of girl are you?" She had been taught to reply, "Strong and smart." I then would ask her, "And what else?" And without hesitation, she would reply, "Beautiful." I wanted her to feel secure in the knowledge that although different, she is unique and full of rich potential.

With my two boys, I also encouraged them, asking, "What do Riggs do?" They were taught to reply, "Never give up." I also would ask them, "What is our creed?" They would then echo the Marine Corps and military service academies' code of conduct, replying, "I will not lie, cheat, steal or tolerate those who do." When putting my children to bed when they were young, I often used the youth creed of the Unitarian/Universalist church of which my family are members, "May your thoughts be wise, may your lips speak truth, may your heart know love and may the work of your hands be blessed all the days of your life." All these creeds, pledges and directives imparted to my children were designed to build moral integrity and self-esteem, a universal quest for everyone that should be especially reinforced with LD-kids.

To realize your potential, you must accept your chemical makeup determined by your genes and the environment that surrounds you. My ADHD did not occur in a bubble and many factors caused it. For a long time, I fought against my identity, but now I embrace my being and do my best to learn how I can do what I put my mind to. I learned to use what I have and not dwell on what I don't. But I have learned to find out for myself what I don't have instead of listening to those who don't know my capabilities, and who think they can tell me what I cannot do. ADHD-expert Dr. Hallowell eloquently states: "Ask for and heed advice from people you trust---and ignore, as best you can, the dream-breakers and finger-waggers."[34] In the end, I hope everyone who reads this book comes to view ADHD/LD in a new, and more positive light.

Takeaways

- If I could succeed at some of the best universities in the world, most anyone can, with the right mindset. Of course, that "mindset" might not take you necessarily on a journey to excellent universities like me, but hopefully it will take you on a path of success. I hope this book will help ADHD/LD-people feel better about themselves, their potential and their brains so they can become more successful than they might otherwise have been.

- The number of LD-children in the U.S. ranges between five and 20 million, depending on how one defines "learning disabled." Our society as a whole must change how we deal with ADHD/ dyslexic-people, because our communities have not corrected the "problem."

- Motivation more than anything else saved me when struggling with learning difficulties. To realize your potential, you must accept your genetic makeup and the environment that surrounds you.

Action Steps

- Read the book. I would encourage you to read it from cover to cover to understand how the lessons therein came from my journey.

- ADHD/LD-types sometimes like to skip around books, and although most of my chapters can stand alone, I would encourage everyone, ADHD/LD and non-ADHD/LD-types, to explore the lessons of this work by reading the chapters chronologically.

The ancient Greeks knew how important it was to know your strengths and weaknesses and be honest about them. They wrote on the portal to the Oracle of Delphi, "Know thyself" (γνῶθι σεαυτόν), a place where Greeks often went for religious worship and self-exploration. ADHD-people need to explore this statement activity and learn how their LD can help them be better people. Photo Credit: AncientGreece.org

Chapter 1:
What Exactly Is ADHD?

I felt a Cleaving in my Mind—
As if my Brain had split—
I tried to match it—Seam by Seam—
But could not make them fit.
The thought behind, I strove to join
Unto the thought before—
But Sequence ravelled out of Sound—
Like Balls—upon the floor.

— Emily Dickinson (1864)[35]

ALTHOUGH DICKINSON WAS NOT WRITING directly about ADHD, her poem aptly describes the condition. Dr. Hallowell wrote, "Dickinson captures with her customary startling simplicity the distress of the ADD mind."[36] He explained that Dickinson's images of the brain splitting and of the thought unravelling are hallmarks of the ADHD-brain.[37] Even though we know much more about the condition now than in 1864, we still have a long way to go until we understand fully what ADHD is and why humans have it. Nonetheless, what we now know gives us a launching pad to reach new levels of understanding as researchers study the ADHD-brain.

Understanding ADHD
Let's review what experts say that ADHD is before examining the historical roots of the "affliction." Dr. Hallowell says that having ADHD "is like being supercharged all the time. I tell kids it's like

having a race-car brain. Your brain goes faster than the average brain. Your trouble is putting on the brakes."[38] Some argue that ADHD, with the word "hyperactivity" inserted, is true ADD (Attention Deficit Disorder). Others say that ADHD is most commonly seen in children, but once grown, they lose their hyperactivity and just become ADD.[39] ADHD-expert Russell Barkley says that this condition is not really a disorder about not paying attention, "but one of self-regulation: how the self comes to manage itself within the larger realm of social behavior." He also calls it a "developmental disorder of self-control" stemming from "an imperfection in the brain" and adds that it is "a failure to regulate one's behavior with an eye toward the future."[40] However, some psychologists advise us to regard his insights with caution.[41] I especially don't like Barkley's term "imperfection," and prefer to describe the ADHD-brain as "different" or "adaptive to high adrenaline environments," which will be explored momentarily.

So, ADHD is a neurological "disorder" that expresses itself in people who are inattentive, hyperactive or impulsive more frequently than "normal" people. It is accompanied by "emotional immaturity, aggressiveness and poor academic performance."[42] The psychiatric profession classifies ADHD "as a mental illness."[43] However, "illness" is defined by the Oxford dictionary as a "sickness" that afflicts one for a period of time. Other medical professionals call it a "psychiatric disease."[44] The Oxford dictionary defines a "disease" as an "illness that causes part of the body to stop functioning correctly." People with ADHD are not sick or afflicted by a "disease" or "illness," and they really cannot "heal" from it if it is *their natural state*. Most often this condition occurs in childhood, although some data show that 60% of those affected with ADHD as children still have symptoms as adults.[45] Boys are six to nine times more susceptible to it than girls. According to Hallowell, recent research, however, has identified

ADD, without hyperactivity as a major indicator, more often among women. And according to his findings, the ratio between boys and girls is closer to 3 to 1.[46]

Ironically, the man who coined the term "learning disabilities," Dr. Samuel Kirk, hated such labels, but "then proceeded to introduce a term that has become, by far, the most frequently used label in special education."[47] Yet, he had an important observation about LD, or any label, especially with respect to children. He wrote,

> I have felt for some time labels we give children are satisfying to us, but of little help to the child himself. We seem to be satisfied if we can give a technical name to a condition. This gives us the satisfaction of closure.[48]

Yet, as Kirk admitted, this process, which is still used today, does little to encourage or motivate the children, or even adults, who have this condition.

What does it tell us about a person ("the expert") who sits around studying defects in others who by his very judgments is claiming that he is normal? This reminds me of Edward Bulwer-Lytton, the English novelist, who wrote, "He fancies himself enlightened, because he sees the deficiencies of others; he is ignorant, because he has never reflected on his own." I would argue that no one is completely normal. We all learn differently. To claim that someone is defective because of how they learn limits that person. Yes, maybe there are challenges when a child learns in ways that are not the standard for most children, but it does not mean that the child is defective, just different. This difference must be encouraged, not smothered. A few LD-experts redefine the problems of using such negative labels in more current terms thusly:

> Postmodernism views disability primarily as a social construction that is based on incorrect immoral assumptions

about difference. Although the notion of a disability is not totally rejected, most postmodernists believe that disability exists more in the perceptions of the beholder than in the bodies of the beheld.[49]

Dr. Tom Lovitt described the origins of LD during a conference on this "disorder" when he said,

> I believe that if we continue trying to define learning disabilities by using ill-defined concepts, we will forever be frustrated, for it is an [elusive] concept. We are being bamboozled. It is as though someone started a great hoax by inventing the term and then tempting others to define it. And lo and behold, scores of task forces and others have taken the bait.[50]

In other words, ADHD should be classified as a "normal variant of temperament."[51]

Some scientists believe "gene abnormalities" cause ADHD. I would argue that they are not "abnormalities," but survival genes. A gene "is defined as any portion of chromosomal material that potentially lasts for enough generations to serve as a unit of natural selection," ensuring survival.[52] Furthermore, "genes exert ultimate power over behavior," according to Oxford University evolutionary biologist Richard Dawkins, and since ADHD describes how one certainly behaves differently than the majority of society, this behavior must be determined, in part, by genes.[53] The ADHD-gene, the "Hunter-gene" if you will, allowed one to live in the wild and hunt and gather food. It ensured gene expression of such populations got passed to the next generation because they were able to survive and reproduce. As paleontologist at the London Natural History Museum Chris Stringer wrote, "DNA does provide a basic template for our behavior."[54] Yet, even though some studies report 95% of the ADHD-cases examined reveal a genetic factor, the "environmental contribution" is thought also to be "considerable."[55] But if people respond a certain way to environmental inputs, then these responses must be in the genes as well, and thus one could argue that that is also an expression of ADHD-genes.[56]

Stringer describes this phenomenon when he wrote, "DNA is more like a flexible container than a mold in the way it determines and sets limits on how we behave," and one might add, respond to environmental inputs.[57] Several studies suggest a list of environmental factors that can cause or exacerbate ADHD, including "lack of oxygen at birth; or from head injury; or if your mother drank too much alcohol during pregnancy; or from elevated lead levels; perhaps from food allergies and environmental or chemical sensitivities; from too much television, video games, and the like..."[58]

On the point about lead levels, for decades cars burned leaded gasoline that emitted tremendous amounts of lead into the air and affected Americans' blood lead levels. Since we transferred to unleaded gasoline, we have decreased the lead levels in our blood, but one wonders how much damage was done to generations born during the 1960s, 1970s and 1980s when lead emissions were high. Lead in gasoline was just one example of many factors in our environment that affect humans.[59] When you ingest something, it hits "your body's greatest exposure to the outside world;" namely, the lining of your intestines.[60] If you could spread this visceral lining out, let's say like a net, it would cover more than 2,000 square feet.[61] That surface area, the floor "of an average house," can collect a lot of ingredients and expose your soft tissues and blood to many things.[62] So, parents, be mindful of what you are putting in and around your and your children's bodies. Our bodies will give substances ingested and breathed a lot of attention, and if they are toxic or synthetic, they can cause ADHD!

Dr. Benjamin Feingold, who is a renowned allergist and pioneer in the field of immunology, documented many chemicals as "predisposing factors," meaning that only when the child came into "contact with the artificial additives" would Feingold observe a change in the child's behavior for the negative.[63] My research indicates that the most often overlooked "environmental contributions" are diet and chemicals which we are exposed to daily. Scientists who study the factors affecting personality generally consider the effects of genetic and environmental factors to be about 50/50 depending on the situation.

So, since ADHD is due to genes and environment, it is a natural condition of humans. It is a misunderstanding to say that it is a disorder. I do not have a disorder. I am just a human, and if everyone were closely analyzed, we would find that we all have some type of "disorder," whether it be poor coordination, bad eyesight, neuroticism or a "learning disability." I like how Dr. Hallowell describes it:

> I don't like the term "attention deficit disorder," although it sure beats its predecessor, minimal brain dysfunction... It is an imperfect label for several reasons. The syndrome is not one of attention deficit but of attention inconsistency; most of us with ADD can in fact hyperfocus at times... Finally the word "disorder" puts the syndrome entirely in the domain of pathology, where it should not entirely be. Although ADD can generate a host of problems, there are also advantages to having it... such as high energy, intuitiveness, creativity, and enthusiasm, and they are completely overlooked by the "disorder" model. The disorder didn't keep me from becoming a doctor, and it hasn't kept many others from far greater success in a wide variety of fields.[64]

Today, ADHD also includes ADD which, according to the diagnostic manual of mental problems, "technically does not exist." By the time this book is published, the term may change again, since the medical community continuously revises the definition.[65] Dr. Hallowell writes, "Most people, even now, don't understand the power, magnitude, and complexity of [ADHD]."[66] In the end, I find the ADHD-terminology demeaning and not helpful in solving the problem. For now, it is the universal way people refer to the condition, and basically means ADHD-brains operate differently compared to those of the majority of people. So, ADHD will be used throughout this book to describe the condition I have and what people can do to deal with it.

Takeaways

- There are lots of theories about what causes ADHD. It can happen in a variety of ways—genetics, lack of oxygen at birth, a head injury, elevated lead levels, food allergies, ingesting toxic or synthetic chemicals, environmental or chemical sensitivity, or too much television or video games.

- ADHD is the clinical term used for the condition and will be used throughout the text although it is not accurate in how it describes the condition.

Action Steps

- Although ADHD is the dominant term, people so affected by it need to look at it as something powerful and unique to them as people.

CHAPTER 2:
ADHD's History and Origins: Exploring Hunters and Farmers

"In the beginning...God created man in his own image, in the image of God he created him."

Genesis 1:27[67]

Note to Religious Readers: Throughout the next sections, I use science to describe the origins of humankind and ADHD/dyslexia. The facts will go against some people's religious teachings. Often religious instruction supports the Creationists' myths about our origins (God made everything in six days),[68] and that the world is 6,000 years old.[69] Science shows this to be untrue. I like what my Phillips Exeter Academy biology teacher, Andrew Polychronis, who was also a Christian minister, said: "The Bible isn't a science book. It reveals things God has done. God made the world. Science is just trying to tell us how He did so. So, no one should be scared by evolution."[70] However, I am not so naïve not to know that this section may make some uncomfortable. I would challenge those who feel this way to think about why God would allow the evidence to be placed in earth's crust that verifies the world has been around for 4.5 billion years and life for 3.5 billion years if it were untrue. If these timelines trouble you, I encourage you to explore them with your minister and or in prayer and ask why you find them disturbing. Moreover, if you are really curious, go to your local natural history museum and talk to staff members about how we can know the earth and life are both so ancient. As one of our founding fathers, Thomas Jefferson, said, "There is not a truth existing which I fear...or would wish unknown to the whole world."[71]

So where does ADHD come from? Why does it exist? Can it be useful? Well, the answer to the last question is that, of course, it can be useful. Where the condition comes from and why it is here are more difficult to answer.

ADHD-Hunters Compared to Non-ADHD-Farmers

ADHD-expert Dr. Hartmann has a useful explanation. He admits that we truly do not know where ADHD originates, but he uses the following paradigm to help us understand this condition historically and conceptually. He simply describes society as neatly split between two groups of mindsets, the Hunters and the Farmers.[72] Dr. Hallowell agrees with Hartmann that this analogy is quite accurate in understanding ADHD.[73]

According to his theory, ADHD is a condition that was "once a useful adaptation but that's maladaptive in modern society (much like sickle cell trait which protects against malaria in Africa but is a liability in malaria-free America)."[74] It is also like the condition of morning sickness, which happens at the beginning of pregnancy when a baby's nervous system and organs are forming. "Among our hunter/gatherer ancestors, morning sickness encouraged pregnant women to eat only those meals they already knew to be safe, and to avoid experimenting with foods which may contain toxins dangerous to the fetus."[75] Thus, such an evolutionary trait helped prevent birth defects and it is "still anchored in our genetic material."[76] And this genetic ADHD-material is an "evolutionary mismatch" with the "current environmental demands" of a Farmer-society.[77]

Those with ADHD have traits that once ensured survival in harsh environments and nomadic cultures. ADHD-people were

Hunters and their behavior was normal, even advantageous, in their surroundings, which required people to move in small bands, "hunting, fishing and foraging for food."[78] Since today ADHD affects a minority, it sets them apart because of their behavior. Although perfectly normal, those affected with such "disorders" are viewed as defective. When this happens, especially early in school, the psychological damage is devastating. If a child gets labeled a troublemaker, or as stupid and useless, he or she will often fulfill those expectations. And if one matches such negative opinions to his life, especially as a child, then he will get caught in a psychological prison where escape becomes difficult—in the world of psychology, this phenomenon is called the Rosenthal or The Pygmalion Effect.[79] The Hindu Saint, Sri Ramakrishna Paramahamsa, once declared that if one only thinks of his "sins, then [he is] a sinner."[80]

Russell Barkley, an ADHD-expert, said ADHD is a "problem," which can cause certain neuroses.[81] I would counter Barkley's claim with, "Is it a problem for the ADHD-person or for the majority of society that is uneducated about how ADHD-people operate?" Moreover, if the "experts" would tell people ADHD-types just have an ancient form of the *Homo sapiens*' brain originally designed to help humankind survive in the wild, maybe this would be a better way of describing it, rather than as "a problem." ADHD-people need to think of themselves not as "sinners," but as evolutionarily unique beings.

For the vast majority of time *Homo sapiens* have lived on earth, they were Hunters, and this ADHD-brain helped them survive. More importantly, it was a byproduct of *natural selection*. Charles Darwin explained in *On the Origin of Species* that "nature favors those best equipped to survive and to reproduce their characteristics by genetic transmission."[82] ADHD-Hunter types were best suited to survive in the wild until mankind started building cities and cultivating farms, and thus changing our way of life and the genetic structures transmitted within populations. Until we had city-states (relatively recent in humankind's existence), the ADHD-behavioral patterns of searching out high-adrenaline activity like hunting, running, and exploring "contributed to the fitness of humans and their reproductive success."[83] Moreover, Hunter-societies also helped *natural selection* along in creating stronger populations by killing infants deemed inferior (i.e., the physically deformed or mentally handicapped). According to some research, ancient Hunter-parents practiced this "family planning" by killing around 7% of unwanted offspring.[84] Although this infanticide sounds immoral today, Hunter-communities could not afford to be handicapped in a harsh world by such members.

So, ADHD is a leftover trait that ensured human survival thanks to the presence of hyperactive, energetic, aggressive, somewhat wild people who were good problem solvers. As the University of Utah anthropologist Henry Harpending said, "The [ADHD] mutation predisposes one to be more active, more demanding, and not such a pleasant person…[and one who] probably does better in a context of aggressive competition." Another way of putting it, citing Harpending's research, "[I]n lean times, violent men may feast while passive men starve."[85] Edgar Allan Poe could have been describing ADHD-types when he wrote,

> I am the descendant of a race whose imaginative and easily excitable temperament has at all times rendered them remarkable; and, in my earliest infancy, I gave evidence of having fully inherited the family character…I grew self-willed, addicted to the wildest caprices, and a prey to the most ungovernable passions…I was left to the guidance of my own will, and became, in all but name, the master of my own actions.[86]

The tendencies described by Harpending and Poe are reflected in the three components that set Hunters apart from Farmers. They are "distractibility, impulsivity, and risk-taking/restlessness."[87] Why do Hunters have such characteristics? Many argue their brains cannot focus on a single task or scene for very long. Many claim ADHD-people have a problem paying attention to anything. In reality the contrary is true: The dilemma is that they *pay attention to everything*.[88] "Attention Deficit," the AD in ADHD, is a misnomer for people classified as such.[89]

For a Hunter, scanning is important. He wants to make sure he does not miss signs that might lead to his next meal, and he wants to be certain that he will not become some other animal's buffet. In other words, the "mental state of constant scanning" is an advantage when a "flash of motion on the periphery of his vision might be either the rabbit that he needed for lunch, or the tiger or bear hoping to make lunch of him."[90] Professor Dawkins further describes this reality:

> In the fierce competition for scarce resources. In the relentless struggle to eat other survival machines, and to avoid being eaten, there must have been a premium on central coordination rather than anarchy within the communal body.[91]

This "coordination" of ADHD-genes also made for the "ability to build efficient survival machines—*bodies*" that were strong, athletic and full of sensory receptors (eyes, nose, hands and ears—seeing, smelling, touching and hearing).[92] In this respect, Dawkins seems to be describing ADHD-Hunter-types' genes "cooperating" by creating good eyesight (especially binocular and color vision), good scanning abilities, good physical strength, and good adrenaline highs, all being desirable traits for this form of *Homo sapiens* to survive in their environments.[93] The ability not only to be able to pay attention to everything in one's environment and process all inputs, but also to want to do so, were desirable traits for an ADHD-person to have in order to survive. His genes had to work together to accomplish this concentration. This heightened sense of awareness ADHD-people have, built on millions of years of evolution, was vividly described by Poe when he wrote, "The disease had sharpened my senses—not destroyed—not dulled them. Above all was the sense of hearing acute. I heard all things in the heaven and in the earth, I heard many things in hell."[94] If Poe was indeed describing the ADHD-brain, he was right to illustrate that ADHD-Hunters are constantly absorbing all elements in their vicinity.

When I was young, I enjoyed hunting on my father's small ranch outside of Lake Texoma, Texas, or on my mother's family ranch in Beaver, Oklahoma. I was good at it and enjoyed running around outside to hunt birds, snakes and rodents. It came naturally to me, so Hunter-characteristics fit me perfectly. When I was in the Israeli Army and the Marine Corps, my Hunter-traits became more evident, as I enjoyed the discipline of learning about war and leadership in martial environments. Moreover, I was also one of the best at land navigation and performed well at the tests they gave us for reading land formations and finding the shortest route between two points, an important attribute for a Hunter-warrior.

Farmers, the majority of society, on the other hand, have evolved to plant seeds, take care of a plot of land, grow fruits and vegetables, tend crops and harvest them. The Farmer-lifestyle depends on predictability and repetition, which a Hunter finds unexciting and spirit-crushing. A Hunter needs the stimulation of the hunt and the knowledge that no two excursions mirror one another. He requires high-intensity, high-risk activities to keep him satisfied with his existence.[95] Such activities motivate him to go out in the forest or jungle and kill animals to eat. As Dr. Hallowell notes, "'[A] restive search for high stimulation' is perhaps the most destructive of the behaviors associated with ADHD in contemporary society."[96] Yes, it is the attraction to danger that helps ADHD-people focus. "They will drive 100 mph in order to think clearly, for example."[97] And this thirst for danger, in ancient days, ensured people got fed from hunting in the wild, which oftentimes was indeed dangerous and required incredible "drive."

Farmers, on the other hand, do not like surprises such as storms, insects or drought. They avoid high stimulation activities, especially since they can "lead to starvation." Dr. Hartmann noted, "Because decisions made by farmers have such long-ranging consequences, their brains must be wired to avoid risks and carefully determine the most risk-free way of doing anything."[98] If a Farmer decided to grow roses instead of corn, it could "lead to tragic dietary problems for the tribe or family."[99]

In war, Hunters take risks and undertake extraordinary missions, even ones that will put them in danger. It is the Hunter-commander who gets noticed. World War II commander General George S. Patton is thought to have exemplified an ADHD-Hunter, while General of the Army Dwight D. Eisenhower epitomized the non-ADHD-Farmer. Patton was the impulsive renegade and rebel commander leading from the front, whereas Eisenhower was the methodical and calm planner leading from the rear. It is not surprising that Eisenhower rose higher in rank and responsibility than Patton, while Patton was more colorful and exciting. No one makes blockbuster movies about Eisenhower, but they sure do about Patton.[100] They were the archetypal examples of their communities. Eisenhower exhibited the traits of a good Farmer: "self-control, dignity, foresight; being patient creator and builder," whereas Patton exhibited the good traits of a Hunter: "embodying the core virtues of masculinity—courage, honor, mastery, and strength."[101]

Even though Hunters were superior warriors, ultimately Farmers came to dominate and/or displace them. "Fewer than 10 percent of hunting society members will normally survive when their culture collides with an agricultural society. And it has nothing to do with hunters' 'attention deficits,' or with any inherent superiority of the farmers," according to Dr. Hartmann. It happens because farming supports larger communities than hunting.[102]

The same acreage of hunting land needed to support 100 people could be used to support 1,000 when farmed, so Farming-communities were superior in growing their populations compared to Hunter-societies.[103] Using evolutionary biological terms, Professor Dawkins writes,

> Natural selection favors genes that control their survival machines in such a way that they make the best use of their environment. This includes making the best use of other survival machines, both of the same and of different species [i.e. Farmers' ability to dominate Hunters and farm animals]."[104]

If a Hunting-nation goes to war with a Farming-nation, the numerical odds disfavor the Hunters. A military truism states that to succeed in the attack, you must have a 3 to 1 superiority in numbers.[105] If the numbers increase to 10 to 1, as Dr. Hartmann claimed was the ratio of Farmer- to Hunter-communities, then almost any group with the inferior numbers will fail in war.[106] Napoleon once said, "God is on the side of the big battalions."[107] And since Farmer-societies were better at organizing large groups to farm, they also were able to organize them for war, and thus these "coalitions of warriors would have been advantageous for group defense and offense," something small, tribal/Hunter-societies were unable to do.[108] Farming-communities can also build food stores to go on protracted campaign while Hunter-communities are less successful in this endeavor. Even without a campaign, the fruits of a Hunter's labors, unlike Farmers' provisions, are less likely to be stored for long periods, leaving Hunters more open to starvation than Farmers.

This Hunter/Farmer conflict is addressed early in our literary tradition, starting with the saga of Cain and Abel in the Book of Genesis: Cain, the Farmer, was the father of cities, and Abel, the Herder (*aka* Hunter), was the father of the hunter-shepherd tradition (Genesis 4:2-17).[109] Herders first had to catch, or hunt, the animals they wanted, in order to domesticate them. This activity would have required one to be a superior hunter in order to catch the animals in the first place, and then smart enough to develop the science of husbandry to control and breed them. Abel would have had to spend countless nights in the wild, finding and navigating new hunting grounds or better pastures. To grow crops, Cain would have had to learn the science of agriculture. He would have had to invent tools to farm with and build structures to store his produce (the beginning of cities). When these men offered up offerings of their respective foods (meat versus plants), it seems God favored Abel's offering over that of Cain's because Abel's piety seemed more genuine (he gave his best compared to Cain's substandard offering), creating jealousy in Cain against his brother, leading to fratricide (Genesis 2:5-6).[110] The Farmer Cain would eventually slaughter his brother, the Hunter Abel (Genesis 2:8).[111] Of course, this story was a mythical, archetypal tale designed to illustrate how sibling rivalry and conflict are a key part of human existence. Indeed, enmity between brothers and kinsmen is underscored in subsequent biblical tales. But the underlying theme in this text was the knowledge that the authors knew the difference between Farmers and Hunters, and how the Farmer-culture, in the end, gets the upper hand against the Hunter-culture.

Although Cain "wins" by destroying his brother, Abel nonetheless was still the favored one in this tale, and his Hunter-lifestyle has proven to be, during the long cycle of evolution, the healthier of the two communities. Anthropological studies cited by award-winning journalist James Nestor have found that when we were Hunters/

Gatherers, we had straight teeth, "expansive sinus cavities" and "enormous forward-facing jaws."[112] Ancient man's skulls show strong evidence that Hunters "very likely never snored or had sleep apnea or sinusitis or many other chronic respiratory problems that affect modern populations."[113] Hunting and gathering food required more chewing when eating wild game or vegetables/fruits/nuts, thus creating stronger jaws and teeth. When we humans started growing our food and then preparing it, most often making it mushy in soups or gruel, this in turn, created smaller mouths, weaker bones and crooked teeth. Humans now, largely living in Farmer-societies, "have misaligned jaws, overbites, underbites, and snaggled teeth, a condition formally called malocclusion."[114] So while growing our food created more of it, it did not necessarily help us develop optimally healthy skulls, teeth and respiratory systems. This dysevolution shows that farming was not conducive to overall health, and, in part, explains why we humans, in general, are "breathing so poorly."[115] Also, plant-based food increased the intake of sugars, rotting our teeth faster.

Moreover, sociologist Emile Durkheim's and philosopher Alain de Botton's research indicate that Farmer-city-states have higher rates of suicide than when people lived in the wild and had more social interaction with one another in Hunter-tribes.[116] And last, it seems Hunter-societies did a better job of maintaining monogamous relationships and strong family ties, whereas Farmer-societies create behavior one could construe as destructive like wide-spread adultery and polygamy.[117]

And it is just not misaligned jaws, poor dental health, higher-suicide rates and destructive family values for which Farmers are responsible. Farmers, although having better immunity to diseases than Hunters, were, in part, also responsible for creating those diseases *in the first place*, especially chicken pox, influenza and measles due to exposure to farm animals where these diseases originated. In other words, many "human diseases were created by proximity to animals."[118] Historian Roy Porter writes,

> Cattle provided the pathogen pool with tuberculosis and viral poxes like smallpox. Pigs and ducks gave humans their influenzas, while horses brought rhinoviruses and hence the common cold. Measles, which still kills tens of thousands of children yearly, is the result of rinderpest (canine distemper) jumping between dogs or cattle and humans.[119]

Agricultural life also seems to have brought on cancers and Alzheimer's.[120] So, in short, Farming-communities are indeed more efficient in creating large amounts of food to support larger populations than Hunter-communities, but they have, in many respects, not helped with making human societies healthier.

Consequently, most Native North Americans and many South Americans (Hunters) died by the millions when exposed to such diseases for the first time through their contact with European explorers and conquerors who came from Farmer-societies. (Although full of nomadic tribes, Central and South America also had their own Farmer-like city-states, including those of the Mayans, Incas and Aztecs among others). Hernan Cortés (1485-1547) and his 600-man army defeated the Aztecs, not through their superior military ability, but due to the smallpox virus they carried, which killed more than half of the Aztec nation of over one million. In this case, living in a dense city-state did not help the Aztecs when exposed to this disease. This event showed one farming community having better immunity than another.

But back in North America, some historians believe that many Indian "Hunter"-tribes "suffered a 90% to 95% population loss within the first century of European[-Farmer] contact." So, when the Hunters encountered pestilence, they died just by the "exposure to the farmers' diseases."[121] In other words, Farmers evolved to better combat disease alien to Hunter-societies. In this respect, farming life is not necessarily good for the betterment of humankind as a whole because it appears that it started most of the diseases we now must fight. Yes, farming increased our population, enabled cities and civilization, created better immunities, and allowed for organized war, but one has to ask whether it has ultimately increased our quality of life with the diseases that can, and have, ravaged mankind like the Spanish Flu epidemic of 1918-1919 or the Covid-19 pandemic from 2020-2021.

Farming-societies provide for larger populations ultimately because the major survival need for food was met. They thus had more stable environments for diverse education, enabling a society to develop technologically, allowing specialized jobs to evolve, such as architects, teachers, ironsmiths and generals. The surplus that farming produced also allowed the development of other professions like draftsmen, tradesmen, soldiers, priests and rulers. A hierarchy was formed not seen in the egalitarian Hunter-society, where a less formal leader, such as a tribal chief, led followers. A Hunter-society usually stays simplistic technologically as well. Since it is on the move, its people do not accumulate many material possessions like Farming-communities and cities (ironically, Cain's name means "possession" and suggests the negative character traits of covetousness and greed). Hunters have to be more in tune with nature to secure food and survive. In the end, the Farmer-cultures throughout history that had better technology came to subjugate Hunter-cultures.[122]

Evolution and ADHD: The History of the Hunter

It is important to know history because it helps us understand our current state. Moreover, it shows us also how to improve our future. The more we understand the history of how ADHD-traits could enter into human genes, the more ADHD-types can feel empowered about who they are and live stronger lives. As a result, it is valuable to do an overview of evolution to analyze how we possibly got to where we are today with ADHD-types and non-ADHD-types besides exploring the Hunter/Farmer dichotomy. The theories below for ADHD-genes might help us better understand why we have ADHD. As the Age of Enlightenment philosopher Baruch Spinoza explained,

> Since nothing happens or can happen contrary to nature, it follows that our judgements of good and bad, better and worse, are always expressions of our knowledge of "the laws and rules of nature."[123]

So, to understand ADHD's "laws and rules," an exploration of how we got here as *Homo sapiens* is necessary. Although, according to Professor Stringer, "there is no single 'right' answer to the question of our behavioral origins,"[124] one can draw conclusions from the data to support that ADHD is part of the *genome* of *Homo sapiens* today; namely, because millions of years of evolution programmed it into us.

For six million years, bipeds (of the hominin line) like us were largely Hunters/Scavengers, and then, around 10,000 years ago, many of our ancestors started to farm. Modern man, *Homo sapiens*, has been around for about 200,000 years.[125] So for the first 190,000 years, the Hunter-brain ensured survival. Due to natural selection, those Hunter-genes got passed down into subsequent populations until we started to grow food, and when this happened, Farmer-genes got transmitted into new populations. Professor Stringer writes that "about 7% of human genes seem to have mutated recently in some populations…particularly within the last 10,000 years."[126] Professor Dawkins explains that specie-populations continue to evolve to create new species "from within."[127] This is what happened with Farmers arising out of Hunter-populations, and these Farmers were more sexually successful in passing on their genes into larger populations. So, using Dawkins' scientific research, Hunter-populations started to be replaced by Farmer-ones 10 millennia ago, and when this happened, the gene-pool of those populations changed, *and new behaviors evolved.* As Stringer wrote, "[T]he fact that farming also entailed self-induced changes in societies, diets, and environments...would have ensured that selection remained a powerful force *for evolutionary change* [author's italics]."[128]

This changing of populations has been a constant during evolution since cells started replicating and creating life.[129] It has always been going on and continues to do so. To illustrate how powerful natural selection is and how ADHD is just one trait out of millions that evolved to ensure life continued on, especially Hunter-life, let's go back into ancient history to give us more food for thought. Although the "fossil record of humans is still very patchy,"[130] I hope my very high-level overview of the march of life below gives a better understanding of how ADHD might have arisen in our genes.

Evolutionary ADHD-Hunter-Genes Timeline

The earliest known "chordate," or vertebrate, is a two-inch organism known as *Pikaia gracilens*, which existed 500 million years ago. One could call "her" the original "Eve" since she gave birth to every organism that has had a vertebra or that has one today, from dinosaurs to mammoths, dogs and humans. Harvard University paleontologist Stephen Jay Gould writes that had *Pikaia* not survived during evolution, then *Homo sapiens*, and all other vertebrates, would have been "wiped out of future history."[131] So, we are alive today because *Pikaia* was able to pass on her genes that created lifeforms with spines. As of this writing, there are 1.3 million species with spines on earth with *Pikaia* being their original grandmother. And having a spine makes an organism more robust and able to hunt. Obviously, spines help farmers too, but our Hunter-ancestors have been on this earth for hundreds of millions of years, whereas our Farmer-ancestors have only been on this earth for 10,000, and that is important to contemplate. The majority of our ancestors were Hunters/Gatherers whose spines developed in response to their need to hunt or scavenge for food.

After *Pikaia*, it would take hundreds of millions of years for something remarkable to happen for humans to become what they are currently. Possibly around 4.5 million years ago (maybe as recent as a million years ago—dating is difficult to do), when our ancestors were perhaps like *Ardipithecus ramidus* or turning into *Australopithecus afarensis* (i.e. like the famous fossil specimen called "Lucy"), chromosome 2 and 3 fused in a group of bipedal species that eventually became *Homo sapiens* (hominin ancestors had been using 48 chromosomes for 50 million years until this mutation-fusion).[132] That is why humans now have 46 chromosomes (we now inherit 23 from each parent instead of 24) and apes, monkeys and lemurs (chimpanzees, baboons, gorillas, etc.) still have 48.[133] We were not created with 46 chromosomes, but rather, we evolved to have 46 chromosomes through *a mutation*! As Professor Dawkins wrote, "Evolution requires genetic change, mutation."[134] Under the microscope, one can see the distorted, mangle if you will, blending of these chromosomes, and according to some evolutionary biologists/geneticists, this is what made humankind different from other primates. This new population of bipeds with 46 chromosomes continued to pass on this chromosomal-blend, creating a different population from within an already existing one. This mutation made us, in part, superior to other bipedal species in intelligence, and in something else, "our capacity for endurance running," which made us *superior Hunters, aka* ADHD-like.[135] Of course, "what triggered the evolution of modern humans in Africa, and why this happened at all, is still uncertain."[136] However, I believe, this chromosome-fusion was one key of unlocking the mystery. Think about this—for 400 million years leading to this fusion, we had "a more-or-less horizontal backbone and walked on four legs." Then, "suddenly," at this time, we started to walk "on our hind legs," allowing us to hunt better by moving faster and more efficiently.[137] This fusion definitely made us different, and possibly provides the reason why we became excellent Hunters using two legs instead of four.

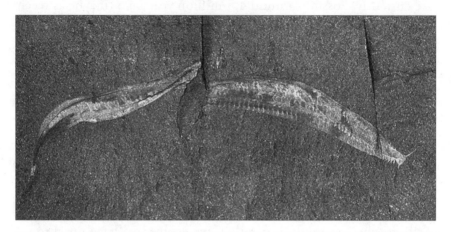

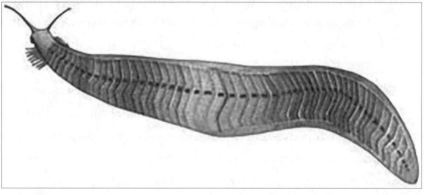

Pikaia is one of the most ancient life forms of the phylum *Chordata* which belongs to the group of all animals with spinal cords and backbones. One could argue that this was the original "Eve" because according to Harvard University paleontologist Stephen Jay Gould, without *Pikaia*, all known vertebrates known to us today would have never have evolved. *Pikaia* was most likely a scavenger, a primitive form of being a Hunter and having a spine helped it in this activity. This drawing, based on fossil records, was done by Mary Parrish from the Smithsonian Institution. Artwork displayed in the Burke Museum, Seattle, Washington/Fossil Image from the Smithsonian

These facts remind me of a conversation I had with my orthopedic surgeon when I was in the Marine Corps. On learning I had a L5/S1 herniated disc (the last disc in the spine) and needed surgery, I asked Dr. Brian Mason at the Bethesda National Naval Medical Center why I had this problem. He replied:

> Unfortunately, our spines are still made for us to be on all fours. The spine has not really evolved to handle us walking on two legs. This, in part, is why you have a herniated disc where you have it. However, I'm still glad our ancestors started walking on two legs because this makes life in many other respects easier. We just need to be mindful of our limitations so we can do our best from preventing back problems, like you're currently experiencing, by knowing we actually have a weak link there.[138]

To quote Darwin, my back problems showed that "even the most highly evolved of us will continue to carry '*the indelible stamp of [our] lowly origin* [author's italics].'"[139]

Besides the changes that helped us walk on two legs possibly over 4 million years ago, more modifications in our ancestors' makeup would help us to be more efficient Hunters. Conceivably around 1.9 million years ago, members of our grandfather species, *Homo erectus*, lost their penis bones, while other primates, like chimpanzees, kept theirs.[140] Why did this happen? One theory claims it was because our female populations bred it out of us. A male with a penis bone could have a healthy heart, or could have an unhealthy one, and still get an erection. Females at this time developed the ability to pick a male without penis bones and mated only with those who could, obviously, still get an erection, proving they were also healthy and likely to be around longer and in a fitter condition to protect them once the baby was born. Erectile dysfunction is a telltale sign of health issues. So, having a good circulatory system made a male more attractive,

and these non-penis-bone genes got transmitted into future generations.[141] How did our ancient grandmothers do this? Well, according
to Dawkins,

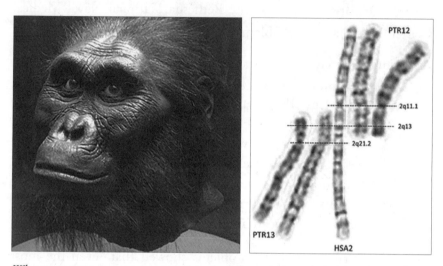

When our ancestors were transitioning from being *Ardipithecus ramidus* to
Australopithecus (i.e. like the famous fossil specimen called "Lucy") over 3 million
years ago, many think we started to walk upright and on two legs. This made us
superior hunters by allowing us to move around more efficiently and faster. This
study believes one of the reasons for this evolution was due to chromosome 2 and
3 fusing in the hominid species during this time that would eventually give birth
to *Homo sapiens* making us have 46 chromosomes (we now inherit 23 from each
parent instead of 24). Apes, monkeys and lemurs still have 48 chromosomes. This
study also believes this fusion had an impact on humans becoming far superi-
or in intelligence than our cousins who remained chimpanzees, baboons, gorillas,
etc.; consequently, this increase of intelligence helped us become better Hunters/
Gatherers, the way our ancient ancestors procured food from their environment.
To help the reader understand the image of the chromosomes here, *Molecular
Cytogenetics* states the following: "[This image shows the] comparison of the band
pattern in human chromosome 2 (HSA2) and chromosomes 12 and 13 of the
chimpanzee (PTR12 and PTR13, respectively). 2q21; 2q13; 2q11.1 are the regions
in our chromosome 2 that, in the fusion area, correspond to chromosomes 12
and 13 of the chimpanzee." The University of Tennessee, McClung Museum of
Natural History & Culture, Knoxville, Tennessee/ BBVA Openmind/ *Molecular
Cytogenetics*

[These women] too were under selection, in their case not
to lose bone but to gain judgement. And don't forget, the
female is exposed to the very same penis when it is not
erect, and the contrast is extremely striking. Bone cannot detumesce (though admittedly they can be retracted).
Perhaps it is the impressive double life of the penis that
guarantees the authenticity of the hydraulic advertisement
[of having a healthy heart].[142]

When women made these mating selections, they increased their offspring's strength, making tougher Hunters by ensuring stronger circulatory systems were passed to subsequent generations. And since Hunters
then were most likely ADHD, these women made sure that ADHD-
traits also got passed down to later generations in stronger numbers.

And yet another theory about the penis bones states that males
lost them when monogamy emerged "as the dominant reproductive
strategy... In monogamous relationships, the male does not need to
spend a long time penetrating the female, because she is not likely
to be leapt upon by other amorous males."[143] One could argue here
again that this sexual strategy provided Hunters a better, faster and
more efficient way to reproduce ensuring that their breeding group
was more successful in passing on their genes than others that have
long since died out.

Then around 500,000 years ago, our ancestors, now called *Homo
heidelbergensis* (evolving from *Homo erectus*), possibly the last evolutionary stage before *Homo sapiens*, developed sophisticated tools,
like flint hand axes, spears and traps. From archeological evidence,
they were "highly capable hunters" killing and butchering horse, red
deer, elephant and rhino.[144] "They could secure the carcasses of large
mammals for the extraction of the maximum nutritional benefit in a
landscape populated by dangerous competitors such as lions, wolves,
and large hyenas."[145] Our Hunter-ancestors had to have the intelli-

gence, strength, willingness, and fearlessness to go hunt and kill elephants and rhinoceroses while also being hunted by lions and wolves themselves—very ADHD-like. Modern elephants can weigh between 6,000 and 12,000 pounds and can run 25 miles per hour and rhinos can weigh between 2,500 and 5,000 pounds and run over 30 miles per hour. Male Olympic sprinters can approach 23 miles per hour running a very short distance, so we are indeed, on average, slower than elephants and rhinos. These aggressive animals are known to gore or trample people who threaten them. Engaging in hunting and being hunted provided the high-adrenaline activity ADHD-types crave and need to *survive* and feel *alive*. And adding to the evidence that *Homo sapiens* improved upon *Homo heidelbergensis*' hunting techniques, our recent ancestors 160,000 years ago developed techniques and tools to hunt one of the deadliest mammals, the hippopotamus. This animal today weighs in between 2,700 and 3,000 pounds and can run 30 miles per hour.[146] By this time, our brain cavities had grown bigger, and according to Professor Stringer, "such size was necessary…if hunting hippos was on the agenda. Even today these temperamental beasts are reputed to be the highest cause of human deaths among all of Africa's mammal fauna [500 deaths annually]."[147] Clearly, our Hunter-ADHD-evolutionary capabilities were growing in tenacity and skills during the march of time ensuring the perpetuation of the ADHD-Hunter-*Homo sapiens* species.

And our evolutionary history also helps answer the question of why men are, in general, bigger than women. As men continued to specialize in hunting, and women in child rearing and food preparation, male *Homo sapiens* became bigger than female *Homo sapiens* as a result of the activities required for them to survive and sexually reproduce.[148] So, one telltale sign of a Hunter-culture, besides being dominated by ADHD, is that the males are bigger than the females. At least this is the case when the males do the hunting—

one only wonders if we would have ended up with the majority of our womenfolk today being Amazons if they had been the Hunters. Interestingly, Neanderthal women and men hunted together, and thus they showed "low levels of sexual dimorphism---that is, males and females were nearly equal size."[149] And here is one reason why *Homo sapien*-Hunters probably survived when their Neanderthal cousins did not; namely, the *Homo sapien*-Hunters *wisely* did not put their "reproductive core—women and children"—at risk on hunts![150] This is one explanation why *Homo sapiens* were superior survivors.

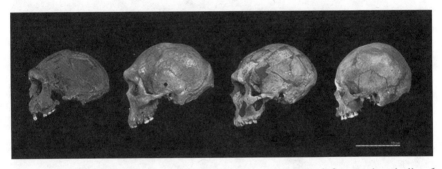

As the Natural History Museum in London writes: "From left to right: skulls of *Homo erectus* [1.9 million years ago], *Homo heidelbergensis* [500,000 years ago], *Homo neanderthalensis* [430,000 years ago] and *Homo sapiens* [200,000 years ago]. The braincase of *Homo erectus* was more elongated than that of later humans. It had a prominent brow ridge, like *Homo heidelbergensis*." All these forms of hominids were Hunters in how they gathered their food, and thus, they had to be very ADHD-like in their daily lives. Natural History Museum, London, England/ Smithsonian

There are other profound evolutionary developments that made us good, and smart Hunters, and thus more ADHD-like. For instance, "in most primates," and "probably our ancient African ancestors," the sclera, the outer eyeball covering, is dark brown.[151] But *Homo sapiens* have "enlarged, unpigmented, and therefore white sclera," which helps us see where others are looking and allows them, in turn, to see what we are gazing at.[152] This "social signaling" allowed for better coordination amongst groups, especially when they were hunting and dependent on stealth when killing their prey.[153] This refinement of expressive eyes helped Hunters be better Hunters as did the evolution of the spine earlier in man's development.

The more I have researched, the more I am convinced that ancient man's brain, that insured survival and superior hunting skills, was ADHD. It was the original brain, if you will, of *Homo sapiens*. According to anthropologists, *Homo sapiens* have been around for 200,000 years. For the first 190,000 years, what ensured survival was being a hunter. Having a none-ADHD-brain that allowed for farming and city building only occurred around 10,000 years ago with the Agricultural Revolution. Such a non-ADHD-mindset allowed for huge population explosions and the building of civilization, but this type of human behavior is a recent evolutionary development compared to what most of our ancestors were like, especially with their ADHD-brains. DG TV/Smithsonian

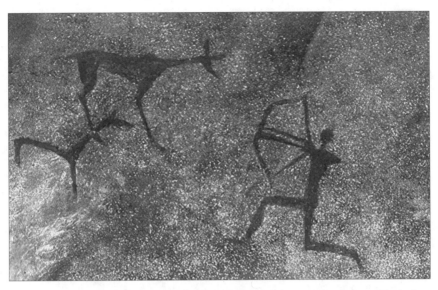

Here is an ancient cave painting done by Hunters thousands of years ago before the dawn of civilization with the Neolithic Revolution (circa 8,000 B.C.E). Before the establishment of cities and farming, mankind had to hunt and gather its food as shown with these cave drawings. ADHD-types were superior at hunting to non-ADHD people. History of Antiquities/Archaeology

So, as man developed new methods of collecting food, a new type of *Homo sapiens*, the non-ADHD Farmer-people, emerged as separate and distinct from ADHD-Hunter-people populations. As these food-gathering changes unfolded, ADHD/dyslexia became an older, and outdated, form of gene expression, and a non-ADHD/ dyslexia-gene expression, dominant in the Farmer-people, emerged as superior in making bigger, more successful human populations. For instance, the human population may have numbered about 2 million 10,000 years ago. Just 8,000 years later, it may have grown to 200 million. Presently, we are nearing 10 billion.[154] Never, in the history of humankind, have there been so many of us, and this population growth came about, in part, by growing large stockpiles of food, enabling us to survive in greater numbers to pass on our genes. As Professor Dawkins writes, "Evolution is the process by which some genes become more numerous and others less numerous in the gene pool."[155] Dawkins further explains,

> [Bipeds] evolved more and more ingenious tricks to increase their efficiency in their various ways of life, and new ways of life were continually being opened up. Sub-branches and sub-sub-branches evolved, each one excelling in a particular specialized way of making a living [i.e., how to find food].[156]

In other words, Farmers were far superior to Hunters as "food-gathering machines"[157] and came to dominate them by sheer volume of numbers because they could feed their communities *en masse*.[158] ADHD-Farmers were doing to ADHD-Hunters what we, as *Homo sapiens*, in general did with Neanderthals.

Homo sapiens 35,000 year ago were superior to Neanderthals "in the extraction of more nutrition from their environments…and this was surely one of the keys to our survival and eventual success in the challenging environments of the north" that eventually led to the Neanderthal extinction.[159] All that is left of the Neanderthals is the limited amount of their DNA that lives in us that happened with crossbreeding before this hominin group disappeared.[160] According to recent studies, between 1% and 4% of the "genomes of non-African modern humans" comes from our Neanderthal cousins.[161] Knowing about this "population admixture"[162] phenomena, one could argue that ADHD-gene markers, like Neanderthal DNA, are still in many *Homo sapiens* since we ADHD-people, even though a minority, have been cross-breeding with non-ADHD-types the past 10,000 years. Like the Neanderthals, ADHD-people are no longer a dominant people on Earth, but our DNA continues to live on within the human population and "might be an anachronic behavioral trait."[163]

This high-level history has been presented to emphasize that we humans continue to evolve throughout the ages, and we will continue to do so. In another 200,000 years, what we consider human now will have evolved once again into something else because life is never static—*it is always evolving.* As Professor Stringer wrote, people for centuries have "wrongly enshrined the view that evolution was simply a progression leading to us, its pinnacle and final achievement."[164]

Further Analysis about Hunter- and Farmer-Societies: Why Did it Happen When It Did and What Does it Mean?

Homing in on ADHD and its history again, we note that many anthropologists describe a shift in populations with how the majority of humankind started to procure food transpiring at the end of the last Ice Age, known as the Agricultural Revolution, or Neolithic Revolution (circa 8,000 B.C.E.). At that time, the human race slowly shifted away from the Hunter-life into an agrarian (non-ADHD) life, again, both in behavior and in genes.[165] Why did this happen at this point in history? Well, at this time, "mutated grasses appeared simultaneously on several continents, probably in response to the sudden and radical change in climate [i.e. the end of the last Ice Age]."[166] These crops were high yield, edible plants that later developed into rice and wheat, food staples of today. Since Farming-communities became larger and did not want to change their habits of "gathering" food, they rejected the hunter-gatherer lifestyle.[167] This transition to farming "altered nutritional composition, culture, and social structure" and brought on "the advent of technology."[168] As history has shown, when Farming-communities encountered Hunting-societies, they usually killed them off, defeated them in war and absorbed the survivors into their populations, or assimilated them into their cultures.

Hunter-survivors of such encounters, once within a Farmer-community, often served as agents of change. Since Hunters in general have more vivid imaginations and restless energy, they tend to think out of the box and to push society into new realms of thought.

My ex-wife often told people that I not only think out of the box, but I also don't even know where the box is. Dr. Hallowell says it another way: "[ADHD-people] don't *choose* not to conform. [They] don't even notice what the standard [they're] not conforming to is!"[169] Tragically though, history has shown that Farming-people will isolate, exile or even kill Hunter-people who try to change the status quo. According to some students of history and sociology, Farmers created war as we know it today. Farmers built walls to defend the people and the land to which they are bound. The surplus food they produced supported non-food producing persons such as artisans, craftsmen, bankers, writers, thespians and engineers. Their civilizations developed hierarchies with emperors, diplomats and generals. War with neighboring states was inevitable. Of course, Farmers also "tame" the environment by clearing, damming, irrigating and terracing. They do these activities because they "own" the land and want to control and defend it.[170]

Before nation-states, created by Farmers, one did not see large-scale wars or massive exterminations. On the one hand, one could argue that this was a byproduct of small populations, and thus there were not enough people to conduct a massive war. On the other hand, one could argue that Hunter-communities, if they encountered resistance, would move to different hunting grounds. Military historian John Keegan wrote that Hunters most often "would have migrated to find fresh prey rather than stay to squabble over the depleted hunting grounds."[171] If a "different" and larger hunting culture continued to bump up against a smaller one, then the smaller one would often melt into the larger one. Farming-communities, on the other hand, have proved to conduct brutal campaigns in order to protect their land and religious/political ideas.[172] Political philosopher, Jean-Jacques Rousseau, wrote,

The first man who, having enclosed a piece of ground, be-thought himself of saying "This is mine", and found people simple enough to believe him, was the real founder of civil society. From how many crimes, wars, and murders, from how many horrors and misfortunes might not any one have saved mankind, by pulling up the stakes, or filling up the ditch, and crying to his fellows: "Beware of listening to this imposter; you are undone if you once forget that the fruits of the earth belong to us all, and the earth itself to nobody."[173]

In the 20th century alone, at least 180 million people died as a result of genocide and warfare. "We are the only species that systematically slaughters its members in large numbers on a more or less regular basis."[174] Almost everyone on the globe knows about the death of a loved one or a friend resulting from war and genocide and, according to Dr. Hartmann, Farmers have caused it all.[175] As Keegan wrote, "The life of a nomad was probably healthier by far than that of the farmer, happier too, and as long as wildlife remained plentiful, more prosperous also."[176] In other words, Hunters did a better job of taking care of the environment and their fellow human beings. Farming-communities tend to divide people and promote the idea of "the other," especially once religion started to support the idea of the superiority of one Farming-community over another.[177] This is not meant to overlook Hunters throughout history who wantonly preyed on the neighboring groups in order to steal animals, women, children and possessions (like the Comanches did against the Apaches in the American Southwest, or the MacGregor and the Campbell clans did to each other in Scotland). My observations here about Hunter- and Farmer-communities are meant to only point out that there were smaller groups of nomadic tribes around the globe that remained small, and often adverse to waging total war, unlike larger groups that developed into Farmer-societies, which, in the end, produced more advanced war-making technology and willing populations for large-scale warfare.

Dr. Hartmann puts forward the radical theory that Farmers "taught that the slaughter of other humans was not only acceptable, but could even be 'a good thing' because it was ordered or sanctioned by their gods."[178] The Crusaders who murdered "heathens" in God's name, or the European Americans who killed indigenous Americans in the name of religion and Manifest Destiny,[179] or the Japanese murdering millions of Chinese during World War II in the name of racial superiority and Shinto/Zen Buddhist doctrines,[180] or the Nazis using Christian institutions, Protestant and Catholic clergy, and even support from the Pope and Vatican, to help them exterminate six million Jews,[181] all show the tendency of Farming-communities to practice such systematic exterminations using religion, in part, to justify such activity.

Although the examples I've shared seem hyperbolic when talking about the current problems with Learning Disabilities, it is important to think about them. With this historical reality in mind, one can understand why problems still exist with integrating ADHD-people (Hunters) into a Farmer-society, especially when such a society tends to impose conformity and practice persecution.[182] Since the U.S. has so many ADHD-people, and that many are having a difficult time assimilating, we have a long way to go to create a more tolerant society. Persecution of another is not just about their skin color, religion or ideology. It can simply be about how one behaves.

Where Does One See the Most ADHD in the World?

In my research, I learn that the U.S. has one of the highest levels of ADHD in the world. Why is this? Well, one prevailing theory states that many "misfits of British society...were daring and brave and crazy enough to undertake the crossing from Europe to America and conquer a new land."[183] The prospects of a new life and such adventurism attracted far more ADHD-types than the Farmer-types who often persecuted them. Consequently, the U.S. probably has a higher percentage of ADHD than the rest of the world because of the profile of many immigrants who then passed on their genes into the population at large. Many were "dreamers" wanting to improve their lot in life. Others simply sought to escape "bad marriages, jail terms and a dreary prospect of life-long poverty."[184] Of course, the American frontier attracted Hunter-ADHD immigrants as hunters, explorers, trappers, traders and prospectors. The large numbers of people with ADHD who came to America probably explains why this "affliction" has been called the "North American illness."[185]

Also, since we know the prison population has a high rate of ADHD, we can extrapolate that many of our forefathers probably had this condition, which led to them being deported to the American colonies. During colonization, Britain systematically expelled its convicts to America justifying this as a way of helping the colonies grow their populations.[186] The entire Crown colony of Georgia was a penal colony. Writing in the *Gazette* in response to this policy, Benjamin Franklin sarcastically wrote that "such a tender parental concern in our Mother Country for the welfare of her children calls aloud for the highest returns of gratitude."[187] Franklin proposed that America, to show its thankfulness for this "kind" policy, should ship a "boatload of rattlesnakes back to England."[188] In the end though, Franklin felt that the British would "get the better deal, 'for the rattlesnake gives warning before he attempts his mischief, which the convict does not.'"[189] With such policies, it is no wonder that our population (including those in our prisons) has a higher rate of ADHD than European nations in general. Our ADHD-forefathers were either *forced* to come to the land of opportunity, or naturally immigrated here for the adventure and chance to make a fresh start.[190] Before they ended up in North America, many in England with ADHD had a difficult time adapting to the new reality of their world, following the "Farmerized Industrial Revolution" going on in Britain, and gravitated to the more Hunter-like environment of exploration, pioneering and adventure that America offered.[191] As Karl Marx, the German philosopher, so "famously" stated, "It is not the consciousness of men that determines their existence, but their social existence that determines their consciousness."[192] In the land of freedom and opportunity, ADHD-types thrived.

Also, many traveled to America to escape religious persecution. These people, often members of new religious sects that probably attracted ADHD-types who were thinking outside the box, like the Quakers, found America welcoming to them and their new ways of worship. My ninth-great-grandfather, Sir John Linton, was disinherited by his father, Sir Roger Linton, for rejecting the Church of England and joining the Quakers. Soon after this break with his father, he immigrated to America in 1699 on the *Canterbury* with his young family, accompanied also by his friend, William Penn, the founder of the Province of Pennsylvania. They arrived in Philadelphia on 10 December 1699 and never looked back.[193]

Another nation with a similarly high rate of ADHD analogous with the U.S. is Australia, which was a British penal colony for a much longer time.[194] "Aussies" pride themselves on being "wild and crazy" and different, the usual ADHD-hallmarks. One just has to watch the late Steve Irwin, the Crocodile Hunter, to see how an active imagination and an ability to think out of the box characterizes people who probably would have never fit into rigid English society. Now there is no evidence that suggests Irwin had ADHD, but he sure did exhibit such behavior. Many watched his shows, although most disagreed with his antics. No one would recommend that his behavior become the norm, since playing with cobras and crocodiles usually results in death.

What Great Britain in particular and Europe in general were doing at this time, essentially setting up penal colonies in the American colonies and Australia, was not unique. To live out of synch in one's culture can lead to devastating and even deadly consequences, whether it is due to learning disabilities, deformities, culturally unacceptable behavior or idiosyncrasies. The Hopi Indians, for example, deliberately drove offenders in their society crazy by punishing them with "derisive laughter." American Shakers shunned those deemed un-Christian or who had "sinned." One may recall, too, how the Puritans treated a defined "sinner" in Nathaniel Hawthorne's book *The Scarlet Letter*. Although Hawthorne's novel was fiction, it was based on historical facts. For example, in 1639, a woman found guilty of adultery in Plymouth "was whipped, then dragged through the streets wearing the letters AD pinned to her sleeve: she was told that if she removed the badge the letters would be branded on her face."[195] In Russia, the Russian Orthodox Church and Christian Tsars utilized their Christian citizens to ghettoize the Jewish populations, and periodically conduct pogroms against them for the "crime" of "killing Christ" (i.e., deicide). Of course, these are generalizations and don't necessarily have anything to do with ADHD. However, when someone is different, which ADHD makes a person, then that individual is often subjected to more persecution than the average person.

Since most American migrants were usually young men, they occasionally later married locals who were often Indians (i.e., more Hunters). In fact, out of the ethnicities tracked for children with Learning Disabilities, Native Americans had the highest level at 18%.[196] Many Americans today can point to a Native American in their family tree. For example, at the beginning of the Spanish colonization, around 750,000 people, mostly young men, migrated to the New World. Since few women accompanied them, these males married "Indians and blacks, unions which produced '*mestizos*' and '*mulattos*.'"[197]

Moreover, many of the Anglo-Saxon immigrants to the colonies owned slaves. Many of these slave owners sexually abused their slaves, passing on their genes into this population, largely a Hunter-one, many of whom came from western Africa.[198] One slave owner, Thomas Jefferson, had his affair with his slave, Sally Hemings, who was the offspring of Jefferson's father-in-law, and thus, half-White and half-Black.[199] Most African-Americans today have mixed heritage, and the ADHD-genes from the original immigrants are widespread throughout all ethnic groups in America with both negative and positive effects.

Why is dyslexia often combined with ADHD? People with dyslexia are superior trackers and hunters so it would be natural that it bonds itself with the ADHD-brain. Dyslexia is described as a brain-handicap, because it makes one flip letters and words around on a page, jeopardizing the ability to read. However, in the wild, if someone is constantly making reverse images, or lateral inversions, of what he is seeing, he can observe more detail than others.[200] Thus, this skill allows one to see more topographical features when tracking an animal one is hunting. So having both ADHD and dyslexia creates a potent combination of killer attributes, ensuring the species' survival. Professor Dawkins writes, "One of the most striking properties of survival-machine behavior is its apparent purposiveness [i.e., in the case of ADHD-dyslexic-types, the purpose of being able to hunt]."[201] One recent study reported, "People with dyslexia have the ability to see how things connect to form complex systems, and to identify similarities among multiple things."[202] Another study found that dyslexic astrophysicists were superior in observing details in the universe, especially around Black Holes, compared with their non-dyslexic colleagues.[203] And dyslexia seems to make one work harder at reading, which actually makes you pay attention more closely to what is being read and, consequently, helping one pick up more knowledge than the average person making dyslexia for reading comprehension "*desirable.*"[204] So, dyslexia, as explored in ancient and modern man, was and is a positive trait. Since dyslexia often finds itself combined with ADHD, then the millions of Hunter-like people coming to the colonies had, it appears, a higher percentage of dyslexia as well as ADHD, compared to other societies.

Conclusion

To summarize, ADHD-people may have been the majority of the human population until the Farmer-communities started to dominate the landscape. ADHD has a historical explanation that originally may have been an important survival characteristic. This history of Hunters and Famers explains where ADHD-people came from and how their minds work. People today with ADHD/LD are not deficient nor do they have a disorder. They have superior Hunter-qualities that can translate into wonderful skills in their modern lives, all probably based on their genes. "To understand is to be able to correct and, one would hope, gain control over our lives" by viewing ADHD as natural and an asset.[205] In fact, since 10% to 20% of Americans are ADHD,[206] evolution is telling us that the genes that are expressing this condition impart "some reproductive advantage to the individual[s] concerned."[207] Ironically, most today can credit their great-grandfathers and great-grandmothers who had ADHD for begetting a strong line of descendants. So, the next time you meet an ADHD-person, thank them for ensuring that you came this far in the march of evolution.

Takeaways

* Some researchers and doctors stress that ADHD-people often express the traits of a Hunter and non-ADHD-types, those of a Farmer. There are three components of ADHD that set

Hunters apart from Farmers: Distractibility, impulsivity, and risk-taking/restlessness.

- Since ADHD is due to genes and environment, it is a natural human condition. It is a misunderstanding that it is a disorder.

- ADHD-people may have been the majority of the human population until the Farmer-communities started to dominate the landscape. ADHD has a historical explanation that originally may have been an important survival characteristic. It helps explain where ADHD-people may have come from and how their minds work. People today with ADHD/LD are not deficient nor do they have a disorder. They have superior Hunter-qualities that can translate into wonderful skills in their modern lives.

Action Steps

- The next time you meet an ADHD-person, thank them for ensuring, in part, that you came this far in the march of evolution.

- If you are ADHD, always remember the evolutionary benefit ADHD had for our ancestors and the gifts it gives you to accomplish so many things in life.

CHAPTER 3:
The Beginning: Turmoil as an Infant and Young Boy

"To remember is to create links between past and present, between past and future. To remember is to affirm man's faith in humanity and to convey meaning to our fleeting endeavors."
— Holocaust survivor and writer Elie Wiesel[208]

I CAME FAST INTO THIS world. My mother, Marilee, started having contractions early in the morning on 16 March 1971, and I was here at 10:05 a.m. When she decided she needed to get to the hospital as the contractions started in earnest, my father, Linton Mark, was at his office in downtown Dallas, so he could not drive her. She then called a dear friend, who would become my first Godmother, Phoebe Hunt, and informed her that she had started her labor. Phoebe said she would drive my older brother and her son to school and then come back and rush her to the hospital. She told her, "Marilee, you aren't going to have your child on your kitchen floor. You get your bag and I'll get you to the delivery room as soon as possible."[209] Luckily my brother's school was around the corner, and after "kicking" him and her son out of the car, she drove to our house and picked up Mom. It was a good thing my Godmother did so because I was delivered 55 minutes to an hour after arriving at Arlington Memorial Hospital. Our physician, Dr. Robert "Brent" Brentlinger, told my mother: "That's the way I like'em, mom. Come in early and be finished by lunchtime."[210] My mom said that my delivery accurately predicted my life in that I have not slowed down since—I was in a hurry from the beginning.

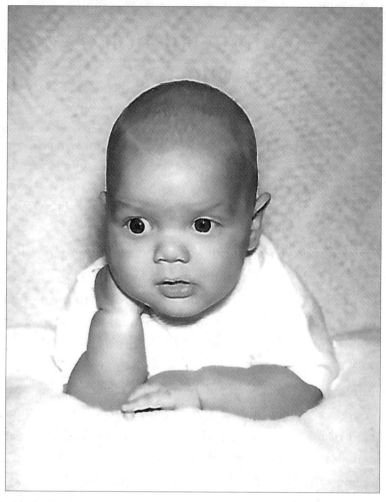

This is my first picture in life soon after I was born on 16 March 1971 (circa two months old).

Actually, I am lucky to be alive at all, because my mother and father had an Rh factor difference.[211] Since my mother's blood was Rh negative and my father's was Rh positive, after they had their first child, my older brother (who had Rh positive blood), my mother's immune system built up antibodies to the Rh factor. She would have three miscarriages before I was born. Nowadays, doctors give mothers who have Rh negative blood and whose spouse is Rh positive a shot that prevents them from building up immunity to a baby with Rh positive blood. Fortunately, I have the same blood type as my mother, Rh negative (actually B-negative, a rare blood type), so I survived. My parents worried about a healthy delivery, knowing my mother's history with her other pregnancies.

Now, if you are looking for a cause of my present condition, other than the fact that both my parents exhibit their own ADHD-like behavior, one can point to the fact that my mother was stressed by this pregnancy, as well as by my father's bizarre behavior at that time. I am sure there is a psychiatrist who has studied this conduct. When my mother got pregnant (six times), my father turned into a strange person, threatening her with divorce and mistreating her. He was also an alcoholic and drank heavily—scotch, vodka, and bourbon and Coca-Cola. My parents did not have a very good marriage to begin with and they ultimately divorced when I was a boy. It is said that stress during the pregnancy can affect a child's brain chemistry.[212] After my birth, Dad seemed to calm down and behave like a normal father, enjoying his new son and bragging to coworkers about his child. My father's behavior during Mom's pregnancies was strange, to be sure, but what family out there is truly perfect or normal? In my opinion, if anyone tells you their family is normal, they are lying and/or delusional.[213]

Even after my safe delivery, my parents continued to be concerned about me. I had colic (acute abdominal pain), was irritable, and did not sleep well. One day, as my father walked by the nursery, he heard my crib slamming against the wall. When he looked closer, he was shocked to see his few-months-old child, banging his head against the end of the crib. Later, once informed of my behavior, the doctor calmed my mother, explaining that this was a "phase" I would grow out of. Little did they know that I would still be bouncing my head, face down, against my pillow until I was 13. Even as an adult, when I become stressed, I bang my head in my sleep, sometimes to my ex-wife's total surprise and horror throughout our 19-year marriage.

When I did martial arts or played football as a teenager, the strong neck muscles I had developed with all that head-banging were an advantage, but as an infant, my parents were frightened by my behavior. I was just agitated and full of too much energy. Obviously, the bouncing was one way I dealt with my overexcited system. Head banging or "crib rocking," as it is sometimes called, is indeed a warning sign that a child is hyperactive. Experts claim a child does this because he is under-stimulated.[214] Now, many children do such movement in their beds, which are self-soothing techniques, but when it seems excessive and goes on for years, like with me, then a parent might want to consult a physician about this behavior.

The other way my excited system would calm down was when my mother or grandmother scratched my back and head. Even today scratching relaxes me. My patient ex-wife and some girlfriends have scratched me while I watched TV, sometimes for hours, which truly puts me into a Zen-like frame of mind. The need for physical stimulation on the skin is common for ADHD-people and helps them process information.

My son Justin, who has inherited my habit and still bounces his head at 19 years of age, needed a lot of scratching to fall asleep as a boy. If he did not get that scratching, he would bounce his head on his pillow just like his father. I remember being at my in-laws and hearing his portable crib hitting against the wall of the room he was in when he was an infant, and entering to find him doing the same head-butt techniques on his mattress that I had done at his age. I declared to my ex-wife, "Well, our son is Satan-possessed just like me. It's in the genes." I then scratched my son's back which seemed to settle him and he fell asleep. And my last child, Ian, has been found several times since he was 18 months old bouncing his head in his crib also, and I often found myself scratching him too when he was very young to calm his nerves. Scratching "stimulates the brain in ways that help integrate sensory experiences."[215] This process, called "brushing," helps children with ADHD "enjoy normal levels of stimulation without overreacting."[216] Studies have shown that massage helps such children as well.[217] But we ADHD-people cannot scratch ourselves, or have others scratch us, 24/7 as the antidote.

When I was an infant, my mom fed me formula, since many doctors in the 1960s and 1970s thought it provided nutrition superior to breast milk. Now doctors and scientists believe "breast is best" and encourage mothers to nurse their babies their first year of life.[218] I mention this because the formula that I drank had preservatives and artificial flavors which likely had a detrimental effect on me. My system is sensitive to anything synthetic. Also, my parents' marital stress probably contributed to my odd behavior. Children are sensitive to their parents' energy, but often can't understand anything more specific than that something is wrong. So, my initial years were full of surprises. No one in the family knew what to make of my behavior.

I did things that tested my parents' patience and made them question their sanity. Today, Child Services might have taken me away from my mother, and she would have appreciated the break. They tried to discipline my wild behavior, but "spankings [were not]… effective at all,"[219] according to a medical report in 1975. Below are a few stories of some of the activities I engaged in as a child that drove my parents crazy.

When I was about two-and-a-half, in late summer of 1973, my mother left me alone briefly in our fenced backyard to play with our dog, a German Schnauzer named Gretchen. After several minutes of silence, my mom looked out through the back door to check on me. To her dismay, she saw nothing. She discovered I had opened the unlocked gate and left with the dog. Panic stricken, she mobilized the neighborhood moms to search for me. Around 30 minutes later, one of them found me two blocks from my house across a well-traveled street. I was lucky I was not killed.

An interesting point to make here is the wonderful support my dog Gretchen was in my life. As I was being destructive and a failure in most aspects of my young childhood, Gretchen was always happy to see me. "An animal does wonders for a child's self-image. It never talks back, scolds, or criticizes,"[220] Dr. Mark A. Stewart says. So, when I did destructive things around the house or even tried to run away, it is no surprise that my favorite partner was Gretchen. I loved that dog and she was significant part of my life while growing up.

My family bought a Schnauzer we named Gretchen when I was born. That dog and I were best friends growing up. Children throughout time have benefited by having pets, but dogs seem to be very helpful for ADHD-kids in developing healthy self-images.

Getting out of the house to go on journeys was something I always enjoyed. During a night full of thunderstorms in 1974, my mom got a call around 6:30 a.m. "Marilee, I'm sorry to call you at this hour, but do you know where Bryan is?" The pounding of her heart was suddenly as loud as the thunder and lightning outside. "No," my mother answered, "Where is he?" "Well," the neighbor said, "He's out in the street playing in the gutter." My mother checked my room, noticed the empty bed and scurried out through the open front door in her robe. She ran down to the street, grabbed me and carried me back inside. I was angry and confused because she had interrupted my play. I was lucky that I did not slip down the storm drain. Soon after this, my mother installed chain locks high up on all the doors.

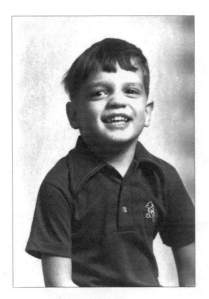

Here I am when I was three years old in my favorite Winnie-the-Pooh shirt. It was at this age that my mother started to worry about me as my ADHD-behavior became more apparent: Not sleeping at night, never taking naps, constant banging of my head on my pillow at bedtime and repeated escapes from the house to run around the neighborhood.

After my mom got locks on our back gate, she would let me play outside for hours. One day, she heard a strange banging on the roof. "It sounded like a 100-pound squirrel," she said. As she walked outside, she saw me, her four-year-old-son, running around the top of the house as if it were a football field. "Bryan, you get down right now." She then watched me grab a tree branch as I climbed to the ground. I had no fear of heights. Visions of her tiny son slipping and falling off the house and breaking his neck filled her mind. A few years later, probably at the age of eight or nine, I prided myself on being able to climb on top of almost every house in the neighborhood. Sometimes this was quite a feat, since many were two stories. I am still surprised today that no one ever caught me in the midst of my spider-man acts. When on vacation in the Caribbean in 1979 off the island of Tortola, I found tall rocks to jump off into the ocean near the shore terrifying my mother once again. And later, in my midteens, when Lake Arlington flooded and the waters came to our back doorstep in May 1989, I climbed atop my roof and jumped into the lake since the house was built on a steep hill that allowed enough depth to cushion my fall.

As an eight-year-old, while on vacation in the Caribbean at Tortola in 1979, I found a tall rock I could climb at the shore to jump into the ocean, terrifying my mother. I was always seeking out high-adrenaline ADHD-activity.

Here I am jumping off the roof of my house during the flood of Lake Arlington in May 1989. I was always searching out high-adrenaline activities as an ADHD-child.

It must be in the genes because my children have been climbing trees and roofs since they were very young. As a girl, my daughter enjoyed walking around Central Park in New York City when we visited her grandparents and bouldering every large rock or climbing every cliff face she could find. Some people would stare in amazement as my little daughter, in a diaper, would scale a ten-foot rock face, with me, of course, standing underneath her as her "belayer" to make sure someone was there in case she fell (she never did). She naturally knew how to conduct edging and fist jams without instruction. And well into her teenage years, my daughter could climb any tree she encountered. Instead of being shocked like my mother by my children's behavior, I came to expect my adventurous behavior to be expressed in my children. As a father, I enjoyed climbing cliffs, rocks, trees and roofs with them. And when in the rain forest in Hawaii during a trip in 2015, naturally my children and I enjoyed jumping off a 20-foot cliff near a waterfall, feeding our ADHD-brains with adrenaline and enkephalins. And when I was an adult, I satisfied my desire even more for heights, obtaining my pilot's license and becoming sky-dive qualified before entering the Marine Corps. I and my kids like heights and the adrenaline from "in person" activities surrounding experiences with gravity, like jumping off cliffs into rivers in Hawaii's rain forests or snow-skiing at Red River, New Mexico.

Since I did not sleep well as a child, I entertained myself at night, often seizing the opportunity to do forbidden things. One night, when I was on one of these excursions at the age of four, the splashing of water awakened my father around midnight. He caught me elbow deep in one of the large aquariums in the family room. I remember planning to put the fish in my toy box for the night, and then in the morning return them to the fish tank before my father ever realized they were missing. I had not learned that if fish remained out of water all night, they would not swim well in the morning. Instead of catching the fish, I received several swats and was told never to bother the tropical fish again.

Sophia and I are pictured here in a large tree outside the library at Phillips Exeter Academy in the summer of 2005 when I was teaching there at the summer school.

In my grand tradition of escape, I often wanted to explore other people's homes. One day, when I was five, I left the house from the front yard where I was playing and went up and down the block knocking on neighbors' doors and asking to look inside their homes. On this block, most families knew one another and kids moved around freely. Many people were good-natured, and they granted the entrance. I remember walking into one house where a toy gun lay on the stairs. I pretended to fire it into the air, thanked the lady and left. I was lucky my neighbors were wholesome, friendly people.

I often baffled my mother with my behavior when compared to other children my age. For instance, when I did start speaking, my speech was incoherent. When she could not understand me, instead of trying to learn how to sound out the words properly, I just yelled my gibberish louder, frustrating both my mom and me even more since volume was not the issue. She could not really understand my words until I was about two and a half. Most mothers understand their children's early speech while other adults have difficulties, but my ramblings simply confused my mother. I started to learn how to speak around three or four, definitely later than most kids, and my speech was severely flawed. This speech problem is quite common among hyperactive children.[221] My erratic speech mirrored my unpredictable behavior.

While I was playing outside with my toy trucks one afternoon, my mother noticed I was getting frustrated. Suddenly, I began throwing trucks around and breaking the ones that remained close to me. As she looked outside, she saw me banging my head out of frustration on the concrete. There was a bloody spot on my forehead and since I reversed *T*'s and *F*'s in my speech, it also sounded like I was cursing. For some reason, the "fucks" were not "working properly." My sudden rage scared my mother and it took her several minutes to calm me down. This excitability is common among hyperactive children, and such tantrums were frequent in my early life. It has been shown that children who have problems with their verbal skills are more impulsive and show signs of ADHD.[222] The faster an ADHD-child can learn how to communicate effectively with words, probably the faster he can start controlling his behavior. When words fail me even today, I feel the frustration build within me.

Whether yelling at my toys or stealing fish, I often did things on impulse that stunned my parents. For instance, as a young child, I was on a sailboat with my father. While cleaning up the boat when back in its berth, I picked up my father's naval survival knife still sheathed in its beautiful leather holster and threw it into the water. My father could not believe his eyes, and started cursing like a sailor. Later, Dad tried to retrieve the knife from the bottom of the lake using his fins, snorkel and scuba mask, but the boat was in around 12 feet of water and it was very muddy. After an hour of trying, having to put his face right up against the murky bottom to see anything, he gave up and made sure nothing of value was ever again in arm's reach of me.

And even when I did not intend to shock people, I still did, as when I asked the babysitter to tuck me into bed. Since I always got my *T's* and *F's* mixed up, she misunderstood my meaning when I said "fuck mee ento beid, pleazze." Later, when my mom was told about this event, she retorted, "Well, he's not being precocious, he just has a lot of problems."

One day my mother heard me knocking at the French door from the backyard. She was busy in the kitchen and yelled out, "One second, Son. I'll be right there." Suddenly, she heard glass crack and me scream. She rushed to the door. I had broken the glass in one of the windows in the door by slamming my forehead against it. My mother stepped outside, grabbed me and yelled, "Stop." As I looked at my mother, she saw the bloody spot on my forehead. I was crying and angry. As one might expect, my mom was often confused about how to handle my behavior.

During this same time period, I must have seen some sword fighting on TV, so I decided to try it myself. I went into the kitchen and pulled out one of my mother's longest knives and began to play *Zorro*. Since I was four, my mother was convinced I was going to slice off a finger or poke out an eye. She rushed over and demanded to have the knife. I had learned from TV that I should guard myself against opponents, and my mother was attacking. So, I started to slice back and forth in the air toward my mother. She leaped toward me to grab my arm and at that moment, I cut her hand. When I saw blood, I immediately handed over the knife and felt bad. In her fear, pain and anger, she yelled and spanked me. Luckily for my family, I did not pick-up sword fighting again.

One morning, my mother walked in my room and noticed a bad smell. "Did you bring in a dead animal," she asked. I said no. Later that night, my father smelled my closet and wondered what was wrong. "Son," he said, "we've talked to you about handling dead animals. I hope you haven't brought one in." I again answered no. A few months before, I was devastated when my mother took a dead Blue Jay I was playing with away from me. I had found the bird under a tree. I thought the blue feathers were so beautiful and was puzzled why it did not fly when I threw it in the air. But I was now telling the truth about dead animals in my room. What my parents did not know was that I was urinating in my closet. I do not know what possessed me to do so, but I thought it perfectly fine. One day, my mother caught me in the act. Appalled, she shouted, "You're only supposed to PEEEE in the toilet, not on the carpet. Your father will hear about this." As she said this, she dragged me into the bathroom for me to complete my business. Later, after Dad was debriefed, he gave me a spanking I have never forgotten. The next day, the carpet was steam cleaned and I never urinated in my room again.

When I was three or four years old, my brother had just finished painting his model airplanes with quick-drying silver spray paint. He left the spray can out in the garage and went inside the house. Unbeknownst to him, I had been watching him while playing in the backyard. The next day, when no one was around, I hurried over to the can, picked it up and began painting my father's three-day-old Volkswagen. Playing Picasso, I sprayed the bumper, the wheels, the back window and the license plate. The silver paint contrasted sharply with the bright red of the car and the black rubber of the bumper and wheels. Hearing no chaotic noise in the backyard, my father soon came to investigate the silence. As he walked out the back door, he was horrified to see half of his brand-new red car painted silver. Then he noticed his son grinning at him holding a can of spray paint. "Daddy, I do good job?" I asked, smiling innocently. My father was not smiling. He picked me upside down by the legs and began spanking me as he carried me back into the house yelling for my brother. I do not remember painting the car, but I do remember being carried upside down and spanked. After spanking me, my father paddled my brother for leaving the paint out. My father had to get the car repainted.

If I was not painting cars, I was doing something to destroy any home decoration that could be harmed. One day things were too quiet again, probably when I was two or three. As a result, my mother knew something wasn't good. As she quickly moved through the house calling my name, she was shocked to walk around the corner of the hallway to find me in the living room unraveling the carpet. I had found the loose end of the carpet in the corner and then proceeded to pull up a pile of weave almost a foot high leaving several square feet of open floor space. My dog Gretchen was frustrated as I had buried her under the mass of thick string and she was twisting and turning, trying to get the threads off her body. Mom yelled, picked me up and then put me in my room, telling me to leave all carpets in the house alone. I didn't listen very well. Soon after this event, I used my mother's red fingernail polish to paint the carpet under the high standing coffee table in our living room. It was time for my family to get new carpet. My family had to deal with this destructive behavior on a continuous basis. As LD-expert Dr. Mark A. Stewart wrote, "Hyperactive children destroy clothing, toys, and household furnishings at an alarming rate, partly because they are impulsive, partly because they give things hard use, and partly because they often let their tempers get the better of them."[223] I fit that profile perfectly.

Besides my father spanking me, my mother often paddled me with an orange, rubber-studded, ping-pong paddle. Often, I would find where she had stashed the paddle and hid it, but she would eventually find it. In my primitive mind, I felt my mom used that instrument because it had "extra grip" to whack my buttocks. When I got in trouble, she would tell me to go to my room and I would hear her rummaging through the kitchen or her bedroom for it as I waited in fear of what was coming. Why did my mother spank me? I don't remember all the reasons, but often they were for being disrespectful to her, or for losing my cool and throwing a temper-tantrum, or for bringing in a water moccasin, a poisonous snake, to skin in the kitchen (of course, I had killed it with my self-made spear beforehand). One day, as I sat in my room awaiting my mother to get her weapon to spank me, my ADHD-mind came up with a brilliant defense. I quickly stuffed my underwear and shorts with extra underwear and socks from my dresser drawer and then courageously waited for my mom to enter to administer the punishment. As she entered, I assumed the position by my bed and waited for the licks. I never even dreamed she would notice my "elephant-man" rear. Well, my mom started laughing, told me to pull down my pants to bare my butt cheeks, and then she swatted me a few times, turned, laughed again, and left. Although I still got my punishment, my shenanigans had diffused the situation to some degree and at least she was not spanking me in anger anymore. I laughed to myself and remembered that invaluable lesson that people punish less if they are not angry.

Having ADHD as a child was not my only struggle. As an infant, I also had problems with my legs and had to wear special shoes and braces (known as a Denny-Brown splint). This splint straightened out the legs of pigeon-toed or bow-legged children. Doctors no longer use them today because they believe that most children's legs will straighten out on their own. Years later, when I stumbled on the splint in a closet somewhere, my mother tried to explain its purpose. All I heard was that in addition to having a "learning disability," I also had a physical deformity. Although my legs and feet were perfectly normal by then, I felt physically inferior and that insecurity stayed with me for some time.

As one can see, I had several problems as a child and my parents did not know how to handle me. I was abnormal in many ways, and not taking naps or sleeping through the night, for example, must have exhausted my mother even more. Regardless of what I was doing, I approached things with high energy and passion. But having the ADHD-gene was not the only thing I struggled with in learning how to live. As a child, I also suffered some trauma. We will examine this sad event and how it affected my ADHD next.

Takeaways

- The faster an ADHD-child can learn how to communicate effectively with words, the faster he can start controlling his behavior.

- The need for physical stimulation on the skin is common for ADHD-people and helps them process information. Peculiar behaviors like head banging at just a few months old and wanting to be scratched are hallmarks of ADHD-types.

- Speech problems are common among hyperactive children. My erratic speech mirrored my unpredictable behavior. Whether yelling at my toys or destroying furniture, I often did things on impulse that stunned my parents.

- ADHD-children often seek out high-adrenaline activities.

Action Steps

- Examine your own childhood. Journal about it and analyze what the events in your life are telling you to do in the future.

- If you are ADHD, learn from looking at your own childhood for methods that can best help your children if they are ADHD. Find healthy, safe and productive, high-adrenaline activities for yourself and your ADHD-children.

Here I am with a Cesena 152 that I learned on to get my pilot's license in 1999. My ADHD-mind loved the challenge of learning new and risky activities and I enjoyed learning how to fly, especially since I was an "air-contract" for the Marine Corps at this time and wanted to learn as much as I could about flying and planes before I went off to military flight school. Willow Run Airport, Michigan, Summer 1999.

Here I am with my flight instructor, Beorn Bricka, before we conducted three skydiving jumps in one day. As I have mentioned all throughout this chapter, my ADHD-brain craved activity where I experimented with gravity and I found sky-diving exhilarating. Summer 1999.

Chapter 4:
Sexual Abuse and ADHD

"Divide each problem into as many parts as possible; that each part being more easily conceived, the whole may be more intelligible."
— Descartes, *Discourses on Method* [224]

"When you talk about your scars, you own them. When you repress your scars and do not talk about them, they own you."
— Clint Bruce, Naval Academy Football captain (1996) and platoon leader in Seal Team 5 (1998-2003) [225]

WARNING: I am not naïve about how this chapter can affect people. When I taught Women's Self-Defense at Exeter Summer School and at Yale University, I was careful with my students because I knew there would always be someone in the class who had experienced some abuse, and simulating situations of what one needs to do in order to protect oneself sometimes could trigger painful memories. When this happened, I would send that person to a school authority to discuss it. Likewise, talking about the crimes perpetrated against me as a child may trigger painful memories in others, and I am sorry if this happens. However, I want to share my rationale. If I can write about my pain in order to maybe help you, maybe you can read about it to see if my experience can give you a compass heading of how to be a better you or how to help a loved one work through the abuse he or she experienced.

✦ ✦ ✦

A trauma I had to deal with at an early age was sexual abuse. People with ADHD usually have several issues they are dealing with, whether it be drugs, depression or emotional or sexual abuse.[226] So I was not unique in that respect. However, speaking publicly about it is unusual. It is also possible this incident of sexual abuse contributed to my ADHD.[227]

I have traveled a difficult journey to get to this stage of openly talking about such matters. Often, sexually abused people, and I am no exception, feel that people will think less of them if they discuss their experiences. This is a common fear when discussing any problem from a person's past. This is especially true, however, with sexual abuse, even though most who have been victims of this crime are innocent and should not feel guilty about it.

The recent Catholic Church sex scandal involving children has shined a bright light on the darkness of child sex abuse. The Church for decades, if not longer, allowed its ranks to include child molesters/rapists, and then protected them when allegations against them surfaced, moving them around to different parishes where they continued to abuse children. The Catholic Church, according to a 2014 United Nations report, has been disgraceful in its handling of these criminals and their victims.[228] So, we still have a long way to go in order to combat this problem in society and its institutions, and to understand its effect on the victims. Since sexual abuse can bring out or exacerbate ADHD-behavior, I bring this up as a contributing factor, and share my story.

Picture of Kevin W. in his high school graduation photo. Now some may find it "mean" to show a picture of the sexual predator who attacked me when I was a child, but one must remember, he sexually assaulted me, and this is part of his legacy. I have tried to prosecute him throughout the years, but the statute of limitations never allowed me to do so. I reveal his picture and tell the story of my sexual abuse to help those who have been assaulted to learn how to heal themselves as I have and to help parents of those so assaulted, because often sexually abused children exhibit ADHD-behavior after the crime. Photo Credit: Arlington ISD, Bowie High School Archives

I was six and seven years old when a next-door neighbor, a teenager named Kevin W., who was ten years older than me and in high school, violated my innocence.[229] As far as sexual abuse is concerned, I was "lucky." I was only assaulted twice. Compared to what has happened to others, I consider myself fortunate. He sucked my penis for maybe a minute on one occasion, and then another time, shoved his penis in my mouth. He also manhandled me during the second assault and grabbed my head and slammed it against the brick wall outside his home when he was trying to get me to continue performing oral sex, but I was able to escape. As I ran away spitting stuff out of my mouth, he said menacingly, "Don't tell your parents or I will kill you."[230] So, in comparison to the child rape perpetrated by thousands of Catholic priests, my abuse might be considered less traumatic than it actually was. Kevin, who violated my innocence, was not in a position of trust with my family and not an authority figure, which would have affected me in a more serious manner. From statistics presented today, one in four girls and one in eight boys are sexually abused by the time they reach adulthood. According to *Darkness to Light*, an organization dealing with child abuse, its research includes data that places the abuse of boys somewhat higher; namely, one in six boys is molested by the time they reach adulthood.[231]

It took me a long time to talk about this event. When in junior high in 1985, I discussed the abuse with Celeste Culver who worked in the district attorney's office as an investigator in Fort Worth, Texas, but she stated that it had been too long, almost 10 years, to do anything about it.[232] I also confided my situation to one of my teachers, Patty Crowley. On learning her daughter had been sexually abused, I thought she could help.[233] Although she gave me a big hug and showed me compassion, she also, like Mrs. Culver, did not know if there was anything I could do to receive justice.[234]

I also shared it with one of my friends when I was a teenager. Her family dealt with foster kids, and hearing about the abuse these children suffered made me realize that I should do something about it. However, she, like Culver and Crowley, did not think the authorities would help. The next time I started talking about it was to my wife in my midtwenties after learning about a close relative of hers having been attacked when young. Also, after my brother and sister-in-law had their first child in 1994, I warned them to be careful with their boy and make sure they knew where and with whom he was spending time especially since Kevin W. had been a friend of my brother's. I used my story to drive home the importance of being vigilant.

It took me many years to be able to talk about my abuse without utter embarrassment. The shame is still buried deep inside me despite intellectually knowing that I as a six- and seven-year-old could not possibly have been at fault, nor should I feel ashamed that I was the victim of another's evil. Eventually, I approached the Arlington Police Department in 2001, when I was 30, about taking some action, because I feared that other kids could be hurt by that same individual. One thing is true about pedophiles, according to John Walsh of *America's Most Wanted*: They do not change and they are almost always repeat offenders. Unfortunately, the officer told me that the new statute of limitations had run out when I had turned 28, and that they could not do anything. In 2005, I filed reports about Kevin W. with the Sherriff's Department in Tarrant County, Texas, and Mansfield Police Department, Texas, where I was told, once again, that the statute of limitations would not allow me to prosecute my assailant. However, while doing research for this book, I discovered that the last legislative session of our government opened up the statute of limitations. As soon as I found this out, I filed a report in August 2021, and as of the writing of this book, a new investigation is underway.[235] Here again, an ADHD-attribute of never giving up and being hyper-focused helped me pursue this case and bring some justice to our society. We must always remember, quoting the Anglo-Irish philosopher and statesmen Edmund Burke: "For evil men to triumph, good men must do nothing."[236]

The more I learn about sexual abuse, the more I feel sorry for this pathetic individual who assaulted me. I often wonder what tragedy occurred in his life to create his depravity. I have always hoped he did not harm his younger half-brother or his daughter. I also question whether our society is doing enough to stop these predators.

Now, I embrace this part of my past and know I am not responsible for it. I am responsible for how it makes me feel. It helps me to be sensitive to those who have been violated. I also approach this event somewhat academically. Sexual identity and what is appropriate and not are difficult things to define. Had I grown up in ancient Greece, I would have learned that pederasty was a mainstay of society.[237] By the time I was a teenager, I would have already slept with an older man. This was accepted in ancient Greece and was considered to be one form of love. Some oriental cultures are just now in the past century curtailing sex between men and boys, while others, like in Afghanistan, continue to practice child rape as being normal and socially accepted.[238]

So, I realize that sexual behavior and norms have changed throughout history. But one thing is for certain: Sexual desire is strong by nature. We as a society are still coming to terms with what society considers moral. Does this justify what was done to me? It absolutely does not. I don't know if Kevin was fully aware of why he acted how he did. Quite often children who abuse other children have been abused themselves. The reason doesn't matter fully now, and the search for answers today is really academic. What really matters the most is the effect it had on me. I learned that I could let this experience shame and eat away at me or accept it and go on with my life, using it to make me a more positive person. This experience inspired me to teach self-defense at Yale University and Phillips Exeter Academy. I also talked to my children about how to prevent sexual abuse and had them attend classes at our church where they learned about their bodies and how to defend themselves against predators. I have allowed my experience with abuse to motivate me to try to better understand the human condition and make my little part of the world better and stronger.

I have mentioned the sexual abuse because it probably had an effect on my neurological system when I was young, contributing to my ADHD. According to psychologist Dr. Kevin Creedon, abuse alters the brain chemistry and creates learning difficulties for children.[239] Dr. Jon G. Allen, a psychologist at the Menninger Clinic, records findings that children who have suffered sexual abuse suffer from hyperactivity, "dysregulation of the HPA axis, and immune system compromise."[240] The HPA axis is short for the hypothalamic-pituitary-adrenal axis and when affected by trauma like sexual abuse, it can lead one to have psychiatric "symptoms [such] as sleep disturbances, restlessness, anxiety, irritability, explosive anger, jumpiness… and difficulty in concentrating."[241] In other words, it can create ADHD-like symptoms. The feelings of shame, fear and anger change the way the brain works, and as a result, victims of sexual abuse struggle with these emotions.[242] Drs. Alexander C. McFarlane and Bessel A. van der Kolk "found that of a sample of sexually abused girls, 28% met diagnostic criteria for ADHD, compared with 4% of a non-traumatized control group."[243]

I cite these facts because with such a high rate of abuse in society and such a high rate of learning-disabled children, many of our children's learning disabilities might have resulted from such abuse or, if preexisting, been aggravated by it. Simplistically, the best solution is to prevent the abuse altogether, but that is unrealistic. A realistic and practical option is to be aware that this is indeed a cause of some learning problems and to treat the effects accordingly. The sooner we let the child know he or she is valuable and important, and that it is alright to talk about the situation, the sooner he or she can accept it and start healing. Dr. Hallowell writes this:

> Many of us have painful memories from our childhood. Many of us are haunted by them even as adults, while others do their best to forget them. I think it is best to hold on to them if you can; just change how they make you feel. Bad memories have something to teach. If you can walk back into the memories, if you can preserve the connection to your past instead of breaking it, you might find that there is some goodness or usefulness left back there, even if it is only in giving you a sense of continuity… The past gives depth to the present, gives it its contrasts, ironies, and feelings of triumph.[244]

In embracing the past, a person is more able to seize the moment each day and live a life with greater energy and meaning. Once the past is embraced, the faster healing can take place. Survivor of Auschwitz Viktor Frankl wrote:

> Everything can be taken from a man but one thing: the last of the human freedoms—to choose one's attitude in any given set of circumstances, to choose one's own way. And there were always choices to make. Every day, every hour, offered the opportunity to make a decision, a decision which determined whether you would or would not submit to those powers which threatened to rob you of your very self, your inner freedom.[245]

When thoughts of defeat or shame enter your mind, refuse them power over yourself. Instead, let them arm you, and the ones you love, with an arsenal to fight against them. Do not let past crimes or misdeeds that have happened to you control your mind. Thoughts of panic, insecurity and pain do not allow you to survive and protect yourself and others, and most importantly, live with meaning. If you embrace your life as it is, and not what you wish it would have been, you can improve your current state to make it better and seize that "inner freedom" to function with a calm spirit and strong determination. Looking to the future as being better and stronger can only happen if you live in the present and learn from the past rather than living in it. As Frankl further stated, "It is a peculiarity of man that he can only live by looking to the future—*sub specie aeternitatis*."[246]

Takeaways

- Abuse alters our brain chemistry and creates learning difficulties for children.

- With such a high rate of abuse in society and such a high rate of learning-disabled children, many of our children's learning disabilities might have resulted from sex abuse, or a preexisting condition of LD may have been aggravated by it.

- The sooner we let the child who has been abused know he or she is valuable, and that it is alright to talk about it, the sooner he or she can accept it and start healing.

Action Steps

- Encourage children who have experienced child abuse to talk about it and not feel shame.

- Encourage children who have experienced child abuse to feel valuable and important.

- If you have experienced child abuse, journal about it, explore it and try to understand it. The sooner you can get control of it, the faster you can prevent it from having any power over you.

CHAPTER 5:

Struggling to Make Friends, Blend with Society, Learn How to Learn and Discover a Diagnosis

"I try to make sense of things. Which is why, I guess, I believe in destiny. There must be a reason that I am as I am. There must be."
— Comedian Robin Williams[247]

"Monsters are real. Ghosts are too. They live inside of us, and sometimes, they win."

— Stephen King, *The Shining*

MY IMPULSIVE CURIOSITY AND QUICK temper exhausted my parents and alienated neighborhood children. The kids on my block did not like me very much, which seems to be common among non-ADHD-children dealing with ADHD-boys and -girls in their age group. As a result, my parents would get complaints from other families on the street. My mom always loved me, but I infuriated her frequently. I was constantly in trouble. She could have said the following: "[Bryan] is a regular boy—only magnified a thousand times."[248] Although my mother never felt this way to my knowledge, mothers of children like me often wish their child was never born. If you are such a parent, do not feel guilty "about not being a perpetual fountain of love."[249] To be otherwise is only human, especially with an ADHD-child.[250] Even my ex-wife and ex-mother-in-law expressed such thoughts about their LD-children. And though my mother never expressed the wish that I had never been born, when her bluish-green eyes turned red, I knew that murderous thoughts were lurking within, although she would never admit to it today. I think all parents, especially mothers, struggle with "sorrow, incertitude, and apprehension"[251] at one time or another during their time raising an ADHD/LD-child.

Many outsiders blamed my bad behavior on poor parenting, which added to my mother's frustrations. Many thought I needed "more discipline, more structure, more limit-setting" and believed my parents were "ignorant, careless, permissive, amoral, antisocial, or, in contemporary parlance, 'dysfunctional.'"[252] My mother often agreed with them. Her inability to control me had shattered all the confidence she had gained through raising my older brother. "With David, Son, I could give him a book and he would go in the corner and read for hours. With you, I could give you a book and within a minute, you were ripping out the pages because you did not like the colors. I didn't know how to control you."[253]

My mother often felt guilty for leaving me where others had to take responsibility for me. For example, she felt awful when she brought me to a mothers-day-out at a local church. She knew the teachers dreaded seeing me come through the door. This was difficult to accept since my mom was doing the best she could and there were few people in the U.S. who knew in the mid-1970s how to deal with children with short attention spans and over-the-top hyperactivity. Even though she knew the ladies did not like me, my mother needed those few hours of peace away from a child who drained her energies. She left me there to torment the ladies.

ADHD does not result from bad parenting, although this is a common misconception. The best parents care so much and try so hard to do what is right for their children that they often hold themselves to unreasonable standards. Although failure to achieve perfection is inevitable, good parents doubt themselves, but still try. Bad parents don't care enough about their children to try at all. A bad parent wouldn't read books like this. And although bad parenting may exacerbate a child's ADHD, "it does not cause it."[254] In the end, remember, raising children in general may seem an "impossibility," but it "usually works out anyway."[255] I believe just showing up and trying to learn how to help your child is 90% of the equation for success.

Even so, at that stage of the game, my mother questioned her abilities and asked herself, "What's wrong with me?" Her confidence as a mother was shaken, and the church and school leaders to whom she looked for help were only pointing fingers. Labeling us as failures did not help our situation. Jane Hersey, National Director of the Feingold Association that deals with LD-kids and diet, wrote the following:

> There are complicated descriptions of behavior problems and an alphabet of acronyms to go along with them... There is blame, there are admonitions, and instructions [by the professionals—doctors, allergists, psychologists, psychiatrists, etc.] to add to the many things you are expected to cope with. You may feel that you have been "jumping through hoops," but none of this effort really makes a difference.[256]

As Hersey goes on to explain, often when we look for help for our child, we ourselves are doing the diagnosis of our child because it depends on whom we consult.[257] In other words, if you assume you know the cause, you take your child to the doctor who specializes in treating that specific cause, even though there could be a dozen or more other assumptions that could just as easily manifest what the parent sees, each with a different medical specialty and solution. Unfortunately, parents of ADHD-children often feel so overwhelmed, exhausted and embarrassed by living with their children's condition that figuring out which experts to consult, or even which questions to ask, is an enormous challenge. I think Hersey above is saying that collecting all the different inputs and making sense out of them can be daunting; *however, it's imperative to get many experts' opinions on your or your child's situation and then do your best to make an educated decision about the best course of action.* Learning to live with ADHD is a complicated process, and experts in many disciplines can contribute to solutions. Doing nothing is not a viable option so ask as many questions as possible and get as many answers to them as you can before you decide on your *modus operandi* for yourself or child. Remember, "A wise man listens to advice" (Proverbs 12:15).[258] Investigate your options and decide on the best treatment plan, but refrain from blaming yourself for the problem.

Parents like my mother have done nothing wrong. As Dr. Feingold wrote, "Parents cannot blame themselves for the very strong probability of a genetic factor, plus the equally strong probability of environmental factors, of which they have no knowledge and very little control."[259] In further exploring behavior of hyperactive children, Feingold basically promoted the theory that kids like me only really need a lot of exercise and good, natural food. This physician's philosophy had a profound effect on my family's operations. He offered my mother understanding, community and, finally, a solution to help me. He was the person with the right advice for my situation. He showed her that she could help me control myself through a natural diet which I will explore shortly.

At her wits' end shortly before my fourth birthday, my mother consulted Dr. Stephen Maddox at the Child Study Center in Fort Worth, Texas. She told him I was "a nervous child," "too active," and had been banging my head on my pillow at night since I was six-months-old.[260] While bouncing my head as a child, I often sang *We Will Rock You* by the rock band Queen since this was one of my favorite songs.

STEPHEN GRIFFITH MADDOX, MD

Stephen G. Maddox

Dr. Stephen Maddox. This caring doctor ran the Fort Worth Child Study Center when I was tested and evaluated there from 1975 to 1979. He worked with my mother to get me to the right school, Starpoint, and proper speech therapy at Easterseals. Fort Worth Child Study Center Archive

My mother often stood outside my door listening to me bang and sing away in my bed, praying to God that He would do something to help me. She also worried about me when I banged my head on the floor, on the grass and against the car seats. Sometimes, my mother thought I was possessed, especially since, compared with other kids, I required so little sleep. My father was always working or drinking, leaving my mother to handle me alone. Each day was a "struggle [for her] to keep some order within herself and in the home."[261]

Dr. Maddox wrote in his notes after examining me in his office that my language skills were "moderately to severely impaired." He added that I was very hyperactive, "stumbled a lot and seems somewhat slow in fine and gross motor skills."[262] Dr. Maddox eventually concluded I had what today is called ADHD, but back then it was described as "minimal brain dysfunction (MBD) with hyperactivity and short attention span." He noted that I also had "a rather marked speech condition, both in expressive language and in articulation."[263]

Had the doctors diagnosed me a few years earlier, MBD would have stood for <u>M</u>inimal <u>B</u>rain <u>D</u>amage, but professionals by 1975 thought that too harsh and changed "damage" to "dysfunction."[264] This sounds absurd to label children as such, especially when the experts believed that kids with MBD "lag in brain maturation... or undetected damage to the brain."[265] Dr. Mark Stewart, an expert on hyperactivity, wrote, "Saying a child suffers from 'minimal brain dysfunction' is, in fact, like describing a child with a sore throat or a skinned knee as having 'minimal physical impairment.'"[266] Dr. Hallowell stated: "One had to wonder whether the brain itself was minimal or the dysfunction was minimal or perhaps whether the understanding of what was happening in the first place was minimal."[267] And before it was known as Minimal Brian Damage, the condition was called "exogenous mental retardation," or "morbid defect of moral control," or "brain-injured child."[268] Since the 1920s, more than 30 different terms have described what is now called ADHD. The more we learn about ADHD, the more the definitional phrases change and grow.[269] In the end, all of these labels do not do much to help the child, and they definitely distress the parents, convincing them they have an abnormal child.

Bryan Rigg
Page 2

REVIEW OF SYSTEMS: He has a reasonably good appetite. He never has had
any somatic complaints.

FAMILY HISTORY: The father is age 42, has a college education, and never
had any learning problems. The mother is age 37 and also college educated.
There is a 12 year old male sibling in the sixth grade who does very well
in school. There is no history of hyperactivity, learning disability, or
retardation in the family.

PHYSICAL EXAMINATION: The weight was 39 pounds, which is at the 75th
percentile. Height was 42 inches, which is slightly below the 90th percentile. FOC was 50-1/2 cms. He would not cooperate for hearing and vision
screen; however, he seemed to hear adequately and vision seemed normal. He
was a rather negativistic child who did not cooperate too well, and most of
the examination had to be done with his sitting on the examiner's lap. He
did have a rather marked speech problem, both in expressive language and in
articulation. Head was normocephalic. Ears: Negative. Eyes: Pupillary
responses were normal. Extraocular movements were full. The fundi were
not visualized. Nose: Negative. Mouth and throat: Tongue motility was
good. Dentition was normal. He had an active gag reflex. Chest: The
lungs were clear. Heart rate and rhythm were normal. There were no murmurs.
Abdomen: Soft, no visceromegaly. GU: Normal male. Back and extremities:
Negative. Skin and mucous membranes: Negative.

NEUROLOGICAL EXAMINATION: This could not be accomplished too well. The
cranial nerves seemed to be intact. There were definitely no motor deficits.
Sensory responses could not be obtained, although he seemed to notice
painful stimuli. He would not attempt any formal tests of gross coordination. His running gait was somewhat awkward, but the walking gait was
normal. He could not catch a ball. He threw it very awkwardly with the
right hand. There were no tremors or obvious defects in fine motor control.
He seemed to tend to use the right hand predominantly.

TENTATIVE IMPRESSION: (1) Probably minimal brain dysfunction with hyper-
                             activity and short attention span.
                        (2) Speech and language problems in both articula-
                             tion and expressive language.

RECOMMENDATIONS: We will proceed with psychologicals, audiological evaluation and speech and language assessment.

Stephen G. Maddox, M.D.
Medical Director
CHILD STUDY CENTER
Fort Worth, Texas

SCM/my

The Fort Worth Child Study Center report on me dated 19 February 1975 is
shown here, giving a tentative diagnosis of "minimal brain dysfunction with
hyperactivity and short attention span" and "speech and language problems in
both articulation and expressive language." Also pictured on the reverse side of
this page is a report of 22 April 1975 verifying that diagnosis. Fort Worth Child
Study Center Archives

Name: Bryan Mark Rigg
Page 2

Lab Data:

X-Ray:

Psychological and Educational Summary:

This child was seen as functioning in the bright normal range of intelligence with the Binet mental age of 4 years, 6 months; however, his social age on the Vineland was 3 years, 8 months, and his Developmental Test of Visual Motor Integration was 4 years, 1 month. He showed considerable scatter on the subtests with the Basal mental age at 3-1/2 years with scatter into the 6 year level. He was seen as a somewhat hyperactive, distractible child who would probably be a high risk for learning disability.

Consultations and Other Data:

Audiological screening using the Bell tone 10dB showed normal hearing bilaterally in all frequencies.

Speech and language evaluation: This showed that he was functioning adequately in the area of receptive language and vocabulary. However, expressive language and articulatory competence were moderately to severely impaired.

Diagnosis and Problem:

1. Minimal brain dysfunction with hyperactivity and short attention span.

2. Delayed speech and language development in the areas of expression and articulation.

3.

4.

Recommendations:

1. Enrollment in a well structured preschool program such as the Early Childhood Program in the Arlington schools or private placement if such can be found.

2. Trial on Milk/Chocolate Elimination diet.

3. Parent counseling.

4. Referral to Easter Seal Society for intensive speech and language development.

I suspect my ADHD is genetic since both my mother and father seem to have the characteristics of this "disorder." My mother is a poor listener and her mind jumps from one topic to the next without any thread of logic, reeling "with a multitude of incoherent thoughts."[270] She does not like to read, rarely finishing books she has started, and has difficulty retaining information unless she is hyper-focused. I am grateful she became hyper-focused on "healing" me (she was a saint in getting me help). She also can be impulsive, having married my father after only dating a few months. Although their marriage lasted 24 years, it was not a happy union. Later, she got engaged for a second time to the husband of her deceased cousin only a few months after her cousin's death. Although everyone thought it strange and unwise, she did it anyway. The marriage was not happy and did not last long. In some respects, it is not surprising why she has been divorced twice since both unions came about in an ADHD-like, impetuous manner. She would have been wise to have lived with both men for a while before tying the knot. Her ADHD also helped her develop positive traits: She has an incredible memory when she takes an interest in something, is very compassionate and has a great sense of humor. She is adventurous and independent. And strangely enough, she becomes an excellent listener at parties when meeting new people for the first time. Famous English writer Joseph Conrad could have described my mother when he wrote: "[She] had the talent of making people talk to [her] freely, and an inexhaustible patience in listening to their tales."[271] My ex-wife and I often joked that if we wanted someone to gather the life stories of people at our parties, then all we needed to do was to have my mother there (very Hunter-like).

Here is my mother, Marilee Gladys Rigg, in 1984 at the age of 47. She was tenacious in getting me help for my ADHD/dyslexia and was a force of nature in finding me a good school and proper therapy.

Like my mother, my father also exhibited ADHD-traits. My father, who died in 2006, was impulsive, needed high risk activities and had an addictive personality, whether it was sex or alcohol. Such activities helped lead to his divorce from my mother in 1984.[272] He also had severe problems with self-esteem, although most who knew him superficially would find this hard to believe. Although a successful executive and a millionaire by 1987, his impulsive behavior led him, after his divorce from mom, to marry an unethical woman (a pathological liar) and go into a business venture that was poorly executed, using his then third wife, unwisely one might add, to help him run this corporation. As someone who worked with both of them said of my stepmother, "Bryan, she is depriving a village of its idiot somewhere in the world." By 1993, my dad had run through all his money and the business was a failure. By 1995, he was bankrupt. By 1999, he fortunately had divorced the "worst-mistake-I-have-made-in-my-life" woman he had married, but he was a broken man with few financial resources. He told me one time as I was helping him learn how to use a computer: "Son, I wish I could push the delete key on my life."[273] His biographical narrative here, unfortunately, is very ADHD-like. When doing something harmful to himself, he didn't know when to stop and often practiced what Napoleon had told his commanders never to do; namely, "Never reinforce failure."[274] The positive sides of my father's ADHD were that he worked well with direction, was driven, had a high energy level and was a superb sailboat sailor. He was also an excellent navigator, with this being his primary job on anti-submarine airplanes (P2Vs) when he served in the U.S. Navy as an officer. He, like me, had an incredible sense of direction and never got lost. Also, he was the proverbial "life of the party" and enjoyed telling stories and making people laugh, which he could easily do. So, by looking at my parents, it seems clear that I got my ADHD from both of them.

Here is my father, Linton Mark Rigg, in 1983 when he turned 50. At this time, he was an accomplished businessman serving as Vice President of Human Resources at Southland Corporation (7-11). Throughout his life, he expressed many ADHD-like behaviors, including being a good leader, an excellent sailor and a tireless searcher for adventure.

Also, both my grandfathers, Wilburn Arnold Davidson and Mark Rigg, seemed to have had ADHD. They were both alcoholics and had problems blending into society. Both were womanizers and got into a lot of trouble throughout their lives. Both were also brilliant men. My paternal grandfather, Mark Rigg, was a pharmacist and was called "Doc" Rigg because he was the pseudo town doctor in Springfield, Pennsylvania, setting broken bones and administering medical services as well as prescribing medications (pharmacists did such things back in the 1920s, -'30s and -'40s). He could quote Shakespeare at the drop of a dime, was extremely charming and was an entrepreneur.[275]

My maternal grandfather, Wilburn Arnold Davidson, was called "Tex" since he had grown up in Texas and was tall and always wore a cowboy hat—which was not uncommon back then for Texans. Since he traveled a lot with religious tours all over the world for decades, people from different regions in the U.S. just gave him this nickname when they were on these vacations. He loved history, philosophy and religion and could discuss a plethora of historical topics and could quote scripture "like it was on the back of his hand" (he was, after all, a son of a Presbyterian minister).[276]

Although grandfather Rigg became a successful pharmacist and grandfather Davidson became an excellent land surveyor, both were also extremely restless.

My grandfather Rigg described his divorce and life to his daughter, Mary Dalbey, née Rigg, as follows: "The divorce was all my fault. I wish I could redo it and many other things in the past. My life can be defined as living on the edge, all the time."[277] As one can see, my grandfather Rigg admitted to his child that he wished he could have re-done his life and that he viewed his mishaps as resulting from his inability to control his risky behavior. He knew his life of alcohol, broken promises, and destroyed relationships was something he horribly regretted. He died prematurely at the age of 53 due to strokes, stemming most likely from his drinking, as well as drug abuse (he was a pharmacist who also gave himself narcotics). The mistakes he had made were very ADHD-like behaviors.

Like grandfather Rigg, grandfather Davidson also struggled with life. He confided in his diary in 1967 the following, powerful self-reflection:

> Very few honest people left in the world—Very few live up to their religion in whatever church or form. That has been proven here—You can see the Dr. Jekyll's and Mr. Hyde's [he was describing people drinking excessively, gambling too much and sleeping around during a Presbyterian trip to Montego Bay, Jamaica, but nonetheless, still attending church on Sunday morning]...Not that I am a citizen to go by. Well, I did not take communion in Jamaica. Hardly do it at home. But I sure wouldn't take communion Sunday morning and then gamble on horse races, drink Bourbon

whiskey and dance to midnight all Sunday evening after dinner---now if that isn't hypocrisy, I don't know what in the hell you would call it....I've done worse than they have, but I wasn't on a Presbyterian tour when I did it. Nor was I within 40 blocks of the Church. I was ashamed to be—I haven't had a drink and they have urged me to go to cocktail parties. I said yesterday, "What you trying to do, get me drunk?" They answered "No, just enjoy life." I said, "You don't know me, but I know myself. If I take a drink, I will wind up drunk. Then you would ridicule me. You would have something to talk about, and I have noticed that some of you have gotten pretty tipsy. You don't have to tell me, because you can't fool an old drunk like me." They looked funny. Because you know they never get drunk, they just get lit. No difference however—I told them and people would tell you, that when Arnold [the name my grandfather went by] is going to church, he is sober. When he isn't, he's liable to be drunk. The more I see it, the more I hate it. [I told them,] "That anybody who drinks is a plain damn fool and how well that I know it. I am better off than you. I know it and you don't. ('But you will find out!'). All you have to do is just keep it up a while longer."[278]

My grandfather Davidson struggled with what he had done and become. His honest assessment of his weaknesses, his regrets and his behavior sum up a lot of what ADHD-people struggle with. As he wrote, "the more I see it, the more I hate it." Obviously, he never got help for his addiction and possible ADHD. Although highly intelligent, his poor self-esteem and weakness for alcohol was evidence for all to see. He had a life full of failure. He attended a prestigious college in Texas, Trinity University, but dropped out after three years, never finishing his degree. He tried growing corn in the panhandle of Oklahoma, but it was an unwise choice for the climate and soil, and this venture financially devastated him and his family. He had affairs on my grandmother and destroyed their marriage, which ended in a nasty divorce. He was estranged from his daughters. And he continued to repeat his mistakes—the definition of a fool. At the age of 60 in 1967, when he wrote this diary entry, instead of looking for ways to improve his life, he was stuck in a weird review of how one should behave when about to go to church, and how one can behave when not going to church. The mind-forged manacles he had about moral behavior and how holy ground should elicit good behavior never actually bore fruit in his own life although he was more than willing to condemn others for their shortcomings. Nonetheless, he was honest about his failures when he wrote, "I have done worse than they have," but then reverted back to his holier-than-thou analysis ending the sentence with, "but I wasn't on a Presbyterian tour." This exchange with himself showed he struggled with leading a disciplined life. And that last line makes me wonder what grandfather Davidson gave himself license to do when not on a religious tour! Like grandfather Rigg, I know much more about grandfather Davidson that is not revealed in this book, but it was a sad tale of never being able to organize an honorable existence. He also had, unfortunately, a very ADHD-like biography. As one of his dearest friends from youth, Dwight Leonard, said, "Bryan, your grandfather was the smartest out of the bunch of us young men in Beaver [Oklahoma]. He by far had the most potential to be the richest and most distinguished of all of us. He just couldn't put it together. He makes me even sad today at 90 years of age."[279] Grandfather Davidson died at the age of 67, drunk in his home in San Angelo, Texas.

Here, my grandfather, Wilburn Arnold Davidson, is looking at the photographer. He is sitting with his newborn daughter, my mother, Marilee,
and his father, Reverend Thomas W. Davidson. My grandfather, although
intelligent, was never able to put his life together and was an alcoholic,
restless and a constant traveler, never settling down in any one place for
long—typical ADHD-behavior. Circa May 1937

Here are my paternal grandparents, Mark Rigg and Leona Rigg, née Parr. Both of them exhibited ADHD-like behavior. Grandfather Rigg was an alcoholic and had constant problems with his relationships. And although a pharmacist, he abused drugs. He would die at the age of 53. Grandmother Rigg constantly had problems dealing with people, was erratic and addicted to drugs. Both lived lives that one could say exemplified ADHD. Circa 1945

And what about my grandmothers? Well, my maternal grand-mother, Edna Davidson, née Barby, was definitely a Farmer-type, unlike my Hunter-grandfathers. She was a wonderful artist and gardener, calm, methodical and probably OCD. Everything was organized in her home and when she died in 1995, she was a millionaire, because she saved everything she could and rarely spent anything on herself. Before she died, she was even still cooking with pots and pans she had bought in the 1930s. She was always well groomed and dressed and did not like excitement. She led a very honorable, but very boring, life.

My paternal grandmother, Lenora Rigg, née Parr, was another story altogether, compared to grandmother Davidson. She was married four times, divorced twice and widowed twice. All her marriages were unhappy. She was beautiful as a young woman, and intelligent, but very unhappy. She was the proverbial "drama-queen," and made my father's, mother's, and other family members' lives miserable when she was around them. She helped in her husband's pharmacy and was, like him, addicted to pills (when she died, she had over a dozen prescriptions). She seemed to live a life between the extremes and never found her equilibrium. Two events illustrate this woman's eradicate behavior. Becoming upset with my father one day when he was apparently going to move out of the home, which, after his father's death, had been turned into a tenant house divided into four apartments, my grandmother threw a fit. He had helped her maintain the place, but he now wanted to go to college. She locked herself in the bathroom and threatened to kill herself. She calmed down eventually and my father moved out and started living his own life. Another time, she visited my parents and my brother while they were living in Detroit, Michigan. Soon after arriving, she became upset about something and insisted my father return her to the airport. He eventually did, and on arriving back at the airport, she went inside to buy a new ticket. My father waited in the parking lot just in case there were no flights departing that evening. After several minutes, she returned to his car and said she had bought her ticket to leave in seven days and that she now would stay at his home until then. My father shook his head at this schizophrenic behavior, drove back to the house and she was delightful for the rest of the week! Obviously, probably something more than ADHD was at work here, but her bizarre behavior was often ADHD-like and shows she had a difficult time with people and life and never got her "ducks in a row."[280]

So, when I research the biographies of my grandfathers, paternal grandmother and father, I can honestly say I come from a tradition of people who were thrill seekers with addictive personalities, and fortunately full of intelligence and energy. Although they were not diagnosed as also having learning disabilities at the time, their behavior and restlessness gave every indication that they had ADHD.

In the late 1970s, my own diagnosis was defined by the federal government in cooperation with the Easterseals Research Foundation as the following:

> [L]earning or behavior disabilities ranging from mild to severe, which are associated with deviations of function of the central nervous system. These deviations may manifest themselves by various combinations of impairment in perception, conceptualization, language, memory, and control of attention, impulse, or motor function... These aberrations may arise from genetic variations, biochemical irregularities, perinatal brain insults or other illnesses or injuries sustained during the years which are critical for the development and maturation of the central nervous system, or from unknown causes.[281]

In addition to MBD, the condition I had was also called Hyper-Kinesis Learning-Disabled (H-LD). As a result, Dr. Maddox warned that my education would be truncated, that I would probably not complete high school and that I would need to be closely watched for self-esteem problems (this fear is expressed by many professionals based on case studies). Maddox knew that if ADHD-kids do not get help, their lives will "likely be filled with failure and underachievement."[282]

Furthermore, Maddox predicted I would have difficulty developing friendships, since I had a speech impediment that made me stutter and mispronounce words, and I would thus struggle in school. Also, because hyperactive children usually have poor self-esteem, they have trouble making and keeping friends. At this stage in my life, I did not have many friends at school or church. Maddox provided literature to my mother that warned her that criminal activity often tempted boys with my problems. This frightening prognosis has been given to many other mothers with children like me. It is a sad truth that there is a large number of people in American jails with ADHD.[283] The Canadian Centre for Justice Statistics documented that the "typical teenage offender is a hyperactive male, with learning problems, poor social skills and low self-esteem."[284] The *Archives of General Psychiatry* published in 1993 reports that males with ADHD have a "significantly higher incidence of antisocial personality disorder (18% vs. 2%) and drug abuse (15% vs. 4%) compared to their peers who had not been diagnosed with ADHD."[285] In short, "children with ADHD are at higher risk for developing long-lasting problems affecting social relationships, academics, and adult life as well as psychiatric symptoms."[286] So the literature my mother read described the worst case scenario of my future based on solid, scientific evidence. Even as a mild case, I was headed for trouble.

Maddox recommended speech therapy at the Fort Worth Easterseals Center. Between the ages of four and five, I saw the reading specialist, Dr. Jean May, twice a week in Irving, Texas. The Fort Worth Child Study Center had discovered that I had problems putting letters together and sounding out words. I still do, but I have worked hard at correcting this problem. I will never forget when reading aloud and mispronouncing some words during a high school drama class, my teacher, Donna Reynolds, stopped me and asked me to repeat one word. I said again "Bif-all-calls." "No, Bryan," she gently said, "you mean bifocals." I still have problems with words, but learning foreign languages like German and some Hebrew helped me a lot with pronunciation.[287] Even today, when I come across new words, it takes several times repeating the word to get its correct pronunciation. Usually, when I find a new word that is difficult, I thrive on learning how to say it and work at it until I get it right.

As a child, I was a poor reader and had difficulty developing the "alphabetic principle." I was also RD or Reading Disabled.[288] With all the abbreviations for "disorders," one wonders how some of us ever survived evolution. Often, ADHD-children are referred to as Alphabet Children because of all the letters that go next to their names to describe their "problems."[289] At age eight, I still could not write the alphabet correctly.[290] According to the experts, I probably had a "deficit in phoneme awareness—the understanding that words are made up of sound segments called phonemes."[291] Dr. May worked patiently with me to help me learn basic sounds and letters. Since my graphophonemic knowledge, "the recognition of the letters of the alphabet and the understanding of sound-spelling relations," was extremely weak, she started with the basics. To obtain "adequate comprehension, word recognition skills need to be initially and explicitly taught to children who are at risk for reading disabilities."[292] This was something I needed to work out.

Dr. May helped me by showing me a letter or a few letters together (phonemic units) on a card and I would have to sound them out and then give a word with that sound. For example, she would show me a card with a U on it. I would then say "you", "uhuh" and then "ugly" to prove I understood how it was used. Then she would show me **NG** and then I would say "ingee," "ing" and then "bring" or **NG**, "ingee," "ang" and then "bang." Then she would have me use the words in a sentence like, "An ugly ant brings a drum to school and bangs on it during class." Speech therapy was fun even though I had to work hard. I was weak in "phonemic awareness," having difficulty "decoding," so this process forced me to attend to "every letter, something readers must eventually do."[293]

Often during these sessions, I became extremely distracted and fidgety, and when this happened, she took me outside and made me run around the parking lot to burn off my nervous energy. Despite Dr. May's help, I still failed first-grade twice. My speech improved, but I continued to confuse *Bs* and *Ds,* and *Fs* and *Ts.* This continued to make for interesting conversation when I called my father "Bad," or when I played with my "frucks," or when I asked the babysitter to "*T*uck me into bed" as described earlier. I also switched words. For example, I said "water" for "weather" and "spill" for "spell" and "walk" for "work."[294] I also would leave endings off of words, writing "sa" for "say" and "mak" for "make." And displaying my dyslexia with "letter reversals and left to right progression difficulties," I would switch, for example, "ni" for "in."[295] Lastly, I had problems with the "scr" sound and instead of asking my mom to "scratch my back," I would ask her to "thatch my back Mommy."[296] In general, letters and words proved difficult for me and my ears.

Even today, I get confused with words. For example, after my ex-wife had our first child in 2000, I expressed to my ex-mother-in-law my relief that my wife had not suffered at all from *postmortem* depression. My ex-mother-in-law responded, "Yeah, it really sucks when you're dead. You meant to say *postpartum* depression." Now, I can laugh at such mistakes.

And when learning German, such malapropisms also were cause for some awkward and funny discussions. When interviewing a German veteran from World War II for my work on *Hitler's Jewish Soldiers,* I talked to a man and his wife about his difficult time and hardships on his first cruise as a sailor in the *Kriegsmarine.* When he arrived in port, I asked him whether he was excited about getting his first official rank of Seaman (*Matrose*) for the trials and tribulations he had experienced while in the Baltic and North Seas. He looked awkwardly at me, and his wife, I could tell, was not very pleased with my question. So, I repeated my question, in true American fashion, louder and with more emphasis on pronunciation. What I didn't know was instead of asking if he wanted the rank of *Matrose* when he got into port, I was actually mixing up German words and was literally asking him if he wanted to get some *Muschi* when he hit port which loosely translated into: "When you got into port, did you want to immediately get some *Pussy*?" He immediately gave me a look that said, "I understand what you are asking, but can we talk about this later." After a few more awkward moments, the couple realized my mistake, gave me a German lesson after which I turned beet-red and then I profusely apologized for my misuse of my vocabulary. We had a hearty laugh and the sweet couple never let me live down my poor understanding of naval ranks and derogatory language for female body parts in *Deutsch*. After leaving their home that day, he escorted me to the train station and as I said goodbye, he said, "As any red-blooded young man would feel, to answer your questions you gave me earlier, well, yes, I wanted both when I hit port after being at sea for months." Like with my mother-in-law above, I can now laugh at the struggles I have had in learning languages, and in learning German, I learned more about how difficult it really is for ADHD-types to learn language.

see relationships of whole to part of whole. ...ne year 16-10 in ability to analyze, relatively familiar material and to would be expected in less than twelve percent of the population. Thus the verbal-visual-motor split and range of scores were atypical. The profile suggests immature neurological functioning (Clements).

Academic achievement, as measured on the WRAT, in word recognition was at the end of first grade. Whole word substitutions were common

(weather/"water", spell/"spill", work/"walk"). Arithmetic scores were at the middle of second grade with difficulty in addition of three sets of numbers. Spelling scores were at the middle to end of first grade with letter reversals and left to right progression difficulties (in/"ni"). Silent letter endings were also omitted (say/"sa", make/ "mak"). Letter formations were fair with size of letters varying.

Listening comprehension, as measured on the Durrell, was at third grade level which was one to two years above grade placement. There were three errors out of a possible seven on the fourth grade level.

Reading comprehension was at the beginning second grade level and thus a few months above word recognition, as measured on the WRAT.

The human figure drawing was in the defective range. There were six Koppitz organic signs which was significant. There were three Koppitz emotional indicators.

SUMMARY:
Child with high average range overall intelligence but with superior visual-motor skills, approximately one and one-half standard deviations above the average verbal skills.

Atypical range of scores.

Achievement similar to grade placement in word recognition and spelling; and above grade placement in arithmetic.

Areas of strength: Ability to analyze, to synthesize whole to a part of the whole, arithmetic skills, WISC visual-motor skills, listening comprehension.

Areas in need of reinforcement: Short term auditory memory, reversals, left to right progression, distractibility, impulsiveness, tendency to manipulate adults, concentration, handwriting, phonics skills, sight vocabulary, alphabet.

Fort Worth Child Study Center report on me on 12 April 1979 showing that I was plagued with malapropisms, doing "whole word substitutions." Fort Worth Child Study Center Archives

Nonetheless, for the vast majority of humankind, people did not have written languages. And even when the "written word" became the norm for most major languages, the vast majority of people still remained illiterate. It only became a social practice in the 1600s and 1700s to teach people in general to read and write in America and Europe so they could read the Bible. In the late 1700s, Thomas Jefferson believed a functional democracy could only operate when its people were literate, and thus he advocated for the public school system in Virginia in particular, and the U.S. in general, something that really only took off in the 1830s under Horace Mann and other educational visionaries. It was only in the last few hundred years that the majority of U.S. citizens could read and write, key skills to have to survive in the modern world.

Here is my "first" first-grade class with Jim Rose. I am on the first row with my chin on my hands. I don't look happy—this first year of school was difficult for me and I struggled with everything.

But for the vast majority of humankind's existence, being literate was not necessary to survive. When the Farmer-societies created writing, they created it with how their brains worked. Hunter-brains, especially those with ADHD/dyslexia, have a difficult time understanding the written word because it was not developed by Hunter-societies and does not conform to the neurochemistry that make up Hunter-people's cerebral matter. As a result, Hunter-ADHD/dyslexic people have a more difficult time understanding Farmer-peoples' written languages, because it was not developed to work with how they actually think and behave. In many respects, learning to read languages separates Hunters from Farmers since it is, in some respects, a *prejudice-learned-behavior developed by Farmers to unify their societies.* Of course, the written word has allowed us to save and store knowledge and communicate in ways that would baffle our ancient ancestors, but it is more difficult to learn for ADHD/dyslexic people simply because their brains have more difficulty learning it than Farmer-types who invented language in the first place.

So, knowing these facts today, I understand why in my childhood, I was consistently frustrated when I could not understand things in the Farmer-classrooms I attended. My first, first-grade teacher, Jim Rose, recalled that I would break pencils at my desk in frustration. Aggravated with learning, I would rock back and forth in my desk so vigorously that I would often fall to the floor.[297] Mr. Rose had to put me in the back row so I would not hurt anyone.

During this year, I was constantly in trouble with Mr. Rose, a Navy and Vietnam veteran. Mr. Rose recently told me, "Bryan, you could drive a teacher to the wall."[298] I had a horrible temper and difficulties with my studies. In his 28 years of teaching, Mr. Rose claims, "Out of all the kids I taught, Bryan, I felt you had the biggest fight on your hands."[299] He also remembered visiting my parents during teacher-parent conferences at my home and seeing how much stress I was causing my father, who clearly felt embarrassed having such a hyperactive, undisciplined son. Mr. Rose noticed that my dad did all he could to keep me out of the room.[300] My mother agreed with Mr. Rose and also felt that my father was in denial about what was wrong with me.

This is a common response of parents of LD-children. Many parents become ashamed of their children, not because they do not love them, but because the "public displays of deficiencies and problems produce... disrespectful treatment from others."[301] Also, fathers often have difficulties accepting their sons as LD because their "boys" are not supposed to be weak, and take it as a reflection of their own failures and identity issues. They usually get defensive and say, "That's just the way I was when I was a kid," as if to justify the behavior of their child.[302] Even if that is true, it doesn't help his child when a father says, "I suffered and survived, you will, too!" In the end, this does not deal with the problem. The problem is not about the father, but about the child and this focus should not be lost. Other parents, in contrast, feel personally responsible for a child's behavior. While they are in a sense partially right to feel this way when the cause is genetic or a direct result of parental behavior, they must also realize that there are factors outside of themselves that can contribute to a child's behavior.[303]

During this difficult stage of my life, in first-grade, the experts had not definitively diagnosed my situation, although Dr. Maddox was convinced it was MBD. However, the adults really did not know how to handle my condition. In doing clinical tests on me at Scottish Rite Hospital in Dallas, Dr. Solomon recommended that my parents ban television in the home (which my mom dutifully did for two years), get me glasses (which the ophthalmologist later determined I didn't need) and make me drink a cup of coffee before school to calm me down (which my mom did for only a few months because I threw fits when I had to drink the "muddy water"). As Dr. Hallowell writes, "The life of a child, and his or her family, with undiagnosed ADD is a life full of unnecessary struggle, accusation, guilt, recrimination, underachievement, and sadness."[304]

And that "struggle" happened often when people simply did not know how to deal with children like me. Back in the 1970s, teachers could still touch children to show affection and to punish. I got many hugs from Mr. Rose, but I also received several spankings from him (unnecessarily according to Hallowell—spankings do not help children, especially ADHD-ones).[305] My father added to my pain by having a policy that whenever I got licks at school, I would also get them at home. I had to tell my parents, because if they found out I had not reported a school spanking, I would get double the punishment at home.[306]

I remember the pain of those school "licks" as the wooden paddle whacked my buttocks. Of course, my teacher did not know my father had problems with alcohol. This sometimes threw off Dad's aim when I got my second batch of swats that night. When my father was drinking, my mother tried to stop him from carrying out such punishments, but her intervention was not always successful. I of course never knew whether Dad had arrived home drunk, and I always dutifully told him about my punishments at school out of fear of getting a double lashing later. Although my dad only hit me across the back a few times, in addition to the swats on my buttocks, those moments still stick out in my mind, especially when my father hit me with the metal buckle of his belt.

It does seem to be the case that some parents of hyperactive children may lose control and take their frustration out on their child. Unfortunately, it has been documented that parents, unable to handle the trials and tribulations a hyperactive child brings into the home, often "beat him cruelly in an explosion of anger."[307] So whether my father was drinking or not when he hit me, what I experienced was regrettably common among many "unprepared" parents of hyperactive children, especially of my generation and prior ones.

Today, when I look back at my school licks, I really do not think I warranted such physical punishment. Mr. Rose today agrees that some of his punishment was unnecessary, because I was just a five- or six-year-old boy. Often normal behavior for young boys is immediately termed ADHD and disruptive when it should just be termed natural.[308] Now Mr. Rose knows there were other ways to go about punishing me (if one assumes punishment was warranted), but back then, he was using the current disciplining methods of the time. Since he, himself, had had a rough past and had been in a lot of trouble in school, and received numerous licks from his teachers, he was just doing what he thought would help us learn best.

I remember two specific occasions when Mr. Rose punished me. Once, I got up from my chair, though he had told me repeatedly not to, and the other time he caught me throwing pebbles at a girl in the class. I can understand why I got punished for throwing stones, because she could have been seriously hurt by a pebble in the eye, but I felt it was unfair for him to spank me for getting up from my chair. I do not remember that Mr. Rose told me not to get up, but I probably did not hear many things Mr. Rose said, and he interpreted my inattentiveness as disobedience. Maybe I simply couldn't hear Mr. Rose since he had placed me on the back row because I fell out of my desk so much.

Mr. Rose recalled that I got another spanking because I kissed one of my classmates without her permission. Before the swats, Mr. Rose always told me, "I don't want to do this, but I think it will help you," and "This is going to hurt me more than you [whatever that meant!]," but I never believed him. He prayed with me afterwards and asked God to help me behave. Was divine intervention really the only thing that could help me change?

As a child, I found this pressure suffocating and feared the paddle. I was riddled with guilt for not behaving properly. I hated the feeling that I was so out of control and did not like school. I remember feeling panic attacks come on right before I left the car to enter the school building in the mornings. The days I left school without being in trouble were some of my happiest moments in life as a first grader.

Although Mr. Rose was a good man and tried to do his best for his students, he said that after his experience with me, he labeled me as learning disabled and did not think I would accomplish much. Mr. Rose now realizes how children with my condition should be viewed and treated differently.[309]

The stigma of being labeled as an ADHD- or LD-child is difficult to overcome and creates in the child a poor self-image. Being hyperactive seems to lead "to emotional problems [feeling like a failure], rather than being a symptom of them."[310] It then takes a lot to break the mirror that tells you that you cannot succeed.

For example, when I was 19 and going off to Phillips Exeter Academy for a fifth high-school year to prepare myself for an Ivy League school, I met up with Mr. Rose while I was wearing a Princeton University shirt. He tells me now that since he struggled with labeling people, he still viewed me as that hyperactive, dysfunctional child and thought about me going to an Ivy League school, "Yeah right, like that will ever happen."[311] Interestingly, Mr. Rose cared for me and really loved me as a student. He did want the best for me, even though he viewed me as headed for failure, as others in my community also did.

My second first-grade year at Pantego Christian Academy under a new teacher, Madeline Teague, produced similar results. Instead of getting licks, she carried a ruler around and would whack me on the arm or hand if I was doing something she did not like. Although she was a sweet lady, I continued to do poorly in school. As she told me years later, "Bryan, we simply didn't know how to deal with children like you in the seventies."[312] As a result, I failed my second year of first-grade. In a parent-teacher conference, she told my mother, "We really shouldn't pass him to second-grade, but we cannot have him do a third year of first-grade at eight years of age."[313] As a result, my mom knew she needed to find another school for me, but she had no clue where to turn.

Here is my "second" first-grade class with Madeline Teague. I am in the middle standing up with the multi-colored stripe shirt. After this year with Mrs. Teague, I failed first-grade again. She told my mother they really could not let me repeat first-grade for a third time and she did not know what to do with me. As a result, my mother knew she needed to find me a new school. Luckily, she enrolled me at the Starpoint School at Texas Christian University which focused on children with severe "learning disabilities."

At that time, I constantly struggled with reading. I was falling behind because I could not master reading as an essential building block to acquire information, build knowledge and enrich my life. When I started to sound out certain words, I was slow and found reading laborious. "The word reading of poor readers is inaccurate, slow, or both," wrote Drs. Joseph Jenkins and Rollanda O'Connor. "Poor readers' inefficient word level processing drains the very attentional resources needed to maximize comprehension."[314] I often read several pages without ever knowing what I had read. This was frustrating and, in turn, had "far-reaching negative implications within the school, family and community."[315] I was struggling to be normal in more ways than one.

Besides having problems with my schoolwork, I also was developing poor social skills. Many kids did not want to be around me. A few years ago, I met up with a man, James Wilde, with whom I attended church when we were children. He had several films of his birthday parties. The first one was when we were all four years old. There was our usual gang all there around the table. However, for his fifth and sixth birthdays, everyone was there except me. I strongly feel that I was no longer invited because I had become a nuisance. I remember in Mr. Rose's first-grade class, I was always on the "bad" team for soccer and never on the "good" team. Kids suffering from ADHD often are "clumsy" with their "interactions with other children."[316] They frequently bump into other children, failing to understand each person's personal space, laughing at inappropriate times and failing to understand the situation at hand. They often have sloppy handwriting and initially have problems "in the use of either fine muscles or gross muscles."[317]

To help with coordination, my mother got me involved with soccer and baseball. During my first year on both teams, I hardly played at all. My baseball teammates actually called me the "Statue of Liberty," because I never swung the bat out of fear of failing. My efforts (or lack thereof) with my athletic endeavors produced the same results as my schoolwork.

Even my parents' efforts to educate me seemed fruitless. My father would sit down with me after work trying to help me read while drinking a glass of scotch. He was consistently frustrated with my performance and kept saying in a harsh tone, "No! No! No, Bryan!!! [heavy sigh] That's not right." He would then sometimes slam the book down on the table where we were working. After a few of these sessions, I avoided doing homework with my father.

My parents were continually encouraged to seek help from an eye doctor since people felt there was something wrong with my vision. This is indeed a reliable initial solution for parents who have a child who has trouble reading in order to rule out vision correction before going to the next level of finding a diagnosis that the child is Reading Disabled (RD). Yet, often kids with ADHD have no problems with their eyes. My vision was 20/15.[318]

During a test at the Child Study Center in Ft. Worth at the age of eight, when asked to write out the alphabet, I wrote the following "A, ꓭ, C, d, e, f, G, 11, M, Q, r, S" and then getting frustrated with not remembering the rest, I "scratched out everything I had written" and said "I can't do it."[319] "I CAN'T DO IT...." This negative phrase shakes me today. Looking back, it is sad that this is what I had learned during my first eight years of life. That was the message I had been trained to accept. Rather than knowing I could adapt and improvise in my learning techniques or that I should never give up, I had simply been taught, "You can't do it."

I met all the conditions of being learning disabled in 1977, according to the U.S. Office of Education's definition at that time when it described it as a disorder "in one or more of the psychological processes involved in understanding or in using language, spoken or written, which may manifest itself in an imperfect ability to listen, speak, read, write, spell, or to do mathematical calculations."[320] And in 1978, the National Joint Committee on Learning Disabilities (NJCLD) defined LD as a "generic term that refers to a heterogeneous group of disorders manifested by significant difficulties in the acquisition and use of listening, speaking, reading, writing, reasoning or mathematical abilities. These disorders are... due to central nervous system dysfunction."[321] I fit all these definitions, but there was little empirical information available to parents to help my mother know what to do, once I was labeled LD. Getting a diagnosis was much different than getting a plan of action for healing. My mother was frustrated with the inability to find a course of action to help me.

Bryan Mark Rigg
Page 2

BACKGROUND AND OBSERVATIONS:

Bryan was referred for educational evaluation by Dr. Stephen Maddox as a child with possible minimal brain dysfunction. The parents of Bryan reported hyperactivity, speech problems at age four, behavior or discipline problems and impulsive behaviors. Bryan was, at the time of assessment, on the Feingold diet. Difficulties sleeping were reported by parents as Bryan "pounds his head to go to sleep". Bryan was reported to still body rock and head bang. Low frustration tolerance and distractibility were problems for Bryan at school and at home. The school reported moderate difficulty in working independently and mild problems with initial and sustained attending behaviors and self-assertiveness. Bryan was repeating first grade at Pantego Christian Academy, however, parents were considering placement in Starpoint school at some later date.

Bryan was a tall, well groomed boy who cooperated for the duration of the testing when firmly managed. He responded quickly and impulsively to all test items and asked several times after each "Am I right? Am I right?" His tolerance for frustration was very low. His responses were loud and lengthy, often without being connected to the original question. When drawing a person, he made three attempts before he stayed with one, quickly scratching over each saying "I can't" and finally drawing a primitive almost stick figure with a hat. The right hand was used for pencil/paper tasks. When asked to write the alphabet, he wrote "A, 8, C, d, e, f, G, 11, M, Q, r, S" while singing the alphabet song to remember sequence, however, was unable to remember and therefore scratched over all he had written. There was difficulty with reversals and left to right progression throughout the testing session. Letter formations were varied in size and shape; pencil pressure also varied.

TEST RESULTS:

Scores on the WISC-R reflected overall functioning in the high average range. There was, however, approximately one and one-half standard deviations between the superior range visual-motor skills and the average range verbal skills. There was a scattering of competencies such that skills ranged from Year 6-10 level of expectancy in short term auditory memory to above the Year 16-10 in ability to analyze, to synthesize, using concrete, relatively familiar material and to see relationships of whole to part of whole. The range of scores would be expected in less than twelve percent of the population. Thus the verbal-visual-motor split and range of scores from the mean were atypical. The profile suggests immature neurological functioning (Clements).

Academic achievement, as measured on the WRAT, in word recognition was at the end of first grade. Whole word substitutions were common

Fort Worth Child Study Center report on me on 12 April 1979 showing that even at the age of eight, I could not do the alphabet and continued saying "I can't" do basic skills. At this time, I was struggling to read and learn. Fort Worth Child Study Center Archives

In 1975 the U.S. Department of Education implemented the Individualized Education Program (IEP). It was not widespread, and it was only executed in public schools, not private ones, like I was attending. Before this legislation, many children with learning disabilities were prevented from attending school! IEP gave rights to LD-students to have special curricula designed for them and it came under the Education for All Handicapped Children Act (EHA), also implemented in 1975.[322] However, programs in schools focusing on children with LD and ADHD really did not gain momentum until the Americans with Disabilities Act was passed in 1990.[323] Thereafter, more LD-programs were implemented throughout the public-school systems. Children today have many options they can benefit from once they are diagnosed with a certain disability. This Act took inspiration from the Civil Rights Act of 1964, recognizing the importance of protecting people against discrimination in any form, from race, to ethnicity, to religion, and last, to how one learns.[324] Obviously, looking at the dates of this legislation dealing with special education, I was born a decade or two too early for these programs to benefit me.

While my mother worked hard to help me, my older brother, who was more than eight years older than me, was not helpful with this aspect of my life. Since my mother spent a lot of time trying to make me normal, she ignored my brother's normalcy. My brother naturally resented the attention I received, as most siblings do in the best of circumstances, and made it a point to put me down, calling me a loser and an "idiot." The difference with me and others with LDs was that everything in my world reinforced his insults, while in many families, it is nothing more than sibling rivalry and would otherwise have carried little weight. Also, since I got into his things and broke many of his toys, he was consistently irritated with me. I often remember fearing to walk down the hallway when he was there because he frequently would make it a point to bump me into the wall, sometimes bruising my arms and shoulders. As a child himself, he did not know how to cope with my unpredictable behavior and it was obvious he disliked me. He hardly paid any attention to me and when he did, it was to pin me down and "fart" on my head, or to see how hard he could throw a football to me during "catch" to try and knock me over. These events, in turn, made me try and avoid him whenever possible. Today, I realize that he was struggling with the dynamics of our home and I understand where his resentment, even hatred at times, came from. However, sometimes his behavior was that of a bully, *basta*. My parents were doing the best with what they had to help me and failed to bring my brother onto the team of support. From what I have heard from families with the same dynamic as mine, often one or more siblings feel cheated at the expense of a "needy," "learning disabled" brother or sister. Many siblings "pull away from the ADHD-child to find some peace from this unruly, intrusive, and domineering person."[325] I understand, to some extent, my brother's feelings from back then, but while I was growing up, having such a poor relationship with my brother affected me deeply. It has been shown that if a child feels that his siblings hate him, that child will develop poor self-esteem.[326]

With such feedback from all those around me, I felt I would never be able to learn or to be normal. An analogy I like to tell to help ADHD-people understand their learning struggles is to think of themselves riding a bike from Dallas to Chicago while another takes a plane. Their end goal, in short, is the same: To arrive at their end destination. The slower traveler might be even stronger physically and emotionally for having gone through more in order to get to the end goal. As a result, he may appreciate that goal even more. Learning is no different. Sometimes it takes some children longer than others to comprehend something, not because they "can't," but because they learn differently. It took me going to a special school, studying under an incredibly successful teacher to help me realize this message, and stamp it on my heart. (Of course, it is not lost on me that the bike-traveler may not make it to Chicago at all and may suffer defeat and humiliation, which unfortunately happens to many with LD and makes this analogy all the more real. Luckily, I would make it to "Chicago," and the story of how I did so, in part, will be told in the next chapter).

Here is my family in 1977 showing me, my father Linton Mark, my brother David and my mother Marilee. I obviously adored my father looking at him with hero-worshiping-eyes. By the time this photo was taken, my mother had been struggling for a year to learn what she needed to do about my ADHD and dyslexia (at the time, the experts said I was suffering from MBD (minimum brain dysfunction) and H-LD (Hyperkinesis-Learning Disabled)). I was "living" up to these definitions at the time since I was failing first-grade and people did not know what to do with me.

Takeaways

- Many outsiders blamed my bad behavior on poor parenting, which added to my mother's frustrations. Many thought I needed "more discipline, more structure, more limit-setting" and believed my parents were "ignorant, careless, permissive, amoral, antisocial, or, in contemporary parlance, 'dysfunctional.'"[327] My mother often felt guilty for taking me where others took responsibility for me. The best parents care so much and try so hard to do what is right for their children that they often hold themselves to unreasonable standards. Failure to achieve perfection is inevitable, but good parents doubt themselves, while bad parents don't care enough about their children to try at all. And even though bad parenting may exacerbate a child's ADHD, "it does not cause it."[328]

- As a child, I was a poor reader and had difficulty developing the "alphabetic principle." I was also RD or Reading Disabled. Often, ADHD-children are referred to as Alphabet Children because of all the letters that go next to their names to describe their problems.

- Once children get "labeled" as ADHD or LD, it is difficult to overcome. Sadly, the stigma that labeling creates produces a poor self-image for LD-children. It then takes a lot to break the mirror that tells you that you cannot succeed.

Action Steps

- Do some genealogy research and interview living family members. When looking at my grandfathers, paternal grandmother and father, I discovered I come from a tradition, unfortunately, of people who were thrill seekers with addictive personalities, and also, fortunately, full of intelligence and energy. Although not diagnosed as having LD-issues at the time, their behavior and restlessness gave every indication that they had both LD and ADHD. If you have similar family trees, learn from them what not to do in life.

- One of the best ways to socialize your ADHD-child, besides special tutoring, is to involve your child in activities with others. Let the adults in charge know some of the issues you have struggled with. Involve these adults, with you, in a team approach to helping your child socialize. Placing ADHD-children in social situations, like in sports or the theatre, is a good technique to help them learn how best to behave on their own and how to interact with others.

- Teach your ADHD-child never to give up on activities that are worthwhile like learning and athletic endeavors. Tell them they can always get better and can learn from everything they do.

CHAPTER 6:
Drugs Did Not Help—
The Feingold Diet Did

"And everybody who has ever had to do with children knows that a suitable diet does more to make them virtuous than the most eloquent preaching in the world."

— Bertrand Russell[329]

Therapeutic Drugs for ADHD:
The Positives and Negatives—Mostly Negative

In 1976, when I was roughly five years old, my mother took me off the stimulant drug Ritalin,[330] an amphetamine that I had taken for six months.[331] Paradoxically, since ADHD-kids are suffering from not being stimulated enough, they take drugs like Ritalin to "jump start" them in such a way that they receive the proper amount of stimulation. In addition to Ritalin, my mother also gave me coffee as mentioned earlier, another "stimulant" that helped me relax.

Although Ritalin seems to help some according to a few studies, it was a nightmare for me, making me catatonic and dysfunctional. I lost my appetite and my mother said I looked like I was suffering from rickets.[332] Other times, according to a next-door neighbor, who was like an older brother, Jerry Boswell, the son of my Austrian Godmother Polli, I looked "drugged," with hollow eyes, a pale face and no energy. He noticed I had difficulty focusing when on the drug and my eyes had a haunted, death-like expression in them.[333] The condition I was experiencing is known as the "amphetamine look."[334] Known side effects of drugs like Ritalin "include nervousness, insomnia, stomachache and skin rash." Other side effects are "difficulty getting to sleep at night, the wan, pinched face with sunken eyes… and sadness." Studies have shown that it reduces monthly weight gain in a child to "less than two-thirds of what would be expected in a normal child" and affects bone growth.[335] Also, children often build up a tolerance to the drug after using it for as little as a month, so the dose has to be increased.[336]

Medications "usually have side effects and nearly always have a narrow range between a useful and a lethal dose."[337] The negative side effects of Ritalin frequently affect children as they did me. As one mother said, the drug turned her child into a "zombie."[338] Also, since ADHD-kids already have a proclivity to abuse drugs, why encourage their use early on? In 2000, the Drug Enforcement Agency's (DEA) listed Ritalin alongside LSD, ecstasy and cocaine as "Drugs of Concern."[339] In short, as some experts ask, why use foreign, synthetic chemicals to "muffle health warning signals" instead of using natural substances that are "inherent to the chemistry of the human body to treat a condition" like ADHD? In other words, "no hyperactive child has a deficiency of amphetamines [e.g., Ritalin] any more than a person with a headache has an aspirin deficiency."[340]

Some studies have shown that Ritalin has a correlation with seizures and "growth retardation." My mother also hated the fact that she depended on drugs to control me. She was even more horrified when she read an article describing the harmful effects on a child when that child is taught, "You're not normal. Take the drug, and then you're normal."[341] For my mother, this was an appalling way to deal with such a problem, especially since she suspected there were other, natural solutions. Dr. Syte Reitz wrote in *Exceptional Children* in 1993 that "The use of stimulant medicine for children with ADD offers short-term improvement for the majority of children, but with potential side effects and no long-term improvement in behavior, learning or social development."[342] Drug therapy can increase "tics, problems with eating and sleeping, and psychological effects on cognition and attribution (the ability to reason and to understand cause and effect relationships)."[343] And it must be noted that the drug has been abused and has been used as a "substitute for cocaine."[344] Dr. Hartmann wrote, "Medicating ADHD Hunter children is very problematic. There's the issue of the mixed message it sends to those people who are most at risk to be substance abusers in later life."[345] In other words, you should do everything you can to pursue all other non-drug alternatives before you take, or force your children to take, a medication to make you, or them, conform to society's perception of normal behavior.

And whereas natural food and even supplements "rarely have any side effects,"[346] drugs are often shown in later studies to have them. In other words, a drug that might be deemed safe today could turn out to be dangerous tomorrow. Ritalin has already been shown to have detrimental side effects as listed above. Let's not forget that in the 1960s, thalidomide was prescribed to pregnant women for morning sickness. For years, young women used this drug until it was proven to cause birth defects.[347] This is just one example of many where drugs thought to be safe today had tragic consequences later.

I am friends with and respect Dr. Hallowell, a renowned Harvard University psychiatrist who is highly esteemed for his work on ADHD (we also attended the same prep school, Phillips Exeter Academy). He believes drugs and diet should be used simultaneously when treating ADHD. We have agreed to disagree on this topic. He claims that if someone suffers from poor eyesight, we do not withhold eyeglasses from him or her: He thinks of medication for ADHD in a similar way. He, of course, is a medical doctor, and I am not, but in my humble opinion, his views about the benefits of drugs for ADHD must be viewed through the lens of knowing he is a trained physician—in other words, he learned about medications far more as a medical student than he ever did about food. Moreover, he has used drugs to help his own children and even himself and has seen the benefit they can bring ADHD-people.[348] After I read several of his books and spoken personally with him, I realized that, unlike Dr. Feingold, Hallowell does not think diet should be used first in treating ADHD, whereas I and Dr. Feingold do. He does mention some of the negative repercussions of drug use, but believes that one should immediately start using drugs at the beginning of therapy instead of looking at other alternatives. He doesn't dismiss the Feingold diet and thinks it can be useful for treating ADHD, but he also thinks drugs need to always be part of the discussion when treatment is started. I think the world of Hallowell, my friend, fellow Exonian and an professional who knows tremendously more about ADHD than I do, but I believe we should ask how drugs are being used, and why our health providers push drugs as the first line of defense for this "disorder," instead of first advocating diet and lifestyle modifications.[349] Dr. Feingold wrote that when treating a behavioral problem, drugs should always be used as a "last resort," though all too often they are the "first measure."[350] In the end, Hallowell does admit that those whom drugs benefit must realize that a drug only "ameliorates but does not cure the syndrome."[351] As nutritional scientist Patrick Quillin, PhD, wrote, "Given the risk/benefit ratio of conventional medicine versus nutrition, nutrition is vastly preferable if it has any chance of being effective for a given condition."[352] Dr. Stewart said, "[I]n actual clinical practice they [drugs like Ritalin] rarely bring about enough improvement to justify the risks of such side effects."[353]

Yes, Ritalin, and other ADHD-drugs, do seem to help some and many claim the drug allowed them for the first time in their lives to control their hyperactive thought processes, "which probably accounts for the common reports of life-transforming experiences as a result of using this drug."[354] Yet, information on Transcendental Meditation teaches how to switch on "a focused state without drugs" and is "similarly filled with studies documenting how people transformed their work and/or personal lives by learning how to activate single-task focused consciousness at will."[355] In other words, if you have a choice between Ritalin and meditation (or prayer if you like), then meditation would be the healthier and safer choice if it works for you. If you have a choice between food and drugs, take food. Dr. Stewart simply said that too many people "are taking too many drugs for too long a time."[356]

Although many professionals will claim that Ritalin is perfectly safe, "no long-term well-controlled studies have been done on its effects among people who use it from childhood through adulthood and into old age."[357] In other words, those who prescribe this drug are hoping that the short-term benefit of behaving "normally" will outweigh any long-term negative effects from using the drug. As Dr. Hartmann wrote,

> Given the pervasiveness of drug use in human history, and the way that over-the-counter drugs are promoted on television as quick cures for everything from arthritis to the common cold, it shouldn't surprise anyone that a first response of our culture to the "disorder" of ADHD would be to administer drugs.[358]

Why are drugs so often used in treating disease? Well, that is what medical doctors are taught in school. According to Dr. David Alkek, a professor at the University of Texas Southwestern Medical School, doctors are educated to seek the cause of the illness or disorder, then use a treatment that evidence has shown can alleviate it.[359] It may be medication, surgery, psychology or if nothing else, rest and a good diet. But many doctors will admit that they know a lot about drugs, but less about nutrition. And according to Patrick Quillin, PhD, "Since [medical doctors] are not trained in nutrition, many physicians express little more than sarcasm for nutrition."[360] Sometimes manipulation of diet is the answer, especially for allergies or intolerances. Medical schools dedicate some time to educating future doctors about the benefits of a healthy diet, but maybe not enough, since obesity in America is a major health problem.[361] They dedicate far less time educating future doctors about the curative effects of a change in diet. Moreover, our nation relies too much on drugs to counter the abuse of overeating or ingesting poor-quality food. A Harvard University study said that, "Our way of life is related to our way of death."[362] We should not create a life that combines a preference for food that is low in nutrient density and eventual reliance on long-term drug therapy. Why have we done this? Quillin suggests that since "nutrients cannot be patented like drugs, the profit picture for nutrients is much less enticing than for drugs."[363] Drug companies obviously profit from Americans who depend on drugs. As of 2015, global spending on prescription drugs topped over one trillion dollars per year, with the U.S. "accounting for about one-third of this market."[364] Too many Americans take "uppers" and "downers." This can easily morph into using cocaine, methamphetamines, fentanyl (earlier known as Quaaludes) and heroin.

What will we say about Ritalin and other drugs used for ADHD in the future? Instead of drugging ADHD-people, Dr. Hartmann writes, we should "find Hunter jobs [jobs advantageous for ADHD-people], school situations, and life situations for these people, and teach them the basic life skills [necessary for them]."[365]

We humans have a long way to go in understanding what is best for us to eat or to avoid. Nicotine is one of the most addictive chemicals out there, but that still does not stop tobacco companies from selling their products. Doctors have warned us about the hazards of smoking for many years. Had there not been pressure placed upon these companies from lawsuits and our government, they would not have been forced to state on their packages that cigarettes are dangerous for your health. According to Dr. Hartmann, it seems that children of smokers have a 40% to 50% greater chance of becoming ADHD than children of non-smokers.[366] So if you smoke and are a parent with an ADHD-child, or are considering having children, stop smoking now.

I am not a drug expert, but I think we should hold to a universal rule that if you can stay away from drugs, do so. Some medicines are indeed necessary to help people live longer and healthier lives, but our nation seems too trusting and too obsessed with pills and their benefits. The pharmaceutical companies profit because of our overreliance on drugs and pills, not because they are necessarily healthier for us. These companies are "laughing all the way to the bank" because of our addictions. For example, although the U.S. population represents 5% of the globe's inhabitants, Americans consume 80% of the opioids in the world.[367] Are we that pain-filled and depressed compared to the rest of the world that we need those drugs that much? And with such drugs killing or negatively affecting so many, one would think Americans would reduce the production of drugs and limit how and why doctors can prescribe them. Since 1999, 400,000 Americans have died due to opioid use. In fact, our government fined the company Purdue Pharmaceuticals, owned by the unethical Sackler family, $8 billion in 2020 for promoting the use of and selling opioids to the public "without legitimate medical purpose."[368] The National Center for Health Statistics reported that overdose deaths in America alone rose from 50,963 in 2019 to 69,710 in 2020.[369] President Joe Biden in his State of the Union address on 1 March 2022 specifically said it was his desire to declare war on the opioid epidemic. Let us hope he wins many battles in this war. Side-effects of medications prescribed in hospitals alone in the U.S. kill "an estimated 106,000 Americans every year."[370] In short, we Americans consume too many drugs. Physicians dispense four billion prescriptions every year to us. "That's about thirteen prescriptions a year for every man, woman, and child."[371] We need to change this trend.

Drugs can put people into a passive frame of mind. And when people depend on such drugs to function, they will start to believe they can only be helped by an outside, synthetic chemical agent that will make their brains work better. This process leads many to believe that their lives will only be good if they accept scientists' and doctors' descriptions of what type of person they are, based on information gathered in the last 30 to 50 years. Society should not force ADHD-types to believe they need drugs to make them more like the majority of humanity. Ritalin, according to Dr. Hartmann, is actually a prejudice drug to "medicate Hunters into behaving like Farmers."[372] And while the drug calms ADHD-people and makes them more Farmer-like, it takes away their creativity, spontaneity, and "sense of the absurd."[373] Maybe Friedrich Nietzsche, the German philosopher, was on to something when he said, "Be careful lest in casting out the devils you cast out the best thing that's in you."[374]

Dr. Feingold believed that there was no evidence to prove that Ritalin would lead to addiction, but he said there was ample proof that such a drug can become a "psychological crutch." Yet, he also noted that "the psychological effects of long-term usage, which may lead to some form of addiction, are still in gray areas."[375] Drugs are almost always the "treatment of choice for ADHD."[376] In 1977, when my mom took me off the drug Ritalin, I was one of "an estimated 50 percent of the diagnosed H-LDs/MBDs in America," who were taking "drugs as a matter of management."[377]

I have heard countless stories of children put on Ritalin as soon as he or she has problems in school. It is a lazy form of treatment and, according to Dianne McGuinness, PhD, the drug has been so over-prescribed that many critics have named it "the teachers' and parents' relief drug."[378] The Deputy Chief of the Drug Enforcement Administration (DEA) said in 1995, "The United States is using five times as much [Ritalin] as the entire rest of the planet combined." The DEA described Ritalin as a Schedule II drug that has a "high potential for abuse and may lead to severe psychological and physical dependence."[379] And according to a National Institutes of Health Report, "Amphetamine use [for ADHD] increased 2.5-fold from 2006 to 2016" from 7.9 to 20.0 tons per year.[380] Is America that badly off that it has to drug millions of its citizens to have them behave normally? Or, is there possibly something more sinister lurking in what we are eating that is contributing to the problem?

Our health care system is not helpful when it comes to weighing the pros and cons of using drugs versus modifying eating habits to allay ADHD-behaviors. Although we spend more money than any other country in the world on health, Americans in general suffer from "rampant poor health."[381] So focusing more on our diets to help us with managing our ADHD is a better solution than drugs like Ritalin. As nutritional scientist Patrick Quillin wrote,

> Rather than placing a hyperactive child on a speed-like drug [Ritalin] for the remainder of his childhood, why not try an optimal eating program first? The drug for hyperactivity can cause lethargy, headaches, and even growth retardation and merely sedates the child while doing nothing about the actual problem.[382]

At worst, putting such a child on a special, all-natural and healthy diet can only make him or her healthier, and at best, it may "solve the hyperactivity."[383]

Some have reported also that they see the same positive results from just half an hour to an hour of aerobic exercise as they do from the drug Ritalin. Endorphins released through exercise have similar neurological effects to Ritalin. It should be no surprise that exercise is an effective healing therapy. It treats hyperactivity, "lowers depression, stimulates intellect, improves self-image, and stimulates alertness, among other beneficial effects."[384]

I believe that my mother taking me off drugs, feeding me a healthy diet and getting me involved with sports gave me the best chance of success. Citing court documents that link school violence with psychiatric drugs, Ross Stewart of the Neurowellness Clinic of North Dallas said, "'We've been able to get every child so far off of medication...I don't like the result in terms of who they turn out to be as adults [when on psychiatric drugs]. Their brains don't form correctly."[385] To emphasize the problem with drugs again, Dr. Hallowell admits that LD-medications can cause a variety of side effects:

> The most common is appetite suppression headache, elevated blood pressure, elevated heart rate, nausea, vomiting, insomnia, the development of tics or twitching, feelings of jitteriness or anxiety, feelings of agitation or even mania, and feelings of depersonalization or paranoia.[386]

So, in other words, there are many problems with drug use for ADHD. And since, according to one study, there are at least 4 million children currently being medicated for some type of LD, it has become an epidemic.[387]

In addition to taking away Ritalin, my mother also discontinued serving me coffee. As mentioned earlier, coffee was often given to hyperactive children in the 1970s for the same reasons as giving Ritalin. Besides the fits I threw when having to drink coffee, I hated how it tasted and was glad to go back to drinking milk or orange juice. She also prevented me from taking aspirin,[388] since it can react badly with sensitive systems like mine, and some experts believe its use may trigger "the often-fatal Reye's syndrome in children" (this syndrome causes swelling in the brain and liver, killing 30% of those afflicted).[389] As a child, I had frequent headaches, and I needed something to help me. My mother used Tylenol and that seemed to do the trick. Looking at my diet at the time, my headaches were probably also caused by synthetic food. Today, the only time I get headaches is when I eat synthetic food (unknowingly) with a lot of dye in it.[390]

People being medicated for ADHD may run the risk of developing Parkinson's and Alzheimer's diseases since both seem to involve neurotransmitters like dopamine. In other words, children medicated today for ADHD may be at a higher risk for such neurologically debilitating conditions later in life.[391] Since my father died of Parkinson's, I am glad that I did not use the drug longer than I did, just in case I have a proclivity for this disease.

As mentioned, my father exhibited a lot of ADHD-behavior through his addictive personality. He enjoyed alcohol and ice cream. He often would eat a whole carton of ice cream at night while downing a few glasses of bourbon. Because both "candy and liquor stimulate dopamine,"[392] I have often wondered whether this brought on his Parkinson's disease earlier than its natural course. Since it seems that individuals with ADHD have lower levels of dopamine, maybe the possible cravings for it was why my father's brain told him he needed alcohol and ice cream.

I think a lot of the evidence just cited argues convincingly that we need to do a better job of avoiding drugs whenever possible and promote exercise, meditation-like practices, and consumption of healthy, all-natural diets as effective alternatives in curing the "ADHD-problem." I think we all know that pills, in general, are never the optimal solution for health problems, especially for ADHD.

The Feingold Diet

After careful study and in the hope of controlling my behavior, my mom eventually put our whole family on an all-natural diet, based on the principles of Dr. Benjamin Feingold. Although there was some controversy surrounding the diet, it saved me. It was the only means of controlling my problem. And studies have found that Feingold's basic concept improves the behavior of hyperactive children.[393]

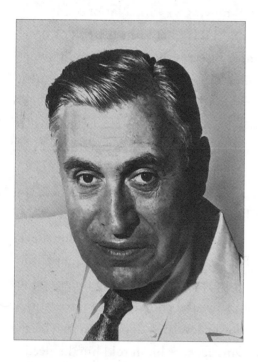

Dr. Benjamin F. Feingold. This pediatrician and allergist inspired a movement throughout America for families to "treat" their ADHD-children with all-natural diets (*aka* The Feingold Diet) instead of using drugs. He motivated my mother to transform our family's diet and it helped me, and my mother, bring my hyperactivity under control. Dr. Stephen Maddox, head of the Fort Worth Child Study Center wrote in my clinical notes that this diet had an excellent effect on me, helping me improve my learning and control my behavior.

Feingold's principles state that there is a direct correlation between what you eat and how you behave. Although this may sound simplistic, it is not generally practiced in our culture today. Most have no idea what they are putting in their mouths. Feingold was a pioneer in his scientific research. One could argue that he operated according to what Hippocrates, the father of modern medicine, advised: "Let thy food be thy medicine and thy medicine be thy food." Even though evidence of how certain diets can have negative effects on behavior have been around for at least 100 years, Feingold brought this topic to the forefront of the scientific community. He stressed that an ADHD-person can live a healthier life by eliminating artificial colors and preservatives from one's diet. Before Feingold's studies, the larger medical community ignored nutrition as a factor in ADHD. Simply put, we know today that what you put into your body can impact your "health and vitality, both now and later on. Nutrition is a logical explanation for how you feel today and how long you will live."[394]

In reaching his conclusions about diet, Feingold observed the "adverse reactions" that people experienced from eating food additives. Interestingly, he found that artificial colors like Yellow #5 (found in Cheetos, for example) are also low molecular compounds that can create allergic responses. Since he knew these synthetic dyes were used in many foods, he felt something was dreadfully wrong with our diets. Basically, humans did not evolve to thrive on a continuous stream of "refined sugar, hydrogenated fat, salt, pastries, bleached white flour, soda pop," artificial colors and artificial preservatives, "yet these are the true staples of the modern American diet."[395] Obviously, calling them staples is an exaggeration, but there is no doubt that there is too much of these in the diets of many westerners.

And here is the scary fact. Ingesting one of these artificial flavors or colorings alone may not be overly harmful, but when combined with other additives (which is usually the case with processed food), it can have serious deleterious effects. One study found that if you ingest mixed synthetic ingredients, you can develop severe health problems. Quillin refers to a study where a researcher fed three groups of laboratory animals different diets: one group with Red Dye #2, the second group with Red Dye #2 and cyclamates (artificial sweeteners) and a third group with Red Dye #2, cyclamates and a food emulsifier (polyoxyethylene sorbitan monostearate). The first group was fine. The second group had diarrhea, balding, scruffy fur and retarded weight gain, and all of the third group died within 14 days.[396] In other words, one can mix natural foods in general without many worries, but mixing synthetic substances which often act like drugs can create a toxic cocktail. Even if you don't die, who wants scruffy fur or baldness?

It appears that only after World War II did the rise of additives invade our food with amazing speed.[397] During the war, the food industry worked hard to ensure its foodstuffs lasted as long and tasted as good as possible, after traveling thousands of miles from America to areas of combat operations in the Pacific and Europe. A by-product was that businesses noticed that preserving food and improving its taste increased their profits.[398] It seems that was when the madness of artificially modifying the food supply started.

Feingold's study documented countless cases of the benefits of removing processed and artificial foods from kids' diets, taking them off drugs like Ritalin and putting them on all-natural diets.[399] After studying Feingold's book, my mother eliminated harmful chemicals like artificial colors and flavors from our diet. Some of the artificial ingredients she removed were synthetic dyes like Yellow #5, Red #2 and Blue #1; artificial sweeteners like saccharine and aspartame; and preservatives like BHT, BHA and TBHQ which are synthetic antioxidants often found in cereals. Many studies have shown these chemicals have a toxic effect on your health. Synthetic antioxidants have even been found to cause cancer. Blue #1 and Red #2 are noted by the American Academy of Pediatrics Committee on Drugs as being bronchoconstrictors (in other words, if you have asthma, don't ingest these dyes). Ironically, many medicines like red-colored aspirin or cough syrup can cause other problems, while they try to offer relief. There is no reason to have the dye in these products except that it is pleasing to the eye. Red Dye #2 may be a carcinogen. Citrus Red #2 is listed by the International Agency for Research on Cancer (IARC) as a group

2B carcinogen, a substance "possibly carcinogenic to humans."[400] If you wonder how you can get some medicines without certain superficial and synthetic additives, talk to a compounding pharmacist.[401] Also children's brightly colored vitamins have unnecessary chemicals. And according to an exhaustive study conducted by California's Office of Environmental Health Hazard Assessment in 2021, dyes result "in hyperactivity and other neurobehavioral problems in some children."[402] My mom became vigilant in reading all labels of food and medicines and eliminated everything with dyes and artificial flavors. She even became the co-chairwoman for the Feingold Chapter for Dallas/Fort Worth from 1977 to 1980, helping other families learn what an all-natural diet can do for ADHD-children.

The dangers do not just stop with dyes and artificial flavors, but include the explosion of sugar substitutes. Synthetic sweeteners like NutraSweet and Equal (aspartame) are often found in chewing gum. They penetrate the blood-brain barrier and have been shown to cause damage to brain tissue, headaches and even seizures. In fact, if you heat up synthetic sugars like NutraSweet, they turn into formaldehyde. You wonder if the cans of sodas people are drinking with this sweetener at one time or another were stored in a warehouse, where it was hot, or if the soft drinks were on a truck baking in the sun *en route* to a store.[403] According to one of Dr. William Pardridge's articles published in the *New England Journal of Medicine*, "a five-fold increase in aspartame consumption by a pregnant woman can lower the IQ of her baby by 10 points."[404] Artificial sweeteners (cyclamates and the saccharin in Sweet'n Low) have all been implicated "in causing cancer" in lab animals.[405] And these synthetic sweeteners have been linked to an increase risk of depression.[406]

These synthetic chemicals interfere with our brains' chemical and electrical functioning. We transfer information between our brain cells via neurotransmitters which are involved in all brain activity. The transmitters are necessary to conduct a nerve impulse from one neuron to the next. Dr. Robert Sinaiko suggests that children with ADHD have problems with synthetic chemicals because they can act as "counterfeit" neurotransmitters. Such artificial molecules like BHA and Yellow #5 can attach themselves to receptors of cells and have chemical structures similar to natural transmitters. As a result, synthetic chemicals can excite your brain's neurons, so they respond in ways we don't intend. "The result of this is like having static or unwanted noise in the brain."[407] Scientific research has proven that by disrupting the function or production of certain neurotransmitters, synthetic chemicals have been implicated in a number of physical problems including Parkinson's disease, multiple sclerosis and melancholy. What you eat directly affects who you are and who you will become.[408] "The risk/benefit ratio of nutrition is far superior to most conventional medical approaches."[409] In short, a healthful diet and good lifestyle choices can help promote good health, making drugs unnecessary.

ADHD seems to have exploded throughout American society in recent years. Obviously, much of the increase since World War II is due to more robust clinical work targeting children's diseases that were previously ignored or underreported, especially behavioral. But the increase in volume that is not related to recognition has to have a source. The growing problems of uncontrolled ADHD-behavior, I would argue, is most likely caused or exacerbated by our poor diet.[410] We know that lower-income families, whose diets are usually poor and include more processed foods, have children with a higher percentage of ADHD compared to families that can afford better, all-natural foods.[411] So, healthy food, according to the study cited above, does make a difference in whether or not a child can learn and behave well.

Once she discovered the apparent links, my mother made sure I ate only healthy food. Soon oranges, bananas, special natural lollypops, orange juice or water were plentiful for me during school or sporting activities when other kids were eating junk food and drinking soda, especially Coca-Cola. My mother warned teachers and coaches about the consequences of giving me candy or Kool-Aid. Since tartrazine, or synthetic dyes like Yellow #5, were in many treats brought to school activities and sporting events, my mother was adamant about taking away such foods. And she was right to do so. One study found that 79% of children tested, whether ADHD or not, reacted negatively to tartrazine. This chemical is often found in bottled lemon juice, soy sauce, pickles, soft drinks and fruit flavored "spring waters."[412]

With the new diet in place, I soon returned to "normalcy," as my hyperactivity and attention deficit disorder came under control. However, during pee-wee football games, my coach, Don Holland, gave me a candy bar to turn me into "a maniac," a tactic that, alas, worked and I earned the nickname "Freight Train." What my coach did not know is that candy can set off a pattern of hyperactivity in me and others like me that can last for days. Behavior and diet cannot be separated. As Dr. Jay Freed, professor at the State University of New York at Stony Brook, said, "Based upon knowledge that I have regarding research into the value of the Feingold diet, we are approaching the dawn of the new era in the linking of foods, chemicals and behavior."[413]

My mom was the key to the success of the diet. Without her vision and courage to speak up, I would not have maintained the diet as well as I did. She got everyone in my life involved (except Coach Holland on game day). As Feingold wrote, "The diet management cannot succeed if parental management is weak or wavering."[414] Besides behaving well on such a diet, I was also healthier for it. The diet was the equivalent of giving me freedom. Using Feingold's terminology, it helped my family prevent our food industry from abusing me. He wrote,

> Most of [ADHD] children don't want to be bad. They
> don't want to be on drugs. They don't want to be in learn-
> ing disability classes. They are not sub-intelligent. In my
> opinion, they are chemically abused. These children are
> normal. Their environment is abnormal.[415]

Often people who are sensitive to such chemicals are "not capable of
functioning normally when they are experiencing a reaction."[416] In
short, Dr. Feingold wrote, "good food control is good health control."[417]

Mom also created a chart listing all the things I had to do and
put it on the wall. She mapped out my chores and my classes, and
thus I had a permanent reminder every time I went to the bathroom
or entered my room, of what I needed to do that day. When I successfully finished a task, my mom would give me a star in the appropriate
box. When I achieved a certain number of accomplishments (making
my bed, staying on my diet, feeding the dog, cleaning the fish tank,
turning in my homework, etc.), she would reward me by taking me
to a movie, buying me fishing equipment or taking me and a friend
to a water park or skating rink. Fishing by the way, although a quiet
activity, is something hyperactive children love. The anticipation of
catching a fish and the thrill of actually getting one on the line seems
to be something that keeps ADHD-children focused (very Hunter-
like). [418] As a result, fishing was a wonderful activity for me.

Whenever I went off my natural diet, my mom easily could see
my behavior change. This is common with kids who try the Feingold
diet. One mother said that when her child went off his diet, she and
her husband were in for three or four days of "whining, foot stamping
and general pitching of fits."[419] My mom would say the same thing
and she would often ask me when I was misbehaving, "What have
you eaten?" I would almost always come clean because my behavior
had betrayed me. I would then get a time-out or have a privilege like
going fishing or riding my bike taken away for a day or so. Usually,

though, I hardly ever went off my diet. Some critics of the Feingold diet say that the positive effects of such diets are due to a placebo effect. The individual thinks the diet helps and so it does. However, my experience, plus that of countless others on the diet, show that if it were just a placebo effect, then a child who has been helped by the diet would not see any negative effects if he or she cheated or accidently ate something artificial.[420]

When I stayed on the diet, my mother made it a point to praise me. She would tell me, "Hey, you're behaving so well, Bryan, I'm proud of you," or "You're doing so well in school, Son, good job. You must be maintaining your diet well."

The diet can even save you money. Highly processed foods are usually more expensive ("potato chips are 1,000% more expensive per pound than potatoes"), but even if they are not, you probably would save more in buying good food instead of investing that money in doctors and medicines to help your child.[421] In general, the less processed the food is, the better it is for you. You should "eat foods in as close to their natural state as possible" to promote optimum health and stay away from "processed foods."[422]

Sadly, even today, "Nutritional management is one aspect that has been relatively neglected."[423] The Feingold diet, or any natural diet for that matter, is difficult to follow. Most families find it too challenging. Luckily, my mother had grown up on a ranch and had been taught how to cook from scratch. She also was a home economics major from Oklahoma State University, and she enjoyed cooking. In today's world, it is often difficult to create such a nutritionally happy home. But even now, my ex-wife and I were able to create a natural food environment for our kids. One of the best ways for us to cook a meal was to throw a whole bunch of vegetables, rice and one or two kinds of meats into a pot and create a stew. My mom also excelled in making soups and stews, and I always had something nutritious and natural to eat. Dr. Frank Lawlis, who wrote *The ADD Answer: How to Help Your Child Now*, recommends home-cooked meals to correct ADD. Ultimately, it just takes a determined family to maintain the diet, and usually that means a *determined mom*, to make the all-natural diet a success.[424]

Although many may tell you that to maintain such a diet is difficult, I have found the opposite to be true. All it takes is learning what foods to buy and how to make about six to eight dishes. The time it takes to read labels and prepare natural food is minuscule compared to the time it takes to recover from dealing with a hyperactive, destructive child or dealing with health issues caused by a toxic diet. It takes time to learn what to buy followed by disciplined vigilance, especially since, according to Dr. Feingold, around 80% of foods in supermarkets have "prohibited additives."[425] Yet, we should feel lucky that we have good options out there and that nowadays we do not have to grow the crops or hunt the meat ourselves.

Some feel that when you put your child on such a diet, you prevent him or her from having fun. I never felt this way. In fact, you will only be depriving your child of developing some possibly serious behavioral problems and health issues. And this is especially the case with sugar. For hyperactive children, sugar—although not synthetic—is "positively correlated with destructive-aggressive behavior."[426] One school nurse reported that during the week of Halloween the number of injuries of children increased by 300%. A study done in over 800 New York public schools and nine juvenile correction facilities discovered that by "increasing fruit, vegetables and whole grains and decreasing fat and sugars, academic performance rose by 16% and learning disabilities fell 40%. Violent and anti-social behavior decreased 48% within the correction units."[427] So, ADHD-children should stay away from sugar, especially refined sugar.

Moreover, reducing sugar improves dental health and quality of life. My mother efficiently eliminated most sugar from my diet. A warning should be given to ADHD-kids that what they often crave is the very substance they should stay away from. Now, if children, especially those with sensitive systems to sugar, eat some sugars after a nutritious meal, they do a better job tolerating them.[428] However, once again, processed sugar is detrimental to our health, so eliminate it from your diet. We need to stop digging our graves with our teeth.

Tragically, ADHD-people are usually "sugar junkies." Sugars give the brain a "jolt" since it is the material needed to run the brain, but if the sugar is processed, it can have negative repercussions. That "jolt" from processed sugar will come crashing down as "the blood sugar is re-balanced by the pancreas and decreases to normal (or, often, even slightly below normal) levels."[429] And the byproduct of eating a lot of sugar for ADHD-kids is that their behavior often becomes erratic. Dr. Feingold brought up an interesting moral question about food companies when he wrote,

> I've wondered whether or not the board chairmen and presidents of certain giant companies really know what is in their products. Perhaps they don't have children or grandchildren. Perhaps they have tunnel vision focused on sales charts. Perhaps they don't care.[430]

One study a few decades ago showed that on average, in addition to the sugar one eats, every American eats five pounds of additives a year, possibly creating that toxic cocktail mentioned above. Since some additives are petroleum-based products, imagine drinking five pounds of engine oil a year. For ADHD-people, "there is no natural body defense against the synthetic additives." In other words, we cannot tolerate or process them. Yet, the food industry does not want you to know about the detrimental effects of sugar and such synthetic additives as artificial colors and flavors. With this in mind, we should never forget that we have "only one body to last a lifetime."[431] We need to stop eating bad food, as medical doctor and nutritional scientist Dr. Michael Gregor writes, "as if the future doesn't matter."[432]

Consequently, during holidays like Halloween, Easter, Valentine's Day and so on, focus on giving gifts instead of candy. Such acts can be just as special and they will not hurt a child's health. During Halloween, my family always gives out whistles, pumpkin-decorated miniature Frisbees, plastic spiders and other holiday-appropriate items instead of candy.

After I started on the Feingold diet, Dr. Maddox noted in his report that I had a "very positive" response.[433] Dr. Maddox also stopped reporting that I had problems with coordination. I improved at sports and became physically stronger. "[S]ports-loving dads" need to realize that an additive-free diet often improves the coordination of children.[434]

I also realized that if I wanted to have friends, do well in school and prevent my mother from having a heart attack, I had to eat healthy foods. After eating natural foods, I felt a distinct change physically. I felt better about myself. I realized that sensible eating habits had a direct correlation with my behavior, and that a healthy diet gave me more self-control. Numerous scientific studies support that when one eats a healthier diet with natural foods, he or she is happier, gets sick less often than others, is more productive and lives longer.[435]

Unbeknownst to me, prior to the diet, one of the frustrations I felt was that I did not have control. Many asked me often with a harsh tone, "Why are you doing this?" or, "Why are you behaving this way?" I did not have answers. The national director of the Feingold Association, Jane Hersey, wrote that typically an ADHD-child who is having a reaction to synthetic food and not doing well in school is told, "'You're such a bright little boy; you could do it if you really tried.'" She goes on to explain that this reasoning is burdened by faulty logic. "If he were in a wheelchair, nobody would say, 'If you really tried, you could walk.' But when a child is experiencing a chemical reaction, the cause is seldom understood."[436] After I followed the natural diet for a while, people noticed a change in me and wondered how I had become a normal kid.

You have to be careful with artificial ingredients not only in your food, but also in your environment. Just as the beverages and food you put in your mouth can cause health problems, what you allow to touch your skin can adversely affect your health. The skin's pores can bring chemicals into the blood stream. Just remember those patches to prevent smokers from smoking or weekend-boaters from getting seasick. The medicine in those patches penetrate the skin. The same goes for touching laminated fiberboard and carpet treated with formaldehyde, scented stickers, fake tattoos or cologne.[437] Often bubble bath soaps have dyes in them that can penetrate the skin. As a result, my mother used all-natural soap for my bathes. We also had to do away with bright blue and red toothpaste. Most toothpastes can retain their natural color of white without blue or red dyes, but companies add these dyes because they will sell more of their product. However, my mom knew that ADHD-kids can be susceptible to such products and she did away with colored toothpaste. I also had to stop my swimming lessons at the local recreational center when my mom found out that I had a negative reaction to the chlorine in the water, often turning me into a raving maniac after practice. And for those of you who enjoy drinking alcohol, you must be careful. Often alcoholic beverages are loaded with dyes or have a red, dyed cherry in them, so stay away from those drinks.[438] I often also avoid red wine because it frequently gives me a headache or makes me stay up all night because of the sulfites that are frequently added to it.

We live in an age with chemicals that have only existed for one or two generations. Our evolutionary development has no memory of how to deal with most of these chemicals. Until now our bodies have never been exposed to them, and have not yet adjusted to them, and quite possibly never will. There is mounting evidence that the reason why male sperm counts have decreased by 50% since 1960 is because of the exposure to such synthetic chemicals, so we need to do a better job of avoiding using plastic containers for our food and beverages and ingesting plastics, artificial colors and artificial ingredients.[439] Some of the worse perpetrators are phthalates and bisphenol A (BPA), "as well as 'forever chemicals' that do not degrade, such as perfluoroalkyl substances (PFAS)."[440] These "forever chemicals" are found "in plastic, vinyl, floor and wall coverings, medical tubing and medical devices, children's toys, nail polishes, perfumes, hair sprays, soaps [and] shampoos."[441] In short, try to make your environment which includes foods and toiletries as natural as possible. By doing so, you not only can help control your ADHD or the ADHD in your children, but you also will be ensuring the *human race continues reproducing in a healthy manner.* Shanna Swan, an environmental and reproductive epidemiologist at the Icahn School of Medicine at Mount Sinai in New York, offers this warning: "Chemicals in our environment and other lifestyle factors in our modern age have harmed our reproductive health to the extent that, in the future, *it may not be possible for most people to reproduce in the old-fashioned way* [author's italics]."[442]

Returning to my childhood, once on the Feingold diet, I began living an active, normal life. I started getting smiles from my parents and teachers instead of frowns. I influenced events and took control of them instead of reacting to them. Before I started on the Feingold diet, I was simply reacting to what I ingested. Once I started learning that what I ate had a direct correlation to my behavior, I put only good things in my body. I received rewards of sporting equipment or books instead of candy or soft drinks, and I appreciated them more because they were healthy and lasted longer. This process, plus having a tough mother and grandmother enforcing the rules, taught me discipline, which is crucial for ADHD-kids. Without discipline you cannot control your environment. Most ADHD-kids on the Feingold diet diligently stick to it. And ADHD-expert Dr. Hartmann, who ran an organization for abused, emotionally disturbed and learning "disabled" children, found that the Feingold diet created excellent results with many of the kids he treated.[443]

I have diligently taught these principles to my own children. My kids have learned to avoid food with artificial flavors and colorings. For example, when my daughter Sophia was five and visiting a church, a man asked if she wanted some candy and Sophia answered, "Is it artificial?" He said he thought it was and Sophia refused to eat it. The man then looked up at my wife and said, "I have never heard that from a child before." I later talked with Sophia about good food and she asked, "Why did you not eat artificial flavors Daddy, when you were a boy?" I explained that as a child, I had to be especially careful because I had problems controlling my behavior and my anger when I ate such food. Since I wanted to always control my emotions, I told her I found that eating well helped me in this pursuit. She soaked it all in.

A few months after this conversation in 2005, I took my daughter and son, Justin, trick-or-treating on Halloween. We let them participate in the activities, but they had to throw away most of the candy they collected. While going from door to door, Sophia continually asked, "Trick or treat. Do you have anything not artificial?" Confused, people often would answer, "I don't think so Sweetie" or "I'm sorry, but this is all I have." After doing this three or four times, I convinced her that she should not ask the people this, and that we would sort out the good treats from the bad ones when we got home. She understood and just enjoyed the holiday while yelling ghost sounds outside (strongly encouraged by me) or running around in her witch costume. A few houses before her plastic pumpkin was full, we started talking with the woman at the home where we had just rung the doorbell. As she handed out candy to Sophia and Justin, my two and a half year old son got greedy and grabbed another handful of candy from the lady's bowl. I said, "Justin, that's enough, Son. Other kids will come to her door as well. Save some for them." The lady said, "That's alright, take a few for your daddy." Without missing a beat, my daughter piped up, "Well, make sure it's not artificial, because if it is, my daddy can't control his anger." I could not suppress my laughter and the kind lady just answered Sophia, "Well, let's hope your father grows out of it." I also thought jokingly, "Well, let's hope Child Services will not be calling me when we arrive home."

Here I am with my daughter Sophia and son Justin on Halloween 2005. My daughter had learned that we did not eat anything artificial because of our LD-issues. I had told her that by eating natural foods, we could control our behavior, especially our emotions like anger. As a result, she often would ask at the homes we went to, "Trick-or-treat! Do you have anything that's not artificial?" We often got surprised looks and laughs at this question. At one house, a lady told my son to take some candy for me. Without missing a beat, my daughter pipped up, "Make sure it isn't artificial because if it is, my daddy cannot control his anger." We all had a good laugh.

When I was young, I would also go trick-or-treating, but I never ate the candy because I knew it was against my diet. I was observant about staying on the diet because of how it made me behave and because people in my life, whom I loved, praised me for doing so. Positive reinforcement was also something that helped me learn proper behavior.

Moreover, once on the diet, I learned that I could take direct responsibility for my actions. I had to be aware at all times of what I ate and how I conducted myself. If I went off the diet, I did not do well. I think this is where kids who use drug therapy can have problems, because it is something outside themselves that can be used as an excuse for failure. Instead of saying, "I controlled myself and improved on my own," many kids who use only drugs for their cure say, "IT made me feel better; IT increased my self-esteem; IT improved my academic performance." Director Hersey writes, "if it's 'IT,' IT is outside of us, and we want something inside that's responsible for successful achievement over the long run."[444] I agree with Hersey and took responsibility for my behavior by watching how my diet helped me to create an ordinary routine and to learn like a "normal" boy. Getting to the stages I have just described was a long journey and I still had a lot of things to deal with, but the Feingold diet played a huge part in controlling my ADHD. With the diet, I could then learn how to use my ADHD as an asset.

Takeaways

- When I was five, my mother took me off the stimulant drug Ritalin, an amphetamine that I had taken for six months. Paradoxically, since ADHD-kids are suffering from not being stimulated enough, they take drugs like Ritalin to "jump start" them in such a way that they receive the proper amount of stimulation. Although Ritalin seems to help some, it was a nightmare for me, making me catatonic and dysfunctional.

- Once my mom took me off drugs to treat my LD, she focused on making my food and environment as natural as possible. In following the principles of The Feingold Diet, she helped me to eliminate artificial additives from all meals and changed my life. In radically changing my *entire* environment by only having me eat natural foods, my mother helped me gain control over my ADHD and live a healthier life.

- If you have a choice between Ritalin and meditation (or prayer if you like), then meditation would be the healthier and safer choice if it works for you. If you have a choice between food and drugs, take food. In addition to diet, some have reported that they get the same effect from just half an hour to an hour of aerobic exercise as they do from the drug Ritalin. Endorphins released through exercise have effects similar to Ritalin on the brain. It should be no surprise that exercise is an effective healing therapy. It treats hyperactivity, "lowers depression, stimulates intellect, improves self-image, and stimulates alertness, among other beneficial effects."[445]

- I believe that my mother taking me off drugs, feeding me a healthy diet and getting me involved with sports gave me the best chance of success. In short, a healthful diet and good lifestyle choices can help head off poor health, making drugs unnecessary. "The risk/benefit ratio of nutrition is far superior to most conventional medical approaches."[446]

Action Steps

- As a parent, create a "things to do" chart for your ADHD-child. Map out chores and classes. By doing so, you create a permanent reminder of what your child needs to do daily. When your child successfully finishes a task, mark a star in the appropriate box. When your child achieves a certain number of accomplishments (making the bed, staying on the diet, cleaning the bathroom, turning in homework, etc.), reward him by taking him to a movie, buying him something or taking him to a water park or skating rink.

- Children of smokers have a 40% to 50% greater chance of becoming ADHD than children of nonsmokers. So, if you smoke and are a parent with an ADHD-child, or are considering having children, stop smoking now.

- There is no reason to have dye in your food products even though you think that it is pleasing to the eye. Red Dye #2 may be a carcinogen. Citrus Red #2 is listed by the International Agency for Research on Cancer (IARC) as a group 2B carcinogen, a substance "possibly carcinogenic to humans."[447] If you wonder how you can get some medicines without certain synthetic additives, talk to a compounding pharmacist. Also, children's brightly colored vitamins have unnecessary chemicals. Became vigilant in reading all labels of food and medicines and eliminate all dyes and artificial flavors.

- Synthetic sweeteners like NutraSweet (aspartame) are often found in chewing gum, cereal, yogurt and other foodstuffs. They penetrate the blood-brain barrier and have been shown to cause damage to brain tissue, and cause headaches and even seizures. In fact, if you heat up synthetic sugars like NutraSweet, they turn into formaldehyde. In short, stay away from artificial sweeteners.

CHAPTER 7:
Starpoint: The School and Women Who Saved Me

"[W]hat makes an act good is that it is unselfish."
— Friedrich Nietzsche[448]

ALTHOUGH MY DIET WAS COMING under control around 1978-1979, I was still struggling with my academics. Appalled at the thought of sending me to first-grade for a third time, my mother, on the recommendation of Dr. Maddox, enrolled me at Starpoint, a laboratory school at Texas Christian University (TCU) in Fort Worth. She later joked that she had nightmares that I would be driving myself to my own sixth-grade graduation at the age of 20, if she did not immediately improve my situation. Since my mom had started early trying to find me help, I had a better chance of improving. "Research has shown that intervention is more effective the earlier it is implemented."[449] I was lucky my LD was diagnosed and *treated* at an early age rather than when I was in junior high school, or worse, when I became an adult.[450] Although my speech therapist, Dr. May, and others helped me a lot, my best treatment came at Starpoint. My mom was doing everything right. As Dr. Hallowell wrote, "[T]he keys to happiness and success in childhood are to have the right parents and find the right teachers."[451] Well, I had the right mother, and the "right teacher" found me at Starpoint.

The Starpoint School at Texas Christian University. This school was founded in 1968 with the purpose of helping children with learning disabilities. When I enrolled there as a student in 1979, there were only two schools like it in the nation.

In general, Starpoint focused on severely learning-disabled kids and, since I met all the criteria, I was accepted. It was almost like a reverse application process: You had to prove you were a bad student to get in. In reality though, the school accepted children with poor school performance, but high IQs. At that time, Dr. Laura Lee Crane ran the school. Her spirit animated the whole place. She was the definition of grace and was the *Grande Dame* of the institution. Entering her presence, at least for me, felt like I was entering an office of the Divine. Students were always on their best behavior around Dr. Crane. She commanded respect and she instilled confidence in us that what we were doing there was good and right.

Starpoint enrolled me in Mary Hale's classroom (now Mary Stewart) where I initially felt inadequate. Mary told me much later, "When you entered my classroom, Bryan, you looked defeated."[452] Since I had always failed in school, I was assuming that this would once again be a place where I would do nothing right. Fortunately, there were no grades in the school and I was placed in Mary's green classroom because of the level of my abilities and her reputation as an excellent teacher. She had a master's degree in special education from Kansas University, one of the best universities for this discipline.

Dr. Laura Lee Crane was the Director of the Starpoint School at Texas Christian University when I attended there from 1979-1980. She was a gifted leader, eloquent woman and compassionate teacher. When you were around her, you felt like you were in the presence of the Divine. You were always on your best behavior around Dr. Crane. She worked at the school from 1968 until her retirement in 1990 and was its Director from 1974 to 1990.

My previous school was at the church my family attended, and during church services every Wednesday night, Sunday morning and Sunday night, my former schoolmates consistently reminded me that I was not like them, but rather a failure. They called me "stupid" or a "freak." One boy used to call me "alien." Sadly, I later used this term for another boy who was probably one of the smartest kids in my group, just quiet and introverted. The adage "abuse begets abuse" comes to mind. I was not socially accepted. The problems with this type of treatment, besides the obvious one of being morally wrong, is that people suffering such maltreatment, especially children, begin to give up on themselves. They internalize what they hear and think of themselves as "bad" or "stupid" or "alien." Historically, society views people with strange behavior as inferior.[453] Tragically, such labeling, name-calling and bullying have led some children and teens to commit suicide.

I will return to Mary Stewart momentarily, but I want to digress here and explore the background of how people like me throughout history were often treated. In ancient days, people similar to me were beaten, imprisoned and often killed. Unfortunately, societies still do this today. Nazi Germans and Imperialistic Japanese did this in droves during WWII.[454] And today, in many Muslim countries, if one is anything but Muslim, there is social and religious justification to persecute and kill the unbeliever. And in many cultures throughout time, especially in China this past century, gender killings of unwanted girls during pregnancy, or right after birth, is commonplace.[455] Regardless of the era, the lethal focus on the unwanted, the inferior or the member of a minority is unfortunately an enduring trait of the human race.

But let's return to our main topic: understanding learning disabilities and its effects on kids and families. For a long time, even professionals believed that parents often caused their children's problems, assuming for a moment that we ignore that the parents' genes are the source for those of their children's. Now we know that those who have "normal" children "are not necessarily healthier, smarter, more organized or more caring. They are usually just luckier."[456] Some "normal" children have good genes and some have good parents. Yet, labeling people is a favorite pastime of humans. An expert on learning disabilities, Dr. Martin Kozloff, wrote,

> What do we usually think of a child who throws tantrums, makes bizarre sounds and gestures, and creates havoc in restaurants or in grocery stores? Do we not stare at the child and think that the child does not know how (or does not care) to behave properly in public? And what do we think of the parents?[457]

We are so vulnerable to people's opinions about us. My mom was constantly reminded of my problems because I did not behave well at stores, grocery markets, church or even in the car. I constantly banged my head against the back of the seat or kicked the ceiling with my feet while in the backseat (I obviously grew up before seat belts were required). She felt that everyone was staring at us. Unfortunately, she was often right. I wonder if she overheard comments like the following: "I wonder if it runs in the family?," "Jeez, what a weird kid," "Has he always acted like that?," or "If he were my kid, I'd tan his hide."[458]

Since my mother also had some difficult experiences as a child, especially after moving from a farm in the Oklahoma panhandle to Oklahoma City at the age of 10, she knew she must help me do better to fit in. She remembered how she had felt when she overheard negative things said about her, especially when her principal said to a teacher, "That Davidson girl [my mother] is the dumbest child I have ever had."[459] Sadly, that principal did not realize that my mother, who has a brilliant memory and probably is also ADHD, had just moved from a country school where she and her sister were the only students. Now they were in a school with hundreds of children, in a large city. Her curriculum while on the farm inadequately prepared her for the city school and she had problems catching up, both academically and socially.[460] My mother never forgot how that principal's opinion hurt her and she refused to allow her son to go through school, or life, with such a lasting stigma. She knew how damaging such comments could be. So, she was inspired to find help for me at the Starpoint School.

During one of my first interviews with Mary Stewart, my teacher at Starpoint, I told her about my experiences. She hugged me and then cupped my face in her hands and said,

You're not a freak and you're not abnormal. You're not learning disabled. You're learning different. There's nothing wrong with being different, but it's up to you to find out how you're different. I'm here to help you discover your strengths and talents.[461]

She spoke with authority and delivered her words quietly, politely and very precisely.

Under Mary's supervision, I discovered my talents and learned that I had imagination and energy. I soon went from being unable to pronounce individual words to reading whole books. With no grades or teacher-imposed time limits, students paced themselves and, upon finishing an assignment, were rewarded by moving on to the next challenging level. The most important lesson I learned was that I was capable of doing nearly anything I wanted and that the barriers preventing us from accomplishing our hopes and desires are usually of our own making.

Mary also taught me to be a contrarian. She told me after I started to read well,

See, Bryan, those kids were wrong who told you that you couldn't read and were stupid. Look, you're now reading at a higher level than they are. Good for you. If someone tells you that you cannot do something, don't believe him.[462]

Most importantly, Mary taught me that when people throw criticism at you, they are usually saying more about themselves than about you. Many know this intellectually, but, I would argue, most do not know this emotionally. She got me over both hurdles. My ex-wife believed Mary gave me a "bulletproof self-esteem."

My Starpoint teacher, Mary Stewart, and I outside the school's entryway. This was the end of the school year party in May 1980. I wanted my mom to make sure to ask Mary this day if she was a Christian so I could be in heaven with her forever. Mary did more for me in teaching me how to read and learn than any other of my elementary school teachers. She was so influential in helping me that when I graduated Yale University, I made sure she was there. She made me believe that I was not "Learning Disabled," but only "Learning Different."

Starpoint also had an effective system of rewards and punishments. Throughout the week, instead of getting grades, we got "chips" for doing certain things well. If we did our reading assignment and could tell the teacher what it was about, we got a chip. If we helped someone in need of assistance, we got a chip. If we did not misbehave for the whole week, we got a chip. The goal was to get 25 chips by Friday so that we could do a special event at the end of the week. Special events often included going to the Olympic-size pool at TCU to swim and jump off the high dive, or to the TCU football stadium to play a pick-up game. Other times we went to the Omni theatre to see educational films or visited museums, the zoo, or Mary's home where we fished in her back-yard ponds.[463] We all wanted to get our number of chips to go on these adventures. They provided a strong motivational factor to learn our subjects and abide by the rules. At Pantego Christian Academy, I was often blocked by an environment where punishment was used instead of rewards, but at Starpoint, I opened up and learned to enjoy the class-room. Starpoint did what English intellectual Bertrand Russell wrote was key for a child's development:

> A child must…not be subject to severe punishment, or to threats, or to grave and excessive reproof…A child must feel himself the object of warm affection on the part of some at least of the adults with whom he has to do, and he must not be thwarted in his natural activities and curios-ities except when danger to life or health is concerned.[464]

Russell eloquently observed that children learn best when they are free to explore information and knowledge in an environment that encourages and loves them, not one that forces pupils to learn through fear and force. Starpoint embraced a Russell-like methodology by re-warding us for good behavior with activities that were fun, positive and educational, and not shaming or punishing us with physical and psychological hurts and reprimands for misbehavior.

At Starpoint, we learned that special events in life are not a priv-ilege, not a right, but something you earn. Our behavior had a di-rect connection to self-esteem. We were not rewarded with candy, but rather, we were rewarded with opportunities to learn something new, all the while helping us accentuate our "natural activities and curiosities." Often after these events, we had to report to Mary what we had gained from the experience, giving us that feeling of "warm affection." Mary explained that if we were having a bad week (i.e. misbehaved or performed poorly on our assignments), she made sure that we felt the taste of failure by not allowing us to go on one of those trips. But she never whipped our buttocks to get her point across. She didn't have to, nor would she have wanted to. We did not want to be left outside the group or experience, and we definitely did not want to disappoint our saintly teacher.[465] I quickly learned that rewards work better than punishments.

Unlike several of my other elementary teachers, Mary never raised her voice or got upset with us. She was brilliant at always redirecting our curiosity and explaining things using eye contact. I joke today that if I had brought a pornographic magazine into the class, she would have responded as follows: "Well, Bryan, the human form is very beautiful. Let's study the human body. Did you know that instead of taking pictures, the ancient Greeks used to take hammers and chisels and make pictures of humans out of marble? How about looking at some pictures of what the Greeks did and then make human figures out of clay?" And during this explanation, she would have gently taken the magazine away from me and had me interested in what the Greeks had done and how I could do something similar. She never let us feel that she was frustrated with us. She always tuned in to our interests and encouraged us to learn through those passions.

For an actual example, I was fascinated with the ship *RMS Titanic* and she motivated me to read about this ship and learn its history. To help me with my math, she had me study how engineers built ships when the *Titanic* was designed; how learning my multiplication tables would help me understand how they riveted hulls together; and how my world geography class would show how skillful navigation helped sailors avoid icebergs when crossing the Atlantic. Using such techniques, she made learning fun. She always asked, "How *can* he process information," instead of, "How *should* he process it?"[466]

Another remarkable educational style of hers was that she never said "no" to us. Of course, if we tried to do something dangerous, like attempting to cross a busy street without looking, she would have grabbed us, pulled us back and loudly stated, "No, don't do that." But in the classroom, she never voiced any negative comments and the words "no" or "wrong" hardly ever left her mouth. If she did not approve of something we were doing, she was nevertheless able to find something positive. She created a world of curiosity, acceptance and kindness.[467] Dr. Hallowell explains that if one creates an environment of love and respect, people will treat one another with love and respect.[468] Mary went further and also created an environment that encouraged learning. She taught us to develop the passion to explore ideas, concepts and events. She made school fun and non-threatening by listening to our interests and encouraging them. She also showed her love for her pupils. As the poet Robert Frost, a teacher himself, wrote, "a teacher begins by loving his subject and ends by loving his students."[469]

Prior to Mary, I had come to fear school and hate learning. But luckily that did not happen in her classroom. Many have had someone who made a huge difference in their lives, and Mary was my saving angel. Her warmth and love surround me now, "giving me the courage to learn new things, to write books, to explore new areas."[470] She made me feel connected and respected. She also helped me accept myself for who I was. "When people grow up being punished for being the way they are, they become damaged."[471] They will lack confidence and fail to perform well in life.[472]

Starpoint healed my wounds quickly. If there is something out of the ordinary with a child, I believe it is important to diagnose any problems early in school. Otherwise, those problems can become an untreated wound that will turn into nasty infections of failure and low self-esteem.[473] Just as a wound heals more quickly when treated immediately, likewise the way an ADHD-child views education early is critical to his or her success, especially since the first 20 years or so of his or her life are spent in a learning environment. The longer an individual is imprisoned in a world of frustration and alienation, the more likely he will lay a foundation of failure for the rest of his life. Put another way, the more success you can ensure a child has when young, the more potential he will realize. [474] The British novelist W. Somerset Maugham said,

> The common idea that success spoils people by making them vain and self-complacent is erroneous; on the contrary, it makes them, for the most part, humble, tolerant and kind. Failure makes people bitter and cruel.[475]

Starpoint knew Maugham's statement to be true and made sure there were plenty of opportunities throughout the days and weeks where we had successes in learning and behaving that gave us great self-awareness that we were valued as human beings with different brains, but brains, nonetheless, that were intelligent and capable of learning.

Mary made me think well of myself, something I had not done until experiencing her encouragement and teaching. Research has shown that people who think well of themselves are indeed successful, happy and confident. Such people are "not burdened by self-doubt"; they radiate self-confidence, which in turn makes them attractive to others. Most importantly, a person who learns these truths respects himself and "is free to respect and love others."[476] In the end, such a person is less likely to exhibit "neurotic forms of behavior that will interfere with his successful functioning."[477]

Another example of how Starpoint helped build my self-esteem occurred years later, in 2003. I had just finished giving a talk about my book *Hitler's Jewish Soldiers* at the main Ft. Worth Public Library. The Director at Starpoint, Dr. Laura Lee Crane, when I was a student there, attended this event. After the talk, I thanked her for all she had done for me by running the school the way she had. She touched me gently on the face and said, "Bryan, I didn't do a thing. You did it all yourself." It was that can-do spirit and focus on taking responsibility for their learning and action that helped each kid at Starpoint develop a healthy self-esteem. According to Spinoza, "Self-esteem is thus said to be the highest thing we can hope for."[478] Starpoint, under Dr. Crane's leadership, fostered a culture of self-improvement and self-empower-ment. It also, unlike at Pantego, fostered an environment of love. As Phillips Exeter Academy English teacher, Harvard V. Knowles, wrote:

> ...a fleeting glance at even a tentative teaching experience will confirm the need for a loving relationship between teacher and taught...For the failure to love [one's students] is a failure to consider them as individuals. And until each one of them is an individual person in the teacher's mind, he will not be able to help him grow in the way in which his individuality demands.[479]

The staff at Starpoint, under Dr. Crane's leadership, understood this and implemented it throughout all the classrooms and activities.

This school also recognized what Dr. Hallowell wrote about ADHD-children:

> [They]...do not stay on track. They stray. But they also see new things or find new ways to see old things. They are not just the tuned-out of this world; they are also tuned in, often to the fresh and the new. They are often the inven-tors and the innovators, the movers and the doers. Good Do-Bees they may not always be, but we should be wise enough not to force them into a mold they'll never fit.[480]

Starpoint helped me embrace what I had and use it to learn. It taught me to dream during the day and not only at night, because in doing so, I gave myself hope.

Many of you may be asking, "How did Starpoint teach me how to read?" Well, in partial fulfillment toward earning her PhD from TCU, Dr. Crane wrote *Code 78*, a Starpoint teachers' guide for improving LD-students' reading, writing and speaking skills.

Dr. Crane's work broke down the 45 sounds in the English language and then taught teachers to use color-coding to help students "distinguish vowels from consonants."[481] The goal in doing this was to ensure each student would "actively participate in learning" and "build a backlog of successful experiences."[482] Right here, at the outset, this "teaching bible" for Starpoint faculty stressed the importance of engaging an ADHD-mind using visual stimulation (different colored letters) and kinematic learning (Hunter-like activity). When I write "kinematic" or when Dr. Crane wrote "actively participate in learning," this all translated into the school having us constantly standing, pointing, writing and speaking as we presented our ideas, our knowledge of new sounds and words, and our written stories. We were in perpetual motion as we explored how to learn English. I was in a perfect learning environment for my brain.

Code 78 focused on working in groups of five to seven children, all at the same level of competency, so they could activity feed off one another as they learned together (again, very Hunter-like, i.e., small, interactive groups).[483] A teacher was instructed to always "look directly at the child" and say "Good" when he or she finished a task successfully, serving as a "social reward" to build self-esteem.[484] Starpoint's techniques focused on the Trigeneric Phonics Scheme which encompassed three components: Sound/Letter Association, Sequencing of Sounds and Blending Sounds into Words.[485] As a result, we learned numerous words daily by breaking them down into their sounds and colors and then building them back up into workable sentences so we knew how to use them. Pictures of nouns were often presented to prompt us to write out what we were seeing. Often, Mary Stewart had us go to a chalkboard and explain what we were writing or stand at our desk and discuss what we just had learned. Every time we did something successful, Mary would say "Good" and then told us to sit down to make room at the chalkboard or shift attention to another desk to give the next student his or her time at learning the lesson "kinesthetically."[486] As mentioned, whether it was reading short stories, using language appropriately, sounding out the pronunciation of words or writing out our vocabulary, we were *always* doing it actively, quite often *while standing*. These were just a few strategies, besides creating a loving environment, that Starpoint implemented to teach LD-kids how to read and write. Remember, I came to Starpoint not even knowing my alphabet, and I would leave it being able to read a truncated version of Hemingway's *The Old Man and the Sea*.

During that 1979-1980 school year, a major event occurred in the world that also impacted me—The Olympics. With my self-esteem returning, I realized, as an underdog, I could rise up and learn at the level of my peers. The Olympics made me take notice of another underdog in the world, our United States hockey team. Every day, after I did my homework, or during the weekends, I watched the hockey games, or the highlights, shown on television. The way the media presented our team made Americans think it would take a miracle to beat the most dominant team in the world, the Soviet Union hockey team.

At Starpoint, we conducted nuclear bomb drills that showed us what we should do and where we should go if attacked by the Soviets. We were all afraid of the evil nation of Russia. We knew that the Soviet athletes were practically machines and older and full of steroids compared to our players. There was so much fear and awe connected to competing against the Soviets that every time our men and women went up against USSR competitors, it was as if little Cold War battles were being fought.

Our hockey team had to beat a lot of other teams to even qualify to play the Soviet Union, much less, beat them. But when we tied Sweden, and beat Norway and West Germany, I got excited. I really got animated when we defeated Romania and Czechoslovakia, two Communist teams! I especially got jazzed about crushing the Czech team because we were told they were almost as good as the Soviets, and we beat them 7-3 (a "massacre"!). And that victory allowed America to play Russia.

Our U.S. hockey team was made up of young college boys, many of whom had only played together for a few months. The Soviet team incorporated Russian military officers who had played together for years. They were older, bigger, stronger, and wiser than the Americans. This game was like having a college football team play an NFL team. There was no logical reason we could beat them, and as an eight-year-old boy, I knew this. But we all had hope that we would win. Also, subconsciously and consciously, this game spoke to the transformation I was undergoing at Starpoint. I was also an underdog, but I was learning how to compete with all those smart kids I had gone to school with at Pantego.

And then it happened. Under Herb Brooks' coaching, we beat the Russians in one of the greatest sporting events in history (the famous phrase at the game's end by the sports announcer, Al Michaels, still rings in my head: "Do you believe in miracles? Yes!"). When our hockey team beat the Soviets 4-3, I jumped up and down in my living room and yelled at the top of my lungs. My mom ran in and asked what was going on and I just replied loudly, "We beat THEM!!" Then, after our team beat Finland in its final game and won the Gold Medal, I took pride in my country and our American players. The game inspired me to work hard and be more than people thought I was. That my ADHD-brain allowed me then to take away the powerful lessons the game taught could have only happened in a place like Starpoint.

So, this school was also helping me to be more positive about myself. Besides now talking about the *Titanic*, I started to talk about America's *Miracle on Ice* team, and Mary, once again, used that event to teach life lessons. One of the biggest ones taught was that without discipline, those boys would not have won the Gold Medal. As a result, I was going to try to be more disciplined in everything I did.

Also, while I was enrolled at Starpoint, my mother became more involved in my schoolwork. My mom helped me with reading, spelling tests and writing. Studies have shown that parents who get involved with their children's schoolwork "increase the rate at which their children learn."[487]

Luckily for me, my parents could afford Starpoint. Many parents of LD-kids do not have the resources to help their child by putting them in specialized schools.[488] Had my family not had the money, I would not have had Mary Stewart. Starpoint did not grant scholarships. What would have happened to me without this school? Would the possibility of becoming a criminal, as some data about ADHD-children predicted, become a reality for me? It's unfortunate that many children fail in life because they cannot afford the opportunity that I had.

This process of finding Starpoint makes me ponder the way we educate our nation. Right now, many of our institutions, in the words of political philosopher Isaiah Berlin, create social inequality. He goes on to write that this inequality rises from,

> [The] evils... from differences of status created by a system of education governed by the financial resources and the social position of parents rather than the ability and the needs of the children... the need to provide for the bodies and minds of as many human beings as possible, and not only of members of a privileged class...[489]

My mother got me to Starpoint on the recommendations of experts. Often, parents of LD-children become frustrated with the experts because they do not give helpful advice. The key here is to find experts who can help in finding solutions by providing useful information.[490] We were lucky to find Dr. Maddox at the Child Study Center in Fort Worth.

Also, getting involved with Starpoint made my mother realize she was not alone. Knowing she was fighting a battle which other parents also were engaged in helped her deal with my situation. She found places where she could go for a sympathetic ear and helpful advice. This is essential in dealing with ADHD/LD-kids. [491]

Similarly, the feeling of not being alone improved how I viewed myself. Starpoint gave me a sense of feeling connected. I was no longer that lonely freak. I was "just different" and that was alright in this place because we were taught that we are all different in some way. This increased connection with a group, a school and a thought process strengthened my emotional health. Such connections with Mary, and my classmates, improved my behavior at home and created the lifelines I needed. I also made friends and even though we had come from difficult school situations, we all accepted one another as we were. My best friend at the school was Greg Guttman, a wheelchair-bound, physically handicapped LD-boy who taught me how fortunate I should feel that my legs worked properly and how I should have a positive attitude like his: He never complained about his condition. The evidence is overwhelming that people who connect with one another live longer and happier lives. Isolation leads to an unhealthy existence, and possibly even to an untimely death. As Joseph Conrad wrote,

> Who knows what true loneliness is—not the conventional word but the naked terror? To the lonely themselves it wears a mask. The most miserable outcast hugs some memory or some illusion... No human being could bear a steady view of moral solitude without going mad.[492]

Had I not had a school like Starpoint, a teacher like Mary and a mother like mine, who was aggressive in finding help, I would have slowly entered a world of isolation, something Dr. Hallowell notes plagues many with ADHD.[493] I was already heading in that direction, but my year at Starpoint turned my ship around. I now knew how to avoid hitting those major icebergs that could slow my progress and further isolate me as a poor reader and slow learner.[494]

Although not aware of it at the time, I had been traumatized by my experience at Pantego Christian Academy. Being labeled stupid and a failure and feeling the stress created by my parents, principal and teachers, I definitely felt like an outsider. According to some research, when I entered Mary's classroom, I may have been suffering from post-traumatic stress disorder (PTSD). My adult self finds this a little bit of a stretch, but it is supported in the literature. According to one study, 10% of ADHD-people attempt to kill themselves and 5% die either from suicide or accidental injury.[495] In 2019, only 47,511 out of a U.S. population of 350 million committed suicide, and 1,380,000 attempted it (.04% of the population). The data suggest that many ADHD-people struggle to find their psychological equilibrium and are at a higher risk of taking their own lives than the general population.[496] Dr. Hallowell documents that having ADHD can lead to "suicide, addictions of all kinds, felonious acts…dangerously violent behavior, and a shorter life."[497] In fact, having ADHD, especially if untreated, has been shown by the research of Russell Barkley to lower a person's "life expectancy…by up to 21 years."[498]

I know this theory that poor management of ADHD may lead to PTSD and lower life expectancies sounds strange. It sounded strange to me, especially since I had only studied PTSD in men who had experienced combat and had difficulties adjusting to life after their war experiences. However, PTSD symptoms are not only combat-related but can also show up after sexual assault, domestic violence, close calls with drowning, animal attacks, surviving severe weather and, as mentioned, from the ostracization that comes from not being able to learn and fit into society.[499]

Some of my PTSD symptoms included "sleep disturbance, irritability, temper outbursts, difficulty concentrating… and fearfulness."[500] In fact, looking at the last symptom in this list, I remember some terrible fears I had as a kid. For instance, I became horrified about death and worried that spiders were going to do me in. My first-grade teacher, Jim Rose, today still remembers how scared I was of this insect.[501] I felt that if I stepped on a spider, its poison would later get me when I took off my shoe and I touched its venom. I even felt that if I walked barefoot on the ground where a spider had walked, I could pick up its poison and die. My fears often made me inconsolable. Mom once again provided the solution that saved me. One day, and I do not know how she figured it out, she told me that when spider poison hits the air, it is no longer lethal. Once she told me this, I calmed down.

I also feared that other children would reject me and call me stupid. This was something that continued to scare me. A characteristic of PTSD involves "intense fear, helplessness, or horror."[502] Moreover, since I was sexually abused as a child, this probably also added to my PTSD, since PTSD results from "a threat to the physical integrity of self or others."[503]

Even if I did not have PTSD and my difficulties were just typical ADHD-symptoms, people still need to know that if a person continues to live in an environment where he is told not only in words, but also by actions, that he is a "freak" and "abnormal," this will take a psychological toll on the person and can lead to PTSD and a lower quality of life. I believe Dr. Hartmann, from whom I have gathered this PTSD information, makes the point that children with ADHD/ LD can suffer from PTSD just as much as a Marine who just experienced an artillery bombardment of his foxhole.

So, Mary's classroom was not only a place of learning, but also a place of therapy for me. I did have a lot of trauma to deal with, and she taught me how to deal with it. She convinced me that my condition was not superior or inferior to anyone else's. I had been taught, even conditioned, to view myself as being minimally brain damaged (MBD). Sadly, this is a common perception today. During a conference on ADHD in the 1990s, a psychologist pointed his finger at an audience of ADHD-people and said, "You people have an illness. You're sick. Don't you get it? Why do you think we call it a 'disorder.'"[504] Relationship expert Melissa Orlov claims that ADHD is a "chemical imbalance" in the brain![505] One father of an ADHD-child who had obviously been given such feedback from doctors like this one said to his questioning son who was on Ritalin,

> Yes, Son. It's a very strong medicine we have to give you because you have this very serious disease called Attention Deficit-Disorder… As long as you always realize that you're different from the normal people that aren't sick like you are, you'll be a lot happier.[506]

The doctor, therapist and father mentioned here all express the view that such an "affliction" is a defect rather than just another way for a brain to work.[507] Even today, ADHD, especially in adults, "is a recognized condition in the big book of psychiatric disorders, the Diagnostic and Statistical Manual (DSM-5)."[508]

In the face of such beliefs in the 1970s, Mary stepped up as one of only a few who were trained to assist me. She helped me know more about myself and to recognize and follow my "Yearning to Know," which is written in bronze on the statue outside the Starpoint building depicting a woman reading to two children.[509] She helped me learn things in the ways that I could.[510] When we start to learn more about who we are and how we process information, we can then grow as human beings. The experience at Starpoint taught me that we must constantly remind ourselves, as Socrates taught, that "the unexamined life is not worth living" and that when one "knows oneself," then and only then, will one know how to learn.[511] After Starpoint, I knew I was smart, funny, well-spoken, capable and worthy. I came in "sick" in 1979 and I left "well" in 1980. Although I still had a lot more healing and learning to do, I knew I could do it all.

Takeaways

- Early diagnosis of any problems in school is crucial. Otherwise, those problems can become an untreated wound that will turn into nasty infections of failure and low self-esteem. Just as a wound heals more quickly when treated immediately, the way an ADHD-child views education early is critical to his success, especially since the first 20 years or so of his life are spent in a learning environment. The more success you can help a child experience when young, the more potential that child will realize.

- Studies have shown that parents who get involved with their children's schoolwork "increase the rate at which their children learn."[512]

- Being labeled stupid and a failure and feeling the stress created by my parents, my principal and my teachers, I definitely felt like an outsider. According to some research, when I entered Mary's classroom, I may have been suffering from PTSD. Even if I did not have PTSD and my difficulties were just typical ADHD-symptoms, continuing to live in an environment where I would be told not only in words, but also by actions, that I was a "freak" and "abnormal" would have taken a psychological toll on me.

Action Steps

- Discuss the best school options with your child's therapist if you have one.

- Do research on the best schools in your area that focus on LD-issues.

- Consult educational experts in your region to select the school and program within the school that best fits your child's needs and will provide help with his or her LD-issues.

CHAPTER 8:
Getting Ready for Mainstream Education

"One must believe in the possibility of happiness in order to be happy."

— Leo Tolstoy, *War and Peace*[513]

AT STARPOINT, MARY STEWART WAS able to do in one year what the experts had thought would only be accomplished in two to three years. I was ready to return to a mainstream school in 1980, but I did not want to leave. However, Mary promised she would follow my progress at the White Lake School nearby. The next year, she met regularly with my new instructor to ensure my successful transition.

Mary, my family and Starpoint were "kicking me out of the nest," so to speak, to get me to a more challenging environment. They saw that I had exhausted Starpoint's curriculum and needed to move on. This is something important to keep in focus when dealing with ADHD-children, or any children for that matter; namely, when they start to learn and have a passion for it, watch for signs of boredom. If that happens, you need to either a). get them into a more challenging class at the school they attend (like AP classes, for example), or b). find a new school (*aka* magnet schools or private academies).

We did this with our son Justin. In fifth-grade, he was bored at Shelton and did not like the school work. Immediately, remembering my experience of transitioning from Starpoint to White Lake, I started looking at other options for Justin, and we transitioned him to Parish

Episcopal in Dallas in 2015, just like his sister, Sophia, had done in 2012. This was what we needed, and the academic rigor increased at this school and Justin started to thrive once again. Nonetheless, a few years later, after attending Phillips Exeter Summer School in 2018, Justin once again became bored with the academics at Parish and realized he needed a more demanding school. To his credit, Justin, with his ADHD-mind, searched out several prep schools and applied to them. He got into several in 2019 but decided to attend Phillips Exeter Academy, one of the most challenging secondary school environments in the world. So, in short, parents of ADHD-children need to watch them carefully, and once they see they are bored with a school's teaching methods, they need to help them find a more challenging academic environment. This was a lesson I had learned early on when Starpoint transitioned me to White Lake, which indeed proved to be more academically challenging than Starpoint.

At White Lake, I did well in school, although I focused more on sports than on academics. I still had some difficulty sitting still and studying, but I earned As and Bs. Much of my time was consumed with playing soccer, football, basketball and baseball. My mother encouraged me in these athletic activities, probably to prevent me from wrecking our house. Also, ADHD-management is aided through sports and physical fitness, so these activities helped me live a normal life. Dr. Hallowell says that one of the best treatments of ADHD is "daily aerobic exercise."[514] Hallowell even goes so far as to say that exercise may go further than medication with some patients.[515] "Exercise stimulates the production of epinephrine, dopamine, and serotonin, which is exactly what the medications we treat ADHD will do."[516] Also, since ADHD-children are four times more prone to violence, having this outlet in sports was invaluable for me.[517] Exercise has also been shown to reduce people's sick days at work or school by 25% to 50%.[518] Exercise also stimulates growth in an area of the brain where

MRI studies show are smaller in ADHD-people; namely, "the central strip down the midline of the cerebellum—called the *vermis*."[519] Exercise not only can tone and grow your muscles, it can also promote "the growth of existing neurons, making them look, on scans, bushier, with more interconnecting branches, like full treetops."[520] In short, exercise is indeed the magic bullet.

By third-grade, while at White Lake, I was a fairly "normal" child and enjoyed my friends, school and athletic teams. My third-grade teacher, Laurie Bodine, remembered the special diet I was on and she helped me maintain it. She remembered me being a "nice boy" who worked hard in class. My fourth-grade teacher Laurie Lakota (now Zuspic) said that I was a sweet and curious boy and she enjoyed having me. She also remembered how rigorous I was with my diet and that I never ate the cakes other parents brought for their children in my class for their birthday parties.[521] My diet and Mary Stewart's philosophies were all working. But Mary told me recently,

> It was a team effort, Bryan. You had a mother and grandmother willing to work with me. Today, teachers most often find themselves at odds with the parents. I was lucky to have a good working relationship with your family. They helped me help you learn and become confident. All too often today, parents want the teachers to raise their children and this will never happen.[522]

Many factors are involved in helping ADHD-kids. Watching their diet, practicing discipline, finding a loving and caring environment and never giving up are the simple, but demanding, life lessons ADHD-parents and ADHD-children must learn for success. To conquer ADHD, I also had to learn that there is a direct correlation between the mind and body, and both have to be nurtured. There is so much truth to the Roman saying, "A sound mind will thrive in a healthy body (*Mens sano in corpora sano est*)."[523] These principles and practices began to take root within my subconscious, beyond my realm of comprehension. Do not forget that if "you have ten pebbles in your shoe and you remove one, you will still limp." Pediatric allergist, Doris Rapp, said this and, although she was focusing on a healthy diet, one can apply it to the other realms of treating ADHD-children, *focusing on their food, attitude and schooling altogether and at once.*

Throughout my elementary school years, I studied at small private schools where I could thrive. Small schools, which are usually private, are where ADHD-kids can have the best chance to do well. Our public schools are simply not set up for ADHD-kids. As Dr. Hartmann writes,

> Our schools, too, are set up along Farmer [non-ADHD-types] lines. Sit quietly at the desk, children are told, while the teacher talks and points to pages in the book. Ignore that child next to you who's sniffling; don't rattle your papers; don't look ahead in the book. To a smart Hunter with a low boredom threshold, this is torture! It's a *prescription for failure* [author's italics].[524]

In other words, in public schools that put at least 15 to 20 kids in a room, the needs of ADHD-children are overlooked. As our schools "are placed under the increasing burden of under-funding and teacher-overload/overwork, Hunter children are increasingly being noticed [for negative and non-conformist behavior]."[525] In a nutshell, I was lucky my family could afford private schools.

Sadly, as my life was getting better, my parents' relationship declined. Like so many other American kids, I had to deal with my parents' divorce while still a child. During my fourth-grade year, my parents separated, and then in my sixth-grade year, my parents finalized their divorce. My teacher, Mrs. Eddie Blackburn, was very helpful to me and my mother, as my family went through divorce. A private school allowed the intimacy necessary for the teacher to reach out to me during this troubling time, just as Mary had done when helping me overcome my learning challenges. Children of divorced families go through a lot. I now realize that the rest of my childhood spent at home, without Mom and Dad fighting, was better for me compared to my older brother's experience, who was always caught in the constant stress between them. In other words, I witnessed less domestic turmoil than my brother by having my parents not being under the same roof during the majority of my childhood. When my father finally left, though, I felt a deep responsibility for it and I was angry. It has been shown, also, that children raised in single-parent homes where the father has left are more prone to express ADHD-behavior, so his leaving would cause me added stress.[526]

I felt so confused and responsible for my parents' divorce, that when I heard that my fourth-grade teacher Laurie Lakota was going through a divorce, I called her up and expressed my hope that I had not caused it. "Bryan, I still remember sitting at my parents' kitchen table when you asked me this and it broke my heart," she told me years later. "It really touched me that you were feeling things so deeply."[527] She informed me that of course I was not the cause of her breakup, but the very fact that I thought I was responsible showed I was dealing with feelings of guilt and confusion.

Yet, during this time, I still needed to engage in activities to feed my desire for risk-taking (typical for ADHD-kids). Although my activities were not as reckless as those of other kids my age, who were involved with drugs, alcohol and violence, I was mischievous.[528] I would take copious amounts of toilet paper from public restrooms in restaurants and shopping markets, hide it in my school bag or under my jacket, store it in my closet and then use it to "toilet paper" people's houses and trees late at night (i.e., "go rolling"). I also enjoyed "door-ditching," where you ring someone's doorbell and then run away and hide. And last of all, I enjoyed tying up people's mailboxes with either chicken wire or with string-pulled fire-crackers and then watching the mailman the next day have either to struggle to get the box open or be shocked when the tiny explosion went off. In becoming the small vandal that I aspired to be, a friend and I during one late night glued a sign "Beware of Dog" to a corvette parked on the street in the neighborhood. And on the rare occasions when it snowed in Texas, I enjoyed throwing snowballs at cars. Although these activities were relatively harmless compared to what I could have done, they provided an incredible sense of adventure. And while non-ADHD-children also can be mischievous, the time I spent doing such things spoke of my desire to stimulate my ADHD-brain.

One day, when my mom investigated my dresser, she was horrified to find about 25 rolls of toilet paper. She confronted me and asked where I had gotten them. I told her why I got them and where most of them came from. After she made me put all the rolls into a bag, she marched me back to the grocery store near my bus stop where I had obtained most of the items, and told me, "Now, you return them to the men's room." I dutifully obeyed and walked into the store with my bag of toilet paper and went to the public restroom. As I was pulling out all the toilet paper and putting the rolls back on the shelves, a store employee walked in. With eyes squinting and his head tilted, he showed his surprise that a young kid—(he may have thought I was a non-uniformed employee)—was stacking rolls of toilet paper. I pulled out the last of the rolls and, as I put them on the shelf, he shook his head. I had re-shelved blue, yellow, white and flowered rolls (some of the merchandise had come from other places). The pyramid of toilet paper rolls, with some of them already half-used, looked very strange. The man stared at me, not knowing what was happening. I felt I had to say something, so I blurted out, "My family doesn't need these rolls anymore so we are donating them."

With that I picked up my bag and walked out of the bathroom. I will never forget the dumbfounded look on the guy's face. He didn't say a word.

Besides the mischief I got into, I also took pleasure in other high-adrenaline activity. For example, I loved taking my 12-foot Sunfish sailboat and, when I got older and stronger, my 18-foot Hobie Cat out on Lake Arlington during heavy thunderstorms (the lake was my backyard). I relished taking the boats on downward legs where I would be surfing the waves (going faster than the waves and jumping over them). I always wore a lifejacket, and sometimes my bike helmet, but it wasn't always prudent to take a vessel out with a long aluminum mast and boom when it was lightening and thundering. Experiencing this risky adventure, I undeniably found it stimulating, fun, exciting and, actually, calming. The feel of the pelting rain hitting my face and arms, the whistle of the wind through the halyards and mast stays and the crashing of the bow and the pontoons through the water made me feel alive. And this was all happening under a ceiling of thunder and lightning, illuminating the bizarre, puffy shapes of the clouds overhead. It created a natural symphony of sound and fury that made my heart race, and I often found myself shouting out with glee as I enjoyed my own company. And when I keeled over with the Hobie Cat in over 20-knot winds on my windward tacks, I took great pleasure in burying the lower pontoon into the waves which would sling-shot me through the air and into the lake as I fully tipped, or rather flipped, the boat over.

As an adult, I would not recommend these activities to young sailors today, but back when I was a kid, these storm-cruises provided full-on, high-octane excitement, and became some of my most powerful memories. When taking physics later, I looked back on the lessons I learned on my boats to help me master the principles of this science. I drew especially on my experience with pulleys, winches, winch handles, Bernoulli's principle (the science of pressure and speed, *aka*, how wind can push boats) and telltales. In other words, like with most people, those with ADHD-traits will master what is taught in the classroom more readily when they can relate first-hand experiences to the topic. Connecting to personal experiences will firmly impress the lesson in their minds and benefit them greatly.

Here I am sailing my 12-foot Sunfish with Danny Farr, my Pee-Wee Football Buddy, circa 1983. I sailed all over Lake Arlington with that boat, and often during thunderstorms. Learning about wind, water, boats, weather, steering, waves and many other things surrounding sailing excited my ADHD-brain and helped me learn about physics, math and meteorology better than any textbook could ever do.

When not sailing, I often applied my knowledge to building boats. During the spring rainy season in 1979, as an eight-year-old, I collected a lot of the wood and styrofoam blocks that floated up along the banks of Lake Arlington to build my own raft, with which I used to fish and hunt snakes. I had three train track logs that I used as the foundation and hammered them together with a patchwork of wood. Underneath, I tied them to large styrofoam blocks, one at the bow section of the boat, and another at the stern. It was my first engineering feat as a child and I used that craft for years to fish off of and paddle around the lake. When I got bored one day, I also built my own sailboat using a rubber dingy as its hull at the water canal where my aunt, Myrna Gregg, née Davidson, lived. It took me hours making sails out of plastic bags and a boom and mast out of sticks from her log pile, but eventually I finished the craft and sailed it around the canal for 20 minutes until a few strong gusts of wind blew it apart. These activities were two of hundreds I did as a child that helped me develop my brain by using my curiosity about the world to learn, in real time, about an activity I already enjoyed—in this case, boating.

Here is the raft I built as an eight-year-old. It is important for ADHD-children to have an outlet to explore their curiosity and involve themselves in projects that satisfy their need for adventure and physical activity. Building this raft taught me a lot about hammers, nails, wood, buoyancy and physics. It took me weeks of working after school to build this craft, but I never gave up. It was the perfect activity for my ADHD-brain to learn how to solve problems and set a goal for myself, and meet it. Summer 1979

At around this time, I started to develop techniques that helped me process information, although I was not aware of it then. I always looked for ways to get extra credit, because that allowed me to do a project on my own time on something that held my interest. Moreover, such a project gave me the opportunity to work one-on-one with a teacher. My high school chemistry teacher, Mary Jo Tyler, often called me, "Mr. Extra Credit." Getting extra credit gives ADHD-kids "an opportunity to learn in a mode that's appropriate to their disposition, and provides them a chance to maintain high grade point averages, even if they're not always consistent in doing their boring homework."[529] All of these factors played into my ability to keep focused and learn.

I also was active in sports, spending an average of 15 to 20 hours a week working out. Between the games, practices and weight room, I was constantly in motion. Often before going to bed, I would go out in the front of my house where we had a basketball hoop in the driveway and several lights, and shoot baskets for 20 to 30 minutes before turning in for the night.

I also started to invent special memory aids that helped me focus on important tasks. I developed techniques to remember things, such as where I had placed my keys or what assignment I needed to turn in. I would focus on the "mission" at hand, repeat it ten times in my mind and then associate it with something in my environment. For example, if I set my keys down on a bench press machine or on the dining room table, I would repeat ten times in my mind where I put the keys and then envision those keys in a strange way with the item I had placed them on. I would see keys bench-pressing over 400 pounds, or see the table eating millions of keys. As a result, I stopped losing my keys or other items I thought important. This points to the value of visualization and memory, especially with those with ADHD.

Here I am in my first year playing pee-wee tackle football. I was in fourth-grade and was an offensive and defensive tackle for the Ditto Elementary Rangers. I loved the physical fitness, the controlled aggression and the thrill of playing games as a youngster. Such athletic activities fed my ADHD-brain that needed risky and high-adrenaline activity. Fall 1981

I would also relate school assignments to something in my room. For a long time, I had a picture of the Baylor University linebacker, Mike Singletary, on my wall. I often would envision DNA pouring out of his eyes or algebra problems spitting out of his helmet when I had a biology test or a math test that week. I also had a picture of a ship above my bed and model World War II airplanes hanging from my ceiling. They also helped me remember things.[530]

While I worked hard to improve schoolwork and my grades, I also excelled at sports. I performed well as the goalie for my soccer team, and improved a lot at baseball, hitting over .350 during my fourth-grade year. Also, throughout my fourth-, fifth- and sixth-grade years, I was one of the star players on my pee-wee football team, the Ditto Rangers. These successes all added to my much-needed self-esteem. Throughout junior high, I played football and basketball and ran track, doing well at all three at my new school, Fort Worth Christian. Besides needing the exercise, I learned how to work in a team environment. I also practiced martial arts at the local Boy's Club, which sharpened my focus and helped my coordination. My improved self-esteem helped me avoid a litany of problems like alcohol, drugs and sexual promiscuity.

As I was developing into a young man, my mother searched each summer for interesting and challenging endeavors for me, knowing I thrived on such activities (and also to get me out of the house to protect it as much as she could). When I was in elementary school from 1978 until 1983, she sent me to 10 to 12 one-week sessions at Camp Thurman summer camp. The schedule was jam-packed with capture-the-flag games, artificial wall climbing, zip-lining, swimming, tent building, horseback riding, archery and BB gun practice. During junior high school in 1984 and 1985, she sent me to summer camps at Goddard Youth Camp in Sulphur, Oklahoma, and to Pine Cove in Tyler, Texas, where I did similar activities. I loved all of it and found it exciting.

After I finished eighth-grade in 1986, with the encouragement of family friends, my mom not only signed me up for Teens Missions International, but she also signed herself up as a counselor. This organization takes groups of kids on mission trips all over the world. Since I was going to start taking French as a freshman in high school, I decided to go to France. Because my mother wanted to see the Holy Land, she signed up to be a leader with the Israel team. As a former TWA flight attendant, my mom loves to travel and explore new cultures, something she has been doing her whole life—very ADHD-like.

Teens Missions International set up teams, which usually consisted of between 25 and 35 children, with four to six adult team leaders, and sent these little groups into the world to proselytize, build wells, construct homes, erect churches and conduct vacation Bible schools. When I was involved in 1986, the organization sent teams to six of the seven world continents. But first, the kids from these teams (numbering around 1,000 teenagers) descended on Merritt Island, Florida, where everyone participated in a two-week "Boot Camp" in the harsh environment of this area. We lived in tents, learned construction techniques and skills, conducted physical training and negotiated obstacle courses as team-building exercises. We also did a lot of Bible studies and verse memorization. We bathed in local ponds, struggled with the heat and humidity and learned to live with armadillos, mosquitoes, snakes and alligators. After Boot Camp graduation, we left for France, and for the next two months, we helped build a Protestant church in Rheims and traveled throughout the country, learning about France and its history. Although today, I don't necessarily agree with the theological mandates of the group at that time, it was an adventure and my mom was doing everything she could to give me these wonderful experiences. For an ADHD-mind, this was how I enjoyed living the most—by doing interesting things and experiencing new cultures or environments first-hand. Before I graduated high school, I had gone on other mission trips to South Africa, Transkei in South Africa, the Bahamas, Romania and Bulgaria, often living among the natives and learning new cultures.

After this interesting summer in 1986 in France, my mother found another camp she wanted to send me to the next summer after my freshman year of high school. It was called Adventure Wild Challenge in Colorado Springs, Colorado, and was sponsored by the Navigators Ministry. Today, it is called the Rocky Mountain Challenge and it is only two weeks long and not as tough as the program I completed. Being a former Marine Corps officer, I think whoever put together the Adventure Wild Challenge in 1987 must have had military training. When I arrived there in the summer of 1987, I thought my mom had sent me to a nice summer camp where we would sleep in comfortable cabins, build campfires to roast our smores and sing *Kum ba yah* while holding hands. Unknowingly, she had sent me to a survival camp, and I would not see either a toilet, shower, sink or bed for almost a month.

The program was three and one-half weeks long. The first week, they ran us in the mountains, made us do hikes, taught us how to set up tents and encampments and made us cook our food out in the open. They taught us about field hygiene, how to build fires and administer first aid. They got us up early, and we did not stop until late at night. I never knew I could take a bath so quickly until I jumped into a freezing river. My technique was simple. I would jump in and then out. Take my bar of soap and lather up. Then I would jump in again and jump out, dry off and then put on a clean set of clothes. It only took about two minutes.

We started with over 30 people, and within one week, we were down to 16. When I was able to call my mother after finishing our "Hell" week initiation, I said to her, "Mom, whatever I did, I'm sorry. I'll never do it again." She asked why, and I responded, "That nice summer camp you sent me to—well, it's not a summer camp, but a military camp with hardships, regulations and beat downs." She asked if I wanted to come home, but I told her I found it challenging and wanted to see if I could finish the course.

During the following weeks, we learned how to survive if we fell into cold water by swimming several minutes in a cold lake (the water temperature was around 50 degrees). We learned how to crawl through underground tunnels, climb steep cliffs, rappel off steep and tall bluffs and precipices, find food in the wild, care for our feet, clean ourselves and outfits in the field, purify water with iodine, read weather from the sky and horizon, work as a team and push ourselves past what we thought possible. We hiked Pike's Peak (elevation 14,115 feet), weathered several thunderstorms and snowstorms, hiked more than a hundred miles and gained self-confidence. The last challenge was a 10-mile run that I completed in 86 minutes. Then we all celebrated our official status as elite campers.

In the summer of 1987, I attended the Navigators' Adventure Wild Challenge, a mini-survival camp in Colorado. During the three-week course, I learned about navigation, mountain climbing, camping, survival skills, backpacking, cooking outside, weather reading and many other activities that my ADHD-brain loved. Here, I am rappelling off of a 100-foot, inverted cliff. Summer 1987

Such activities fed my hunger for adventure and helped me enjoy my ADHD-brain. I encourage parents with such children to find outdoor activities to teach a sense of self-reliance, physical fitness and problem-solving techniques. Being in the wild helped me learn how to deal with my environment, enjoy the outdoors and meet others who liked being challenged. It was perfect for making my ADHD-mind stronger. I have encouraged my children to participate in similar training, going on dozens of campouts with them and sending my oldest son twice to Camp Cheley in Estes Park, Colorado, and my daughter to horse camp in Vermont.

By the time I entered high school, although very physically fit, I knew I would not become a professional athlete. Although I still spent a lot of time training for my sports teams, I started to focus more on academics, obtaining mostly As. I also had another incredible teacher, Donna Reynolds, my drama teacher. She started to instruct me in 1985 as an eight grader and continued doing so until I graduated from high school in 1990. She taught me self-reliance and how to present myself in front of an audience and lead others. Since I had a speech impediment, working on rhetoric, articulation and pronunciation helped me improve in skills that were more difficult for me. Often ADHD-kids have a difficult time leading others, because they struggle relating to people around them. In forcing me to understand the motivations of characters we played in drama class, Donna helped me do something vital for my social development. Donna's teaching helped me empathize with my fellow human beings. Donna forced us to look closely at how people behave, because if we understand them, then we will start to understand ourselves, all important attributes to have as a thespian. Moreover, working alongside diverse individuals in creating a realistic play forced us to work intimately with each other, teaching us why people were behaving the way they were.

In teaching theater, Donna Drama, as we liked to call her, told us that to become a better actor, we needed "to own" our feelings. She focused on the Stanislavski theory of actor's recall. She consistently asked us to go into our past, feel our emotions and then analyze them. Only then, she told us, could we truly understand what our characters were going through and thus make them believable. In having us do this, she helped us consciously deal with our lives and learn from our past.

She also taught us to keep our dignified bearing and to think on our feet. The best way to do this was to have confidence. To be confident, she taught us basic psychology. She explained that to understand people and to relieve the stress we felt about speaking in front of others, we had to remember how we felt when we watched someone on stage. Instead of wanting people to fail when they get in front of us, we usually root for them and hope they do well. Nothing makes an audience more nervous than to listen to a nervous speaker. And, most often, when a person gets up in front of others and experiences stage fright, that person becomes self-absorbed. He or she wonders what others are thinking and how he or she might fail. Yet, this is just the opposite of how one should view the situation. Donna taught that keeping one's presence of mind is critical not only on the stage, but also in life. It is never as bad as one might think, and the worst thing is to give up. The "play must go on," she often said, and so too with life.

Through her teachings, I learned that life will often deal us a lot of "crap," but the key to it all is to learn from the experience and move on. To perform to our full potential, she taught that we need to free our minds from problems. As a result, we would do a symbolic game of taking our "crap" off our shoulders and throwing it out the door of the drama building before class in order to free ourselves of its influence so we could focus on the class or rehearsal.

Pictured here are Donna Reynolds, my drama teacher from eighth-grade until twelfth-grade, and me. We called her Donna Drama and she was one of my most influential teachers. She taught people to care about one another and how to perform. She helped us learn how to explore plays and characters by exploring our own psychology using actor's recall of emotions (the Stanislavski theory of acting). For years, our school dominated the Christians Schools Tournaments at Abilene Christian University in all acting and performance competitions, including One Act Plays, Dramatic and Humorous Duets, and Bible Reading. Under her tutelage, during my senior year, we won the best play out of all the schools and I was named best actor playing Cyrano de Bergerac. Learning my lines and overcoming stage fright helped me with my speech impediment and gave me another high-adrenaline activity my ADHD craved. Circa June 1989

She also instructed us that the most important person on stage is your partner, not yourself. You need to feel that person's energy and hear his or her words. Most often the greatness of acting, just like in life, is not what you are doing, but how and why you are listening. You can do a play, give the lines and act, but it is the true artist and, by extension, the true liver of life, who can not only act, but can also respond to others' actions in an appropriate way. As she often taught, "Half of acting is reacting."[531] Through these lessons, she taught that it is not about "me" in life. If "we" do not do well, then the "play" fails. When we let others down, we let ourselves down, and therefore "the play" does not go on.

Another of her lessons was to be who you are. When you get up before people, you may be acting a part, but if you can truly feel the emotion, the action behind the words, then people will listen. That is the honest way of dealing with life. If that means embracing things in your past that are unpleasant, you must do it because by doing so you can control them and thus prevent them from having a hold on you.

Although I didn't consciously realize it at the time, her teaching methods and philosophies would become more meaningful throughout my life. Hardly a day goes by that something Donna taught me does not influence the way I do things, and it is always for the better. Those five years of her teaching awakened in me another talent I never knew I had; I could act and speak in public. But she also taught so many lessons for life in her class that went beyond drama and rhetoric. They helped shape who I am more than any other teacher except Mary Stewart. She was a shining light at the Fort Worth Christian School (FWC), which was generally lacking in academic rigor. Even though I graduated in 1990 with honors, I was still woefully unprepared for the challenges of a tough college environment.

When I applied to Yale and Princeton for the first time in 1989 from FWC, I was an honor student in academics, All-State in Drama,

All-State Running Back in Football, All-State Forward in Basketball and All-State in Track. Looking at my clumsy athletic beginnings, I shake my head as I look at my senior statistics as a running back, when I ran for 1,500 yards and score 21 touchdowns. [532] Of course, I had a good offensive line and a great coach, Cam Prock, who allowed me to do all this.[533] These achievements were key to keeping my self-esteem healthy, more than I realized.

At Fort Worth Christian, I was captain of my Football team (#87) and helped lead them to the TAPS (Texas Association of Private Schools) playoffs in 1989. Here I am leading the team onto the field with co-captain Jackie Hemby (#1). Playing sports helped me deal with my ADHD and added to my self-esteem. Photo Credit: Cal Gaines Circa September 1989

Here is a picture of me dunking a basketball during my senior year at Fort Worth Christian (1990). I was captain of my basketball team and was one of the highest scorers and rebounders. We made it to the playoffs and had a winning season. Attending a small school where I could play many sports was extremely beneficial in dealing with ADHD. Participating in organized sports in schools, I believe, is one of the best ways for an ADHD-child to build camaraderie in the school, learn about leadership, stay physically active, and receive the stimuli necessary to help the child deal with the daily stress of having a mind that needs a lot of stimulation. Photo Credit: Cal Gaines Circa January 1990

This is my *BotraMama*, my Slovenian Godmother, Charlotte Bercé in 2010. She was my next-door neighbor when I was a child. She grew up during WWII and, as a young woman, she and her family fought with Tito's partisans against the Nazis. In the 1960s, she moved with her husband and children to America from Yugoslavia. As a child, I was at her house weekly for several hours learning about life, philosophy and discipline. When she uttered her words, it was like the voice of God and I always listened to her and obeyed everything she told me to do. She treated me like a son, and I loved her like a mother. Fall 2009.

I had another incredible woman in my life during my youth, my next-door neighbor, who became my *BotraMama*, Slovenian for Godmother, Draga "Charlotte" Bercé, née Poljanec. Since nobody in the United States could say her first name correctly, and since she was tired of frequently being called Dragon, she used the name, Charlotte. She was my second Godmother. She grew up during World War II in Bled, Yugoslavia, and she and her siblings helped Josip Broz Tito's partisans fight the Nazis. She was a tough woman who did not stand for any nonsense. She was the only person who could control me as a child and I found myself over at her house almost every day. She found ways to teach me to be honest, tough and hard-working by listening closely to what I told her and studying how I acted. She was always teaching me to refine my behavior. For example, one day I accidently rode my bike into her iron gate and broke some of the bars that had been welded into cross beams. No one saw me do so, but I was devastated that I had broken something of my godmother's. When I told her, she embraced me with those big Slavic arms and said, "Bryan, you good boy. You could've been coward and hide. You're strong and told me. You good." That meant so much to me and reinforced to me the power of being honest.

Another day, I told her I was German and she grabbed me and said,

No, Bryan. Germans did bad things in war. They have many things to ask forgiveness for. America win the war. America stands for freedom. You American. Never forget you're American. I don't want to ever hear that you think you're German. Promise me?

She helped teach me the value of what it means to live in a land of freedom and with a strong history, and she did so by teaching me that the U.S. destroyed Nazi Germany and had brought it democracy. "Germans didn't do this," she said in her tough Slavic voice, "Americans did. You American. You be proud to be American—not German."

And yet another time, when I had some trouble with a girl-friend, she asked me to explain the situation and then said: "If you not willing to take bullet for girl, you leave her. There're many fish in sea. Don't waste time for girl who you don't care about." She always made sure I was learning how to improve my behavior. And she always made me look at a situation differently with realistic eyes.

Here is my Austrian *Patentante* (god-mother), Leopoldina Hedwig "Polli" Boswell, née Ladits. She taught me how to play chess, ping-pong, fish and speak German. She taught me about history and knew a lot about it since she lived in Vienna during the war and experienced several Allied bombings of the city. Circa 1980.

I also became very close to another European next-door neighbor on the other side of my house, whom I thought of as yet another god-mother of mine (I needed a lot of godmothers obviously). She became my Austrian *Patentante*. Her name was Leopoldina Hedwig "Polli" Boswell, née Ladits, and she had come from Innsbruck, Austria, after she had married her American husband, Herman. She also loved me a lot and taught me how to play chess, how to speak German and French, and how to play ping-pong and fish. We often sat at the end of her dock on Lake Arlington and caught perch and catfish; she taught me the valuable lesson of how to set a hook in a fish's mouth as it nibbled on the bait. During these times, she talked to me about astronomy, reincarnation and art. She also talked to me about the German military and industry from World War II since her father, Karl Ladits, had built machines for the *Wehrmacht*, especially the Goliath (the first remote-control anti-tank vehicle that was used to maneuver under tanks and explode them from underneath). Having grown up under the Nazis in her city of birth, Vienna (Austria was untied with Germany in 1938 with the *Anschluß*), she told me stories of it being bombed, resulting in her one time having been stuck in a basement with several dead people for three days, until she was rescued from the ruble. After another bomb attack, she discovered a family in her building at their dining room table, still sitting where they had been playing cards, but now dead with blood oozing from their noses and ears due to the concussion bomb that had hit the structure. As a result of these stories, I was never again allowed to light bottle-rockets on her dock during July 4th celebrations because the small firecrackers reminded her too much of when she had been bombed in World War II. I will never forget the night she told me these stories as she pulled my friend, Richard Shoults, and me off the dock with tears streaming down her face and her arms and hands shaking as she asked for us to "Pleaze stopp it. It is painfaul to lizten to you do zhe fireworks. Come inside my home and I will tell you why." After she told us her war stories, she ended, "*Krieg ist sehr schlectht* [War is horrible]." For years as an adult woman, whenever a city alarm system went off, she would become catatonic with fear. Obviously, she suffered throughout her entire life with PTSD.

Polli also told us that before the war, everything had started with much fanfare when Hitler came to power. She had actually been one of those young girls who had met him at the border when he took over Austria in March 1938 and was able to give *der Führer* some flowers. He was so taken with her blond hair and blue eyes, that he took her onto his lap and had some pictures taken of himself with her. I will never forget her declaration after telling me this,

> Of course, vee had no knowledge in 1938 of vvhat zhe evil Hitler would later do, but in zhat moment, as an eleven year old girl, I knew I could never love another man as much as I would Adolf Hitler. He had zuch a charismatic voice, piercing blue-eyes and a crowd of adoring fans. He vas amazing.

After this admission, her husband, Herman, in the other room, a strong American patriot and U.S. Army veteran, yelled out, "God forbid, Polli, that is crazy. Don't tell people that!" Well, through Polli, I loved exploring history, especially World War II.

Luckily, I had many women like this in my life. My grand-mother, Edna Davidson, whom I mentioned earlier, also deserves my gratitude. She was a daughter of pioneer and Cowboy Hall of Famer Otto N. Barby. As a native of the panhandle of Oklahoma, she was resourceful and tough. She would tell me, "Bryan, if you watch the pennies, the dollars take care of themselves" and "Remember, if you point a finger at someone, three are pointing back at you." She taught me the virtues of being thrifty and resourceful. Often during the month, I would have to bring my shirts, skivvies and socks that had holes in them to her, and she would have me sew or darn them up. You never threw things away around her and you always found ways to save money. One day finding me with a lot of change in my Halloween pumpkin, she made me roll up the money and deposit it in the bank because "coins in the closet don't earn interest, but money in the bank does." I will never forget that after one high school basketball game, where I had one of my highest scoring games of over 30 points and at least 10 rebounds, she pulled me aside afterwards and said, "I'm proud of you, but before your head gets too big, you need to remember that you missed three easy baskets and two opportunities to make good passes to your teammates." With this declaration, she was telling me that there was still room for improvement and that my best was never my best and that I could always do better.

Here is my grandmother Edna Davidson, née Barby. I called her Ganny, since my brother and I had problems with r's, and could not say Granny. She supported me throughout all my trials as a young boy and was always there to offer sage advice when I needed it (which was often!) Summer 1989

It takes a village to raise a child and these women, all from different parts of the world and with varied experiences, rallied around me to help me be a better person and believe in myself. These women taught me how to act properly, and be self-sufficient and confident, and I hungrily absorbed their teachings. One theory states that ADHD-persons are very "independent, and tend to dislike being told what to do. They prefer to think for themselves..."[534] Well, "thinking for myself" and doing my best for self-improvement have stayed with me throughout many difficult decisions in life, and women like my mother, grandmother, Slovenian godmother, Austrian godmother, Mary Stewart and Donna Drama, all helped shape such a mindset.

So, in all honesty, in view of my experience with ADHD, I feel that I was an exception to most rules. I became a contrarian. If someone told me I could not do something, I did it anyway to prove that I could. My teachers and family members gave me the strength to recognize the trade-offs. So, after I received Yale's and Princeton's rejection letters for my application in the spring of 1990, I refused to accept the rejection as final, although my college counselor at FWC thought I was setting myself up for failure and reaching beyond my abilities. Disregarding her opinion, I knew I was good enough for Yale and Princeton. It was just a matter of convincing their admissions offices that I was Ivy League material.

So, not accepting "no" for an answer, I called the head football coach at Princeton, Steven Tosches, and asked him what my options were. I told him I could do the work at Princeton and needed to know what I could do to prove it to the admissions office. He mentioned that some kids do a second senior year at prep schools up "North" to better themselves academically, and he encouraged me to do so. Soon after this, I applied to Phillips Andover Academy, Hotchkiss Academy and Phillips Exeter Academy. All three accepted me, and after careful deliberation and visiting all three campuses, with my father, I decided to accept Exeter's offer.

In 1990, I enrolled in Phillips Exeter Academy for a postgraduate year to better myself for admission to Yale University. I set my sights on Yale after looking at that Ivy League university more carefully and the football program under Coach Carm Cozza. Many Texans warned me that I was wasting a year and that the "North" would pollute my mind. One of my FWC teachers pulled me aside one day and said, diplomatically, "Just remember that those people up North sit on the pot just like you." Another one, a devout Christian, warned me: "Be careful, Bryan. Many people up North have rejected Christ and live secular lives. They are going to Hell, so be careful." Everyone felt petrified about the North, as if it was Sodom and Gomorrah, or even worse, a land of Democrats (which was largely true, of course). I did not place much stock in their concerns, since my father and his family came from Pennsylvania and New Jersey. In fact, one ancestor of mine, my ninth-great-grandfather whom I mentioned previously, Sir John Linton, helped establish Philadelphia since he was, as mentioned before, a close friend of William Penn. And his progeny would help establish the towns of Burlington and Beverly, New Jersey. Another ancestor, my twelfth-great-grandfather, "The Deacon" Samuel Chapin, was one of the founders of Springfield, Massachusetts.[535] Through him, I am related to abolitionist John Brown, anti-Slavery writer Harriet Beecher Stowe, President Grover Cleveland, President Howard Taft, American poet and playwright T. S. Eliot and famous musician Harry Chapin. So, I had strong roots in the North and wasn't worried about the people hurting me "up" there.

During my year at Exeter, an incredibly good school combining a caring atmosphere with academic excellence, I improved my test scores and academic portfolio. My experience there proved the opinions of many of my Texas mentors dead wrong. People "up North" were willing and able to help me and cared about my success.

Here I am standing next to the statue of "The Deacon" in the middle of Springfield, Massachusetts. "The Deacon," or Samuel Chapin, was my 12th Great-Grandfather and one of the Puritan founders of Springfield. He was a major leader of the settlement and showed he could lead and think out of the box with his unorthodox religious beliefs and governance, very ADHD-like behavior. 8 September 2019

Without Exeter, I would not have made it into Yale. This school's philosophy was simple—love learning. Its founder, John Phillips, said more concretely, "goodness without knowledge is weak and feeble, yet knowledge without goodness is dangerous."[536] I was blessed to have gone to Exeter as a postgraduate, or PG for short. Many of the four-year seniors at Exeter were burned out by the time they reached their final year. However, coming in as I did, fresh and with a goal in mind, and having an incredible challenge set before me, allowed me to relish the opportunities that the school presented. Also, this school invented and implemented pedagogic techniques and interactions in the classroom that encouraged discussion and debate around a large oval table called the Harkness Table, where we could look at one another. Such a classroom environment was perfect for my ADHD-brain. Every teacher there demanded that you work hard and rewarded you for creativity and energy. If all schools could do half as much as Exeter does from a philosophical point of view, in getting students engaged in active learning while in the classroom, we would have a thriving secondary educational system.

After being at Exeter only a few months, I applied to Yale University again, and in the winter of 1991, I was accepted. It was a lot of hard work and seemed like I had traveled a long road, even in those few months. Exeter helped groom me properly for re-applying to this Ivy League school, and I had a wonderful college counselor, Tom Hassan, who guided me through the process. (One of the first people I called when Yale accepted me was Mary Stewart. I told her, "We did it, Mary. *We* got into Yale.")

In April of 1991, I still had several months before I left for Yale and was enjoying my time at Exeter. I had two English teachers, David Weber and Harvard Knowles, who had a strong impact on my life and probably influenced me more than anyone to think about writing.[537]

My beloved English teacher from Phillips Exeter Academy David Weber, pictured here in 2020, taught me to love writing and to explore language.

Mr. Weber often took the time to meet after class and follow my progress with careful attention. He knew that as a post-grad at Exeter, I had gone there to improve myself in the hope of getting into a college of my choice. He had wonderful clear eyes that radiated kindness. During my classes with Weber, I learned how much knowledge, power and passion can be expressed through the written word.

We humans learn most about our world and how to operate in it through the printed word, and thus things that we write and read have an incredible impact on the way we view our reality. Mr. Weber went beyond the call of duty to read and reread my essays, teaching me the importance of "showing" (or describing) and not just "telling" when writing.

He also proved his selfless devotion to me and other students by showing us how much he cared about our hearts and souls. He often met with me before class to work through SAT word problems with me to help improve my test-taking skills. When I got into Yale, he gave me a big hug and said, "I knew you could do it, Bryan." He gave me that type of positive energy throughout my entire year at Exeter. He also told me that although my writing was weak when I arrived, especially since I had hardly done any of it at my Texas high school, I had improved immensely. He further explained that although I still had much to learn about writing, I had a lot of passion and energy in my words. He said, "Bryan, you can learn how to improve your writing, but something you cannot teach people is how to have passion in what they write, and you have that."

Mr. Weber taught me that it is passion that makes the difference. Tragically, most are scared to follow their passions because of fear of failure, or because they are not aware of what they are passionate about. This may be due to social pressures, concern about money, or inability to analyze themselves. While I had dealt a lot with my ADHD up to this stage in life and was able to function in a competitive academic environment, Mr. Weber helped me find even more techniques for learning.

While discussing Thoreau's *Walden*, one of Weber's favorite books, he taught that we should not live our lives and then at the end discover that we have not sucked out the marrow of life.[538] It is up to us to learn what gives our lives meaning. He wishes he could put *Walden* into a pill form and give it to every Exeter student before she or he left the school. In teaching Thoreau, Mr. Weber taught about the importance of learning how to live with meaning. During the summer of 2005, I had the opportunity to travel to Walden with Weber and retrace Thoreau's steps while I was teaching at Exeter's Summer School. It was great to go with this wonderful teacher to the place where Thoreau wrote his masterpiece. It brought home the importance of doing away with words like *"stress, not enough time, busy* and *becoming rich."*

And in the spirit of *Non Sibi* ("Not for oneself, but for others"), the motto of Exeter, I reconnected with Mr. Weber in 2019 and 2020 and asked for his help with my book *Flamethrower*. Over several months, he read chapters from my 800-page book and sent me back detailed notes and copyedited corrections. And through his analysis of my research into Japan's Holocaust and the Pacific War, he once again helped me think about morality, ethics and the "good life," just as we had done when studying Thoreau. In reviewing and editing my book, he again showed his selfless nature, continued kindness and mentorship. Weber has learned, over the past 30 years, how I best process information, and has helped me utilize my ADHD-traits to improve my skills as a writer and thinker. He is a true friend.

Another wonderful teacher I had at Exeter was Harvard Knowles. This salty character looked like a figure from the early 19th century. He wore tweed jackets, and beautiful, colorful, pressed shirts with bow ties. He had mischievous, clear blue eyes and never failed to find the sarcastic angle of any situation. Yet, he had a big and caring heart. Often in class when things would get out of control about a passage on sex or women or something titillating, you could hear him exclaim loudly, "Excuse me. Excuse me. Let's get back to the text. What does it mean? What is the author telling us?" He would bring out an important point about a book and then assess how it touched your heart and how it should speak to you. One of the favorite books we read was Robert Pirsig's *Zen and the Art of Motorcycle Maintenance.* Through this book and under Harv's guidance (we all call him Harv now), we learned that much of what we do mirrors how we feel about others and ourselves. The more we care for our hearts, the more we will get out of life. This pursuit is a daily activity. He was helpful in getting us to look at how the text related to our own desires and how we could draw meaning from it. Using Pirsig's book, Harv helped me understand that "small minds always know what they are thinking and know, while big minds don't always know what they are thinking, and they know that they do not know."[539] This is the beginning of wisdom.

Harvard Knowles and I after enjoying a Thanksgiving Dinner at The Colony Hotel in Kennebunkport, Maine, 22 Nov. 2018. Harv, as we all call him now, taught me how to analyze texts of famous authors and explore human behavior. Moreover, besides being one of my best teachers ever, he taught me the Harkness method of active teaching when I was a teacher at Phillips Exeter Academy's 2005 Summer School. The pedagogic technique is one of the best ways for ADHD-types to learn because it creates an interactive environment for learning.

Harv created an environment of intellectual curiosity, not only about the subjects we explored, but also about ourselves. As he wrote about his teaching philosophy in 1971,

> The teacher who cares doesn't imprison his students in his system or bind them to his ideas of what they ought to be. On the contrary, he seeks to free them to be themselves, to develop in themselves what is unique. The good and loving teacher cherishes what is different in each person and never sees him as part of the mass.[540]

Although Harv did not realize it at the time, the way he taught was absolutely perfect for a Hunter, ADHD-person like myself.

After Exeter, Harv wrote often and encouraged me to pursue my studies. I especially remember his letters while I was a college junior in Germany, working on my book *Hitler's Jewish Soldiers*. He gave me words of encouragement and presented me with several questions to help with the research. Once I returned to the U.S., he had me over to discuss the project and had me give several Assembly talks to the entire student body at Exeter. He continually helped me with my work and explored ideas with me. He also was my advisor, imparting to me how to teach when I was an instructor at Exeter Academy during the 2005 Summer School program. He wrote in his review after the session had concluded:

> It was good to see you this summer and especially to work with you… As soon as I walked into your classes and felt the energy of your students, I knew they were in the hands of a professional. Your experience shows your poise, confidence, and commitment kept you in full touch with the members of your classes. These qualities enabled you to make quickly and fluidly any necessary adjustments. Whatever was going on in the classroom before you arrived, you had the students' attention once you entered the room. Once the

class began the students were alert, interested, energetic, and respectful of you and of the material. I had the sense in watching them and you at work that they were aware of the quality of what they were getting and wanted more. Once you and I had talked about some strategies to keep the discussion flowing and on topic, then the students did talk across the table to each other, did put questions to each other, did challenge one another, and appeared less dependent on you as teacher. Enabling students to see each other as resources is one of the goals of Harkness teaching. The more explicit a teacher's authority is, the more likely it is that the class will be content with the "right" answer, with the teacher's declaration, with the summarizing certainty that discourages inquiry. The more students do in class, the better off they will be in a class. Your students this summer confirmed but once again to me the truth of that assertion. As I mentioned to you this summer, ***never do for students what students can do for themselves*** [author's italics].[541]

Having Harv's mentorship and praise meant the world to me, since I tried my best to conduct the classroom just like he had done with me as a student 15 years before. During this summer, he taught the value of having the students debate and explore historical events, ideas and figures to find out for themselves the lessons from the military history we were learning. Ironically, he used the Harkness technique on me to teach me the Harkness method and to explore ideas about how to help me help kids learn. By getting me to really understand the value of getting students to speak, debate and explore events in the higher pursuit of understanding them, I was able to engage the active part of their brains. And when they struggled together to understand the material, they mastered it. By getting students to practice active learning, I understood even more how people should learn, especially ADHD-types. They do so by learning the material in order to debate it, not in order to regurgitate it on a test or in a rote response that gives the pro-fessor what they think he wants. Learning to teach with Harv made me a better father, teacher and scholar. As the old adage goes, if you want to learn a subject, teach it. Well, teaching military history and the Harkness method took me to another level of understanding both of these disciplines, which, in turn, helped me later in my classrooms at Southern Methodist University and American Military University. One could not have asked for a better mentor and friend than Harv. His support and influence continued after that summer in spades.

Here I am with Harvard Knowles at Herman Melville's home in Pittsfield, Massachusetts, which is now a museum. We are standing in the room and next to the desk where Melville wrote *Moby Dick* from 1850-1851. This is one of Mr. Knowles' favorite books which he feels is one of the greatest works of American literature giving us a strong piece of American culture. He often said this book reads us just as much as we read it, meaning, it forces us to think about who we are, why we are here and what we should be doing with our lives. Exploring *Moby Dick* in the classroom with Mr. Knowles engaged my ADHD-imagination and this book has shaped the way I view life, attested by how often it is cited in this book. 12 February 2022

I want to show how the spirit of Exeter (*Non Sibi*, again) continued with me long after I graduated. When I returned for my 20th class reunion in 2011, a couple of football buddies, Adam Rand and Marty Tucker, and I were discussing one of Harv's favorite books, *Moby Dick*, with him and decided to do a "long-distance" class together. Harv had taught that book for over four decades and we decided that since we had not studied it with Harv, we would do a virtual book club. So, soon after the reunion, my buddies Adam and Marty in Massachusetts, Harv in New Hampshire and my ex-wife Stephanie and I in Texas would call up on my conference line every Sunday night and study *Moby Dick* under Harv. It was one of the most interactive and richest learning experiences I have ever had. I learned much about myself and my LD-brain and how one should approach some matters about life and humankind. For ADHD, I think Herman Melville nailed it when he said, "Ignorance is the parent of fear."[542] Quite often, people, and in many cases children, who struggle with LD, learn to fear school, reading and other people. They do not trust the system or the people who are benefitting from that very system. Accepting this reality is important, and *Moby Dick*, of all things, in its exploration of whaling in the 19th century, helped me explore issues of humanity and how best to navigate life and learning.

Moreover, Melville wrote that in order to live a healthy life, we have to learn how to be content with our own "companionship" and always be equal to ourselves (especially with ADHD-types).[543] In other words, we must learn we are not broken, but are unique and capable of productive and intelligent activity just like everyone else. It is a long journey for some to obtain this self-awareness, but it is critical for ADHD-people to have this outlook, if they are going to take the first step toward a life where they are "equal" to themselves.

Through reading this classic piece of American literature, I learned more than anything that the pursuit of truth is truth itself.

If you ever think you have the Truth, which is often expressed by the ultra-religious, then you stop growing. As Melville writes, "But clear Truth is a thing for salamander giants only to encounter."[544] Thinking you know something in its entirety kills your ability to grow and you then are not standing on the shoulders of giants, but sitting on the backs of "salamanders." Just think if we had stopped medical advancements in 1800. If that were the case, we would still be treating people with leeches, bleeding them needlessly; handling birthing mothers with dirty hands, causing many of them and their babies to die; and hacking off limbs because of simple infections. Thankfully, we have made advances medically and hopefully we will continue to do so with brain science and learning differences. With our cerebral diversity, as I like to hear ADHD referred to, we need to realize that there is no ultimate truth, and that what lies out there to be discovered is a large world without boundaries.

Maybe we will learn of ultimate truth when we die, but as Shakespeare claims, the realm beyond death is "the undiscovered country from whose bourn no traveler returns."[545] In the meantime, we must realize there is so much to learn in life. And what helps me see this truth? Well, I believe it is in learning how to die that we truly treasure life. We must realize that we all are dying each day, just at slower or faster rates than others. It is a reality many try to avoid. As King David said, "Teach us to number our days aright, that we may gain a heart of wisdom" (Psalms 90:12).[546] Helping my clients as I do with their legacy and estate planning and insurance, I find many of them unwilling to discuss their mortality. It is a difficult topic, but I firmly believe that bringing death into focus allows us to understand what is really important in life. We all have to deal with the breakdown of the mind and body, but if we can fight it as long as we can and embrace the knowledge with dignity, then we can face that great unknown. This was one of the many lessons from *Moby Dick*

Harv taught me. The realization that life is finite gives me strength, and in many ways, helps me develop "the good life" in general, and understand my ADHD in particular. We all pursue in some shape or fashion the ultimate prize, the Great, White Whale if you like, of living a good and balanced life. *Moby Dick* brought home the truth that death is an ever-present reality, especially with our loved ones and friends dying around us, and thus we have to face our own mortality whether we like it or not. Embracing this reality should help us, in the end, live a "good life."

In exploring this theme of facing our demise, Sigmund Freud wrote in *Reflections on War and Death* in 1918 that men would live better if they knew that death had something to do with them. He quoted the ancients: "*Si vis vitam, para mortem* (If you wish life, prepare for death)." American author Stephen King said it another way, "If being a kid is about learning how to live, then being a grown-up is about learning how to die."[547] Melville eloquently explored this idea when he wrote, "Our souls are like those orphans whose unwedded mothers die in bearing them; the secret of our paternity lies in their grave, and we must go there to learn it."[548] In conclusion, when we understand life is fleeting and death is a debt we owe that will never be forgiven, then we will start to learn how valuable life is and enjoy what we have, instead of what we do not have. If we can confront our biggest fear, death, and do away with it, then maybe all the other lesser fears of life will fade away.[549] For ADHD-people, this viewpoint is critical to learn. After all, we have so much to give to others and so much fun to have with them. And the experiences we offer can often be unique and unorthodox.

I also want to explore here an essay that Weber and Knowles collaborated on in 1978 titled *The School Community as a Moral Environment*. It explains the power of their teaching philosophies. A colleague of these men, Jack Herney, said this essay is a "classic treatment on how one should behave as a teacher of children and young adults."[550] I would also say their tactics are beneficial to ADHD-types, just like the small Harkness-Table classrooms of Exeter were ideal for people with my type of brain. Their vision as teachers and the environment of Exeter where they taught offer powerful lessons to teachers who focus on teaching LD-children.

To assure success in the classroom, Weber and Knowles in this manifesto wrote that a school must always provide two things: "both high academic standards [and] humane or moral values [such] as compassion, fairness, and courage."[551] They further explained that an academic setting should provide a nurturing environment that will not only create well-educated citizens and potentially future leaders, but provide students a capacity for "generosity of spirit and prin-cipled decision-making."[552] These themes demonstrate something critical for an ADHD-person. These teachers were creating an en-vironment, expressed in their article and witnessed by me in their classrooms, of having the student buy into the hypothesis of making themselves better by looking at what they can do for others. This was a message of empowerment, something all children need, but espe-cially those with ADHD who, in general, struggle with feeling that they can't make a difference. Both these teachers taught that the most important thing to do in the classroom, and in life, is to learn "how to live with one another."[553]

Moreover, they also embraced the teaching method that one should never humiliate a student when he or she was wrong or strug-gling to explore ideas.[554] They wrote, "The teacher who puts down students not only demeans the object of his contempt or fear, but di-minishes his own humanity at the same time."[555] They taught that en-couragement and questions should be used to help the student figure out for himself or herself how to deal with a problem or how to see the error of their ways. In getting across this point, Knowles and Weber quote Shakespeare's Hamlet: "We should treat others better than we deserve to be treated: 'Use every man after his desert, and who shall scape whipping?'"[556] This sense of inclusion allowed ADHD-types, and non-ADHD-types, to blend into a single classroom and explore ideas together, a Hunter-like way of doing things. Farmer-types can always learn in a Hunter-like environment (interactively), but Hunter-types have a difficult time learning in a Farmer-like environment (with static, passive, traditional classroom instruction).

Moreover, Knowles and Weber warned against labeling others with negative terms. This is especially true for ADHD- and LD-people, because, if these labels are not eventually discarded, a person can carry them throughout life like a congenital hump. They wrote:

> No student who is liked and respected will ever be called a lout, a slut, a loser [or learning disabled]—all invidious terms that come too easily in too many schools. In creating a negative language, we attack adolescents where they are most vulnerable. Not only does labeling deny humanness, it encourages a person to display the very negative behavior that the label demands.[557]

The implications for those with ADHD and LD after their names are self-evident. In short, both these teachers helped me, unknowingly, to discard those labels I had grown up with and had in my brain from my early days. They also, like Mary Stewart, helped me deal with my mind as it was and embrace its potential instead of "displaying" the negative traits such labels demand.

These two Exeter teachers, more than anyone, got me interested in writing and ideas. Although I did not know it at the time, I was on the road to becoming an author and thinker, something for which I was never conditioned, nor believed I could do. Writing was and is a hard discipline. Yet, in meeting the challenge, I started to discover a calling and a passion. The lessons I had come to learn with ADHD were reinforced. If I felt I could not do something that I wanted to do, then it was up to me to at least try and see if I could succeed. Harv taught me more than anyone else what school and learning should be about. He wrote:

> Education doesn't impose, it elicits. It doesn't mold, it creates an environment free enough to enable the individual to assume the shape consistent with his own potential, his own inclinations. It ought not to impose discipline from the outside; it should free the student to find his own restraints, to impose his own restrictions. It should encourage him to be himself and not what someone else wants him to be.[558]

These Exeter philosophies about how one learns helped me develop the discipline to graduate from Yale with a BA, and finish my MA and PhD from Cambridge University. Exeter provided a huge building block for the foundation of my life despite my ADHD, and I found myself, in general, happy with my state of being after graduating from there.

Takeaways

- Many factors go into helping an ADHD-kid. They are simple, but somewhat demanding. Watching your diet, practicing discipline, finding a loving and caring environment and never giving up are life lessons that one must learn for success. In order to conquer ADHD, I had to learn there is a direct correlation between the mind and body. Both have to be nurtured and, although these things were happening beyond my realm of comprehension when I was a child, they were taking root within my subconscious.

- High-adrenaline activities for ADHD-people are pleasurable. I spent an average of 15 to 20 hours weekly working out, practicing with my team, or playing in games as a child.

- I also started to invent special memory aids that helped me focus on important tasks. I developed techniques to remember things, such as where I had placed my keys or what assignment I needed to turn in. I would focus on the "mission" at hand, repeat it ten times in my mind and then associate it with something in my environment. This points to the value of visualization and memory, especially those with ADHD.

- It takes a village to raise a child so look for mentors. My mentors rallied around me to help me be a better person and believe in myself.

- In order to live a healthy life, we have to be content with our own "companionship" and always be equal to ourselves. We must learn we are not broken, but are unique and capable of productive and intelligent activity. It can be a long journey to obtain this self-awareness, but it is critical for ADHD-people to have this outlook, if they are going to take the first step of being "equal" to themselves.

Action Steps

- Small schools, which are usually private, are where ADHD-kids can have the best chance to do well. Our public schools are simply not set up for ADHD-kids. If you have a child with ADHD, do your homework on where to send him or her. I would encourage parents to explore charter schools and private schools as the best choice for ADHD-children because of their smaller, and thus more intimate and active classrooms.

CHAPTER 9:
The Power of Religious Belief for Better or Worse

"Heaven and hell are within us, and all the gods are within us."
— Joseph Campbell, *The Power of Myth*[559]

SINCE BELIEFS PLAY SUCH AN influential role in how people deal with problems, I have felt the need to openly explore this issue. If you are a Christian, what I am about to explore in this chapter may seem disturbing. Nonetheless, it comes from years of study, thinking and reflection. While many of the issues about child-rearing and religion I explore apply universally, parents with ADHD-children need to be extra careful with the religious institutions they expose their ADHD-children to, since LD-children often have overactive imaginations.

As a child, my schools, churches and relatives raised me to view everything through religion, even my ADHD. They taught that God had created things to challenge us that remained inexplicable, like disease, hardships, loss of loved ones, etc. Church leaders often explained that my struggles as a youth were evidence that God was testing me. I was told that when I got in trouble or was sick, God was punishing me for my sins. One child with LD was "certain that God 'hated her because he would not let her mind [obey]."[560] I often thought as a kid that my "learning disability" was God's curse for something I had done. I continued to pray for forgiveness. In some societies in our past, ADHD-misbehavior was viewed as signifying "satanic possession or a moral infirmity deserving punishment."[561]

| 237

So, it is not uncommon for children to view their ADHD as a defect or divine punishment.[562] Sadly, such beliefs and practices can cause ADHD-children to suffer extreme trauma.

Because I also believe religion has a powerful effect on ADHD-kids, I need to return to my youth and give some history of the ideas I was brought up with. My family attended Pantego Bible Church in Arlington, Texas. When I was eight years old, salvation was explained in simple terms. The Church leaders said that to receive salvation all I had to do was ask Jesus to come into my heart. If I did so, I would have eternal life and be able to live in Heaven with God and my family forever. In Heaven, there was no pain or suffering, no sickness or death, no ADHD. Church leaders and relatives explained that if I did not ask Jesus to come into my heart and recognize that he was the Son of the Almighty and died for my sins on the cross, I would go to Hell, which was described, by Jesus himself, as a place of wailing and gnashing of teeth (Matthew 13:42).[563] My Sunday school teachers described this underworld as having huge pools of bubbling human flesh that could reach up and grab your legs. Lucifer, the Lord of this place, would ensure that a lifetime of earthly suffering would be nothing compared to a second of time in his lair. Visions of feeling hot molten lead falling on my head and body, making my skin bubble off the bones, made me fear death and Satan. When I asked about certain non-believing family members and what would happen to them when they died, I was told that some in my family tree would indeed go to Hell. I wondered if we—who would live in Heaven—could be happy about this "fact" of knowing some of our relatives would be in eternal misery. I never received a satisfactory answer to that question.

I am not alone in learning about such horrible images. A famous Irish writer, James Joyce, imagined a preacher describing Hell as follows:

Now let us [understand] the nature of that abode of the damned which the justice of an offended God has called into existence for the eternal punishment of sinners. Hell is a foul-smelling prison, an abode of demons and lost souls, filled with fire The prisoners are heaped together in their awful prison, the walls of which are said to be four thousand miles thick. They lie in exterior darkness. For, remember, the fire of hell gives forth no light. Imagine some foul and putrid corpse that has lain rotting and decomposing in the grave, a jellylike mass of liquid corruption. And then imagine this sickening stench, multiplied a millionfold and a millionfold again from the millions upon millions of fetid carcasses massed together in the reeking darkness...[564]

Joyce has the preacher continue for several more pages. This type of picture is how Hell has been described to millions throughout history. I was one such victim who succumbed to the fear of Hellfire similarly described by Joyce's character. Many preachers control their flock through the fear of sin and its punishment.

Jesus also used such techniques, and many of these preachers follow his example (Matthew 11:24).[565] One just has to watch modern televangelists to get a feel for the poisonous language they use to scare people. As Herman Melville in *Moby Dick* wrote, "It's an all-fired outrage to tell any human creature that he's bound to hell."[566]

Melville might have been further thinking about this Christian ideology when he wrote,

I have no objection to any person's religion, be it what it may, so long as that person does not kill or insult any other person, because that other person doesn't believe it also. But when a man's religion becomes really fanatic; when it is a positive torment to him; and, in fine, makes this earth of ours an uncomfortable inn to lodge in; then I think it high time to take that individual aside and argue the point with him.[567]

The preachments of Hellfire and damnation makes the world for millions of children "an uncomfortable inn." It is "high time" to challenge preachers of such traumatizing doctrine for their ignorance and their abuse of and crimes against children.[568] Yet, I did not possess such sophisticated thought when I was a child, and Hell paralyzed me with fear. What I felt as a child is best described by Edgar Allan Poe when he wrote, "It was in vain I endeavored to banish these reflections [of Hell]...The more earnestly I struggled *not to think* [of Hell], the more intensely vivid became my conceptions [of damnation], and the more horribly distinct."[569]

Unfortunately, my mother, who was helping me so much with my diet and education while dealing with my ADHD, was also one of the people I struggled with when discussing Hell, damnation, salvation and religion in general. She saw everything through the lens of Fundamental Christianity and threatened me that I would go to Hell if I did not do things properly and behave. As Nietzsche said, Christianity was also teaching me "cruelty against oneself and against others; hatred of all who think differently; the will to persecute."[570]

For a child, the choice between Heaven and Hell, between accepting Jesus, or rejecting him, was for me, as an eight-year-old boy in 1979, a no-brainer. I decided to ask Jesus into my heart and beg for forgiveness for my sins. Wow. At that moment, I felt such relief having my fire insurance. Soon after receiving salvation, I was baptized before the whole congregation to affirm my belief in Christ.

During my education at Pantego, religious leaders also taught me about unforgivable sins. The first one was simply not accepting Jesus as the son of God. The other unpardonable sin was blasphemy. If you cursed God or misused his name, you would go to Hell. Jesus said, "[A]nyone who speaks against the Holy Spirt will not be forgiven, either in this age or in the age to come" (Matthew 12:32).[571] Since the doctrine of the Trinity and the Nicene Creed from 325

C.E. declared that Jesus, God and the Holy Spirit shared the same godhead, then anything negative said about the Holy Spirit was also saying it about *Yahweh* and Jesus Christ or vice versa.[572] When hearing this at a summer camp run by Pantego at Pine Cove, Texas, probably in 1981, I broke out into a cold sweat. Suddenly, I remembered that I had cursed God as a small child.

Remember, ADHD-children are given to fits of rage, and God had made me angry when I was out on an adventure capturing insects. It was a sunny day at my house on Lake Arlington as I played outside catching butterflies with my net. One beautiful, yellow butterfly continued to elude my attempts to catch it. So, I did what I had been taught. I prayed to God and asked him to grant me the wish to acquire the yellow butterfly. After praying for what seemed like minutes, I continued the hunt. Yet the butterfly avoided my sweeps with the net, and flew away. Angry, I said, "I hate you, God."

I must have been around six years old when I cursed God. Then at the age of 10, at the Pine Cove summer camp, I was informed that I was going to Hell during a Bible study for what I had done during my butterfly hunt. I started crying. A camp counselor came to see what was wrong. I explained I was lost for all eternity. He realized he had a serious situation on his hands. Remember, ADHD-children usually have potent imaginations, and mine was working overtime. He took me into one of the cabins and prayed with me. I was still inconsolable (a strong bout of religious OCD).[573] Explaining how this particular sin has caused much trauma for people, English intellectual Bertrand Russell wrote the following:

[It] has caused an unspeakable amount of misery in the world, for all sorts of people have imagined that they have committed the sin against the Holy Ghost, and thought that it would not be forgiven them either in this world or the world to come.[574]

At this stage in my life, I felt I was in the unforgiven category.

Acknowledging the difficult situation he had to deal with, my camp counselor got a few more of his colleagues, and they all began looking into their Bibles to help with my crisis. They soon convinced me I was saved because I had repented of my sin and still loved God. I need not worry because the truly unforgivable sin was not accepting Jesus as Lord and that he rose again on the third day "conquering Death." All sins that one recognized, I was told, were forgivable. Assured that I was alright and going to Heaven, I went back to my friends and started playing ping-pong. Since I was a young child, the concepts of salvation and damnation and Heaven and Hell played a significant role in my imagination. Being ADHD, when I got fixated on something, I became hyper-focused. When I felt my soul was in mortal danger, I became even more vigilant about how to save it from damnation and often went to bed wondering if I really was going to Heaven or not.

Any religion that brings in such dreadful concepts of eternal damnation, Hellfire, Satan and demons needs to be carefully taught and explained to children, especially ones with ADHD. I already felt that my ADHD was a punishment from God for some sins, and I spent years in fear for believing so. I often was obsessed with doing all I could to prevent my name from being erased from the Book of Life (i.e., documented assurance that salvation was secured). Chapel and Bible classes at my later school, Fort Worth Christian (FWC), reiterated these doctrines on a weekly basis from fifth-grade until I graduated from its high school in 1990.[575] My obsession affected me up to the time I entered Phillips Exeter Academy.

At Fort Worth Christian, a dogmatic Church of Christ school at that time, I had always been taught that we knew the truth about religion and everyone else did not. In fact, many teachers there taught that most of humanity was going to Hell for not believing properly in Jesus Christ. Its version of theology demanded no musical instruments to be played in church and full body baptismal emersion as a prerequisite for legitimate salvation. As my former Exeter Academy teachers Mr. Knowles and Mr. Weber wrote, a school like FWC "that identifies itself with a religious tradition, of course, risks parochialism,"[576] and FWC was the very definition of being parochial. Bertrand Russell said it another way,

> "Religion prevents our children from having a rational education. Religion prevents us from teaching the ethic of scientific co-operation in place of the old fierce, doctrines of sin and punishment."[577]

In fact, at Exeter, the religious legalism I had been taught at FWC started to fall away from my thinking as false teaching, and as "impotently anachronistic, tautocratic, constricting, [and] arbitrarily narrow."[578] Through Knowles and Weber, I realized that many FWC values concerning theology and life were shallow ways of viewing the world. As American author and philosopher Robert Pirsig wrote,

> You are never dedicated to something you have complete confidence in. No one is fanatically shouting that the sun is going to rise tomorrow. They know it's going to rise tomorrow. When people are fanatically dedicated to political and religious faiths or any other kinds of dogmas or goals, it's always because these dogmas or goals are in doubt.[579]

Pirsig further started me thinking about why people at FWC preached that people who didn't believe like they did were headed for Hell. This was not moral instruction, but bigotry. We need to remember that what a person believes is not private, because beliefs are a "fount of action *in potentia*."[580] Beliefs, like "Jews killed Christ," or "non-believers go to Hell," or "homosexuals are sinners," or "my religion is the one and only true religion" were taught at FWC. These belief systems in exclusivity gave birth to dangerous historical episodes like the Crusades, the Inquisition, the Thirty-Years War, and the Holocaust. In short, learning absolute truths about God, Heaven, Hell, Unbelievers and Believers prevented us from learning that there were other ways to live and think. In exploring these unhealthy religious concepts, I realized there are other "learning disabilities" besides ADHD. Pirsig echoed this when he wrote,

> If your values are rigid you can't really learn new facts. If you have a high evaluation of yourself then your ability to recognize new facts is weakened. Your ego isolates you from the Quality reality. When the facts show that you've just goofed, you're not as likely to admit it.[581]

The beginning of a good education is simply to know that you don't know. Russian writer Leo Tolstoy expressed this theorem in *War and Peace* thusly, "All we can know is that we know nothing. And that is the acme of human wisdom."[582] Dogmatic religion, like I had been raised with at Pantego Bible Church and Fort Worth Christian, taught the opposite of what Tolstoy espoused for one who wanted truly to be wise and educated.

In wrapping up this chapter, I would encourage those with ADHD-children not to attend a church where the leadership uses certainty, guilt, sin, eternal punishment and Hell as motivating concepts. Such vivid ideas are like telling a young ADHD-child that there is a monster under the bed before turning out the lights and closing the door. In other words, try to find a church where the focus is on forgiveness, love, tolerance and questioning.

At a time when I as a young person should have been focused on learning how to live in the present with a feeling of security, I was preoccupied with my church's teachings about the afterlife, sin and death. At a time when I should have been enjoying catching butterflies, playing with Legos and relishing my youth, I shouldn't have had to worry about whether I was going to Hell or not. Oxford Professor Richard Dawkins wrote,

I am persuaded that the phrase 'child abuse' is no exaggeration when used to describe what teachers and priests are doing to children whom they encourage to believe in something like the punishment of unshriven sins in an eternal hell.[583]

While at Pantego Bible Church and FWC, I had been abused.

As Dr. Hallowell said, "Fear is the most pernicious learning disability. It is also by far the most common."[584] I would say the fear of Hellfire used by a church to motivate and control believers is one of the worst fears a person can have. Thus, fear is a horrible learning disability and one that I had to overcome. Luckily, I did so, and I hope others will take a closer look at this religious problem and how it can create ADHD or make ADHD worse. Bertrand Russell wrote,

An education designed to eliminate fear is by no means difficult to create. It is only necessary to treat a child with kindness, to put him in an environment where initiative is possible without disastrous result, and to save him from contact with adults who have irrational terrors [i.e., religious zealots].[585]

Children need to be around teachers who are open-minded, curious and kind. Children do not need to be around adults who preach fear, damnation and Satan. They need to be around teachers who know they don't know and are searching for new knowledge, instead of teachers who claim they know it all and are convinced that their beliefs about life, the afterlife and God are the right ones for everyone. These are concepts that can harm a child's development, especially a child with an ADHD-mind full of energy and imagination.

Takeaways

- ADHD/LD-children's psyches may be harmed when they are raised in a religious environment that focuses too much on fear, shame and guilt. Just as families fight hard to find the right school environment for their LD-children, they must also find a religious setting that focuses on positive aspects of God, not Hellfire and damnation for sins. The more an ADHD-child can experience freedom to grow and explore who they are, and not worry about the fear of the Almighty sending them to Hell for their sins, the more they can flourish as human beings.

- Any religion that brings in such dreadful concepts of eternal damnation, Hellfire, Satan and demons needs to be carefully taught and explained to children, especially one with ADHD. I already felt that my ADHD was a punishment from God for some sins, and I spent years in fear for believing so.

Action Steps

- I would encourage those with ADHD-children not to attend a church where the leadership uses certainty, guilt, sin, eternal punishment and Hell as motivating concepts. Such vivid ideas are like telling a young ADHD-child that there is a monster under the bed before turning out the lights and closing the door. In other words, try to find a church where the focus is on forgiveness, love, tolerance and questioning.

CHAPTER 10:
Learning How to Learn, Cope and Adapt

"Go where your body and soul want to go. When you have the feeling, then stay with it, and don't let anyone throw you off."
— Joseph Campbell, *The Power of Myth*[586]

WHEN I STUDIED AT YALE, I had a difficult time writing. Several professors were unkind to me after I turned in essays, saying I could not write, like Mark Shulman and Henry Ashby Turner, Jr. I would have preferred them to have shown me how to write. Of course, there were many others who were kind (especially my writing tutor Elizabeth "Betsy" Sledge, and professors Leslie Brisman, Liselotte Davis, Cathy Caruth, Richard Selzer, Jeffrey Sammons and Lieutenant General William Odom (USA)). But this adverse treatment by Shulman and Turner heightened my thinking about my disabilities when I was beginning my Yale career.

ADHD/LD-people make up anywhere from 3% to 20% of any society ("depending on how you measure it and whose numbers you use"),[587] and many, especially the "experts," look at us as deformed and unsavable. And often, we struggle with learning how to write. Now I should not blame my negative Yale professors too much because I should have been a better writer by that time. But of course, their behavior was not helpful. To use a phrase from James Joyce, LD-people are "living in a skeptical and… thought-tormented age: and sometimes I fear that this new generation, educated or hypereducated as it is, will lack those qualities of humanity..."[588] I doubted myself and did not understand why I could not write like others. ADHD/LD-people often doubt themselves because others do not understand them, and question whether they are normal. It is a vicious cycle of negative reinforcement that spirals down into a burning hole if we are not given new wings of hope. As Joseph Conrad wrote, "Woe to the man whose heart has not learned while young to hope, to love—and to put [his] trust in life!"[589] This hope, this "trust in life," should be reiterated to those with ADHD/LD to reinforce their awareness that they are excellent and extraordinary just the way they are. The "salvation of personality" will only be realized when one embraces and recognizes his or her own "selfhood."[590] ADHD/LD-people must be aware of why they are the way they are. And sometimes, we ADHD/LD-types must just work harder than the average person, *basta!*

My Yale Professor, Lieutenant General William E. Odom (USA), a warrior intellectual. He did independent studies with me on World War II and taught me how to write, requiring me to read Strunk & White's work *The Elements of Style*. He wrote on this photograph: "To Bryan Rigg—My excellent Yale student, a great scholar and Marine. Wm E Odom."

Learning these truths was a long, trepidatious journey for me that started in earnest at Yale. During my high school years, I was ashamed to admit that I had failed first-grade twice, but I had started talking about it as college approached, sharing my story when appropriate. Also, midway through my sophomore year at Yale, I discovered that independent study with professors was available in most departments and gravitated to these one-on-one options. When I could interact with a professor in a personal relationship, I could actively develop and modify my bibliographies, writing assignments and tests. When this happened, I started to thrive at Yale. I was able to study one on one with some of the best minds in the world, like Geoffrey Parker, Paul Kennedy, Paula Hyman, Cathy Caruth, Richard Selzer, Jeffrey Sammons, Liselotte Davis, Henry Turner and Lieutenant General William Odom. I benefited greatly as an undergraduate by reviewing my writing with Mrs. Sledge, the writing tutor at Yale's Silliman College. Every residential college at Yale had writing tutors, but strangely enough, few students utilized them. Fortunately for me, since few students used my tutor, I often had Mrs. Sledge all to myself. She helped me make good arguments, use active language and utilize diversified words; and my writing improved by leaps and bounds. She was always happy to see me, read my papers judiciously and cared about me. Once again, I was finding ways to learn in an intimate environment that improved my ability to process information. When I continued my studies at Cambridge University, I was blessed to benefit from the British tutorial system, which was perfect for my ADHD-mind. In short, I found that ADHD/LD-people learn by actively getting involved in debating and discussing the subject matter being explored, not by passively listening to someone lecture on it or solely relying on reading a book to learn it. Reading and lectures help, but personal hashing out of the facts is imperative for an ADHD/LD-person's knowledge retention. Realizing this learning *modus operandi* helped me thrive academically and made me look at my ADHD/LD more closely.

My Yale University writing tutor Betsy Sledge (pictured here) worked with me in a one-on-one setting and helped me improve my thinking, arguments and writing as I prepared my research papers. Learning how to improve my writing with her was ideal for an ADHD-person—i.e., learning actively while sitting next to her at her desk. Photo Credit: Yale University Summer 1996

I also started to think critically about my "learning disability" when researching World War II and the Holocaust as a Yale undergraduate, culminating in my PhD from Cambridge and my first book, *Hitler's Jewish Soldiers.* Doing such historical work required a lot of writing, and I knew that to do justice to this topic, I would have to become a good writer. When I first started the project, which eventually led to five books, several professors, including the German historian Henry Turner and English professor Geoffrey Hartman, the head of Yale's Fortunoff Holocaust Archives, claimed that I could not write and that the research was a waste of time. Turner said I needed *Sitzfleisch* (literally "sitting meat," but meaning patience to sit still and study for long periods of time or write for hours on end). Well, I did not have a lot of *Sitzfleisch*, but I knew I could do the research because I had the hyperactive energy and thinking out of the box that ADHD gave me and my research required.

For most undergraduates, this negative criticism probably would have stopped them. But I was not to be deterred so easily. If someone said I could not do something, I often accepted the challenge. Consequently, I adapted my skills to conduct the research I needed that aptly utilized my strengths and downplayed my weaknesses. Instead of spending most of my time in archives, I went out and found the people I wanted to interview. I took my people skills as an ADHD-person and applied them to research and archive building. I biked around Germany, sometimes for over 70 miles during one day, to get interviews. I often carried my portable studio on my back, 70 to 80 pounds of gear, that included a computer, printer, camera, tripod, radio, cassette tapes, videotapes, electrical transformer, clothing, and food—everything I needed to conduct my interviews. I not only did this to complete my study, but also to prove to those doubting Thomases professors that I could do something they said I could not do.

There is a fine line between ignoring groundless negative criticism and rejecting good advice. I found that many who offered advice were revealing more about themselves than about me. As a developing writer, I learned to distinguish productive or positive criticism from the destructive and harmful kind. Someone who says your work is terrible, childish, poorly constructed, and of no value is not helping you. A person who points out your weaknesses and mistakes and advises you on how you can correct them and improve has given you positive criticism. I listened closely to those who loved me and wanted me to succeed, and who had a genuine desire to help people like me. Sadly, I came to discover that many authority figures who criticized me were of the former, not the latter. It reminds me of what a German writer, Gotthold Ephraim Lessing, wrote, "For people are not always what they seem. But rarely are they better."[591] When people negatively criticize others, it makes them feel better by making others feel worse. It can usually be translated as, "You're not good enough," or "I'm better than you." However, they rarely notice the harmful effects on you when they do so.

That type of attitude that Turner, and others, showed did not sit well with me. Without the challenges of my childhood and throughout college, I would not have gone on to write several books. Without embracing my ADHD and learning from it, I would not have had the skills or mindset to research or write about a profound event in human history, or to graduate with honors from Yale and earn an MA and PhD from Cambridge. I did all my studies in an unorthodox way, which is typical for ADHD-people. You must find ways to let your ADHD shine and I learned how to do this effectively during college. Much of the drive came from what I had learned at Starpoint, and I began to behave in a way that ensured my success as an ADHD-person. Yet, I did so subconsciously because I genuinely did not understand ADHD-success strategies at that time. I just gravitated to them subconsciously, as when I chose independent study options at Yale. I followed my mind when it told me what to do. I developed my methods of study and learning by harnessing what came to me naturally or through trial and error. I had learned not to take no for an answer, knowing there was usually another path to follow with a green light saying, "Yes, you can do it." When I allowed my mind to take me where it wanted, I instinctively turned to methods that just worked for me.

Had I listened to the "experts," I would not have accomplished any of the things I have achieved. So, within reason, I encourage those with ADHD to follow their passion and listen to their inner voices instead of what others say they should do. Once an ADHD-person finds his or her passion, incredible things can be accomplished.

While at Yale, I learned how best to apply my skills. During my freshman year, I decided to major in history and English. Since I had injured myself in football and doctors ordered me to stop playing contact sports, I channeled my energy into my studies. To hang up the cleats was difficult, especially since I wanted to play for Coach Carm Cozza, who today is a member of the College Football Hall of Fame. However, it was a valuable lesson. I quickly found that there was life after football and other ways to nurture my sense of self. I could no longer deal with my ADHD by playing sports. I had to motivate myself to stay in shape and find new cerebral ways to deal with my situation. Until recently, I had always regretted not having played college football. However, with all the research about CTE (cerebral traumatic encephalopathy) and brain trauma resulting from football, I may have dodged some irreparable cognitive damage.

At Yale, independent study courses truly enlightened me and expanded my learning abilities dramatically. All my life, I had preferred to learn in this autonomous way and Yale offered options for me to continue in such a fashion. Out of my 50 courses (36 were required), 15 were independent study courses with renowned scholars. Dr. Hartmann agreed that one-on-one mentoring is how ADHD-people learn best. At Cambridge, I worked closely with professor Jonathan Steinberg during my entire graduate study program. We often met in his office and discussed historical issues one-on-one. I never had to sit through a lecture or work as a research assistant during my years at Cambridge. The ADHD-Hunter model fits this method perfectly. Hunters usually learned their craft from fathers, grandfathers, or tribal elders in a one-on-one teaching experience. The way I searched out education fits perfectly with my genetic mindset.[592]

At this point, I must mention my academic advisor, Dean Susan Hauser. This tough lady pushed me and encouraged me in these endeavors. Since I was in the habit of collecting godmothers in life, she became my Yale godmother, advising me on my studies and helping me apply for my scholarship for graduate studies at either Oxford or Cambridge. This survivor of the Holocaust was a serious, no-nonsense type of mentor, and I often found myself in her office to discuss my next strategy at Yale or my next independent study project. She also understood how I learned and encouraged me to explore such methods that my ADHD-mind needed. She helped me navigate the sometimes confusing waters at Yale when deciding which professors and courses to choose. And as I let my ADHD help me go where I learned best and find the professors who understood me the most, my ADHD enabled me to excel at my studies. At Yale, I discovered how to use my ADHD to uncover how best I learned (one-on-one), and found those people who believed in me and wanted to help me like Susan Hauser—people like Mary Stewart.

Dean Susan Hauser, pictured here, was head of Career Services at Yale University. She was my academic advisor and helped me with my Henry Fellowship that got me into Cambridge University. As one of my biggest supporters, she was always there to offer tough advice, sincere support and honest friendship.

Also, while at Yale, and later at Cambridge, I developed another technique that helped me learn. I noticed how much time I spent walking to classes, or to the library, or to the gym from my dorm room or townhouse. I also observed how much time I spent in lifting weights or running, or working at my recycling job on campus, and thought to myself, "I could be learning during this time." So, I took my Walkman cassette player and played tapes of some of the best professors in the world lecturing in their specialties. I particularly liked the political science series by Barnard College professor Dennis Dalton, as I learned about Socrates, Plato, Aristotle, Machiavelli, Rousseau, Marx, Freud, Hitler and Ghandi. In addition to these lectures, I also listened to my Berlitz German language tapes. Many at Yale laughed at seeing me always wearing my headphones walking across campus. However, I took pride in getting another hour or two of learning in each day during my waking hours. I would also record my notes I took in class on blank cassettes and then listened to them before exams.

In learning how to find the right people to help me learn, another mentor I found needs to be mentioned. While finishing up my PhD in Germany at the *Bundesarchiv/Militärarchiv* (The German Military Federal Archive), the head of World War I and World War II documents, *Oberarchivrat* and former *Bundeswehr* Lieutenant Colonel Günther Montfort, noticed my unorthodox ways and met with me several times. We quickly developed a dear friendship and he became fascinated with my work. However, he knew what I had in imagination and drive was countered by my lack of how to really cite sources and do proper bibliographic cataloging. This kind man, who became, what in German is called my *Doktorvater*, or my German PhD supervisor, actually proof-read my work almost a dozen times making sure it was properly presented to Cambridge for my PhD and to the public when it was published as a book. Knowing about my ADHD-mind and where I was weak had taught me to seek out people who could help me learn and make my weaknesses my strengths.

I am with *Oberarchivrat* and former *Bundeswehr* Lieutenant Colonel Günther Montfort. This man was my German *Doktorvater*, or PhD advisor, and made my book *Hitler's Jewish Soldiers* academically "kosher." He was a heaven-sent advisor who helped me correctly cite all my sources and produce a first-class piece of scholarship. November 2017

Here is our first family photo. I had just become a Marine Corps officer and was very proud of my newborn daughter, Sophia. Winter 2001.

I believe my ADHD also helped me thrive during my time in the Israeli Army and the United States Marine Corps. In both militaries, I always performed well when faced with land-navigation problems, and physical and psychological tests. I entered these militaries physically fit, athletic and well educated, which also helped me perform well. And having the ADHD-Hunter mindset aided me tremendously. Although my Marine Corps career was cut short due to an injury, I graduated from Officer Candidate School (OCS) with honors, placing 6th out of an original class of 278 candidates. I strongly believe ADHD-types should serve their nations and have this Hunter-like experience on their resumes. ADHD-persons thrive in such environments. In fact, Melissa Orlov, a therapist and ADHD-expert who has given lectures at military bases, has been told by several authorities that the military looks for ADHD-types when it does its recruiting.[593]

Here I am in my Israeli Army Marva unit in the Negev desert near our base Sde Boker during training. Summer 1998

Also, the ability to overcome hardships by finding new ways of being productive that I had learned from Mary Stewart helped me while I was in the Marine Corps. I originally was an air-contract for the Marines. This meant that once I finished OCS, I had secured a slot to go to flight school. If I successfully completed flight training, then hopefully I would have become an F-18 fighter-pilot or Cobra helicopter attack pilot (my first two choices). My recruiting officer told me I achieved one of the highest scores on the flight exam she had ever seen. There were several math problem-solving questions on the exam, for which I learned a ton of mathematics. Also, on the exam were special awareness and visual recognition questions, which I thrived at answering correctly. My ADHD-mind helped me tremendously. The section I often would ace was the one showing pictures from a cockpit of an airplane requiring me to ascertain whether the plane was in a dive, turn, ascent, roll, etc. I easily recognized the patterns and rarely answered a question incorrectly---the Hunter-mind at work.

However, while at The Basic School (TBS) for the Marine Corps (a six-month school all Marine officers go through before they go to their specialization schools for further training), I got injured. During field exercises, I herniated the last disc in my spine (L5, S1) and was in traction for six months. I never gave up trying to return to active duty, but after two back surgeries and months of rehab, the doctors at Bethesda National Naval Medical Center medically discharged me. It was hard to leave the Marine Corps, especially with the hopes and dreams I had for a military career, but my ADHD-mind and past experiences had taught me to do the best with what I have and look forward to the next chapter of life.

I am thankful for the support I received at this time from a distinguished Marine, General Al Gray, the 29th Commandant of the Marine Corps from 1987-1991. When transitioning out of the Marines in 2001, my then boss, Colonel John Allen, and General Gray helped me with my new activities at American Military University. In conversations with General Gray, I told him how disappointed I was to be unable to fulfill my dream of serving as a pilot in the Marines due to my injury. I had been at The Basic School (TBS) for almost two years in the holding company (Mike Company) hoping to heal enough to return to active duty. However, during this time at TBS,

Colonel Allen made sure I used the academic skills I had acquired during my PhD program. I managed the library on base, gave lectures to fellow officers and developed professional guides for books on the Commandant's Reading List, all duties I had while working in the Warfighting Lab at TBS under Major Brian Gudmundsson. Hearing how disappointed I was not to be able to finish my time in the Corps, General Gray said: "Whether a librarian or pilot Rigg, you have accomplished something few people do and many people envy and that is you have earned the title Marine. Never forget that." I have never forgotten those words and I am honored that General Gray, at 91-years of age, gave me insightful feedback on and an endorsement for my book *Flamethrower*. As possibly the only "Librarian" in the history of the Marines, I hope I have used my skills well to write a book on the Corps and the Pacific War justifying all the time I spent in the TBS library and at the Al Gray Research Center at the Marine Corps University. As luck would have it, during the time I spent in the Warfighting Lab, I was able to organize my own schedule as I saw fit. Working one-on-one with my commander, Major Gudmundsson, allowed me to use my strengths as an ADHD-person to provide TBS with unique study guides and a distinctive lecture series. I taught courses on the Holocaust, Nazi Germany, and ancient Greek history. Many fellow Marines said this was the first time they had learned about the Holocaust or ancient Greek warfare. It was an honor to impart the knowledge I had gained from Yale and Cambridge to fellow Leathernecks and give back to the Corps while it was taking care of my injury and trying to return me to the "Fleet."

General Al Gray, the 29th Commandant of the Marine Corps. He helped me transition from the Corps to American Military University. He later helped me in not only endorsing my book *Flamethrower* and giving me feedback on its content, but he also honored me with writing a Foreword for it. In this photograph, he wrote, "For Bryan Mark Rigg. Officer of Marines and Marine Warrior! Many thanks for all your many contributions to our Country and to our Nation's Corps of Marines! Semper Fidelis, Al Gray, Marine 29th Commandant"

During a Military Expo at the Marine Base, Quantico, General Gray posed with me at the American Military University booth when I gave him a copy of my book *Hitler's Jewish Soldiers*. I thanked him for helping me find a job at American Military University which I was then representing. Summer 2002.

General John Allen, while in charge of TBS as a colonel, took care of me and made sure I got the medical treatment I needed when injured. He also put me in the Warfighting Laboratory where I could use my skills as a historian and lecturer. I am honored he wrote on this photograph, "Bryan Rigg. Thank you for all you've done for our Country and Corps! Semper Fidelis. John R. Allen, LtGen, USMC, Deputy Commander US Central Command."

Clearly, both my independent studies at Yale and Cambridge and my experiences in two militaries helped me start to see where my ADHD could shine and how best to use it. Introspection on these experiences has empowered me to help others, especially my college and prep school students, and my children. I enjoyed giving my students special time to discuss their writing, helping even a few get published.[594] With my children, I have often put them into challenging situations like placing them in schools in China, Germany and Iceland, or putting them in classes or clubs for broad and diverse learning experiences ranging across math, English, Icelandic, German, Chinese, Spanish, martial arts, scuba diving, camping, archery, horseback riding, swimming, rifle marksmanship, rowing, baseball, basketball, tennis, football and track and field. When traveling, I always take them to museums or archeological sites in order to improve their general knowledge. I have supported my son Justin's activities in the United States Naval Sea Cadets Corps, which have included training for a week on a large sailboat with a Royal

Canadian officer on Lake Huron, and learning special warfare tactics at the Naval Special Warfare Orientation Course, under the tutelage of Navy Seal instructors. When Justin enrolled in the Special Warfare Course, I conducted the academic lectures there and completed the program with him using my skills as a teacher once again. I have gotten involved in all my children's activities and tried to find them mentors so they too can learn one-on-one with the experts, whether that means hiring tutors, tour guides or private coaches. Knowing how I best learned, I wanted to help my children develop these same skills early on so they would be smarter and better than me.

Here I am with my children, Sophia, Justin and Ian at Xichen Itza, Mexico, by the main Mayan pyramid there. I enjoy active, ADHD-learning with my children, including teaching them history during vacations. 26 June 2017.

Here I am with my sons Justin and Ian Rigg at Mt. Suribachi, Iwo Jima, Japan. We are standing at the spot where the famous flag raising occurred and below us are the landing beaches where the Marines started their invasion on 19 February 1945. 23 March 2018.

Here I am in the far right in the picture, back row (without a hat/cover), standing next to my son, Justin, during the Naval Special Warfare Orientation Course that the Sea Cadets conduct for two weeks. I was the academic instructor teaching American history, amphibious warfare and military concepts. At this training, my son received personal attention from Navy Seals on such topics as vessel boarding, small unit tactics, zodiac surf passages, weapons handling, teamwork, scuba-diving navigation and amphibious infiltration techniques. I often get my children involved with unique activities that teach them to build discipline, overcome hardships and gain skills. And in doing so, I often get involved myself. All very ADHD-like activities. 26 June 2021

Here I am with my children at the Castle Outside Burg FluhenStein. We were learning about Medieval Germany and how castles were built and defended. I am here with my sons Ian and Justin and daughter Sophia. December 2016.

Picture with my son Ian Rigg at the U.S. Marine Corps War Memorial at Arlington National Cemetery, VA. This sculpture is a copy of the Rosenthal photo of the famous flag raising done on Iwo Jima from 23 February 1945. I taught him that his great uncle, Frank Rigg, fought the Japanese during World War II at Angaur and suffered an injury that left his right hand crippled and how America was the primary country that brought Hirohito and Hitler to their knees by 1945. Freedom is never free and I take opportunities like this to teach my children historical lessons and family history. 24 July 2017

Takeaways

- While at Yale, I learned how best to harness my skills. At the end of my freshman year, I decided to major in history and English. Since I had injured myself in football and doctors ordered me to stop playing contact sports, I channeled my energy into my studies. Since I could no longer deal with my ADHD by playing sports, I had to adjust my workout schedule and motivate myself to stay in shape, and find new cerebral ways to deal with my situation.

- ADHD also helped me with my military service, although it was very short. I firmly believe that I thrived in the Israeli Army and the Marine Corps due to my ADHD. In both militaries, I performed well when faced with land-navigation problems, and the physical and psychological tests. Having the ADHD-Hunter mindset also helped me tremendously. Although my Marine career was cut short due to an injury, I graduated from Officer Candidate School with honors. I strongly believe ADHD-types should serve their nations and have this Hunter-like experience on their resumes. ADHD-persons thrive in such environments.

- Both my independent studies at Yale and Cambridge and my experiences in two militaries helped me start to see where my ADHD could shine and how best to use it. Introspection on these experiences has empowered me to help others, especially my children.

Action Steps

- Find schools and environments where there is interactive learning. Avoid passive learning situations.

- Knowing how I best learned as a student, I wanted to give such skills to my children early on so they would be smarter and better than me. As a result, I put them in summer outdoor or sports camps to challenge them physically. I also enrolled them in foreign schools, military youth programs, tutoring programs and language schools to challenge them academically.

I am pictured here with my son Justin Rigg at the German U-Boat U-995 at Laboe, Germany. This is one of the best-preserved German submarines from World War II and we were there visiting the large memorial and museum dedicated to this branch of the German naval service from World War I and II. I had enrolled him in Berlitz German school in nearby Kiel. I enjoy finding adventuresome ADHD-activity for my children to expand their learning and horizons. 23 July 2019

Here I am with my daughter Sophia Rigg at a monument for American Professor Minnie Vautrin of Ginling College on the grounds of the University of Nanking, China. During the "Rape of Nanking," Vautrin helped save the lives of hundreds of people and prevented numerous people from being raped and killed by hiding them from the Imperial Japanese soldiers. She bravely confronted the Japanese and refused to be cowered by their threats and demands. The Chinese government would recognize her for her heroics after the war awarding her the Emblem of the Blue Jade for saving lives and being an up-stander. I have enjoyed educating my daughter about strong female historical figures like Vautrin. She was there in China as my interpreter helping me with my research for my book *Flamethrower*. 11 May 2019

I am here with my boys, Ian (9) and Justin (13) teaching them about sailing with a Hobie Cat-16 while we were on vacation in Cancun, Mexico. An important trait for ADHD-individuals to learn is to teach one-on-one things they have learned to those they love. This is the best method for ADHD-types to retain information and I do this often with my children. We ADHD-people learn by doing, not by hearing. 21 March 2016

Here are my children at the Nazi Concentration Camp Dachau, right outside of Munich. My son, Justin, had two of his friends with us, Nik Knapp (gray sweater) and Micah Lampert (black jacket with hood). I do my best to impart difficult knowledge to my children so they can help the world to "Never Forget" one of the biggest tragedies of mankind, the Holocaust, and so that that they may also do more than others to try and make this world a better place. December 2016.

CHAPTER 11:
The Benefits of ADHD

"We are all born mad. Some remain so."
— Samuel Beckett, *Waiting for Godot*[595]

ADHD-TRAITS DO NOT ONLY CREATE efficient Hunters, but can also produce amazing, creative artists and thinkers. In recent times, people with ADHD-minds, who many would argue were "tortured souls," have produced powerful literature or art. A few examples are Edgar Allan Poe, Ernest Hemingway, Jackson Pollock, Stephen King and Robin Williams.[596] Their lives present strong evidence that they were ADHD, self-medicated people. All had significant drinking and drug problems and all were creative geniuses.

Some medical experts, like Dr. Hallowell, have argued that those with alcohol and cocaine addictions, for instance, are often seeking to medicate themselves. Interestingly, as already mentioned, cocaine has similar effects on the body as Ritalin.[597] Had Hemingway, Poe, Pollock or Williams learned of their condition and developed less destructive coping techniques, they might have lived longer and happier lives. As it turned out, Poe never really knew success in life and drank and drugged himself to death.[598] Hemingway, continually fighting depression, also abused his body with drugs and alcohol, eventually committing suicide. Pollock, sadly, died while driving drunk. Williams abused drugs and alcohol his entire life. Some have suggested that the Lewy Body Dementia (diagnosed as Parkinson's during his life) he struggled with at the end of his life might have been brought on or exacerbated by years of substance abuse. While fighting this disease and depression, Williams, like Hemingway, killed himself.

Interestingly, accidental death and drug abuse (Poe), alcoholism and suicide (Hemingway), substance abuse and suicide (Williams) and reckless actions causing death (Pollock) haunt ADHD-people more than the average population.[599] Steven King, fortunately still with us, abused alcohol and drugs for years. Had his family not intervened, he might have killed himself too, just like Poe, from an overdose. Yet, it seems that such minds reached beyond known boundaries and pushed us to new areas of thought and exploration. Poe was the father of the modern detective story.[600] Hemingway was one of the greatest American writers ever. King has become the best horror writer in the English language. Pollock, one of the fathers of the modern art movement, revolutionized the way artists paint. And Williams became one of the best comedic geniuses of all time.

While the stigma of ADHD persists in our society, in a few other cultures, the thinking about ADHD has gone in different, and sometimes, more positive directions. For example, in India, some consider ADHD as a sign of greatness, and those who have it are deemed holy and "old souls, near the end of their karmic cycle."[601] In other words, how the ADHD-person is treated by others, as well as how he views himself, is significantly influenced by the cultural environment. In the U.S., unfortunately, ADHD-people are not considered "old souls" at the end of their "karmic cycle."

In earlier times, great men like Socrates, Plato and Aristotle defined such ADHD-traits as unusual imagination, associative thinking, heightened creativity and excessive energy as unique "powers."[602] One need not forget though that the Athenian government accused Socrates of "corrupting the youth" and sentenced him to death for his unorthodox teachings and spreading his ideas to the youth of Athens.

However, without Socrates, one could argue, we would not have had Plato, his student, or Aristotle, Plato's student, or Alexander the Great, Aristotle's student. If Socrates had ADHD, his life would provide dramatic evidence of how ADHD-people serve as capable agents of change, not only by how he influenced Western thought, but also how he helped mold his "offspring" of Plato, Aristotle and Alexander the Great into agents of change themselves. These three men likewise transformed the Western world even more than Socrates with their philosophical writings, political science, rhetoric and military strategy.

Today, one would not label these thought-leaders as outcasts, but back then, that was what they were in many respects. Today one could argue they have shaped philosophy, political science, military strategy and rhetoric more than most in our history. *What is considered abnormal often lies in the perspective of a specific time and culture. The difference between a disorder and a skill is in the eyes of the beholder as well as in the brain of the person in question.* Often, it all comes down to how you perceive ADHD. The positive ADHD-mindset has a real gift for embracing new ideas, rather than refuting them. Taking on this mindset depends on whether you take on a positive attitude about having ADHD in general. Whether you take on a positive ADHD-mindset or not, also seems to depend on whether or not you're a person who is continually seeking to learn and to grow.[603] For most, but especially for ADHD-types who struggle with learning, there seems to be a correlation with being *positive* and with collecting knowledge. Moreover, there is an even bigger correlation with being positive and applying knowledge once it is gained. That is the ultimate goal of learning.

ADHD can, then, be an advantageous condition when one wants to be a pioneer and push the boundaries of thinking, learning and behaving. ADHD-people have the energy and vision to see opportunities and vistas that remain in the dark for many without

ADHD. This uncanny ability to use their creative powers allows ADHD-people, if they have the confidence, to make a massive difference in their chosen field of interest, whether it be literature, art, philosophy, business or science.

However, when starting in life, this vivid imagination of ADHD-people can sometimes be a handicap. Yes, it can become a powerful force for an adult, but it must be watched closely in the young. For example, when I was a small child, I felt that I saw ghosts. That was how the right brain worked for over 200,000 years in humans. History is full of seers, shamans, witch doctors and oracles who saw and heard spirits, and throughout mankind's development established their versions of religion and worship. Perhaps, too, they were the harbingers of today's ADHD. One can make a viable argument that Zarathustra, Buddha, Abraham, Moses, Jesus, Mohammed, Joseph Smith, and L. Ron Hubbard, just to name eight major religious figures, saw and heard many things in the supernatural realm and exhibited ADHD-like behavior, utilizing and being influenced by over-active imaginations.[604] However, one may also note that this possible tendency of ADHD-people for creating religious movements is not necessarily a positive one, because one can argue the world needs less superstition rather than more, and less religions bigotry and condemnation and more reason and tolerance.

I now know it was my imagination working overtime when I thought I was interacting with the supernatural, but at the time, I was scared—my church, with its focus on "spiritual warfare," also didn't help my situation much. Luckily, I grew out of it and no longer believe in the paranormal, having discarded these beliefs as many children do with such myths as Santa Claus, the Boogie-Man, or the Tooth-Fairy. I just add to this list ghosts, demons, angels, saints, zombies, vampires, spirits, goblins, witches, gods, etc. The Austrian-British philosopher Karl Popper said that if you cannot prove or disprove something, then it is a waste of time and should be ignored. His exact phraseology is this: "In so far as a scientific statement speaks about reality, it must be falsifiable; and in so far as it is not falsifiable, it does not speak about reality."[605] In short, the supernatural, paranormal or mystical world that the imagination can give birth to quite often, if not always, is very unscientific and thus needs to be discarded. Now, my ADHD-imagination does help me look at historical events from different angles, sharpening my analytical skills and my conclusions about people and events. Luckily, I have prevented my ADHD-imagination from making me a religious zealot, something that ADHD-types need to be careful about.

But, as I mentioned, such an imagination in an ADHD-child that explores things deeply, can get carried away. For instance, I was on vacation in the Caribbean, sailing around the island of Tortola with my family when I was eight years old. My older brother, David, who was 16, had brought his best friend, Cary Bauer, on the trip. One day, as we all were in the back of the boat, Cary showed me a quarter, put it with his hand behind my ear, then snapped his fingers and showed me his hand. There was no quarter there. He then told me he had put it in my ear. Suddenly, I started to panic. I asked him to take it out, but he refused to do so. Then, I began to have pain and knew that the quarter was stuck in my head. I started to yell, "Take it out. I can feel it. Ah, it HURTS. Take it out, PLEAZZZ." My mother came up on deck and asked what was going on. With tears streaming down my face, I pleaded with my mother to have Cary take the quarter out of my ear. At this stage in the game, both my brother David and Cary were on the floor laughing uncontrollably. Seeing a quick solution to this difficult situation, my mother held back her laughter and said, "Cary, take out the quarter from Bryan's ear." Huddled in the boat's starboard bow corner, I screamed that the quarter hurt and that it was in my head. Laughing, Cary came over and did another little trick behind my head and then showed me the quarter. I felt instant relief. The pain was gone. I never let Cary do another trick again.

This story demonstrates that the imagination that ADHD-children possess, which makes them wonderfully successful later in life, can be a problem when they are young. Those with ADHD or parents of ADHD-children need to learn about their children's over-active imaginations. Yes, it can give birth to incredible artistic expression later like Poe, Hemingway, King, Pollock and Williams have shown, but in childhood, the imagination can create demons that can harm a child and cause mental anguish.

In other words, the earlier a child is educated about his ADHD-mind's unique features, the better off that child will be in adapting his behavior to his environment. *Only when I learned that my condition made me different, not defective, could I begin to lay the building blocks necessary to explore my mind and accept its way of thinking.* Such awareness will also ensure that the child is quicker in developing a healthy self-confidence, which we all need so desperately as children in order to live successful lives as adults.

ADHD, then, can be a beneficial condition to have if the person in question learns early about how to develop and nurture the positive aspects of his thinking and control the destructive parts of his impulses. ADHD-children are just like everyone else in this respect, but times 10. I think Bertrand Russell was thinking of ADHD-children when he encouraged people to let these children be who they are when young, writing:

> Busy grown-up people cannot be expected to endure a continual racket all around them, but to tell a child not to make a noise is a form of cruelty producing in him exasperation leading to grave moral faults. Much the same thing applies to the necessity for not breaking things. When a

boy climbs on the kitchen shelves and breaks all the china, his parents are seldom quite pleased. Yet his activity is of a kind that is essential to his physical development. In an environment made for children such natural and healthy impulses need not be checked.[606]

So, if an ADHD-child can explore who he is and learn to accept his condition, I think such a child is positioned to do great things. I believe that some people who have shaped the world for the better, like history's heroes, often have ADHD. These people, if they can control and embrace their ADHD, are natural-born leaders and thinkers.

Yet, even though ADHD might be benefit for many, it is difficult to identify, since it is often over-diagnosed today. Dr. Hallowell writes that "there are schools and regions where every child who blinks fast seems to get diagnosed with ADHD."[607] I believe "labels" like ADHD are nowadays used too often for kids who do not fit the mold society would like. And the facts usually show later that society's early perceptions of a person were wrong. Many so labeled believe this "hardship," or even "brain disease," is their "problem".[608] This is wrong. ADHD should be viewed as unique—that is all. Philosopher Spinoza wrote about universal rights of human beings, supporting their freedom to express who they are by nature. He said,

> "For whatever each thing does according to the laws of its own nature, it does with supreme right because it acts as it has been determined to do according to nature, and cannot do otherwise."[609]

Spinoza was discussing moral action of questioning established religious beliefs and governmental rules and how this questioning is natural behavior. However, he also discussed how such behavior can get squashed by society when the majority thinks a person is not acting according to what is thought to be orthodox. Of course, Spinoza would not justify murder or cruelty as something being performed "according to the laws of its own nature," which someone could argue about a sociopath. In short, Spinoza was exploring the fact that many behave differently from one another in society when it comes to exploring how one learns and processes information, and that difference is to be welcomed, not repressed.

We have come a long way in understanding and accepting differences. It was only a few decades ago Jews and Blacks were only allowed to study at certain schools. Until recently, women were not permitted to study in several universities and preparatory schools. We have explored emotional intelligence, learning styles and emotional tendencies, and have concluded that there are many ways of learning. Regardless of ethnicity, sex or socio-economic background, all minds can learn. In the end, when it comes to education, we should know that how one thinks or learns doesn't change what one can do, but how one should learn to do it. After all, we are all *Homo sapiens* and have the same basic brain structure.

Although I use the term ADHD, I disagree that it applies to many who are "diagnosed" with ADHD. Simply put, the abbreviation of ADHD should be replaced with a more positive one, perhaps UFP for "Unique with Full Potential." People are not aware that the upside of ADHD is "originality, creativity, charisma, energy, liveliness, an unusual sense of humor, areas of intellectual brilliance, and spunk" just as expressed by Socrates, Plato, Aristotle, Poe, Melville, Nietzsche, Hemingway, Pollock, King and Williams, just to name a few here. As Dr. Hallowell writes, "[ADHD] is often the lifeblood of creativity and artistic talents."[610] Others insist that people like Thomas Edison and Albert Einstein, who struggled in school early on, may have also had ADHD. He goes on to explain that "many people who *don't* have ADHD are charter members of the Society of the Congenitally Boring. And who do you suppose advanced civilization?

Who do you suppose comes up with new ideas today? People with ADHD, of course," the natural born leaders.[611] Former senior executive and IBM Chief Information Officer of its Hardware Division, Robert E. Corley, said that most of the people in senior management positions, including himself, were definitely ADHD, which, in his opinion, allowed them to keep track of several things at once and envision where the company needed to go, all of which made them natural born leaders.[612] With this in mind, one will not find it surprising that famous CEOs like Bill Gates (Microsoft), Richard Branson (Virgin Atlantic), Walt Disney (Disney), Ingvar Kamprad (IKEA), David Neeleman (Jet Blue), and John T. Chambers (Cisco Systems) all have ADHD. And not surprising, Branson, Kamprad, Neeleman and Chambers have dyslexia too.[613] We must realize that "our actions are not the product of will but of understanding," and *how* we come to understand that something. In this case, we need to understand that ADHD is an asset and not a defect.[614] So being diagnosed with ADHD is a sign that a person has incredible gifts. But we are a long way from a society that truly believes this. As ADHD-expert Russell Barkley said, "Our understanding of the psychology of ADHD is far from complete."[615] Since this is the case, why not focus on its positive aspects and give it a name that is full of positive rather than negative words? Living in a Farmer-world for a Hunter is full of more challenges than most realize. A Hunter must at times work twice as hard to adapt to society's prevailing expectations.

Although what I have written about non-ADHD-people might sound like I am praising the Hunter too much and bashing the Farmer excessively, one must remember that I married a Farmer and, for some years, felt very fortunate for doing so. For ADHD-people to survive, they need to make friends with Farmers. In fact, I would encourage some Hunters to pair off with a Farmer because this could be a Yin/Yang relationship and can sometimes prove beneficial to both.

A courtship of a few years should confirm whether the relationship would genuinely benefit from this "opposite attracts" type of union. What I want to impress in general is that we Hunters need to learn to assert our differences as being acceptable and that Farmers need to know that we are not defective, just different.

Labels like ADHD, although negative and often harmful, are the only words we currently use to describe the condition. It gives us a window from which to view ADHD by defining it. I hope in the future we could use an acronym without deficit or disorder in it. In addition to the other abbreviations I have suggested, maybe we can also call it ADHP for Attention-Different and Hyper-Productive.

In conclusion, we as a society need to tread carefully on the ground that creates two realities, separating those who are declared "normal" from those defined as "defective." We need a society that strives to understand that people learn in many ways and to encourage different methods of opening a child's mind. Knowledge is not only to be gained from books, but also in the ultimate power of confidence and imagination. If an ADHD-child learns to admire his mind and gain confidence in his abilities, he will be able to achieve more in life than a child who is forced to conform to an environment that incorrectly tells him that he is deficient. As we have seen with several famous ADHD-types, when the power within their brains was harnessed and accepted, it accomplished great things. As Joseph Campbell said, "Identify your notion of yourself with the positive, rather than with the negative."[616] When ADHD-people do this, they accomplish amazing and unique things in life.

Takeaways

- In recent times, people with ADHD-minds, who many would argue were "tortured souls," have produced powerful literature or art, for example: Edgar Allan Poe, Ernest Hemingway, Jackson Pollock, Stephen King and Robin Williams. Their lives present strong evidence that they were ADHD, self-medicated people.

- The positive ADHD-mindset has a real gift for embracing new ideas, rather than refuting them. Taking on this mindset seems to depend on whether you take on a positive attitude about having ADHD in general. Whether you take on a positive ADHD-mindset or not, also seems to depend on whether or not you're a person who is continually seeking to learn and to grow.

- The imagination that ADHD-children possess, which makes them wonderfully successful later in life, can be a problem when they are young. Those with ADHD or parents of ADHD-children need to learn about their children's overactive imaginations. It can give birth to incredible artistic expression later on like Poe, Hemingway, King, Pollock and Williams have shown, but in childhood, the imagination can create demons that can harm a child's life and cause mental anguish.

- We as a society need to tread carefully on the ground that creates two realities, separating those who are declared "normal" from those defined as "defective." We need to strive to understand that people learn in many ways and encourage different methods of opening a child's mind. Knowledge is not only to be gained from books, but also in the ultimate power of confidence and imagination. If an ADHD-child learns to admire his mind and gain confidence in his abilities, he will be able to achieve more in life than a child who is forced to conform to an environment that incorrectly tells him that he is deficient.

Action Steps

- Be ever mindful that the ADHD-mind, although full of incredible creativity, can also make one struggle with who he or she is as a person. As a result, be aware of self-loathing or depression and fight those two imposters whenever possible.

- ADHD should be admired and embraced as unique.

Socrates, Plato, Aristotle, and Alexander the Great were all men who thought out of the box and changed society in major ways, a very ADHD-trait. In discussing this issue with famous Political Philosopher and academic, Dennis Dalton, he thinks I am on to something by calling all four of these men ADHD-types. They viewed the world differently than most of the people around them and were able to become, in ADHD-expert Dr. Ned Hallowell's phraseology, "agents of change." Photo Credit: Kunsthalle zu Kiel, Germany

CHAPTER 12:

The Impact of ADHD on My Marriage and Divorce: ADHD + OCD = Trouble

"Love is the meaning of life—it is the high point of life."
— Joseph Campbell, *The Power of Myth*[617]

"Know one another? We'd have to crack open our skulls and drag each other's thoughts out by the tails."
— Georg Büchner, *Danton's Death*[618]

"You have no right to complain about something unless you have a proposed solution."
— Prominent Texas Family Law attorney, Charles Robertson, quoting his mother[619]

Note to Reader: Numerous people have reviewed this chapter. Most have encouraged me to keep it, while some think it belongs in an autobiography. Nonetheless, many therapists think it profoundly explores issues that ADHD-types have with relationships. They think it can help others prevent similar problems I experienced. Others just think this chapter reveals too much. However, when asked how something truthful that explores many ADHD-minefields can be problematic, I have been dissatisfied with their answers. I have found that when this chapter, like the one on sexual abuse, reminds people of their pain, then this section becomes painful for them. I find these revelations telling and would encourage all who have such a response to ask why this chapter may do this to them. In other words, this chapter makes many question difficult issues in their lives---and that is why I have written it. As relationship therapist Dr. Stephanie Lang explained after reading this section: "This chapter forces people to really analyze how they treat one another, especially ADHD-types, something we people need to do more of in our relationships in general."[620] Furthermore, sexuality counselor Rabbi Dr. Edgar Weinsberg wrote, "Chapter 12 is a moving, instructive demonstration of the onerous, perilous position ADHD-folks and their non-ADHD spouses often unwittingly put themselves in, when a generally healthy relationship, with inherent but unnoticed personality conflicts, descends into dishonesty and self-delusion due to a lack of sufficient self-awareness and mutual awareness."[621] He further states, "This chapter will help many ADHD-relationships be stronger by knowing what to do and what not to do when conflict arises (which it invariable always will). It is a must read for ADHD-people who have married non-ADHD-people."[622] Since the divorce rate is over 50%, anything that strives to help others have healthier relationships should be welcomed. Consequently, I have chosen to share this important epoch in my life.

My Marriage and Divorce Odyssey

It's a truism that all marriages have their ups and downs. But when a couple consists of at least one ADHD-partner like me, the outcome can be heightened joy on one hand, or catastrophe on the other. In short, a marriage like mine is bound to produce higher highs and lower lows. Putting this differently, all marriages involve a continuum of emotions: The great, the good, the bad and the ugly. But when ADHD is added to the mix, that which is good can become really great, or conversely, what's bad can get quite ugly. That was certainly true in my case. In this chapter, I explore many personal details in the hope of helping others avoid the mistakes my ex-wife and I made. As a historian, I am trained to report facts, names, pictures and situations that surround important events. Consequently, I have approached this period in my life similarly, and although I have tried to remain objective, I know no one can truly remain objective about his or her own history. I have struggled with how to present the facts from this time in my life, and you may feel my anger, bewilderment, and frustration as you read through this chapter, but I hope you also find insights that will help you deal with ADHD while managing a healthy relationship with a partner.

One lesson I learned as my marriage suddenly turned into a debacle of pain and resentment is that if you have trust without intimacy, you have set yourself up for disaster. With my ADHD-mind, I had built my relationship with my wife on duty-bound love focusing on fulfilling my raw obligations like earning a good living, supporting my children, and creating wonderful memories during family trips, etc. I had failed, however, to earn more *agape-* and erotic-love from my wife, more personal support from her for my endeavors and more space in her heart for memories of just us two. The story below has many elements of a Greek tragedy. It deprived my family of years of happy memories and robbed my children of an innocent, and health-ier, childhood. This is usually the story of divorce for many families, especially ones with ADHD. I sure wish I could redo this chapter in my life, and I would think my ex-wife would wish the same. That redo may not have saved us as a couple, but I am sure we would have done many things differently for the betterment of our children and us individually.

Stephanie and me on our wedding day, 4 January 1997. Highland Park Methodist Church, Dallas, TX.

As I moved through life and overcome most of my obstacles, I became more of a spokesman for ADHD. In 2014, my then wife and I became the lead couple for a fund-raising campaign for the Shelton School, the leading school in Dallas/Fort Worth for learning differences and one of the best in the world for LD-issues, especially for grades K-12. All our children have attended this school. I often spoke at the school about overcoming learning disabilities, encouraging students and teachers in these worthwhile pursuits. My wife was usually in attendance and supportive, often sitting next to my mother and Mary Stewart, who also attended. I often praised her for her support in dealing with my ADHD and dyslexia; our daughter Sophia's autism, dyslexia, anxiety and sensory integration issues; our eldest son Justin's ADHD and dyslexia; and our youngest son Ian's anxiety and mild ADD.

Stephanie and I were the 2014-2015 Capital Campaign co-chairs for the Shelton School, a school that focuses on children with LD-issues from kindergarten through twelfth-grade. All our children have attended Shelton and benefited from its teaching techniques and caring environment. Photo Credit: *The Horizon*, December 2015.

As my son Ian has told me, this is the last photograph showing when "we were a happy family." It was shot in December 2014, a few months before I discovered my wife was involved with someone else.

I am proud to report that my daughter Sophia eventually received a 1300 SAT score as a sixth-grader and entered the Duke University TIP Summer School system (Talented Identification Program). As a high school junior, she scored a 1570 out of 1600 on the SAT and became nearly fluent in Mandarin Chinese after her one-year learning abroad through SYA (School Year Abroad), a prestigious national study abroad program for high school students. She graduated at the top of her class from Greenhill School in 2019 and, as of this writing, attends college in New York City at the School of Visual Arts. She struggles with issues relating to her anxiety and autism, but she is a successful college student and an incredible 3-D animator and artist. She also is a deep thinker, thoughtful person and hard worker. My older son Justin has performed well academically and is currently studying at one of the world's best high schools, Phillips Exeter Academy. Like his dad, he uses the skills he has obtained dealing with his ADHD and dyslexia to make him a high-performing student and athlete. He is a varsity crew rower, receives A's and B's in his classes and completed the challenging United States Sea Cadets Special Warfare Orientation Course in 2021. During his year abroad in Germany at Louisenlund Stiftung in 2020-2021, he developed a working knowledge of German language, culture and society. He also is a humorous young man, considerate person and kind-hearted. My younger son Ian is an A student in junior high at Parish Episcopal, where he thrives, playing basketball and football, and running track. He also is a sensitive young man, an empath to a high degree and a strong leader. I am proud of my children and their accomplishments "despite" some of the genetic material they inherited. I wanted to digress and tell how my children are succeeding in spite of their "handicaps" or because of them, and also acknowledge the support my wife gave me and them before our divorce.

For years, my ex-wife praised me in front of teachers and parents at Shelton to illustrate what a person with ADHD/dyslexia can accomplish. I felt she was proud of me, and of what our children were achieving, as she often claimed. However, later she admitted she secretly resented the fact she had to deal with so many learning-disabled people within her own family.

My ex-wife is a quintessential "Farmer." She is a very organized, rule-oriented, introverted and shy. She often prides herself as being one of the smartest people in the room. Many view her as overly calm and, more often than not, people have called her the proverbial "stick in the mud." She was at the top of her class academically, but not very outgoing, at Trinity High School in New York City, a prestigious private school. While at Yale University, she continued to earn academic honors and graduated *summa cum laude*. She was a passive learner and rarely got involved with her teachers or engaged in debate.

The following story is telling and offers an insightful account of our Yin/Yang relationship. At the end of our last college semester, Stephanie got a B+ in her German history class. After I read her Blue-Book essay, which was the final test for the course and graded by her professor's teaching assistant (TA), I told her the TA was wrong to give her such a low grade and that she should take it up with the professor. My Hunter-mind kicked into high gear as I told her how to approach this situation. She didn't want to rock the boat, so to speak, and felt nervous about doing so. I, being the impulsive ADHD-type, said she should take this directly to the professor, Henry Turner, and protest. The TA in question did not like her and had an attitude problem. Moreover, if she did not get this B+ upgraded, she would not have been able to graduate *suma cum laude*, a coveted honor for high-ranking students. So, reluctantly, and with me pushing her from behind, Stephanie went to Turner's office to request that he review her exam. Turner was never known to be generous with his grades, but he was indeed a fair man, and he actually saw what I had seen; namely, my fiancé deserved a better grade. He upgraded her score to an A- and this allowed her to graduate *suma cum laude*. I still remember her walking across "Old Campus" after she had received the upgrade, then running into my arms as she shared the good news. I picked her up and swung her around. We both laughed with glee at her triumph.

So, my ex-wife was very educated, but she was not very aggressive in her dealings with others and she was reluctant to take risks when it came to meeting people, debating with them or engaging in controversy, very Farmer-like. At first, my type of support and aggressive help was welcomed in our relationship, but later, it became a burden. This event is one example of how I helped her throughout life (later, I would help her get her first two jobs, once again pushing her from behind, but hey, that was my "job" in the relationship). Also, since I exercised all the time, something she had not done in life, I also started to help her develop her own exercise regime (in our first six months, she toned up and lost ten pounds). She, in turn, dutifully, and enthusiastically, edited my writings for years since she had a lot of *Sitzfleisch*. We loved and supported each other in our unique ways, blending our methods of living life, helping each other to be stronger and more confident. We rarely, if ever, fought and never raised our voices in anger with each other.

And while at Yale, we seemed to prove that opposites attract, and we fell in love. At that time, she enjoyed my zest for life. She went to parties with me, practiced martial arts at my dojo, worked out with me lifting weights and crewed for me on the Yale sailing team. She often told me that had she not married me, she would have become a hermit. I found her smart, well-traveled, beautiful, kind and affectionate. We got engaged in only a few weeks (typical ADHD-impulsive behavior). She followed me to Cambridge, where I had received the prestigious Henry Fellowship to conduct graduate studies. In turn, I thought I was the luckiest man alive since I had found such a woman who wanted to be with me.

Now, to be honest, we did face some major obstacles from the outset. In my opinion (and even hers) and one of our counselors, she has OCD, and that does not usually create a good combination with an ADHD-person like myself, according to sexuality counselor

Rabbi Dr. Weinsberg.[623] Her controlling behavior could turn her into a nag when she got irritated with my hyper-responses and when I did not conform to what she thought normal behavior. Frankly, our personality "quirks" sometimes rubbed each other the wrong way and diminished our respect for each other over time, although the growth of that irritation was glacial at first, picking up momentum over the years. This is something ADHD-relationship expert Melissa Orlov has noted with couples like Stephanie and me, writing you need to be mindful to avoid "forcing yourself or your habits on a spouse without consent," as this disrespects that person and violates his or her trust.[624] Orlov says this often happens when the non-ADHD spouse tries to make the ADHD-spouse non-ADHD-like.[625] This is no doubt what occurred between Stephanie and myself. Being a controlling person with OCD works well in organizing projects and completing demanding tasks. However, it generally does not serve either person well in personal relationships. And ADHD, of course, can also wreak havoc, unless it is tempered by some measure of control and understanding.[626] The tension between these character traits can cause serious problems if not tended to, something Stephanie and I obviously failed to do which will soon become apparent.

Other factors besides the clash of OCD and ADHD-personalities (and maybe because of them), affected us too, primarily in the bedroom. Our earliest years of courtship and marriage were great, except in the realm of sexual intimacy. Stephanie struggled with a few sexual dysfunctions that started to wear on me by the third and fourth year of our marriage.[627] Initially, I had been patient, thinking things would eventually change. Indeed, I had enjoyed several wonderful, loving and sexually healthy relationships before Stephanie, positive experiences she did not have. I wanted to share that with her. I never gave up on her, and she repeatedly asked me not to leave her, despite knowing she was struggling in completely giving of herself to me when we were intimate. Eventually, by our eighth year of marriage, we were having serious problems, but after some intensive couples therapy, we found a way to please each other sexually. Still, the sexual struggles she had with me and others before we met might account for some of her eventual actions that I will describe later. This all came up in therapy sessions.

Apparently, Stephanie had unresolved abandonment issues due to her father's absence during her formative years. This further complicated her capacity for intimacy, not just with me, but with others before me. Above all, though, my hyper-sexual-energy, typical of many with ADHD,[628] eventually intimidated her and turned her off years later, although it is likely that this same high-energy had attracted her to me in the first place. Obviously, such issues disrupted our relationship. The turmoil we experienced in this arena has left me with one profound conclusion: If you do not find someone who is sexually compatible with you, you should leave such a relationship as soon as possible, while of course trying not to hurt the other person or yourself in the process. This complication can often happen to couples if one person is ADHD, so be aware of this danger.[629] It's true that at the outset of our relationship, we were not as sexually compatible as we had wished; but we thought that with time we would grow in this area. In fact, we both tried to do just that over many years. Looking back, I realize we were probably both deluding ourselves despite our best intentions. To have avoided the heartache we endured, it would have been prudent to have called it quits while in college before prolonging our commitment, as difficult as that might have been.[630] For better or worse, Stephanie and I can be quite stubborn.

From my experience as a man with ADHD, whose wife was OCD with several sexual hang-ups that disrupted intimacy, it is incumbent on those contemplating marriage or a long-term relationship to explore all potential obstacles and jointly determine if they can be resolved or not, before deciding to continue life together. Maybe had Stephanie and I explored each other's needs and personalities more honestly before we got engaged, we would have discovered then the potential complications that could arise later during our lives together. During the process of finalizing our divorce, for example, I found out that Stephanie was bisexual while reading her long email exchanges with her lover with whom she was having an affair (she had never once divulged this information to me during the two decades we were together). Had I known sooner that she might become more attracted to women than men, I would not have been able to stay with her, unless we had decided to have an open relationship, which is something I would have opposed.[631] Maybe this was one of many sexual awakenings for her, but during the later years of our marriage, I know that it would have further exacerbated the tensions in our household. Maybe we could have survived this, but it is all academic now. In the end, we sometimes cannot help whom we fall in love with, as I will explain further in reference to Stephanie and me. All the considerations just mentioned, and the fact that we got married right out of college, indicate that neither of us was sufficiently aware of our differences, and we were not really ready to enter a lifelong commitment. *Thinking long-term is something ADHD-types sometimes don't do well at a time when that is all they need to be doing.*

Yet, despite everything just mentioned, I have to acknowledge that for 19 years Stephanie and I had a respectable run. We built a good life from the little we started with. We had a lovely home in Dallas, two cars, a successful business and three wonderful children in great private schools. For many years, I felt I was on top of the world and a proud husband, father and businessman. But apart from Stephanie's issues, I myself, like many others with ADHD-traits, thrive on a high-energy lifestyle and crave adventure, and these traits can exhaust those around us. Now I understand more clearly, as the old saying has it, that "It takes two to tango" if we wish to sustain any long-term relationship. As Socrates taught, we must know ourselves because only in self-awareness, coupled with fuller knowledge of the other, can we make our partnerships enduring.[632] Well, unbeknownst to me, my ADHD and Stephanie's OCD, along with other issues, were about to clash in such a way that it would shatter our relationship into pieces.

As the adage goes, what you love about someone and hate about them is usually the same thing.[633] Like many men, I was clueless about some of my ex-wife's struggles, raising three children with complicated genetics, while trying to keep up with me. I was building a successful business and active on two prestigious boards. Many have noted throughout the years that my energy level is something they have never seen in another person.

As it turned out, this energy in exploring new ideas, participating on prestigious boards, writing books, doing new things with my business, playing with my kids and getting them involved with sports had exhausted Steph.[634] On the surface, she held everything together, putting on a brave face and pretending we were one of the best families at the Shelton School. We had excellent answers to questions about LD-children and how to make a successful marriage in spite of them. People often asked me for marriage advice since, it seemed, we were a "power couple." People called us Ken and Barbie. I might add, immodestly, that we did make a handsome couple.

Now, if you look at the entirety of our marriage, we had our ups and downs as mentioned before, but up to one year before our divorce, I thought our marriage was the best it had ever been. She even told me this. I felt like a king. She seemed to love me for who I was and had embraced my ADHD/dyslexia as unique things. These traits had allowed me to perform well at Cambridge, write books, build a business and provide a great life for our family. For years, I was in the top five of financial advisors out of 200 working at Broker Dealer Financial Services, and she often told me how proud she was of me. I thought I was the luckiest man alive to have a wife who was a witness to my life and proud of my accomplishments. We were still intimate twice a week at least, held hands, went on vacations often and gathered at special events with our respective families. She seemed grateful that I earned enough to allow her to remain home and raise our children, and I thought it wonderful to have a Yale-educated mother raising them. And despite our hardships, I was proud we had stuck together. And I not only loved my wife dearly, but I also loved her family. Everything seemed perfect on the surface, and then it happened—the divorce hit.

As my grandmother used to say, "When things are going well, Son, remember to still look over your shoulder." I got complacent and believed everything was alright. Also, at this time, I was hyper-focused on writing my fourth Holocaust book and building up my business even more. I was still coming home at regular hours, going on family vacations, coaching my son's basketball team, mowing the yard, going to church, dating my wife, etc., but I failed to notice that my wife was drifting away, had taken her affection elsewhere and was having an affair.

However, my situation was out of the norm, since my wife had fallen in love with a 73-year-old, overweight married man, Charles B., who was 34 years her senior.[635] For months, and unbeknownst to me, she was meeting him in parks, at my office, in our house and in his home. I was clueless. Reading texts and emails between them provided a fascinating insight into the real woman I had been living with for 19 years. I did not know this person existed. The information devastated me.

Before discovering the affair, I had noticed a change in Stephanie when I returned from a trip with our son Justin to Iwo Jima to commemorate the battle's 70th anniversary. I thought I would return home to a hero's welcome after taking our son on an incredible journey, exploring the Pacific War in general and the historic battles of Guam and Iwo in particular.

During the trip, I sent back photos and reports of our activities. Since Stephanie's father rarely spent time with her as a child, I thought the most significant "love languages" I could show her, besides spending time with her, was to spend time with our kids, which came naturally to me. However, instead of enjoying the photographs, she was taking this opportunity to meet with her lover. She brought him into our house while I was gone and introduced him to our other children, and even had him for dinner with the family one night. She went so far as to lock the two children in their rooms one evening and enjoyed Charles in our bedroom while I was teaching Justin history and bonding with him 7,000 miles away. While studying the Marine Corps' attack of Iwo with Justin, my home base had been invaded in more ways than one.

When she picked us up at the airport on 25 March 2015, I immediately noticed something had changed. There was an iciness in her eyes I had never seen before. They were fish-cold snake eyes. Every evening for the next month, after we put the kids to bed, she took the time to complain about everything in her life, neglecting, of course, to tell me about her affair. Among the many hurtful things she said, the worst were that:

A. She hated her "busy doctor" dad for never being there for her. She now felt she had married her father, since I also worked a lot.[636]

B. Her "narcissist" father had angrily told her mother about not being home enough, "Why should I be home? Here, I'm shit. At the hospital, I'm God."[637] She also felt like "shit," feeling she was only a "sex doll, CPA and maid."[638]

C.   Her mom made a mistake marrying her father and she had done the same with me.[639]

D.   We should have dated longer. Had we done so, she would never have married me because of my hyperactivity.[640] Consequently, maybe we should divorce.

E.   Our son Justin was her biggest burden in life since he was ADHD/dyslexic.[641]

F.   Had she known I could pass on my LD to Justin, she would have never married me. This was BIG news and the most devastating thing anyone had said to me.[642]

This last two shattered me. I asked, "Steph, wait. You're saying you wish Justin was never born and that you wish I'd never met you." Instead of seeing her gentle spirit, she snarled, "You both have ruined my life."[643] Although I asked her to consider that maybe the dyslexia came from her family too, since her brother and grandmother were severely dyslexic, she didn't listen. I was the guilty one, according to her.

Now, in reviewing how my Hunter-mind and her Farmer-brain worked, I must own some of these problems. Stephanie had not made this list overnight. It had been gestating in her for years. Obviously, my inability to see she had these problems probably, in part, stemmed from my heavy focus on being a kid around the children (I loved playing and doing activities with them) and my busy work schedule—both very ADHD-like behaviors.[644] I now own my role in not creating an environment where Stephanie could have shared these problems in a spirit of love instead of now in a spirit of hate. My hyper-focus mechanism with raising the children and building a good career prevented me from seeing that the credit I had built up throughout the years with my wife had run out. She needed me to hear what her needs were and I needed to be able to act on what she needed, but we failed each other in creating a team approach with a good feedback loop. Yes, her clues throughout the years were often nonverbal, which are hard for ADHD-types to pick up on; nonetheless, I could have seen them had I tried harder.

Stephanie, in making her list of woes, was doing what ADHD-relationship expert Melissa Orlov has described when she wrote: "Often, in frustration, a non-ADHD partner points out every failure the ADHD spouse encounters and uses it as further proof of incompetence."[645] Frequently, what relationships become reflects what people focus on. We humans make a choice everyday with our relationships either to focus on good or bad things. Stephanie never focused on a list of good things during this time of complaint. This probably happened because her lover was supporting her heavy emphasis on the negative, as both of them relished discussing how much they loathed their spouses.[646] I failed in getting her to focus on the positives of our relationship probably in part because she felt I had not paid sufficient attention to her needs. Often, ADHD-types can do this to their partners. Taking care of a relationship is akin to how a good gardener tends his garden daily, weeding unwanted vegetation, watering the good plants and pruning and harvesting when necessary---something very Farmer-like, and not very Hunter-like. Once a relationship is established, then the everyday details of shopping, working, paying bills, doing the laundry, and taking care of the children's needs are the tasks necessary to make a relationship work, and most often, these are things Hunters do not pay close attention to. My wife was good about the details, but she was tired of having to do them, in her opinion, all on her own, and I failed at seeing this. I also failed to see that my zany-humor, hyperactivity, new ideas and high-powered schedule were wearing her out. Orlov further writes, "ADHD affects the non-ADHD spouse more than can be imagined [and often negatively]."[647] Non-ADHD spouses eventually can feel "unloved," "angry and emotionally blocked," "incredibly stressed out," and "exhausted and depleted," which sums up precisely how Stephanie was feeling at this time.[648] Of course, there is always a lot of negatives we can list about anyone we know well. As Geoffrey Chaucer said in his *Canterbury Tales,* "familiarity breeds contempt."[649] So as our marriage unraveled before my eyes, I was unable to keep our focus on the good, and, at this moment, everything I was and had done was bad in Stephanie's eyes.

Permit me to provide some commentary here about relationships, especially involving ADHD-people. The only way we can respond intelligently to issues "and not allow [our] emotions to govern [our] behavior" is to understand the root cause of any event.[650] "To act rationally or deliberately and not emotionally is a positive enhancement of our power not only over events but just as decisively over ourselves."[651] During traffic jams, we often can get frustrated by what we think caused it or what it was that is now preventing us from arriving at our destination, which causes even more stress if we are now going to arrive late. However, if we know the root cause of the traffic mishap was an honest mistake done by another driver (which we ourselves have done), or a woman going into labor, or a car's mechanical problem, etc., then we can understand the traffic jam's cause and alter our "response to it."[652] In other words, instead of "succumbing to road rage," we "can accept the situation for what it is and in this sense free [ourselves] from purely feelings of anger and frustration."[653] Well, although Stephanie had known about my ADHD/dyslexia since the beginning of our relationship together, instead of looking at my habits as a byproduct of who I was, she looked at them as a burden she no longer wanted to carry. And I had failed to see how much my ADHD "afflicted" her. The traffic jam of our life was now fully my responsibility according to her and she was experiencing rage over it. In her opinion, I had made bad decisions while behind the wheel the past several years traveling along our relationship road.

I had collided with many events we shared in such a way that I had created a mile-long pile up on our highway of life. Her list of my errors made it clear that this accident was something I could never recover from. It was a game changer that would irreparably damage and ultimately "total" our relationship.

So, with these thoughts in mind, let's return to Stephanie's list of issues. Many couples go through divorces and often say things that are downright mean but not necessarily 100% true. Some of the issues she raised fit this category. But what shocked me about this exchange was that she was also going after our ADHD-son too, who was a wonderful boy. He was just a child; why attack him? Everyone loved him. But Stephanie hated his energy and resented the time and effort she had to put into making him "normal." And once again, she *hated* my unorthodox LD-ways, especially since I apparently had given all those issues to Justin too, my little-mini-me. Suddenly, our whole marriage at that moment revealed itself as being a lie. After I had discovered the affair on 22 April, Stephanie admitted she had fantasized about leaving me for over a decade (right at the time when our sex life started to take off), and that it was only when she met her true love, Charles, that she realized she needed to get away to have her own life. Moreover, she did not leave earlier, she said, "Since we didn't have any money. But now that we do, I'm gone!"[654]

Wow! My life turned upside down. At first, I did all the wrong things one should when his woman has taken her love elsewhere. I tried to get my wife to fall back in love with me and work out the problems she identified. As an ADHD-person, I became hyper-focused on this and made every effort to save my family. I was even willing in that moment to forgive her for taking up with an old married man. However, the worst thing you can do with a woman who is emotionally cut off from you is to love her when she doesn't want your love. *If you are not in a woman's head, you will never receive her affection.* All my efforts to love my wife just drove her away. And I really couldn't change what she needed me to change; namely, my ADHD. I was devastated. The one woman who I felt was my best friend and biggest supporter turned out to be the person who loathed me the most. I even said, "Steph, you're my best friend, why are you doing this?" She replied, "I may be your best friend, but you've never been my best friend."[655] Did my ADHD-mind make it impossible for me to see that I had been living with a spouse who *never* had thought of me as her best friend? Obviously, my ADHD-mind was partly to blame. At this stage, my vacuity became apparent to all, including me. Once my partner pulled away, I had a difficult time switching my hyper-focus mechanism to that new reality.

Our last "date" was telling. A few months before she filed for divorce, Stephanie slyly suggested, along with her mother, that maybe "we" could fix things. Secretly, they were vying for time as they planned the divorce. On our last "date," ostensibly to put things "back together," we dined at our favorite restaurant. Before we ordered, three people who knew me randomly came to us and said a few nice things like, "Your husband is a great guy," or "Your man can fight well [this guy was my martial arts sparring partner]," or "You must be lucky to have this man," or "Your husband often brags about you." My wife was pleasant, but I could tell that instead of making her proud, she was seething inside. When they left, she said in a caustic manner, "Everyone loves you."[656] The tone of her words made it sound like these comments were the worst things that could have been stated at that moment. I asked, "Do you mean, 'Everyone loves you,'" saying it in a normal voice, "Or, EVERYONE LOVES YOU," saying it now with disgust. She just turned away. At that moment, I knew it was over although she did also indeed say during the course of the night that "maybe we could put things back together." But she was just giving lip service to this concept, and I knew it, but still, strangely enough,

I wanted it to work, even though I knew it would not. Intellectually knowing that our relationship was a corpse and emotionally accepting this reality were two different things. As a result, I struggled with the situation. I knew that my ADHD and other personal qualities were partly to blame for her turning away from me, and I was, for the first time in my life, at a loss about what I needed to do.

Soon after our last date, we went to our first, and only, marriage counseling session on 1 June 2015. Stephanie had suggested we should go to repair our marriage, but in reality, she and her mother thought that would be the best place to announce the divorce. We entered the gentleman's office and sat down. He asked what was going on. She explained excitedly that she had already filed for divorce. I was shocked and the therapist was slightly annoyed since he had also been misled. He asked, "Well, since you have paid for the hour, let me hear both your stories." Stephanie explained her side of things. Then I described my history with Stephanie and how I had felt we were in the best place we ever had been until just recently, and that she had just a few months ago told me how great I was and how strong our marriage was.[657] After listening to me, he asked Stephanie, "Is anything false about what Bryan has said?" She answered, "No, he is accurate in how he described us." The psychologist then asked half curiously and half sarcastically, "Are you just the best actress ever?" Stephanie didn't answer this question, but when her nostrils flared, I knew she did not like his question. She quickly announced that our session was over. With that, she got up and left me there to pay the bill as she walked away, with a skip in her step.

As I paid the bill, the psychologist said, "I'm sorry you're going through what you are. It sucks." As I walked to my car, each foot felt like it was a hundred pounds. Crossing the 50 yards or so from the office to my parking place felt like it took an eternity. I thought back on the time when I could run 50 yards in a matter of seconds as a running back, but now it took forever, and I literally felt like I could not even open my car door once I had finished the exhausting journey to my vehicle. I also thought that by doing so I was unlocking a new dimension that I did not want to enter. Nonetheless, I knew I still had to turn the latch and step through the portal to enter a new world that I did not want to explore. As I sat in the driver's seat, I felt a few tears stream down my face, off my nose and onto the leather wrapped steering wheel of my BMW. I dried my eyes on my sleeve, looked up at the sky with the occasional cloud floating by and thought of how happy we had once been, especially during our first week of lovemaking when we started to date, or when we became engaged, or on our Yale graduation day, or on our wedding day, or when our children were born. I reflected, "This is the saddest day of my life and the beginning of the death knell of my family." I started the car, and after a few tries, finally put the stick into first gear and slowly drove out of the parking lot. I didn't want to drive home, because, quite simply, it wasn't home any longer.

One thing that I had failed to realize at this time was Stephanie's cheating was probably an overt act "to blow up" our relationship that made her "feel trapped in some way," a common reason for why women cheat according to Charlynn Ruan, Ph.D., "a clinical psychologist and founder of *Thrive Psychology Group*," a group practice that specializes in women.[658] Ruan further explains what Stephanie was most likely doing at this time was acting "out to end the relationship," end of story.[659] And there is no doubt, her acts did indeed blow up and kill our relationship and we were on the fast track for divorce (eight months later, it would be done).

In the meantime, the thought of going through a divorce and splitting up the kids was horrifying since I had experienced my parents' divorce and remembered it vividly. Moreover, the idea of her breaking up Charles' family and marrying him horrified me, and I feared how it would affect my kids. When Justin found out about the affair, he rocked back and forth, exclaiming, "This doesn't happen to our family. This doesn't happen to our family." His body shook with pain. Later, he declared, "Why is she going to marry a 73-year-old man? He'll be dead in five years!"

Justin has the ability like me to hyper-focus on things he is passionate about or troubled by. My younger ADD-son, Ian, has this ability too, even though it is not as strong as Justin's and mine. Nonetheless, the divorce traumatized my boys. Ian has told me recently that he was depressed for years and Justin has declared that experiencing our family's divorce has taught him that he "should never trust someone fully because everyone has the potential to let you down." My boys continued to plead with me throughout 2015, and with their mother, to not get a divorce. I promised them I would do my best. However, it takes two to make a relationship work and I was on my own. In addition to my ADHD-hyper-focus nature centering on my wife's betrayal, I now was using it to concentrate on my children's depression, affecting my own mental health even more.

One thing that ADHD-types usually like is to feel in control. When dealing with ADHD early on, one so "afflicted" often feels out of control. As a result, once an ADHD-person has learned to use it effectively in life and has it under control somewhat, then the feeling of being out of control feels scary as if the negative aspects, the demons if you will, are coming back to plague you. All people are like this to some degree, but I would argue ADHD-types, once they find a good rhythm in life, hate going through major changes they cannot control. Well, with the divorce staring me in the face, I felt out of control. The secure life I had given myself and my children now was shattered. I felt lost. I also felt I could no longer help my children feel protected. My children withdrew to their rooms and did not really interact with anyone for a year. The boys now tell me that the process of going through a divorce robbed them of their childhood. I agree with them somewhat (my childhood was also somewhat taken from me by my parents' divorce), but in life, you cannot force someone to remain married to you. As far as Steph was concerned, she no longer loved me and definitely did not want to be married any longer. And in America, everyone has the right, and privilege, to not be married any longer regardless of the reasons. In some respects, this is the beauty of America securing individual rights for its citizens. However, knowing our law system protected people's rights to go through divorce did not help me emotionally with the situation I found myself in.

When Stephanie and I later discussed her affair, instead of admitting it was a mistake, she doubled down and said her new boyfriend truly understood her and that they were in love.[660] I felt like a thousand daggers entered my heart as I heard her declarations of adoration for Charles. In struggling with this, my ADHD-zany-humor came to the rescue, and I asked her, "Since Charlie has four children and three grandchildren, how will you like being called not only stepmother, but also step-grandmother?" She flared her nostrils at me. I then gave a typical ADHD-humorous retort to her scowl with, "Well Steph, if you had only told me to wear Depends to get you sexually aroused, I would've done so... Just be patient. I too will be an old man in three decades, and then, can give you what you need." To say the least, she did not like my humor, and although I was laughing hysterically in one side of my chest, the other side of my chest heaved with pain. As my stepsister, Lori Mayfield, noted on seeing Charles' picture:

> The old guy is certainly no Harrison Ford or even on the bald end, Sean Connery. He's like a non-animated form of Elmer Fudd, your typical old guy at IHOP ordering the Rooty Tooty Fresh n' Fruity. There's not any ounce of appeal from the pleats in those slacks to camouflage a Depends adult diaper to the size-too-big-belt with six extra belt loops

and the Mitch McConnell jowl. No doubt he's as creepy as they come and having a spouse cheat on you is one thing but to have someone cheat with someone especially creepy adds insult (and bewilderment) to the betrayal.[661]

My stepsister's psychological insights were spot on in describing how I was struggling to understand my new reality.

Here is a photograph of my ex-wife's lover, Charles B., who was 34-years older than she. Unfortunately, my ADHD-mind hyper-focused on this bizarre turn of events. It was hard for me to get past her rejection of me for this man with whom she had actually fallen in love.

Stephanie's parents quickly justified her behavior. When talking with my ex-mother-in-law about the bizarre turn of events, she said, "Well, Bryan, Stephanie's taking up with Charles shows you how miserable she was."[662] I replied, "Wait a minute. Your daughter hasn't always been a princess, but when she behaved poorly, I didn't go sleep with an 80-year-old woman in a walker to get over it." Although I again exhibited my zany ADHD-humor, my then mother-in-law did not like my response. I'm surprised. Everyone else usually laughs at that retort!

My ex-father-in-law was not much help either. Although he is an elder in his church and has touted the mandate that married people stick together no matter what, because that is God's will, he supported the divorce. When asked why, he said, "Because your family is now destroyed."[663] I thought that strange and said, "I didn't have an affair and I'm not the one who wants a divorce." He responded,

> Stop saying she had an affair!!! She was involved with the old man, but it won't go anywhere, and your guys' marriage is on the rocks. And moreover, and I'll regret saying this, but you are a narcissist, and that's why you're divorcing.[664]

And I replied,

> Wait a minute. You've known me for 20 years and we have had many candid discussions. You have often said you love me as a son and are proud of me. And now, you suddenly come to the conclusion that I'm a narcissist. Why not tell me this years ago, or did you just come up with that to justify the situation because your daughter has revealed that she likes to sleep with a geriatric because of the daddy issues you gave her?

He, like my ex-mother-in-law, did not appreciate my ADHD-humor. Surprisingly, we calmed down and continued talking. I said, "I believe there's always a way to mend a relationship and I'm willing to do anything to keep my family together. I believe in miracles." I will never forget his response. With the vitriol of a disgruntled old man, he hissed, "How can you believe in miracles? You don't even believe in God!!!"[665] He then hung up the phone. My reality was quickly changing.

As a sidenote here. My ex-wife and I had raised our children in the religious tradition of Unitarian/Universalism, embracing tolerance. We raised our kids as ethical humanists and my ex-father-in-law took the opportunity during this dark time to let me know how disgusted he was with "my" parenting techniques not having raised our children as fundamentalist Christians. Consequently, he showed himself to be a bigot. Had my ADHD also blinded me to how he really felt about me and my parenting skills? Losing him as a second father was almost as devastating as losing my wife. And to add insult to injury, my ex-mother-in-law even had encouraged and then helped Stephanie destroy our home computer a month before she filed for divorce when I was at the office so I would not find anything else incriminating. They claimed it had "suddenly crashed," and that is why they took it to the store to get "recycled" within a *few minutes* of it crashing, but I knew otherwise. In short, the entire family structure I had relied on for support deteriorated in front of my eyes. I felt horribly abandoned.

Within the perceived sanctity of family, where I thought I had been safe, a Cain-like, latent animosity, raised its ugly head and bashed me to the ground. The problems I was experiencing would be difficult for anyone, but for an ADHD-person, my hyper-focused nature enabled me to home in on multiple betrayals and I was traumatized. The people whom I had lived with for 20 years, and with whom I had gone on dozens of trips, celebrated the births of my children, enjoyed milestones, leaned on during hardships, supported during sufferings, gathered with during holidays and talked with regularly were now not there for me at all. I started thinking, "Who else in my life tells me they love me who really doesn't love me at all?" Such thoughts shut me down, and I suddenly became a hermit. It took me years to once again fully engage with humanity like I had before the divorce, although now, I am much more guarded. Nonetheless, I am still working on trusting others like I once did, but it is still a process. As my mother declared, one cannot blame my ex-in-laws for their behavior, because, of course, "they would stand by their daughter no matter how pathetic her behavior was."[666] As the German medieval phrase rightly declares, "Blood is thicker than water (*Blut ist dicker als Wasser*)."[667]

I have discussed my divorce for two reasons. Firstly, ADHD-people need to be ever vigilant in their relationships and make sure they are tending them. Everyone needs to do this, obviously, but ADHD-people need to make extra efforts with their loved ones, especially if their spouses are non-ADHD-types. ADHD-types can sometimes forget to treasure those closest to them, and I obviously had failed in this area. One study asserts ADHD-types are "almost twice as likely as one who does not have ADHD to be divorced."[668]

Secondly, I included this chapter because the one thing I had not been conditioned to expect in life, especially when I had strong women in my corner like my mom, grandmother, godmothers and teachers, was to think of them as no longer loving me once they had joined my "team." That my wife had jumped ship, was no longer in love with me and resented all the success I had achieved was something I could not take my mind off. This hyper-focused nature of an ADHD-person (let's say in my case while serving in the military or doing a PhD) can be an excellent ally, but when going through trauma, it can be an albatross around the neck. For months, I could not sleep or eat. I went from a 200-pound, physically fit male to a 165-pound, demoralized man. My hair turned even grayer. I was more devastated when I read a text my ex-wife had written Charles describing my pain and laughing about it. The reality that my family's castle had been invaded, and in many respects, defeated, created a great weariness in my soul. Moreover, a touch of animal terror seized me because *this defeat* had occurred due to an *inside job* by my closest confidante, my wife.[669] Unbeknownst to me, I had been sleeping with the enemy for a long time: My ex-wife confessed to me she had actually checked out back in 2005. How could someone live a lie for so long, I thought?

I struggled to turn my love into hate, or even better, indifference, but for the life of me, I could not. I believed in the Stephanie

I thought I had been building a joyful life with, and I was slow to accept that she was now a phantom, or worse, had never even existed. ADHD can make people naïve if their hyper-focusing mechanism fails to focus on the truly important things. I had obviously been missing clues about who my wife really was for years, and I now own those mistakes of judgement. Moreover, I had failed in her eyes to become the husband she wanted, due in part, to my ADHD. It appeared, and her emails bore this out, that she had only married me for the status I offered her during our university time with all my Yale successes (being a Henry Fellow going off to Cambridge, and receiving many awards and a lot of press coverage during our senior year), while she was struggling to find a job during our last semester and having little direction about her future. She had made a decision long ago to bond with me because I looked good on paper. As she told me, "At Yale, I jumped on your coattails of success and that was a mistake."[670] Could such a marriage then evolve into a long-lasting relationship? Maybe, but obviously her personality and my ADHD-brain made strange bedfellows.

My ADHD, in this case, had blinded me from seeing the relationship for what it really was—unhealthy, and apparently, doomed from the outset. Of course, anything is possible when it comes to relationships and maybe Stephanie and I could have found a healthy way to love each other, but if you are blind to the problems, you cannot fix them. Well, the divorce definitely made me aware of things about my marriage I had been oblivious about. As comedian Robin Williams said, "You'll have bad times, but they will always wake you up to the stuff you weren't paying attention to."[671]

Now, some of the trauma I went through is not unique. Many divorced people go through the "divorce diet" and lose weight, and many take years to recover from a breakup. And many rewrite the history of their relationships in order to justify their breakups, turning from defining them as wonderful and loving to eventually poisonous and broken. However, how my ADHD-traits possibly prevented me from seeing that I should not have gotten married in the first place to the person I did, or, in the end, caused the divorce, or how my ADHD caused me to incorrectly respond when faced with the divorce are things I *do not wish* on anyone. Replays of the marriage and what I could have done differently continued to run through my head, tormenting me. As Edgar Allan Poe wrote, "Either the memory of past bliss is the anguish of to-day, or the agonies which *are* have their origin in the ecstasies which *might have been*."[672] Poe could have been further describing me when he wrote, "Who does not remember that, at such a time as this [traumatic event], the eye, like a shattered mirror, multiplies the images of its sorrow, and sees in innumerable far off places, the woe which is close at hand?"[673] It has taken years to remove that "sorrow" from my inner eye because I was unable to compartmentalize the pain and intellectualize the process. Here, my hyper-focused attribute worked against me. I still mourn the union that once had been my family, even if now I realize it to be, in part, a myth.

In the end, there were obviously some serious issues my ex-wife had that came to a head in 2015. I cannot lay blame on my ADHD for all of them.[674] However, how I responded to the trauma, because of my ADHD, was not healthy, and I want to help others avoid my mistakes.

So, what do I recommend to ADHD-people to help defend themselves from a divorce or the traumas of going through a divorce? Well, know that a person can sour on you at any time. Not preparing for a worst-case scenario during my marriage gave me a false sense of security. It has been said that it is better to be prepared for a situation and not have it, than to have the problem and not be prepared. I think ADHD-people need to know that when they marry a non-ADHD-person, that non-ADHD-person sometimes will later have difficulty keeping up with the new ideas, the sense of adventure and the quirky humor that initially drew that person to the ADHD-type. And sometimes the non-ADHD-person will ignore "personal boundaries" and try to change the ADHD-person into a non-ADHD-person. But as therapist Melissa Orlov reminds us, "[A]s you already know, you can't change someone else."[675] I now feel I married the wrong person for me. I should have married someone more like an ADHD-person, who would not tire of keeping life exciting. As my ex-wife told me when she left me with two little boys crying in my lap, "I just want a quiet life, drink wine with Charles and be left alone."[676] With that declaration, she walked to her car from our house, literally singing a happy tune to herself, as incredible as that seems!

So, what are my tips for ADHD-types who want to build healthy relationships and prevent divorce?

A. From my experience, since most ADHD-types are extroverted, do your best, if you have ADHD, to marry a fellow extrovert, so he or she can keep up with you and appreciate who you are. Of course, this is not a universal mandate, but I think it should serve as a guide when picking a partner.

B. Explore how your potential spouse handles high-energy children. Do they find them fun or burdensome? My ex-wife struggled to keep up with our children, and they ultimately exhausted her. She blamed that on me. If you are a non-ADHD-type contemplating marrying an ADHD-type with the potential of passing on those genetics, then interview the mother of your potential partner about what type of child they were. Had my mom been interviewed, she would have told Stephanie I was a handful. This is important to explore since ADHD seems to be a dominate gene with almost an 80% heritability rate.[677]

C. Once married, do everything you can to prevent divorce. Regularly confer with your spouse about what you are doing and if she or he is all right with it. Be proactive in this arena. For example, have a quarterly "business meeting" to discuss whether you guys are on the right track or not.

D. Continue to think about divorce and what that would look like. Don't take anything for granted. Realize that some people at some point in the relationship just will not like you anymore. That is OK, not desired of course, but sometimes, inevitable.[678] I made the mistake of embracing the romantic view of "happily ever after."[679] I think had I realized that divorce was a possibility every year of my marriage, I would not have been hyper-focused on trying to save it. Once she filed in June 2015, I suffered a PTSD response. My health was affected for months, and ironically, or logically if you will, my ADHD got out of control and everything I had done in life up to that point to harness the positive attributes of the condition unraveled and many of the negative traits started to plague me (distractibility, forgetfulness, hyper-hyper focusness, etc). I could only start putting the pieces of my life together in August. If you go through divorce, find meaning in it as soon as you can. As Holocaust survivor Victor Frankl wrote, "To live is to suffer, to survive is to find meaning in that suffering."[680]

E. As prominent Texas family law attorney, and a person who had a 60-year successful marriage, Charles Robertson, quoting his grandmother, said, "Only fools seek out confrontation."[681] He goes on to explore the reality that we will have enough conflict in life without looking for it. One way of preventing divorce, I believe, is to not get angry and fight with your partner. Although Stephanie and I rarely fought when married, we definitely have made up for it during and after the divorce, unnecessarily causing hardships for one another and our children. ADHD-people usually don't like conflict, but when it happens, they sometimes can "enjoy" the environment due to the adrenaline high it gives them and for which their minds thrive at having. So do all you can to avoid conflict. When married, try asking questions instead of being bossy and declaratory with your concerns,[682] and if divorcing, try to find a good mediator who can help you get to the finish line of divorce with the least amount of arguing and conflict.

F.   Always "treat each other with respect, even in the most difficult times."[683] If you find yourself not respecting your partner, then you must get that back or the relationship is doomed. Respect for each other's humanity, personality and brain is the hallmark of a healthy relationship. If divorce becomes your plan of attack, do so with kindness if possible. For example, when you begin divorce proceedings, do not serve your spouse, especially while he or she is at work, "by a sheriff, constable or private process server."[684] And once the divorce happens, try to always ask what you would do if in the other person's shoes. This will help you remain more kind than probably otherwise would be the case.

ADHD-people need to remember they need a unique partner in life. Most cannot handle living with a person who is "on" all the time, so probably living together for a few years would be a wise thing to do. For example, Stephanie grew tired of how I wake up full of energy. Although this seems minor, it was another one of her "major" complaints when our marriage went on the rocks.[685] My divorce was indeed traumatic, but the ADHD-reaction I had to it was excruciating. I want to prevent people from going through what I did.

Looking back today on our life together and assessing both the hefty highs along with the painful lows that have culminated with the god-awful dissolution of our relationship to a point where we now abhor each other, I doubt if I would have embarked on my marriage in the first place had I known what those 19 years would bring (except for having my children). In short, while we had good times, in the long run, my marriage was a big mess I wish I, my wife, and our kids could have been spared.

To end on a positive note to this rather painful chapter in my life, I do believe in love. It is rare, and few have enduring romantic love, although, ironically, most want it. As Ernest Hemingway said, "[Love] is the most important thing that can happen to a human being."[686] When someone has true love and loyalty throughout life, it is a rare gift and I wish that for everyone if possible. As Holocaust survivor Viktor Frankl further noted:

> The truth—that love is the ultimate and the highest goal to which man can aspire. Then I grasped the meaning of the greatest secret that human poetry and human thought and belief have to impart. The *salvation of man is through love and in love.* I understood how a man who has nothing left in this world still may know bliss, be it only for a brief moment, in the contemplation of his beloved.[687]

Most throughout their lives want to love and be loved. It is one of the greatest, and basic, human wants. After all the pain and confusion we have in life, we somehow believe it will be all worthwhile if only we can have someone to hold, kiss and adore. Loving someone often gives us a reason for living. And since ADHD-people become hyper-focused when they are excited about someone, they can, I would argue, love more deeply than the average person. But if they want that love returned in equal measure, they must focus on their partner's needs first. I want that for my ADHD-cousins. It is not easy, but it should be a goal, however lofty it may be.

Takeaways

- Relationships for those with ADHD/LD are often more complicated than for the average person. ADHD-people need to be ever vigilant in their relationships and make sure they are tending them. Everyone needs to do this, obviously, but ADHD-people need to make extra efforts with their loved ones, especially if their spouses are non-ADHD-types.

- When an ADHD-person marries a non-ADHD-person, that non-ADHD-person sometimes will later have difficulty keeping up with the new ideas, the sense of adventure and the quirky humor that initially drew that person to the ADHD-type. Since most ADHD-types are extroverted, do your best, if you have ADHD, to marry a fellow extrovert, so they can keep up with you and appreciate who you are.

- Once married, do everything you can to prevent divorce. Regularly confer with your spouse about what you are doing and if she or he is all right with it.

- Continue to think about divorce and what that would look like with your spouse. Don't take anything for granted. Realize that some people at some point in the relationship just will not like you anymore. That is OK, not desired of course, but sometimes, inevitable.

Action Steps

- Before you get married, explore how your potential spouse handles high-energy children. Do they find them fun or burdensome?

- If you are a non-ADHD-type contemplating marrying an ADHD-type with the potential of passing on those genetics, then interview the mother of your potential partner about what type of child they were.

- ADHD-people need to remember they need a unique partner in life. Since most cannot handle living with a person who is "on" all the time, try living together for a few years beforehand.

- Once married, have a quarterly "business meeting" to discuss whether you and your partner are on the right track.

- *Remember, never run after those who do not want you.*

CHAPTER 13:
ADHD, My Historical Research and this Book

"History…is philosophy teaching by examples."
— Thomas Babington MacAulay[688]

"Knowledge is better than ignorance; history better than myth."
— Ian Kershaw, *The Nazi Dictatorship*[689]

I ENDED CHAPTER 11, AND I will end chapter 18, by telling my fellow ADHD-cousins, that if you follow your passions and embrace your condition, then something creative and wacky might happen. I am speaking from experience. Nothing illustrates this more than the stories behind the writing of my history books and this manuscript. With the unique ways ADHD/dyslexic people look at the world, I was given a "blessing" as a historian to always get into "trouble" by documenting provocative subject matters. It *never* starts that way, but as I have looked deeper into every subject I have explored, I have always found new sources, uncomfortable truths and heated controversies. *Welcome to my ADHD-life.*

Research for *Hitler's Jewish Soldiers*
In 1992, when I started researching Jews and men of Jewish descent who served in the German Armed Forces of World War II (*Wehrmacht*), I immediately encountered opposition. At the time, everyone thought I was crazy for investigating Jewish soldiers in Hitler's

military. "Impossible," they said. "Hitler killed all the Jews. What's wrong with you?" Several Yale professors were negative about my work. On hearing such criticism, I went back to what Mary Stewart had taught me—I was a contrarian and needed to find out the truth for myself. There was purpose behind my curiosity and instinct told me there was something to be discovered.

The story opened in a Berlin movie theater and followed a trajectory along a decades-long obsession with this topic that led me from a Yale undergraduate thesis, to a Cambridge master's and doctoral dissertation, to five published WWII books.

In May of 1992 when I was at the Goethe Institute in Berlin to learn *Deutsch* and research my ancestry, one of my teachers recommended viewing *Europa Europa (Ich war Hitlerjunge Salomon)* to improve my German. This film tells the story of Shlomo Perel, a Jew who, as a teenager, falsified his identity and served in the *Wehrmacht* from 1941 through 1942. Then, after being adopted by his commander, he returned to Germany to study at an Adolf Hitler Youth boarding school from 1942 to 1945.

Before the film began, I entered an empty auditorium, and while waiting for the movie to start, I heard the doors open behind me. When I turned around, I saw an elderly gentleman walk in. He was unsure of his footing, and it was apparent his eyes had not adjusted to the darkness as he leaned against the wall for support. With my good, Texan upbringing, I went to him, asked if he needed help which he accepted, and I sat him next to me. The man was Peter Millies, and in our ensuing conversation, he offered to translate any section of the film I did not understand because he spoke English. Essentially, he translated the entire dialogue, and since we were the only ones in the room, we did not bother anyone. After the film, I noticed he was emotional and asked why. With the occasional tear running down his cheek, he shared that the film reflected much of his own story. He asked if I was interested in hearing his account. I excitedly accepted.

Over a few beers, Peter recounted his life. He was a "quarter-Jew" who was drafted into the *Wehrmacht* in 1941 and spent three years on the Russian front. After the war, the Russians took him prisoner, and he did not return to Germany until 1950. Our conversation made me wonder if there were others like him and Perel.[690]

During this summer, I also discovered some Jewish heritage in my family, which further piqued my interest, driving me to investigate this subject even more. In one of the Lower Saxony towns where I conducted genealogy research, a World War I monument had a list of veterans, many of whom had my family's surnames. If these men were Jewish, I thought, how could they have so valiantly served in WWI, only to be exterminated in the Holocaust a few years later? Over 100,000 German-Jews served the Fatherland between 1914 and 1918, with 12,000 of them dying in battle.[691] How could Germany be so ungrateful?

I also wondered what were the odds of going to a theatre to watch a film about a Jew who served in the German army only to sit next to a man whose own life mirrored this very tale? How could that be a coincidence? Moreover, what were the odds that a month later, I would discover my own Jewish heritage? Was destiny telling me something?

When I returned to Yale for my sophomore year in the fall of 1992, I researched the subject matter despite being discouraged by professors about its feasibility. Henry Ashby Turner, Jr., who was my professor of German History, told me, "Stop chasing after some curious anomalies that won't add anything to our understanding of the history of the Nazis and study some serious German history!" However, my contrarian, ADHD-mind kicked into action. I knew the burden was mine to prove that Turner was wrong to doubt me. When I learned that he had never explored this history, and knew of no one else who had either, I decided to give it a go. I believed if I could find 20 men like Perel and Millies, I would have enough material to write an interesting senior essay.

After my sophomore year, I returned to Germany and lived with *Herr* Millies for a few months in 1993. I learned how it was possible for him, his brother and many of his cousins to have served. I learned through one-on-one discussions what it was like living under Hitler when having Jewish heritage. I also studied history in the local libraries and museums. When not at these centers, I talked with as many older Germans as possible by visiting retirement homes, or by searching them out in parks in order to learn about WWII. My ADHD-impulsivity helped me because German eyewitnesses were usually reluctant to talk to strangers, especially regarding the Second World War. Yet, I went out on "hunts" daily, speaking with new people and learning about the past.

By the end of my junior year in 1994, I convinced some Yale residential colleges to sponsor a Holocaust seminar with Shlomo Perel, the protagonist of *Europa Europa*.[692] We flew Perel from Israel and had three days of events. By this time, I had identified seven living *Wehrmacht* veterans of Jewish descent, and an additional 12 who had died in battle or were otherwise deceased. I knew more existed. I also realized that locating the living veterans meant a race against time because these men were dying off. Driven by this "ticking clock," I applied for and received several scholarships, which allowed me to pursue my project. The Dean's discretionary fund scholarship was the most prestigious. When Dean Richard H. Brodhead presented it to me, he said, "Bryan, I believe in what you're doing and think you're on to something. Go make us [your dean and Yale] proud."[693] Those kind words lived with me throughout my research.

I decided to take a year off between my junior and senior years to live in Germany to conduct more interviews and collect documents. As mentioned earlier, I bought a laptop computer, a printer, a video camera, a sleeping bag, a mountain bike, an electrical transformer and a large backpack. My goals for the year were to interview 30 Jewish veterans, find supporting documents in the archives and become fluent in German.

Before I left for Europe, Professor Turner again told me I was wasting my time. Another professor, Lieutenant General William E. Odom (USA), was more supportive and felt I was exploring something interesting. Still, he thought that taking a year off would only delay my education, and he worried I might not return to Yale to finish my degree. One of the nastiest conversations I had with a professor was with the co-founder of the Holocaust Fortunoff Archives, Geoffrey Hartman. After I asked for his help, he dismissed me from his office and told me I was on a fool's errand. When leaving his office, he demanded, "Shut the door when you leave," while shaking his head. The head of the Judaic Studies Program, Professor Paula Hyman, was the only scholar who encouraged me without reservation.

Despite getting more negativity than encouragement from Yale faculty, I still felt there was something there to explore. If I, a lowly undergraduate, had discovered almost 20 men who fulfilled my criteria, then the total number of those who served had to be bigger than anyone thought possible. I believed if I could document several hundred, then people might take me seriously. This research posed many historical questions. Why were these men serving? How many served? Did they know about the Holocaust? What did this tell us about Nazi racial policy? How Jewish did one have to be to be sent to the camps? How widespread was German-Jewish assimilation in Germany by 1933? What did my research tell us about German-, Jewish-, and Nazi-identity during the Third Reich? My ADHD-brain became hyper-focused and fully engaged in finding the answers to these questions.

Paula Hyman, my beloved Yale professor and head of Judaic Studies. She supported me and encouraged me to research "Hitler's Jewish Soldiers" and the Nazi rescue of Rebbe Joseph Isaac Schneersohn. She wrote the Foreword for the Schneersohn book, *Rescued from the Reich*, published by Yale University Press in 2004. Photo Credit: Yale University

However, I had a problem. Yale had given me enough funds to support a summer's worth of time, but I was now determined to spend a whole year in Germany. So, I created a budget to know exactly how much I could spend monthly, allowing me to accomplish my goals. To save money, I circumvented the need for public transportation by using my bike, and sometimes I slept in public parks, using hotel or public restrooms to clean up in the mornings. I got most of my food from open markets where it was cheap, primarily buying tomatoes, cucumbers, bread, jam, peanut butter and bananas. After a few months, I started to develop networks in the major cities and I soon had a lot of "German grandparents" who provided hospitality when I was in their city. Often, these kind people had been interview-partners. My ADHD-Hunter mind knew no fear, so I just went out, met people and became their friend.

My research started with momentum. In the first month, I documented 30 living veterans and dozens of others who had passed away. My research benefited from the snowball effect. Most I met entrusted me with the names of friends and family members who were also Jewish *Wehrmacht* veterans. I primarily traveled throughout Germany and Austria, interviewing such men and collecting the historical documents they provided me. My ADHD-brain enjoyed every minute of it, and daily I awoke excited about the new adventure, or rather, the new hunt, I was about to undertake. Also, learning how the Nazis had documented men of Jewish descent (*Jüdische Mischlinge*) enabled me to discover more archival material.[694] I would then use a CD I had of the entire German telephone book and wrote to people whose names I had found. I sometimes sent over 100 letters a week to find new leads. Often, when writing families, I could not locate the person in question, but my initial contact would lead me to another *Mischling* who had military service. In the archives, I researched Jewish names that led me to document hundreds more.

During the fall and winter of 1994-95, I resided in Berlin and studied at *Die Neue Schule* language institute. Because many interviewees lived in Berlin, I scheduled meetings there on weekdays. I also frequented the *Deutsche Dienststelle* in Berlin, which housed a database on World War II soldiers. On weekends, I traveled to other cities to interview veterans I had contacted during the week utilizing a Eurail train ticket. When on trains, I adopted the habit of sitting next to elderly folks, and during conversations with them, found half a dozen new cases during this year. Because my methods were yielding so many successes, I realized this was bigger than my doubting professors believed.

Using my bike in a city was always faster than taking the bus or underground systems—and it saved me money. Sometimes, I could conduct two to three interviews in a day. And often, biking, quite simply, was the only way to get to someone. But biking also required me to carry a fresh set of clean clothes in case I sweated too much or got rained on.

I once biked around 100 miles round-trip to reach Alexander Stahlberg, Field Marshal Erich von Manstein's adjutant, who lived in a castle in the town of Gartow.[695] Stahlberg was of Jewish descent and claimed Manstein also had Jewish ancestry. Moreover, Stahlberg told me I could stay in his home and that I better hurry since, "I have one foot in the grave and one on a banana peel. If you want to interview me, you better *Mach schnell*."

When I looked on a map to see where Gartow was, the closest train link I found was at Wittenberge, 100 miles northwest of Berlin. Gartow was 40 miles of rural roads away from Wittenberge. That was a long distance to bike with 40 pounds of equipment, especially over dirt roads. But, my ADHD-brain said, "No problem." Being 6'2", over 200 pounds and physically fit, helped me bike to appointments, and carry documents. This methodology of conducting historical research was unorthodox. Professor Turner later claimed I was the only student he ever had who created his own archive.

On 3 December 1994, I took the train to Wittenberge and arrived in the afternoon. Since this was northern Europe, the sun went down a little after four in the afternoon and I soon found myself biking in the dark. Half-way to Stahlberg's castle, I turned onto a dirt road. Every 30 minutes or so, I would stop, pull out my map, and verify I was on the right road using a small flashlight. The light on my front wheel would frequently turn off when I rolled over rough gravel. This was especially hazardous on the dirt paths with no streetlamps. Once when this occurred and I had not seen a pothole, my bike's front tire dropped down into it, stopping the bike abruptly and flipping me over the handlebars. When I hit the earth, the weight of my pack slammed my chest and face into the road's surface. The metallic taste of blood oozed into my mouth, and I rolled onto my side to regain my wind. I unstrapped my backpack, moved it and my bike off the road, waited for my lungs to fill back with air and gazed at the stars. I asked myself, "What are you doing?" As I sat there dusting off myself, I again heard Stahlberg's voice in my head saying that he had one foot in the grave and one on a banana peel, so I put my backpack on, mounted the bike and pushed forward. I was determined to get to him before he died and find more sources. My determination was emboldened by my ADHD-brain and gave me the drive necessary to barrel through obstacles like that dark road.

When I arrived at the castle, I was a disaster. I was sweaty, covered in dirt and had dried blood on my face. As I entered the courtyard, I could see Stahlberg open the front door and walk out on top of his steps. Displaying the military bearing of a Prussian officer, he was smartly dressed, wearing a tweed jacket, colorful bowtie and ironed slacks. His hair was neatly combed and parted on the side, and his face was clean shaven. As I got closer, my appearance surprised him. After describing my adventures, he said, "You probably would like a shower before dinner." I gratefully accepted, cleaned up, changed into fresh clothes and then had a lovely evening with him and his wife. I was glad I had not been deterred from my purpose!

After the meal, we moved to a separate room with a table which had numerous documents on it. Stahlberg brought out maps and showed me what Manstein did after Stalingrad with the hundreds of thousands of men under his command. He discussed Manstein's Jewish heritage, the Holocaust and the war in Russia. He gave me hundreds of documents. The following day, we walked around his estate talking about the war in Russia. After a few days, I packed my backpack which now weighed over 60 pounds, mounted my bike and returned to the station using the paved, northern route instead of the southern one I traveled from a few days before. I didn't want to hit those dirt roads again.

One month after visiting Stahlberg, his wife informed me he had died because of his frail health. This was one example of many that prompted me to interview as many men as possible before they took their stories to their graves, forever lost to history. Dozens of men I had previously interviewed died throughout this year, always leaving me with extreme gratitude that I had been able to interview them before death carried them away. A few times, I even interviewed men on their death beds. It made me wonder how many had died before I ever started this quest.

During the winter, spring and summer of 1995, I lived in Freiburg in southern Germany to be near the military archive there. I continued my German classes during the week at the Goethe Institute in town and traveled every weekend to interview more veterans. My dorm room started to overflow with material. What was unfolding before me excited my curiosity, and I continued to collect as many documents and conduct as many interviews as I could. By the summer of 1995, when I returned to Yale, I had interviewed more than 200 Jewish-*Wehrmacht* veterans and had documented hundreds more who had already died. My archive numbered over 10,000 pages of materials. I displayed numerous "trophies" from my hunts to mount on my walls, including documents about high-ranking *Wehrmacht* officers who Hitler had "Aryanized." For example, "half-Jew" Erhard Milch became a field marshal and ran the *Luftwaffe*. I interviewed his daughter and one of his Nuremberg Trial interrogators, and gathered information no one else had.[696] "Quarter-Jew" Bernhard Rogge became a vice-admiral and was the most successful WWII surface raider captain sinking or capturing 150,000 metric tons of shipping. I interviewed his widow, a nephew and two of his close friends, and was able to collect more documents about him.[697] And last, "half-Jew" Helmut Wilberg became a *General der Flieger* in the *Luftwaffe* and had developed the operational concept of *Blitzkrieg*. I met Wilberg's son and daughter and gathered papers from them.[698] In short, I found that many in my research were not "curious anomalies," but had played significant military roles.

When I started my senior year in August 1995, I met with Professor Turner. I took a cache of documents, some of which had Hitler's signatures, to show him. Entering Turner's office, I opened my bag and placed documents, a sword, a Luger pistol, medals and photographs on his desk. Turner asked, "Where in the world did you get all this?" I explained my adventures. Much of the history I showed him, especially a list that one of Hitler's adjutants had put together that named numerous high-ranking officers of Jewish descent, shocked him. I asked, "Now will you be my senior essay advisor?" He replied, "Ok, you have convinced me."

During this year, I worked hard in my courses, improving my writing and research skills. In December of 1995, my college Rabbi, James Ponet, who had also supported my work with a scholarship (the Horowitz Award), wanted me to go with one of his staff to pick up a guest lecturer, Michael Berenbaum, who was going to speak to us about developing the Holocaust Museum in Washington, D.C. and Steven Spielberg's *Shoah* Foundation.[699] I had been a member of Yale's Hillel Jewish Life Center since 1992 and Ponet wanted to help me grow my contacts. I sat next to Berenbaum at dinner before the lecture, and took this opportunity to discuss my project with him.

As I did when meeting Turner, I selected key documents to share with Berenbaum. He patiently listened to my stories, read my documents and debated my estimation that more than 150,000 men of Jewish descent served in the *Wehrmacht*.[700] Berenbaum was polite, but like Turner, very skeptical. However, he issued this challenge: "I don't think you will find much. But, if you turn this into a PhD, get in touch. I will then want to read your dissertation." I replied, "Yes, sir, I'll do so." Later, I listened to his incredible lecture thinking, "I hope one day I too can become a lecturer and help people learn from the past."

My hyper-focused ADHD-mind went into high gear and throughout that year, I continued to write people in Germany to gather additional material. Every school break, I returned to *Deutschland* and conducted interviews and collected more documents. In the fall of 1995, I had the honor to meet and interview the former chancellor of Germany, Helmut Schmidt, who was a "quarter-Jew" and a *Luftwaffe* officer. He was so impressed with my work that he wrote me an endorsement letter. During the winter break, I met the famous Nazi-hunter, Simon Wiesenthal, in Vienna in January 1996. When I told him about my research, instead of supporting my work, he told me not to write about it. I wondered why, and he replied that the investigation would be misused. I asked, "How can the truth be misused?" I don't remember his answer, but it did not convince me.[701] And by the end of my Yale studies, I was well known in the history department for documenting a new chapter of WWII.

Here I am with Helmut Schmidt, the former chancellor of West Germany, after interviewing him about being a "quarter-Jew" and a *Luftwaffe* officer. 22 November 1995

Nonetheless, although I graduated with honors in history, had received an A- on my senior essay, been awarded the McKim Prize for unique research and won the prestigious Henry Fellowship to study at Cambridge, Turner still did not think I could become a historian and had even tried to block my scholarship. Well, not to be deterred, I decided I would do more research and perfect my writing while in England. Unlike Turner, one of my Cambridge professors, Jonathan Steinberg, gave me extra time to help me develop the skills I needed to become a successful historian. To paraphrase Dr. Hallowell, listen to those who encourage you and ignore those who don't believe in you.[702]

At Cambridge, Steinberg was so intrigued with my research that he came up with a brilliant idea to expand my investigation. He had a former student, Tim King, who was a journalist with the newspaper *The London Telegraph*. He convinced King to do a lengthy article on my work. Steinberg had two reasons for doing so. Firstly, the story would give me and the project international visibility and reach many people I otherwise would never have exposure to. Otherwise, I could only do so much research since I was able to focus only on one person at a time. Using mass media, I could reach thousands who could help by responding directly to me after reading the article. Secondly, since I needed more scholarships to conduct further research, positive publicity would give me credibility when I applied for such awards.

On 3 December 1996, the article came out on the front-page under the title *Secret of Hitler's Jewish Soldiers Uncovered*.[703] The article commanded three full pages of the newspaper. The response was so great, the newspaper did a follow-up article the next day. After that, my phone rang off the hook and numerous letters poured into my mailbox. The mailman knew me by my first name within a week's time after delivering a few hundred letters. The BBC interviewed me, and follow-up articles were printed in the *Los Angeles Times, New York Times, Die Zeit* and others worldwide. And it indeed helped me receive scholarships to conduct research in Germany. Steinberg's plan worked beautifully.

My Cambridge University professor Jonathan Steinberg. The Henry Fellowship I received from Yale gave me the option to study at either Oxford or Cambridge. Paul Kennedy, my Yale professor, told me, "Choose Cambridge; Steinberg is your man," and boy was he ever. Steinberg guided me in my learning using the British tutorial method, which was ideal for my ADHD-brain. He helped me grow my archive for my work *Hitler's Jewish Soldiers* and taught me the value of exploring new ideas and tough subjects. He got me on the front-page of *The London Telegraph* in 1996 which helped me gather thousands of pages of primary sources and establish contact with dozens of interview partners who all helped shed new light on this unknown chapter of history. MCT/SIPA USA/PA Images

He also stood by me when I got hate mail. For example, in response to an aggressive attack by a Dr. Lisl Goodman who had published a demeaning article about me in the *Sarasota Herald Tribune*, Steinberg responded professionally but firmly to her when she questioned my methods.[704] He answered her question, "Since when is Hitler's racist definition of 'who is a Jew' recognized by historians?" with his typical dry sarcasm and scholarly acumen writing,

The answer is since 14 November 1935, when '*die 1. Verordnung zum Reichsbürgergesetz*' appeared in the *Reichsgesetzblatt* and made the racist (actually religious) definition of the Jew definable by the number of Jewish grandparents an essential part of the legal framework of the German Reich.[705]

When she questioned my methods and said it was only a theory, Steinberg once again dropped the hammer, writing:

[The story of the German soldiers of Jewish descent] is as much a part of the historical past as anything else and needs to be understood. Rigg has no 'theory'; he has facts. They may be uncomfortable, but they are facts and facts are what historians ought to recognize.[706]

Not surprisingly, Goodman never responded to Steinberg's letter. With such a mentor and advocate, my research blossomed and I was honored to have him teach and defend me.

I also had scholars in Germany attack me, most notably Winfried Meyer and Wolfgang Benz. Meyer accused me of taking material from one of his books to write my master's thesis. Luckily, while working with *The London Telegraph*, the photographer who was traveling with me, Ian Jones, had documented me at the very archive Meyer accused me of never visiting, having taken pictures of me there. Furthermore, I had the order slip for the file he said I never looked at. Nonetheless, Cambridge, in response to Meyer's accusations, had to do an investigation. I had made mistakes in my citations, but luckily, the very errors I had made in citing Meyer properly, he had *actually also done in his work* titled *Unternehmen Sieben* that he said I had used to "steal" sources from.[707] Eventually, Cambridge absolved me of any wrongdoing. Through it all, Steinberg coached me on how to handle these people. What was my mistake? Instead of citing his book, I had thanked Meyer in a footnote for pointing me in the right direction toward where I could find a source. Now that was innocent enough, but when Meyer then accused me of not even looking at the source archive myself and just appropriating the information from his book, then that became a serious accusation. This might seem minor to the reader, but as the old adage says, "In academia, the fights are so vicious because the stakes are so low."[708] I learned from this experience, so when I submitted *Hitler's Jewish Soldiers* to my publisher, my book had almost 300 pages of footnotes and 270 pages of text. My editor, Mike Briggs, told me that in the history of publishing, my book would be the first with more pages of footnotes than text pages and that I needed to cut it down. I did whittle it down to 106 pages of footnotes, but my experience with Meyer made me hyper-focused on being anal-retentive about citing all and any source that I ever laid eyes on. Today, I have a reputation of being a footnote enthusiast *extraordinaire*.

As was the case with Meyer, historian Benz used his institute's yearbook to attack me and question my historical findings. Once again, Steinberg was by my side and berated Benz for his unwarranted criticism. In regards to Benz, his is a bizarre case. Due to recent controversies when Benz invited anti-Semites like Sabine Schiffer to speak at his center and when it was revealed he had kept secret that his mentor, Karl Bosl, was a Nazi, his sources need to be used with care and his character questioned. Even when confronted that the public knew about Bosl, Benz refused to distance himself from his "Nazi doctoral supervisor" or condemn this man who was a "high-level member of the Nazi party and an energetic ideologue of Hitler." He even failed to recognize the danger of Islamic fanatics, equating anti-Semitism with "Islamophobia." Due to these controversies, he had to leave his research center at the Technical University in Berlin.[709] So knowing these facts, and that Benz supported Meyer's attacks against me, I take pride that I worked tirelessly on my rebuttals to both of them, winning my case.

Throughout these struggles with Meyer and Benz, I never gave up and continued to focus on my work. I knew that once I could put these assaults behind me, I could get on with documenting history. My ADHD-drive helped me stay on track. These events illustrate that life often gives one hardships, but never surrender when you can still fight. You must always get up one time more than the number of times you have been knocked down. That is what my ADHD had taught me.

World renowned Holocaust scholar Michael Berenbaum. He has supported me throughout the years and has inspired me to continue to be a better scholar, writer and human being. Back in 2002, he encouraged me to research and write *The Rabbi Saved by Hitler's Soldiers* and wrote its Foreword. Since he also struggles with learning disabilities, (ADHD and dyslexia), he encouraged me to write this ADHD-book. Photo Credit: Michael Berenbaum

For years, I worked hard to transcribe my interviews, organize documents, make notecards and write my PhD thesis. Moreover, I sent early drafts of my manuscript to interview partners, getting their feedback (over 100 of them reviewed it). When I had a working draft in 2001, I got back in touch with Berenbaum and asked if he remembered our conversation. He did and reviewed my work and was "shocked" by the information I had found. He wrote a fantastic review which, in part, stated: "Startling and unexpected, Rigg's study conclusively demonstrates the degree of flexibility in German policy toward the *Mischlinge*, the extent of Hitler's involvement, and, most important, that not all who served in the armed forces were anti-Semitic, even as their service aided the killing process. An invaluable contribution."

My book *Hitler's Jewish Solders* was the lead title for the University Press of Kansas' spring catalogue for 2002. In 2003, it received the William E. Colby Award for the best book on military history for the previous year. Renowned military historian Sir John Keegan wrote: "The revelation that Germans of Jewish blood, knowing the Nazi regime for what it was, served Hitler as uniformed members of his armed forces must come as a profound shock. [Rigg's work] will surprise even professional historians of the Nazi years."

My PhD was conferred in February 2002, and my thesis was published as a book in April of that year. Thereafter, I went on a lecture tour just as I had hoped when I had listened to Berenbaum in 1995. Also, in the spring of 2002, NBC *Dateline* aired a documentary on my work called *Hidden in Plain Sight*. During the program, Berenbaum said my methods to gather sources showed the "Triumph of Perseverance." I also received the *William E. Colby Award* for the best military history book for that year. All my years of hard work, academic fights and painful bike rides were paying off, and I had my ADHD, in part, to thank for it.

During this time, several Farmer-like professors who had doubted my abilities came around to support me. For example, after *Hitler's Jewish Soldiers* was published, Yale threw a party for me at the behest of Dean Brodhead. Many professors, deans and writing tutors who had helped me attended---even Professor Turner. After I spoke, people started to tell "Bryan Rigg stories." They talked about the thief I apprehended at Yale in 1993, or the time I rappelled off the main tower in Silliman in front of people's classrooms in 1992—all very ADHD-like activities. We laughed a lot, and people were so kind to welcome me back as a "favored son."

Then Turner's turn came to speak. My heart rate rose. He, unlike the others, stood up. As always, he was immaculately dressed. He looked around the room with a wry smile. He held up my book with many pages marked with post-it tags and then declared, "I've a confession to make." I swallowed hard and looked at my academic advisor, Susan Hauser, who knew about the whole saga with him. She smiled and her clear eyes told me to be calm. Turner continued:

> "I'm glad Bryan didn't listen to me many years ago. For had he listened to me, this first-rate piece of scholarship would've never been written. My compliments, Bryan, on an excellent work on German history."

With that, he smiled, nodded to me and sat down. I could not believe my ears. Turner was a brilliant historian and demanding teacher not known for being kind. This was one of my proudest moments, when despite Turner's discouragement throughout the years, I had persisted. And for a professor who never admitted a mistake, for him to do so in a public forum, was amazing, gracious and impressive. My

ADHD had told me years before to take up the challenge and it had not been wrong. I not only persevered, but I was also a huge success. Turner's compliments were my crowning glory up to that point of becoming a scholar.

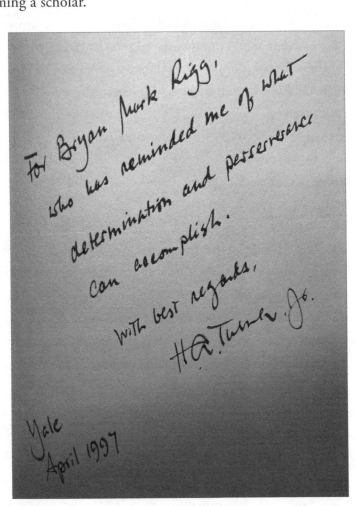

Professor Turner's note to me written in the front page of his book *Hitler's Thirty Days to Power: January 1933* which he gave me as a gift. Turner was not known to give compliments and it was rare for him to write such words of praise.

Professor Henry Ashby Turner, Jr., one of my Yale professors, is considered to be one of the most distinguished scholars of German history of the 20th century. His works include *German Big Business and the Rise of Hitler, Hitler's Thirty Days to Power: January 1933* and *Germany from Partition to Reunification.* He taught me how to search for primary sources and never compromise by looking for what one wanted to find, but rather, to report the findings so discovered. For his scholarship, he received the Commanders Cross of the Order of Merit *(Bundesverdienstkreuz)* from the Federal Republic of Germany. Photo Credit: Turner Family

Dean Brodhead also recognized my abilities. In a recommendation, he wrote, in part:

> While in college, Bryan became interested in the phenomenon of Jews and descendants of Jews who served in Hitler's army. Few people suspected that there even were such people, but by dint of resolution and persistence, Bryan succeeded in tracking such figures down and bringing a hidden corner of history to light. I was sufficiently impressed by his project that I found funds to support his research early on. As the project has matured, Bryan's work has won acceptance and admiration from a wide range of distinguished experts. Making a historical discovery of this sort is no ordinary feat for a person in his or her early twenties. But Bryan did far more than have a bright idea. In

characteristic fashion, he delivered the whole force of his mind and character to following the idea through.[710]

This ability to deliver the "whole force of [my] mind and character" resulted from having an ADHD-mind, and I am honored that Brodhead recognized this attribute of mine. Having the praise from scholars like Turner and Brodhead, and many others, strengthened my confidence and made me aware that I was indeed a scholar and could explore topics in unique and powerful ways. My next project would prove this once again.

Research for *The Rabbi Saved by Hitler's Soldiers*

After I finished my book *Hitler's Jewish Soldiers*, I decided to revisit an essay I had written for a Yale undergraduate course on the Holocaust taught by Professor Hyman in 1995. I later expanded this essay into my MA at Cambridge in 1997. For years, Hyman, Berenbaum and Steinberg had encouraged me to develop the story into a book, which I dutifully did.

In 1992, I came across the story of a "half-Jew" and *Wehrmacht* Major, Ernst Bloch, and how he had, at the behest of the U.S. government, rescued the "Pope of the Jewish world," Rebbe Joseph Isaac Schneersohn. The story seemed unbelievable. Schneersohn led the largest Hasidic community in the world called Chabad, but also known as Lubavitch. Bloch served as an intelligence officer in the *Wehrmacht*'s Secret Service called the *Abwehr*.

Historians and journalists have examined Schneersohn's rescue from various angles. However, my work was the only study that synthesized sources from the Lubavitchers, German and American archives, and oral and written testimonies into a single account. This information appeared for the first time in my book *Rescued from the Reich* published by Yale University Press in 2004. Thereafter, new documents about the rescue, especially about Max Rhoade (the leading lobbyist in Washington D.C., supporting this rescue) and Bloch, surfaced. These were included in a second edition re-titled *The Rabbi Saved by Hitler's Soldiers* in 2016.

Rebbe Joseph Isaac Schneersohn (1880-1950). He was the sixth Lubavitcher Rebbe and was rescued by Nazi military officers during WWII. It was probably one of the most remarkable rescues of the Holocaust. In this picture, he is sitting at his desk in Brooklyn in 1949. He was a religious fanatic and a bigot.

"Half-Jewish" Major Ernst Bloch (later Colonel). The horrible wound on his face is quite pronounced although he had several surgeries to repair it. He took a bayonet through his mouth and jaw in WWI. He received Hitler's *Deutschblütigkeitserklärung* (German-Blood Declaration) and worked in the German Secret Service *(Abwehr)* under Admiral Canaris. He saved Rebbe Schneersohn and a group of his followers and family members.

To conduct research, I interviewed dozens of eyewitnesses, collected thousands of pages of documents made available to me in people's homes and researched thousands more in public and private archives in the U.S., Israel, Germany and England. It took me over 20 years to collect everything I did to write the story.

I describe how I negotiated this complex labyrinth to collect my sources to help the reader understand my ADHD-research mind. With the Hunter-ADHD-brain, I followed every path, scent and footprint that might yield information. Berenbaum describes me as "an archive rat." If there is a source to find, I will find it, and again, I have my ADHD-Hunter-mind to thank for this. However, this ADHD-brain often gets me in trouble, as you saw with *Hitler's Jewish Soldiers*. This happened once again during the investigation of the Rebbe.

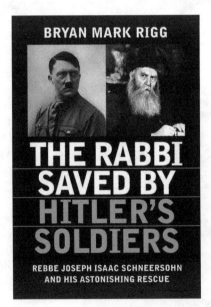

Cover of *The Rabbi Saved by Hitler's Soldiers*. According to historian Michael Berenbaum, my book documents one of the most remarkable WWII rescues. Berenbaum wrote, "Were this story a novel, it would have the character of an implausible fable, but as often occurred in the Holocaust, reality exceeds the imagination."

In my research, I found that the Rebbe was a weak leader who missed countless opportunities to rescue lives because of his religious convictions. Ironically, my research here turned some beliefs about the

Holocaust upside down. My investigation showed a few Nazi soldiers and diplomats being the "good guys" in the effort to save Jews, and Chabad rabbis and Lubavitch hierarchy being the "bad guys" triggering division within the American-Jewish community and failing to rescue Jews who were suffering and dying under Hitler. In short, the Lubavitchers caused a lot of unneeded bickering and disunity within different religious groups trying to facilitate rescue efforts instead of focusing on saving more Jewish lives. They caused this chaos by condemning the bulk of American Jewry, especially Reform Jews, and their leadership for their theology and religious practices instead of uniting with them to rescue *all* Jews suffering under Hitler. As one can imagine, this account of this discord did not win me friends in the Lubavitch movement. Jews are *always* supposed to be the good guys, and the Nazis are *always* supposed to be the bad guys. However, my research often showed that things were not always as they seemed during the Third Reich and history never plays out in black and white schematics. Life is never simple, and humans are complicated creatures. When studying history, therefore, one will encounter many gray zones.

My experience with the Lubavitchers was frustrating and not dissimilar to the experiences of many other scholars who have found their condemnation of Reform and Conservative Judaism *reprehensible*, their theology that preaches Gentiles are inferior creations of God *abhorrent*, their claim that non-Orthodox Jews caused the Holocaust *false*, and their belief that their leaders and doctrines are superior *primitive*—Lubavitchers, in many respects, are racist, bigoted Jews.[711]

Well, my ADHD-brain, which is informed by my belief that we must protect human rights, does not like it when I see discrimination in any form. And here we have an ultra-religious, Jewish group practicing discrimination. I wanted to know why and I started searching for answers.

Their ahistorical approach reveals itself when the record of events detracts from their organization's image. When something reflects negatively on them, they claim it is a false interpretation of the documents, an explanation from those who hate them, or an indication of inadequate understanding of their movement. For them, to question their Rebbe is "worse than sin." Moreover, when they do not like something in the documents, they often censor the material. They have also fabricated sources when they think they can get away with it.[712] As historian David Myers observes, modern critical thought has challenged traditional Judaism by encouraging Orthodox Jews to depart from the "tenets of inherited faith. The more one knew about the past, the more reasons there were for abandoning it."[713]

When the Lubavitchers let me into their community, they failed to see I was taught to question everything as a person with ADHD and as a secular historian. I came to their community with an open mind intent on reporting facts. I have done my best to remain faithful to that goal. However, as I challenged their theology, I received threats to destroy my reputation, and one rabbi said I better not ever show my face in their neighborhood, or else!

Knowing that some of what I uncovered was unflattering about their history, I did not expect to make all the Lubavitchers happy, but I was shocked by some individuals' responses. I was offered money if I took out everything negative about the Rebbe. I was told that if I only praised the Rebbe, I would have a book tour with honoraria from hundreds of communities, making me rich. Instead of giving in to such inducements, I stuck to the truth. I was even threatened with lawsuits if I talked derisively about the Rebbe. I think my ADHD taught me not to fear such things, so I ignored the threats. During many talks, Lubavitchers exclaimed I was committing "*lashon hora*" ("evil tongue"). How could I, a mere mortal, question Rebbe Schneersohn? When I told Professor Hyman about this, she responded, "These people are nuts. Just ignore their threats and stick to the facts. Facts always protect you."

I think my ADHD-way of looking for patterns allowed me to understand Hyman's opinion and to see these people for what they were—religious zealots without the ability to use reason to study their past. And I did indeed set the historical record straight, and for that, I became a *persona non grata* in this community. I did show with remarkable clarity that it was people like the Rebbe who not only did not rescue but rather also prevented the rescue of Jews during WWII. In the end, most Americans for various reasons also behaved the opposite of what was required to save Jewish lives suffering under the Third Reich from 1933 through 1945; some remained silent out of ignorance, some out of anti-Semitism and some out of religious bigotry. My book showed the latter conclusively when studying the Lubavitchers during World War II.

I guess I am living proof of what Dr. Hallowell said ADHD-types are often like; i.e., agents for change.[714] Moreover, according to Berenbaum and Hyman, using my wacky ADHD-mind, I documented one of the most remarkable rescues of the entire war. I wrote this book, just like my first, with a lot of opposition, derision and controversy. But hey, that type of excitement is what my ADHD-mind craves, and often, in the throes of my research, I can see the larger picture of an event that others might miss. To quote Reinald Rose from his play *Twelve Angry Men*, "It takes a great deal of courage to stand alone."[715] Often, ADHD-people have to stand alone because they see the world differently. Changing people's views about sacred beliefs is tough, but my ADHD-mind seems to enjoy the challenge of doing so.

Research for *Flamethrower*

When my second book about the Rebbe's rescue was published in 2016, I had already begun research on another work. I was both excited and relieved as I was certain that my new topic would steer me clear of any possibility of a controversy. Although I knew my

ADHD-brain would bring a fresh analysis to this project, I was confident that I would not uncover anything controversial as I had in my previous books. Boy, was I in for a surprise! This new project would launch me into the biggest academic, and legal fight of my life.

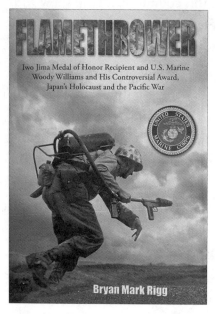

Iwo Jima Medal of Honor Recipient and U.S. Marine Woody Williams and His Controversial Award, Japan's Holocaust and the Pacific War

Bryan Mark Rigg

My book *Flamethrower* received the endorsements of two Marine Corps Commandants, General Al Gray and General Charles Krulak, and a former CentCom Commander, USMC General Anthony Zinni. General Kurlak wrote, in part, about the book: "Rigg has done something most authors of 'war stories' are totally incapable of doing in *Flamethrower*...he has neatly tied all three levels of conflict into a single package (i.e. tactical, operational and strategic) and done so in a magnificent manner...And in the cases of both General Kuribayashi and Corporal Williams (the two main characters of the book), as with every combatant on Iwo Jima, Rigg shows that neither was a saint nor a sinner. Each had his own flaws that have been masterfully researched and documented by the author."

In 2015, when I started my research into the war in the Pacific in WWII, which would eventually culminate in the publishing of *Flamethrower*, my intention was to both venerate and highlight the U.S. Marine Corps and this period in U.S. history. I wanted to honor one particular hero from the Iwo Jima battle, U.S. Marine and Medal of Honor recipient Woody Williams. I also wanted to study General Tadamichi Kuribayashi, who commanded the Japanese Iwo Jima forces and is reputed to be one of the toughest Imperial Japanese Army (IJA) leaders our Allied command encountered. Not surprisingly, though, along the way, I uncovered troubling facts about both warriors, causing me to struggle with a different sort of battle: The pursuit of evidence against self-interest. As always, my ADHD-mind focused on revealing evidence.

Initially, I expected to present Woody without flaws, and Kuribayashi as an ethical and ingenious leader. Unfortunately, I discovered Woody's autobiographical reporting to have many discrepancies, and uncovered horrible atrocities committed by Kuribayashi. If I could have presented Woody without failings, there would have been Marine Corps events honoring Woody accompanied by much fanfare. Likewise, if I could have written about Kuribayashi without his criminal past, the Japanese government and society most likely would have supported my work "praising" *their* hero as they did when Clint Eastwood's film *Letters from Iwo Jima* came out in 2006 glorifying Kuribayashi. Just as people had discouraged my pursuit of researching *Hitler's Jewish Soldiers* and others had encouraged me to falsify my findings for *The Rabbi Saved by Hitler's Soldiers*, I was told by many, even by two Marine generals, not to reveal my findings about Woody and Kuribayashi. They wanted me to bury history, but my ethics and ADHD-mind refused to let me do so. If one fails to honor the truth and remember the victims of the past, he desecrates history.[716]

First, let me describe the controversies with Kuribayashi. His grandson and prominent Japanese Liberal Democratic Party (LDP) politician Yoshitaka Shindo was interviewed for this book. Once he saw I was uncovering his grandfather's criminal past, he tried to discredit me with some of my U.S. contacts by rescinding what he had revealed to me, apparently, in a moment of weakness during the interview I conducted with him in April 2018.[717] Shindo even told the Iwo Jima American Association he would close Iwo Jima to American tourists in 2019 if its members did not force me to adhere to his demands (a violation of the 1968 agreement between the U.S. and Japan).[718] I later learned I should not have been surprised by Shindo's behavior because he is not only a right-wing nationalist, but also a member of *Nippon Kaigi* (a sort of "Japanese Holocaust" denial group) that disavows that Japan committed World War II atrocities.[719] This book and perhaps the potential political fallout seemed to have him worried.

Shindo may have also taken offense when I challenged him on not doing enough to conduct DNA testing on the human remains found today on Iwo Jima. There are hundreds of MIA (Missing-in-Action) Marines whose bones are in this battlefield. He is one of the most prominent politicians who supports Japan's efforts to gather the fallen and cremate them, adhering to Japanese religious death rituals.[720] Shindo admitted *no DNA-testing* is being done on the skeletons found and did not take kindly when I told him that this was wrong (ADHD-minds tend not to have filters).[721] Apparently, when bones are found on Iwo, they are put together in a pile, set on fire and offered up to Shinto gods. Unfortunately, probably several Marines' remains have been improperly burned along with their enemies. If Shindo was offended by these questions, that might explain why he tried to hinder my research. I have consistently encountered people who have tried to prevent my research throughout life, so I was not surprised by Shindo's behavior. As soon as I felt Shindo was reluctant to discuss his grandfather's past, my ADHD-mind smelled blood, and I looked into the general's past with more determination.

Next, I discovered that Medal of Honor (MOH) recipient Woody Williams should have never received his medal. Due to his self-reporting, with numerous inaccuracies, I found countless cases where Woody misled people about his life. Unfortunately, his Sea Tales made it into the official record. But in the summer of 1945, upon seeing the inconsistencies that I was now uncovering in 2018, the Fleet Marine Force commander, Lieutenant General Roy S. Geiger, and the Pacific Fleet commander, Fleet Admiral Chester

Nimitz, and their boards tried to block Williams from receiving the MOH. Nonetheless, due to political pressure, the normal process of awarding Williams the Medal of Honor was bypassed. Geiger and Nimitz were removed from that process and it was fast-tracked through the channels in Washington in order to quickly award this medal due to pressure put on the Secretary of the Navy by the White House. In other words, the process of review and approval was such a huge mess that under normal circumstances the medal should never have been awarded to him.

Woody Williams and the author at the *USNS Hershel "Woody" Williams* ship-christening ceremony on 21 October 2017 at San Diego.

When all this conflicting information surfaced about Williams and the narrative of his heroic acts that led President Truman to award him the MOH in October 1945, he and his family attempted to prevent my book's publication first by threats and then by litigation.[722] Williams tried, unconstitutionally one might add, to silence me through prior restraint of my book's publication by filing a federal lawsuit against me.[723] My attorneys responded to his intimidations thusly: "Your threats to tortiously interfere with Mr. Rigg's book contract are…unlawful" and "violate the First Amendment [of the U.S. Constitution]."[724] Luckily, the Judge in the U.S. Federal Court of West Virginia in Charleston thwarted Woody's attempt to prevent the book's publication when he denied Williams' request for a temporary restraining order. Moreover, leading scholars in America supported me, including UCLA professor and constitutional law expert, Eugene Volokh, who filed an *amicus* brief with the court. Williams would be wise to adhere to Thomas Jefferson's mandate, which says: "Our Liberty depends on freedom of the press. And that cannot be limited without being lost."[725] After I completed three years and thousands of hours of painstaking research preparing the final manuscript, which included trips to Iwo and other locations, Williams attempted to force me to give him censoring rights.[726] And lastly, he also demanded to be *personally* financially compensated for his story rather than using book proceeds to support his charitable organization, something initially offered. Although we discussed the possibilities of sharing royalties, Williams' terms were unacceptable. Moreover, as became clear as I started to see problems with Williams' self-reporting, had I allowed him to have the final say on this book, there would have been much misinformation placed in this work. I found Williams' obsession with trying to control his narrative suspicious. Unfortunately, my research would show many problems with his history, and I was wise to keep my autonomy as a historian. While I prevailed in court, the road ahead would be fraught with continued obstacles to getting the book published.

As a result of these controversies, Regnery Publishing declined to publish this book, fearing legal retribution.[727] I then took my manuscript to the University Press of Kansas, which had published three of my books. My factual assertions were backed by research, and I had documented Williams' story as a public figure. Although the university's legal department found nothing wrong with the scholarship, the press became uncomfortable with publishing a work against which Williams had threatened litigation. Although my editor had communicated her commitment to publishing the book, other staff members put pressure on her to rescind their offer unless I omitted certain sections. Rather than supporting my research and the freedom of speech, the press chose to avoid controversy and declined to move forward. Next, I went to Stackpole Books, and despite the problems with Williams, it decided to work with me. Once again, Williams pursued his legal bombardment against me and along with his grandsons and legal team continued to attack me and my now third publisher. My findings were being litigated in a federal court and the conflict between Williams and me now made the rounds throughout the media.[728] When Williams directly threatened to take on Stackpole Books, the higher-ups got nervous and asked me to *actually* mislead the public and write a piece that would stop the legal action (i.e., not reveal the truth).[729] I could not do so because it would mislead my readers by not revealing the truth. I then went to the self-publishing arm of Simon & Schuster called Archway Publishing. At first, they wanted to publish the book, but once again, the executives got scared and decided while there was pending litigation, they did not want to expose the company to potential legal ramifications, so they chose not to publish my work.[730] As a result, I set up my own publishing company, Fidelis Historia, in order to get this book printed. My ADHD-mind and the lessons Mary Stewart had taught me so long ago to be a contrarian kicked in once again, and I became hyper-focused on finding a way to publish my findings. I have adhered to the principles espoused by my cantankerous Yale Professor Henry Turner: *Follow the evidence* wherever it goes and present conclusions based on *empiricism*.

It was a struggle to gather the truth and finally publish *Flamethrower*, but it faithfully portrays the Japanese soldiers and U.S. Marines whose stories are told therein. One would think that the problems I encountered in the land of James Madison and Thomas Jefferson who helped form and write the First Amendment to the U.S. Constitution guaranteeing the freedom of speech and of the press would not exist today in America.[731] Ultimately, as historians Philip A. Crowl and Jeter A. Isely at Princeton University wrote, "History is of value only if it helps to solve pending and future problems."[732] But if one does not reveal the untarnished truth of these "problems" because to do so might offend someone, then future problems cannot be solved.

As you may imagine, *Flamethrower* was written with much soul-searching, heartache and many a sleepless night. Without my ADHD-mind, I probably would not have found the truth during this study, and I would not have had the drive to self-publish the work.

As a historian, I believe in two principles: It is better to deal with uncomfortable truths rather than beautiful lies if we want to learn from history, and we should rise above threats to censor the truth. As I have quoted Thomas Jefferson earlier in the text, "There is not a truth existing which I fear…or would wish unknown to the whole world."[733] My works have followed Jefferson's mandate of facing the facts without fear. In the face of controversy surrounding some of my books' content, I consulted numerous experts, both general historians and those specializing in military history, to verify that what I discovered was correctly presented and analyzed. Experts have endorsed my books in their fields of study and I have benefited from their feedback, including three of the most distinguished generals the Marine Corps has produced: The 29th Commandant, General Al Gray, the 31st Commandant, General Charles C. Krulak and former CENTCOM commander General Anthony Zinni. The courage I needed to go to them and ask for their advice came, in part, from Mary from Starpoint, who taught me the benefit I could gain by listening to those who care about me and my projects. In the end, the major magazine of the Corps, the *Marine Corps Gazette* in 2020, and the Marine Corps periodical *Marine Corps History* in 2021 both wrote up glowing reviews of my work, giving it the kosher stamp of approval that my book was indeed a legitimate work of Marine Corps history.[734] The lesson of "never give up" that my ADHD had taught me was proven yet again.

The 31st USMC Commandant, General Charles C. Krulak, provided invaluable feedback and advice for *Flamethrower*. I was honored, too, that he wrote the book's Foreword. We both not only attended the same prep school, Phillips Exeter Academy, but we also resided in the same dorm, Peabody. He not only showed he lived by the Corps' motto of *Semper Fidelis* (Always Faithful) with his support of my work, but he also showed he lived by Exeter's motto of *Non Sibi* (not for oneself) in giving me countless hours supporting my research.

Research for *Conquering Learning Disabilities at Any Age*

And while doing research for this book, I once again experienced headaches. Although I had to set up my own publishing house, Fidelis Historia, to publish *Flamethrower*, I wanted to return to the traditional publishing world to publish *Conquering Learning Disabilities.* Although I liked the quality of work produced by doing my own publishing and the freedom of working at home, I also realized that some publishing houses just have better marketing and PR capabilities and are more successful in getting a new book out to the public. So, I decided I needed help in finding the best option for me. I elected to use Author One Stop run by Randy Peyser. She had developed this consulting firm that prided itself on getting book proposals and books to a professional level in order to then go and pitch them to traditional publishing houses. I told her about this book, and she became excited about the project. She felt enthusiastic not only about this book, but also about another I had been writing for the past 20 years on theology and the Third Reich. She quickly wanted my money to start the process of sending the drafts to her editors, asking them to evaluate the chances of successfully pitching the books to major publishers. After her two editors/gatekeepers said the books were excellent and she should take me on, she once more got excited and took more money from me to allow her to move to the next stage of getting my books ready for the publishing houses she had in mind. However, one of the reviewers of *Conquering Learning Disabilities* raised concerns about the issue surrounding Woody. When I talked to Ms. Peyser about this, I told her to look at the section herself and let me know her thoughts since I discovered, in the meantime, that she had not looked at anything I had written. When she did review that small section, she suddenly said she could no longer help me since I had named publishers that had refused to publish *Flamethrower.* I found her response strange and asked her about it and she said she did not want anything negative about any publishers mentioned in my book even if they behaved poorly. We, of course, parted ways.

After this negative experience with Peyser, I then went back to Archway, and its sister company, Balboa, both of which are under the parent organization called Authors Solutions. After explaining my projects to two gatekeepers, whom I really liked, they became excited about the prospect of working with me and started the process of onboarding me. However, once again, their content review team, headed by Trina Lee, found problems with *Conquering Learning Disabilities*. They wanted me to falsify the whole situation surrounding my abuse as a child and to remove content that would reveal the sex of my attacker, the place of my attack, the year and time of the attack, and any reference to any name that might disclose my attacker's whereabouts. Although I had police reports on this man and legal justification for mentioning him and protection in case he came after me, Ms. Lee refused to work with me on this manuscript unless I made the changes. She, and her team, also asked for a release permitting me to include information about my father although my book clearly stated he had been dead since 2006. They also wanted releases permitting me to use details from my own medical file that I had obtained from the Child Study Center in Fort Worth, Texas, although I had already provided them with the release information in the manuscript. And last, but not least, the content review team under Lee did not want anything discussed about my *Flamethrower* legal battles with Woody, something that had already been published in newspapers, magazines, periodicals and in the book itself. Obviously, Ms. Lee's team was very slapdash in their review techniques. So, once again, I decided to *adapt and improvise* and publish this book under my own imprint *Fidelis Historia*. My grandmother often told me if you wanted to do something right, do it yourself. Well, I learned this lesson in droves dealing with this company and two of its entities. In the end, this book has benefited from the research of one of the leading experts in ADHD, Dr. Edward "Ned" Hallowell, and his willingness to write a Foreword for the book giving it the kosher stamp of approval for being a book that adds to our ADHD-knowledge. Had

I relied on the traditional publishing world, then this book would have never happened. Again, when doing something worthwhile, one should never give up. ADHD-minds, in my opinion, do a better job of never giving up when they are focused on something---just make sure the activity is positive and worthwhile.

Conclusion

In conclusion, I have shared these stories behind the research and writing of three of my history books and this memoir/self-help book to demonstrate how an ADHD-mind can do valuable research, and how an ADHD-brain can persevere even in the face of adversity. Obviously, I benefited greatly from having intelligent and ethical people support me. Without my ADHD-Hunter-like-mind searching out the truth and sticking to my guns, I would have never received others' encouragement. What makes a book of scholarship worthwhile to the reader? It is a book that brings new information, insights and analysis to the subject matter being explored. Moreover, a good historian never cowers in the face of people telling him to give up or falsify history. Having dealt with ADHD, I had learned that I see things differently than most, but in seeing things differently, ironically, I manage to see things more clearly as they actually were and are. Seeing things in a novel light, and as they really are, is the greatest gift a writer can give his readership. Without ADHD, I would not have been able to do so. For this, I am grateful.

Takeaways

- An ADHD-mind can be used to do valuable research. My ADHD helped me document and write three major historical works. Each one of my projects encountered incredible opposition from experts and from some of the people documented, or their followers, due to the presentation of truths about an event that debunked established historical claims thought to be true. The ADHD-brain sees things differently, and quite often more clearly, enabling me to consider new angles and threads in my research.

- Often, ADHD-people have to stand alone because they see the world differently. Changing people's views about sacred beliefs is tough, but ADHD-minds seems to enjoy the challenge of doing so.

- Without my ADHD-Hunter-like mind searching out the truth and sticking to my guns, I would have never received others' encouragement.

Action Steps

- Don't be afraid to explore what your ADHD-mind sees in research or life that others don't see.

- Don't be afraid to stand alone in what you are pursuing and exploring. ADHD-types usually are unique in how they view things, so embrace this about yourself instead of avoiding it.

- Remember, when people tell you that you cannot do something, they often are telling you more about themselves than they are about you.

The London Telegraph's article on my work about "Hitler's Jewish Soldiers" which featured me on its front page on 3 December 1996. My backpack, equipment and bike that I used for my studies are seen here. The un-orthodox manner in which I conducted my research, or one might say, the ADHD-manner in which I conducted it, helped get me noticed by one of the most prestigious newspapers in the world.

CHAPTER 14:
ADHD and My Experience on Wall Street

"If you have a mind driven by curiosity and informed and tempered by the impulses of the heart, then your education, however you have achieved it, will continue to light your way."
— Harvard V. Knowles, Phillips Exeter Academy
Graduation Talk, 2003[735]

IN 2005, I HAD BEEN a college professor at American Military University and Southern Methodist University for almost five years and had come to realize that being an educator was a tough life to choose due to the limited budgets academic institutions have to pay their staff and teachers. Quite frankly, schools in general, not only universities, treat their teachers poorly when they do not offer them good salaries. If America was to do one thing to improve itself, it should focus on paying its secondary and college teachers twice as much as they presently earn. Finland and Luxembourg are excellent examples of what can happen for a society that financially and professionally rewards those who dedicate their lives to shaping the next generation. We should take care of people who focus on helping children. But I digress.

With the realization that being a teacher would barely provide for my growing family, I explored a field I had always been fascinated by, namely, finance. I was particularly interested in private wealth management. I consulted with friends in the industry, and from the end of 2005 through the beginning of 2006, I interviewed with nine

Wall Street firms. I received several offers, but I decided to join the Private Bank of the Swiss firm Credit Suisse. It offered an excellent six-month training program, half of which was spent at their American headquarters in New York City. I was excited! My starting salary was four times what I had earned as a professor. Since my main responsibility in this job was to meet people, my ADHD-personality loved it. Just as I took great pleasure in interviewing all those men in Germany to write my books, I was now able to go out and meet new people all the time, listen to their stories, gain their trust and help them manage their money. It was Hunter-like activity once again, and I thoroughly enjoyed it. It was a natural fit for someone with ADHD.

For three years, I thrived at Credit Suisse and led my class of 15 members, managing $100 million in assets. Compared to many seasoned "relationship managers" (what they called us), my book of business was small, but compared to the other Credit Suisse "freshmen," I felt I was doing well. My first boss, David Holmes, was good to me. He was a former Air Force officer and F-4 Phantom fighter pilot. Since I had also served in the military, we connected. He encouraged me and helped me learn the industry. Two years into my tenure, however, he became ill and had to leave. Credit Suisse brought in a new person, who many in the office called "Nazi," playing off the name he had that had a somewhat similar pronunciation, and accurately describing his character. He was a religious bigot, homophobic and sexist. He even made it a point to tell me when he found out about my Jewish background and my ethical humanist values that I was going to Hell. Of course, I embrace freedom of religion and freedom of speech just as every other American should, but his behavior in a professional setting was unethical and disturbing. With my typical ADHD-behavior (i.e., not having a filter), I let him know how I felt about him when he attacked my beliefs and ethnic background. Naively, I believed that since I was at the top of my class, I would be left alone as long as I avoided this new boss as much as possible, and just focused on my clients and bringing in assets.

When the subprime mortgage crisis hit us in 2008 and 2009, and the Dow Jones Industrial Average dropped from its high of 14,164.43 (9 Oct. 2007) to 6,594.44 (5 March 2009), Credit Suisse reduced its workforce by 15% (approximately 7,000 employees). Since my boss did not like me, I was one of the first of my class to be "let go" (administratively laid off). Since I managed the most assets among all other members of my class, it was clear that the man over me took this opportunity to get rid of me, not for performance, but out of spite. At least, this is what many colleagues who stayed in touch with me believed, as my colleague Bruce Lee in Chicago verified. I was shocked and devastated.

For three days, I was in a funk and did not know what to do. But then, my ADHD-brain kicked in. I had a roster of clients who had trusted me with their assets and depended on me for advice. I had three children to raise. I had a wife who looked to me for security and income. I was not going to let them down.

My ADHD-energy went into overdrive. Contacting several people in the industry, I learned how I could become an independent financial advisor. I worked 18-hour days for weeks and devoured all the literature I could to understand how to become an independent wealth professional. I called everyone I could to learn how best to set up my new organization. I made 10 to 20 calls daily. With help from the independent arm of Fidelity Investments (Institutional Wealth Services) and a registered investment advisor (RIA) here in Dallas, I was able to set up my firm within three weeks (Rigg Wealth Management, LLC). I transferred almost all my clients within two months. I became hyper-focused on getting my clients away from Credit Suisse, who had essentially abandoned them by leaving them orphaned without me, their quarterback, to take care of them. I firmly believe that this can-do attitude came from my ADHD, and it helped me get ramped up and energized to transform myself in a short amount of time. Moreover, being independent and taking my clients away from Credit Suisse was natural for me. (We ADHD-Hunters are independent creatures.) My income increased dramatically since I was not also supporting a network of managers who did not care about me or my clients.

Since leaving Credit Suisse, I have been disappointed in the negative public announcements about the bank's activities. The incidents that stand out are Credit Suisse receiving the largest fine by the US with respect to violating our economic sanctions with Iran (2009), receiving another fine by the US for "bundling mortgage loans with securities [and] misrepresenting the risk" of those "mortgages during the housing boom" (2012),[736] receiving the most recent fine of a staggering 2.6 billion dollars that the Justice Department levied against the bank for violating our tax laws (2014) and last, but not least, receiving world-wide attention recently with leaks revealing the bank had accounts with human-traffickers, criminal businessmen (i.e. Russian Oligarchs), corrupt autocrat Egyptian President Hosni Mubarak, Nigerian dictator Sani Abacha, corrupt Filipino dictator Ferdinand Marcos, head of the *SS, Reichsführer* Heinrich Himmler, Italian Fascist Dictator Benito Mussolini, and 12,000 accounts of former-Nazis who fled to Argentina after 1945.[737] Also, the more I learn about how the bank treated Holocaust victims, stealing their assets and not returning them to their surviving families, I regret that I ever worked at that firm. Since then, my dear friend and mentor, Holocaust historian Michael Berenbaum, has educated me about how Credit Suisse pursued anti-Semitic policies and got away with one of the largest "robberies" in history.[738] The reparations paid in the 1990's leave a lot to be desired. In short, since leaving the firm, I came to learn that the bank's policies, and Switzerland's banking secrecy laws, "are immoral."[739]

Before starting at Credit Suisse in 2006, I had talked to Berenbaum about working at Credit Suisse in light of its dealings with the Nazis and its mistreatment of Holocaust victims. At that time, he thought the 1.25 billion dollar settlement in 1998 was a good step toward rectifying the crimes of the past that the Swiss banks in general and Credit Suisse in particular committed against Holocaust victims.[740] Follow on research since the late 1990's unfortunately reveals the extent of the crime to be larger than many had previously believed and the reparations should have been dramatically more.[741] So with these facts in mind, it was a blessing in so many ways that I left this firm to find a better way to take care of my clients, my family and myself.

In conclusion, when I was "kicked out on the street" in 2008 by Credit Suisse, I was able to adapt and improvise quickly and find a new, independent home for my clients. My Hunter-like mind allowed me to explore how to hunt down and take care of my accounts and then move quickly, with a lot of energy, to develop my firm. My teacher, Mary, taught me to view myself as a determined individual who just does not know the word "quit." I am still navigating my firm as the captain of my ship. My ADHD gave me the drive and incentive to do this. It is my belief that if you follow the inclination that your ADHD calls you to pursue, then you will find the calling that best fits your life. I did.

Takeaways

- An ADHD-brain can help you adapt and improvise to take care of yourself and your family. Since an ADHD-person can get hyper-focused when necessary, when I suffered a life-changing event while employed at one of the most prestigious financial institutions in the world, Credit Suisse, it pushed me to start my own business, yet another ADHD-like trait.

Action Steps

- Don't be afraid to be your own boss and set up your own business. ADHD-types usually do not work well under people or within organizations that do not care about them. Since ADHD-types are usually more creative and passionate than the average person, they often find that traditional work environments can be stultifying. Often, being in charge of a company is most conducive for an ADHD-person to truly realize his or her potential.

CHAPTER 15:
Adolf Hitler and the Misuse of ADHD

"There will never be an adequate explanation... The closer one gets to explicability the more one realizes nothing can make Hitler explicable."
— Emil Fackenheim, Jewish Philosopher and Reform Rabbi[742]

THROUGHOUT THIS BOOK, I HAVE often praised ADHD and what it can do for a person. I have given examples of remarkable Americans and ancient Greek thinkers who probably "struggled" with ADHD and perhaps as a result of it were able to bequeath to humanity great philosophy, military strategy, literature, art and entertainment. I have also mentioned a few incredible business leaders who have probably benefitted from having ADHD/dyslexia to create amazing enterprises. Although I do not consider myself on the same level as all of these individuals, I am convinced my ADHD helped me research and write five books that have contributed to the body of knowledge about World War II and the Holocaust. However, as Dr. Maddox once told my mother, and as Dr. Hallowell and Dr. Hartmann have documented, ADHD, if not properly harnessed, can create criminals.[743] Countless studies have shown that if ADHD does not get addressed early in a child's life, he will develop poor self-esteem that can lead to failure, anger, illegal activity and contribute to an overall pathology of bad behavior. In other words, some of our worst criminals, using their intelligence, drive, hyperactivity and unique ways of thinking, are probably, often, at least in part, misusing their ADHD. As a result, one must be very deliberate with ADHD-types. If they are not nurtured and encouraged to develop an understanding of who they are and how they think, they will never develop a healthy self-esteem and can instead become full of self-loathing and, indeed, egregiously violative.

In this picture, later General Gotthard Heinrici (far left), is saluting Chancellor Adolf Hitler in 1937 at a gathering at the *Reichstag* in Berlin. As numerous books have shown, Hitler had several psychological problems he never got help for during his life. In discussing him with Dr. Fritz Redlich, former Chairman of the Department of Psychiatry and Dean of the School of Medicine at Yale University, Redlich believed that Hitler struggled with ADHD. Redlich wrote one of the definitive medical works on Hitler entitled *Hitler: Diagnosis of a Destructive Prophet*, and he believes Hitler used some of the powerful attributes that ADHD can afford someone for evil purposes like hyper-focusing on killing the Jews.

This realization was brought home to me on 9 September 2000, when I sat down and had a long discussion with Dr. Fritz Redlich, former Chairman of the Department of Psychiatry and Dean of the School of Medicine at Yale University. Redlich was a Jewish immigrant who came to the U.S. in 1938 after Hitler took over his country of birth, Austria. Six of his relatives were not so lucky, and they would perish in the Holocaust.[744] Redlich loved America and transformed the Department of Psychiatry at Yale into a world-class leader in its specialty. He was one of the pioneers in "social psychiatry."[745]

Redlich lived in the same retirement center as my beloved Aunt Mary Dalbey, née Rigg. She was also a medical professional from the Yale School of Nursing. When she told Dr. Redlich I was conducting graduate research at Cambridge University on the Third Reich and Hitler, he told her he wanted to meet me. When I next visited my aunt, I took the time to spend a whole afternoon with Dr. Redlich in his apartment at Whitney Center in Hamden, Connecticut. He had just published his 20-year study on Hitler called *Hitler: Diagnosis of a Destructive Prophet* with Oxford University Press and he wanted to give me a copy.[746]

He was a dignified gentleman, soft-spoken and immaculately dressed the day I sat down with him for the first time. We discussed Hitler's anti-Semitism, upbringing, potential Jewish background, invasion of Russia, and weird sexual behavior among other topics. Dr. Redlich is considered the world's expert on Hitler from a medical perspective, and I eagerly soaked up knowledge from him while taking copious notes. During our conversation, he excused himself briefly, and I started flipping through his book and came to the section about Hitler's hyperactivity and possible ADHD. When he returned, I asked, "Dr. Redlich, in your book, you state that Dr. Shlomo Aronson diagnosed Hitler with ADHD, and you write that Hitler was indeed hyperactive as a child. How did you both come to these conclusions?"[747]

He explained, "Well, Hitler had problems as a child focusing in school. He was rambunctious. He got into fights. He wasn't well-liked. He was a loner. And he wasn't very good at school. These are

ADHD-traits, and he had a hyperactive mind. In my book, I write that I didn't necessarily agree with Aronson's conclusion about Hitler, but today I think I was wrong about this. Hitler probably did have ADHD, undiagnosed then because it did not exist as a medical condition. But one can say today his ADHD-like behavior caused many of his problems, because he never got help for it---and mind you, he didn't get help for a lot of his problems!"[748]

I inquired, "Dr. Redlich, why are you now changing your opinion about Hitler?"

He responded, "Well, Bryan, I have received so many wonderful letters of support and admiration after this book was published two years ago. Naturally, I also get a lot of articles people have written about Hitler and psychology. They have influenced me. During the course of thinking about this more, I believe Hitler did have ADHD, and if I live long enough to have a second edition, I will change that section in my book. I only dedicate a few paragraphs to it, but I think it's important to note. Why are you so interested in this aspect of Hitler?" he asked.

As one can imagine, I shared my story with Dr. Redlich. We laughed at my stories, and he shared his thoughts with me about ADHD. He believed some of the most creative and gifted people have it. Then he turned serious and returned to Hitler.

"As we talk about ADHD, I agree with what that doctor told your mother about poor self-esteem coming from failure to deal properly with ADHD, or any disorder as a child, and how that can lead to bad decisions later in life. In the case of ADHD and Hitler, this probably was one of the reasons why he had such an erratic work schedule, bizarre sleep patterns, and the inability to focus on important issues at hand. However, sometimes he could hyper-focus on random facts like how powerful some howitzers were and other technical details of his weapons and divisions. For example, I remember reading how he became obsessed with demolitions and how they can blow up bridges. Sometimes, as you will see in my book, he would hyper-focus on things that didn't make any sense in light of current world events, like when, in 1945, he was working on how he was going to rebuild his hometown of Linz after the war, just as his whole empire was crumbling around him.[749] But unfortunately for humanity, he also became hyper-focused on slaughtering all the Jews in the Holocaust and he was very successful at doing so. So, in thinking about these issues, he indeed had ADHD. As you will discover with your book, you will find many things you would like to change once it gets published. Luckily for me, I have a file here of some changes I will make for the next edition, and it's not very long. After 20 years of research, I think I did a pretty good job of covering everything I could about Hitler's mind and behavior. But a book is never finished."

I responded by saying, "Dr. Redlich, they say Einstein failed as a child, but he went on to do great things. Why did Hitler go in the opposite direction if one can say his hyperactivity and ADHD caused him to fail a lot as a child and this in turn, led to some of his horrible pathology later in life?"

"Good question. Of course, Hitler had a lot of things he was dealing with. His father beat him.[750] His father was an alcoholic.[751] His mother, although very loving, wasn't a powerful personality. She died of cancer when he was young. Hitler didn't have a strong family to lean on, and when homeless, it seemed very few, if any, relatives reached out to help him. He didn't make friends easily. He had a traditional Austrian-Catholic upbringing, focused on shame and guilt. I know this, since I was raised Catholic in Austria also [Redlich's Jewish parents raised him as a Catholic to try to help him assimilate into Austrian society]. Hitler suffered in the trenches of World War I and was wounded three times. All these issues, and many more, led to problems later in life. So, although his hyperactivity and possible ADHD caused many of his later problems, he had many other issues he was dealing with. Hatred is a horrible learning disability, and Hitler had a horrible hatred for the Jews drilled into him in our virulent anti-Semitic environment in Austria."

"Could one say that Hitler is a case study of how ADHD can help one do good or evil?" I asked.

"Well, everyone has the potential to do good or evil. Hitler is complicated, as you know from your studies. But I think you're right to note that he used the positive ADHD-traits of hyperactivity, hyper-focusing and thinking differently in unique ways to do, unfortunately, incredible evil. I firmly believe that without Hitler we wouldn't have had the Holocaust. He was indeed the driving force behind that whole extermination process. Such energy. Such focus. Such evil."

Hitler also abused amphetamines, an affliction that many ADHD-types develop when they self-medicate.[752] His abuse of such drugs could have brought on his Parkinson's disease.[753] I met with Dr. Redlich several times from 2000 to 2004. He proofread my book *Hitler's Jewish Soldiers* and gave me valuable feedback. It was a proud moment in 2002 when I handed him my book, one of the first copies off the press. When I presented the copy to him, he smiled, shook my hand, and then said, "Welcome to the club." He was a kind and wonderful man.

What I took away from my discussions with him about Hitler and *der Führer*'s hyperactivity, and his likely ADHD, was that we as a society need to be careful with ADHD-types. As Dr. Hallowell said, ADHD-types are agents of change[754] who can work toward good or bad effect, as Hitler so clearly illustrated. I agree with Redlich that without Hitler we would never have had the Holocaust.[755] As Redlich wrote, "Hitler was the most important anti-Semite. Only he had the stature to unleash the forces…that resulted in the genocide."[756] The hyper-focused energy, leadership skills, and ability to think outside the box that is so often demonstrated by ADHD-people can be incredibly positive attributes. *However, if ADHD is not attended to and, as a result, a child develops self-loathing, ADHD can transform a person into a monster.*

Takeaways
- There are people who use their ADHD-skills for evil. When doing research on Nazi Germany, I met with Dr. Fritz Redlich, a world-renowned Yale University psychiatrist who had done an in-depth, medical study of Hitler. He concluded in all probability that Hitler had ADHD and used it for evil instead of good. Of course, Hitler had many mental problems, but the fact that he had issues with ADHD, which apparently were not dealt with properly, reveals interesting lessons for one who studies ADHD or who is dealing with it.

- If not properly harnessed, ADHD can create criminals. Countless studies show that if ADHD is not addressed early in a child's life, that child will develop poor self-esteem that can lead to failure, anger, illegal activity and an overall pathology of bad behavior. In other words, some of our worst criminals, using their intelligence, drive, hyperactivity and unique ways of thinking outside the box, are probably, often, in part at least, misusing their ADHD. As a result, one must be deliberate with ADHD-types. If they are not properly supported and nurtured to develop healthy self-esteem and an understanding of who they are and how they think, they can become instead, full of self-loathing and, indeed, egregiously volatile.

- ADHD-leadership skills, thinking outside the box and hyper-focused energy can combine to be incredible attributes for one to have. However, if ADHD is not attended to and, as a result, a child develops self-loathing, ADHD can transform a person into a monster.

Action Steps

- Teach ADHD-types the importance of kindness.

- Be aware that sometimes ADHD-types can become angry at the world since it seems not to understand them. When this happens, try to redirect that anger into positive activity.

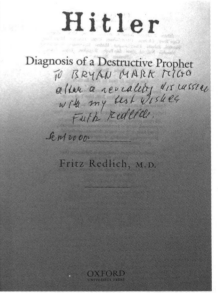

On 9 September 2000, I sat down and had a long discussion with Dr. Fritz Redlich, former Chairman of the Department of Psychiatry and Dean of the School of Medicine at Yale University. Redlich was a Jewish immigrant who came to the U.S. in 1938 after Hitler took over his country of birth, Austria. Toward the end of his career at Yale and during his retirement, he dedicated twenty years of his life to doing research on Adolf Hitler. Redlich is considered one of the foremost experts on Hitler from a medical perspective. During my discussion with Redlich, he was convinced Hitler had ADHD and used it for evil purposes. At the end of our afternoon together, he gave me a gift of his book *Hitler: Diagnosis of a Destructive Prophet* and wrote, "To Bryan Mark Rigg after a revealing discussion. With my best wishes, Fritz Redlich, Sept. 2000."

CHAPTER 16:
Applying My ADHD to Discover Hidden Relatives

"Remember the days, consider the years of many generations, ask thy father and he will shew thee; thy elders, and they will tell thee. For one who takes advice from elders never stumbles."

— (Deuteronomy 32:7, King James Version)[757]

THROUGHOUT THIS BOOK, I HAVE explored ADHD-benefits and how my use of them have helped me perform at various activities. They also allowed me to discover one of the dearest people in my life, my Aunt Mary. The story of how I found her is a strange and sad one, but I am convinced that without my ADHD I would have never known her.

Sometime in late 1983, my father got a phone call from his aunt, my great-aunt, Gladys B. Potts, née Foulks, who was suffering from lung cancer and she wanted to tell him something important before she died. Her husband had just passed away, my great-uncle Ridgeway (a World War II grumpy old Army Tech Sergeant), and she could finally tell my dad something she had wanted to tell him for a long time. Apparently, my great-uncle did not want my father to know that my father had an older half-brother. Now that Uncle Ridgeway was dead, Aunt Gladys was free to tell my father this secret. My father looked up his older half-brother, Frank H. Rigg, and they met. I later learned from my Aunt Doris, Frank's wife, that at this re-union the two men hugged each other, cried and had a great evening getting to know one another.

Apparently, my grandfather, Mark Rigg, also had a family between 1915 and 1920 that he had never disclosed to my father or
to my grandmother Leona, who was, I learned later, his third wife.
I would later do research on Uncle Frank, and when I discovered he
was an Army World War II platoon leader who fought the Japanese
at the battle of Angaur (17-30 September 1944), I included him in
my book *Flamethrower*. He would suffer an injury to his right hand
that he never recovered from. I wish I had known him, but family
dynamics prevented me from meeting this war hero.

Well, the Rigg saga would get even more soap opera-like. A
few years later, in 1987, my father moved back to his hometown of
Philadelphia and was living outside the city in Villanova. On one of
his business trips, he stopped in the town of Ambler, Pennsylvania, at
a barber shop to get a haircut. The man cutting his hair was elderly,
in his 90s, and as he and my father were talking, he piped up with,
"You know Mr. Rigg, we also had a Mark Rigg living here back in
the 1920s. And he was a pharmacist too, just like your father. And by
the way, he has a daughter in town." As my father put two-and-two
together, he realized that there were not many pharmacists in that region at that time named Mark Rigg. The barber gave him the number
of the woman who it turns out is my Aunt Irene and he called her
up. Sure enough, after a few minutes of talking, my dad realized he
not only had a half-brother but two half-sisters. I would later get to
know both my Aunt Irene and Aunt Janet and learn more about my
grandfather's second family.

A few years later, in 1994 and 1995, as I was conducting my
genealogical research for my book *Hitler's Jewish Soldiers*, I discovered many hidden families in Germany that were the result, at least
in part, of unknown affairs, multiple marriages and attempts to hide
Jewish backgrounds. What I discovered was that many secrets were
hidden away in family closets, and shockingly, most never become

known. Well, as I started thinking about this more in 1995, I had a conversation with my father that went something like the following:

"Dad, from 1983 until 1987, you found out you had two half-sisters and one half-brother. It seems that grandpa Rigg was a busy man. Do you think there are other siblings out there you don't know about?"

"Well, I don't know. Before my brother died, he did talk about an estranged sibling he had—a sister. I even have a vague memory of her actually visiting me when I was a small child, but I didn't know whether she was a sister or an aunt because I was so young. I do remember her name was Mary."

"What, another sibling, Dad! Why haven't you told me about this?"

"Well, I just never thought it was that important. As you can see, strong familial bonds in the Rigg family just don't really exist when your grandfather had three wives and died early, at 53. I was only 13 when he passed away and have hardly any memory of the man."

"Well, regardless, we need to find this sister. Did you have any information on her?" I said.

"Well, during one of my conversations with my brother, he did mention that she had gone to Yale."

"What? Dad!!!! I've been attending Yale University since 1991," I responded, "and now you tell me I have an aunt who went there too. I am going to find her."

During the next few weeks, I worked with the Yale Alumni Office, and found my father's last lost sibling, Mary Dalbey, née Rigg. She attended the Yale University School of Nursing and even taught there and worked at the hospital attached to the school for decades. She was then currently living in a retirement center right next to the university, Whitney Center. Once I obtained her telephone number, I gave her a ring.

"Hello."

"Hello Mrs. Dalbey. This is Bryan Mark Rigg. I'm a student at Yale and I've recently learned that we might be related. My father is Linton Mark Rigg. My grandfather was a pharmacist in Beverly, New Jersey, [Aunt Mary's hometown] and then in Ambler and Springfield, Pennsylvania. His name was Mark Rigg. And my great-grandfather was Frank Rigg, a butcher in Beverly, New Jersey."

There was silence on the other end of the phone. Then after a few seconds, she took a deep breath and said, "Well, I think you're right. We're related. How about you come out here and have lunch with me?"

I excitedly agreed. A day later, I rode my bike from Silliman College (my residential college at Yale) to her retirement complex, Whitney Center, where we sat down for several hours over lunch and talked about our family. We quickly ascertained that she was indeed the sister of Frank H. Rigg and the first child of my grandfather. We laughed, even cried a little, and had a wonderful time. She was the type of person some people have in their lives where the chemistry and connection were just there from the beginning. For the next year while I was a senior at Yale, I would have two to three lunches or dinners with her weekly and she helped me with my essays, gave advice about girls, imparted knowledge about my family, and explored my plans for the future. I even had Christmas with her that year by a tree in her apartment that we had decorated together.

She experienced a lot of disappointment in her life. After her father left her family, her mother struggled to make ends meet. Aunt Mary did very well in school and felt that was her way out of poverty. She eventually married her college professor from Rutgers University where she was getting a master's degree at the same time she was studying at the Yale School of Nursing. Today, she admits she married this man who was 22 years her senior probably due to the "daddy issues" she had with my grandfather. Nonetheless, her much older husband was a stable and secure man and she wanted to start a family. She had always wanted six sons, but for some reason, she was unable to conceive any children. Tragically, her first husband died 10 years into the marriage from a brain aneurism. Soon thereafter, she once again married an older man, a retired minister this time. After around 20 years of marriage, he died from cancer. Eventually, she met her third husband while she was in her late 50s. This time her new husband was closer to her age, and they were together for around 20 years until he died from complications from Parkinson's disease. She always laughed when explaining that while many people struggle to have one good marriage, she actually had three! Here is an interesting sidenote: She is buried between two of her husbands at St. Mary's Episcopal Church in Beverly, New Jersey. She was an elegant, beautiful and smart woman, and apparently all three of her husbands knew this and cherished her. She always regretted not having her six sons, but after she got to know me and my hyperactivity and ADHD-brain, she started calling me her "Six-Sons" since I had the energy of at least six human beings, if not more!

From the time I became close to my Aunt Mary in 1995 until she died in November 2011, I sent her flowers every Mother's Day, Valentine's Day and on her birthdays. I also made sure I celebrated Christmas with her and took my children to meet her. My daughter Sophia gave a reading at her memorial service and my son Justin spoke at the graveside. I, of course, gave her eulogy. She was always there giving me advice and support about marriage, children, careers, books and family. She was a pillar of strength and without my ADHD, I am convinced, I would not have had the drive and curiosity to have found her. Having a brain that sees how different patterns in life reveal the truth about a situation is a trait of a Hunter. Well, just as I have done in my historical research, I used my skills as a historian to find Aunt Mary and I am glad I did. This ADHD-skill set allowed me to pounce on an opportunity to bring to light a family secret and connect with one of the dearest relatives I have ever known. Maybe if I had been a Farmer, I would have done the same thing. However, I don't think so. My ex-wife's great-grandfather had a second family in the small Texas town where my ex-mother-in-law's family is from, and no one to my knowledge in her Farmer-family has ever done research to find out about their lost relatives. My Exeter teacher Harvard Knowles' father had a son in town with his mistress, but his family, like my ex-wife's, refused to pursue a relationship with this relative and he today doesn't even know the name or whereabouts of his half-brother. I have had many tell me that they have heard about "lost relatives" in their families, but few, if any, have ever done anything to find them during my research when writing my book *Hitler's Jewish Soldiers*. I think my ADHD provided the drive and curiosity I needed to "hunt down" my lost aunt who had remained in the shadows for years.

Takeaways

- A unique event in my life allowed me to discover a lost relative I never knew I had while at Yale, who in turn became one of my closest relatives, my Aunt Mary. My ADHD's curiosity and ability to see unique patterns in life allowed me to do so.

Action Steps

- Don't be afraid to look into things about your family's past. You never know what you will find.

Here I am with my Aunt Mary Dalbey, née Rigg. She was a graduate of Yale School of Nursing and was the first child of my grandfather Mark Rigg. I only learned of her in 1995 when I was a senior at Yale. My ADHD-fueled-curiosity and -drive allowed me to find her and she became one of my most closest relatives. Summer 2000

CHAPTER 17:

How My ADHD Helped Save a Life

"Our actions are not the product of will but of understanding."
— Steven Smith, *Spinoza's Book of Life*[758]

"Knowledge is a form of power that not only interprets the world but changes it."
— Steven Smith, *Spinoza's Book of Life*[759]

POLICE OFFICERS, FIREMEN, EMTs, MEDICS, medical doctors and naval Corpsmen, just to name a few, save lives daily and they do not have to be ADHD to do what they do. However, I do believe that an ADHD-mind, when armed with knowledge about lifesaving techniques, might be better able to use those skills to save lives. I believe my take-charge ADHD-impulsiveness did indeed help me successfully confront the emergency situation I describe below.

Before I joined the Marine Corps, I became CPR certified by the Red Cross. I also learned basic first aid in the Israeli Army and the Marine Corps. During a fathers' campout in East Texas on 16 October 2010, a friend of mine, Philippe Semprez, started choking on some meat. Of the few dozen men in the area, none knew what to do. Once I ascertained that he was about to suffocate on the piece of steak lodged in his throat, I stood him up, raised his arms and performed the Heimlich maneuver on him. It took me three times performing this technique before the piece of beef blocking his airway popped out of his mouth. When this happened, he took a deep breath, turned around, and gave me one of the most compassionate hugs I have ever received from a person. Everyone around me did nothing, but my training and my impulsive ADHD-brain immediately recognized the danger and I acted: I am convinced that had I not had ADHD, I would not have acted so quickly as I did. After a few seconds of stunned silence, the crowd that had gathered around erupted in applause. Ironically, Philippe's brother-in-law, Thierry Mollet, had died at a train station after choking on a sandwich a few years prior. So, Philippe, who was a well-known artist, was grateful beyond words and painted a picture of the event that he presented to me a few years later.[760]

So, although not necessarily the only requirement, it would appear that ADHD-types who thrive on high-adrenaline activity would make good candidates for jobs where quick thinking is required to save lives. Maybe that is why some research shows a high percentage of ADHD-types pick law enforcement or the military as their chosen vocations.[761]

Takeaways

- ADHD gave me the skills to save a man's life during a campout. Although thousands of people save lives daily in the world, I believe my ADHD allowed me to act quickly and competently in order to save this man from death when there were only minutes to spare.

Philippe Semprez's painting showing how I saved his life during a campout in 2010 by performing the Heimlich maneuver to dislodge a piece of meat stuck in his throat. I actually had to do the Heimlich on him three times before the steak logged in his throat popped out—hence, why Semprez painted three figures (which are actually the same person) in different positions being held by me. This event shows how the impulsive nature of many ADHD-people can sometimes be beneficial. I reacted quickly to help him while everyone else around Philippe seemed uncertain about how to respond. Of course, I relied on the first aid training I received in the military and from the Red Cross, but my quick response can be attributed to my ADHD.

- I do believe that an ADHD-mind, when armed with knowledge about lifesaving techniques, might be better able to use those skills to save a life. ADHD-types who thrive on high-adrenaline activity make good candidates for jobs where quick thinking is required to save lives.

Action Steps

- ADHD can give people the drive to seek out and thrive on adrenaline-filled activities. Explore careers where you find them each day, such as in the military, in the FBI, the CIA, as a policeman, a fireman, an EMT, or a medical doctor.

- If you have not taken a Red Cross Adult and Pediatric First Aid/CPR/AED class, do so immediately. This is especially the case if you have children. This training saves lives.

Here is a picture of many of the fathers during the campout when I saved Philippe Semprez's life. I am standing second from the right in the picture with the military, brown shirt on and Philippe is on my far left at the end of the line with the long, gray hair and white shirt.

CHAPTER 18:
Living with ADHD Today

"What does not destroy me, makes me stronger."
—Friedrich Nietzsche[762]

"[Death] is what happens to everybody… This is the way we will all finish." For Whom the Bell Tolls,
— Ernest Hemingway[763]

ON A COLD MORNING IN February 1991, the topic in my philosophy class at Phillips Exeter Academy under the tutelage of Kathy Brownbeck was Plato's cave. Plato tells an evocative parable of people trapped on multiple levels in a cave unable to turn around with a fire burning behind them. All they can see are shadows of people on the cave's wall. Their reality is the world of shadows. But then one hardy soul leaves the cave and experiences the outside world. Upon his return, his explanation of the natural world is met with disbelief. Those trapped in the cave cannot transcend its limits. Such is often the world of ADHD when described to an "outsider."[764]

My coming of age is comparable to the story of Platonic discovery. I too left the security and warmth of my cave at different stages in my life, which helped me to embark on a journey that changed how I viewed myself and the world. My symbolic cave was the identity given to me by my family, society and religion. When I returned after journeying forth, friends, relatives and scholars were puzzled by my new ideas. It seems I have always been an exception to the rules, especially how I learned to think about my learning disability as a child.[765]

Although you might classify this book as motivational, it is not the traditional kind that tells you how to make a fortune. I have not explained how to earn millions, reach new spiritual levels or achieve your wildest dreams, although those three things might be byproducts of what you have learned here. I want you to realize how to touch souls, especially your own, and make them better because this is what matters most.

Defining problems to overcome and setting goals for ADHD-people are keys to success. This is especially the case when the question arises of what course in life is best. First of all, what is essential in life? Most would probably say money. But money itself has no value. The happiness, security and health it buys have value. But no one dies wishing he had more money. Most die wishing they had made more of a difference in people's lives or had a more fulfilled life. A great sage, Rabbi Akiva, suggested that to maintain equilibrium in life, you should remember that you come from a putrid drop, you go to the grave and then you are worm food.[766] You came into this world naked and will leave in only the clothes the funeral home employees put on you. What you leave behind in helping others and making a better world is what matters. Keeping this in mind will help you realize that most problems are not worth getting upset about. The more you keep things in perspective, the better you can know yourself. I believe this is a key realization for ADHD-people. By doing this, you will see which problems are worth overcoming and which goals are obtainable. Never forget: "a little work, a little sleep, a little love-and it's all over."[767]

And in keeping things in perspective, one must realize the importance of living in the now. Often an ADHD-person can be haunted by past mistakes. Instead of letting the past drag you down if you have made some bad blunders, take those experiences and grow from them. Learn from the past in order to strengthen your present state of being. In other words, do your best to live in the present. Do the next right thing for yourself and others because all you have is your "right now." As Ernest Hemmingway wrote,

> There is nothing else than now. There is neither yesterday, certainly, nor is there any tomorrow. How old must you be before you know that? There is only now, and if now is only two days, then two days is your life and everything in it will be in proportion... And if you stop complaining and asking for what you never will get, you will have a good life. A good life is not measured by any biblical span.[768]

For an ADHD-person to "suck out the marrow of life,"[769] he must learn to live in the now and enjoy what he has in the present and not what he wishes he had. Regretting what might have been does not allow you to seize the day and make yourself better. As Hemingway wrote, a good life can only happen when you learn to be present in the moment. If you don't live in "the now," then to quote Stephen King,

> [Your ghosts will] sit undramatically by the roadside like poor beggars, and we see them only from the corners of our eyes, if we see them at all. The idea that they have been waiting there for us rarely crosses our minds. Yet they do wait, and when we have passed, they gather up their bundles of memory and fall in behind, treading in our footsteps and catching up, little by little.[770]

In other words, if you don't live in the present, you will carry a lot of baggage, or "bundles of memory," that will not help you live in "the now." And eventually, they will catch up to you, "little by little," and weigh you down, making it more difficult to march into the future confidently with eyes wide open for new and better opportunities.

Next, keeping things in perspective is difficult for ADHD-people. ADHD-persons must listen to what is going on inside instead of listening to those on the outside, who are labeling them "freaks" and "disabled." In other words, the more self-awareness you have, the stronger you can become, and the more focused you will be in knowing what you should be doing in life. By knowing what and who you are (understanding your ADHD), you free yourself of uncertainty and indecision. As the German philosopher Hegel wrote, "I am free when I am within myself. This self-contained existence of Spirit is self-consciousness, consciousness of self."[771] Surprisingly, "Who am I?" is a question many do not ask themselves although it is incredibly important. As psychologist Dr. David Grossman wrote,

> Philosophers and psychologists have long been aware of man's basic inability to perceive that which is closest to him. Sir Norman Angell tells us that "it is quite in keeping with man's curious intellectual history that the simplest and most important questions are those he asks least often."[772]

Self-knowledge is not explored nearly as much as is necessary for ADHD-kids. They are bombarded with criticism about who they are and what they can or can't do, so they must overcome this by examining themselves. The unexamined life may be worth living, but it will be a colorless life reacting only to what the world throws at it.[773]

The great thing about self-awareness is that it helps one know how to help oneself and others. Dr. Hartmann quotes a Catholic monk who once said, "When we discover our own being, our own purpose, we help others discover theirs, too."[774] Hartmann further explained that "success isn't about doing successful things, or even things that will bring us success. Instead, it's about being success-full. And that comes from defining first what we want to be. Who we are. What's at the center of our lives. What excites and drives and animates us."[775]

Ultimately, as mentioned above, I learned that to suck out the marrow of my ADHD-life, I needed to realize I will die someday. This helped me put ADHD into perspective, i.e., I can either see how to use it to create positive experiences in my life or let it become my crutch. Life is too short to have mental crutches, and the finality of death helped me see this truth.

I want to share an insight into death by using some of the themes mentioned in Chapter 2 about ADHD's evolution that might give one a unique perspective to our impending demise, thereby helping us live more fully. In short, our deaths help the next generation using *natural selection*. Let's think about this. If cars, for example, stayed in their 1880s development, we would have automobiles that could only drive 30 mph with numerous safety hazards. That would create many perils on the roads today, and we are lucky that each generation of cars since then have slowly evolved to be faster, safer, bigger and more fuel efficient. Automobiles today look somewhat like those from the 1880s, but they have evolved into being better machines. Living organisms are like the history of cars. Through *natural selection*, subsequent generations are more suited to live in their environments than previous generations, and this happens when older species breed and then die.

So, death is a good thing for the collective whole of future humankind and should be embraced. We have evolved and improved from when we were *Pikaia* 500 million years ago, or *Ardipithecus ramidus* 4.5 million years ago, or *Homo erectus* 1.9 million years ago, or *Homo heidelbergensis* 500,000 years ago to now when we are *Homo sapiens*, and this march of evolution has been good. And it will continue. *My genes only improve with passing them, after mixing them with another, into future generations,* not by me keeping them as they are for perpetuity. My current state, like those 1880s automobiles, will someday be outdated and inefficient if I were to live forever or if my progeny were clones of me, so it is best that I die giving my future progeny the ability to adapt and evolve for the forthcoming environments they will experience that will, indeed, be different from mine. Consequently, I must welcome death as something advantageous to ensure the health of upcoming generations. Just think, we would never be where we are today if *Pikaia* or *Ardipithecus ramidus* lived for eternity and stayed in their evolutionary states, thereby preventing *Homo sapiens'* evolution. If this had happened, you would not be here, and modern civilization would *never* have arisen. We would still be slithering as *Pikaia*s or walking on all fours, sometimes on two, like *Ardipithecus ramidus*, and neither species would have been capable of culture, science, medicine, space travel, etc.[776]

Thinking about death in such ways has helped me stop feeling down for having ADHD, understanding now its origins and roots. In other words, ADHD arose by populations evolving and then dying out to create it within the human genome in order to improve life. Without the death of previous generations, ADHD would have never evolved to help humankind, in part, to be superior Hunters and thinkers. Ironically, we are fascinated with death, yet we harbor the unrealistic notion that it has nothing to do with us. As Sigmund Freud said, "At bottom, nobody believes in his own death."[777] The sooner you stop ignoring your death, and the sooner you give your life and coming death meaning, the better you will live today and with more passion. Hegel said that "nothing great in the world has been accomplished without passion."[778] Contemplating death, ironically, gives me that passion now to live life to the fullest.

Moreover, I think finding that passion will also prevent people from hating their ADHD. Many regret they have it and wish it away, instead of dealing with it and using it for good. As Dr. Hallowell said, "If you don't get help, ADHD can curse you and make you wretched. But if you work it right, ADHD can enhance your life and make you sparkle."[779] The tendency to see ourselves as destitute is common, especially among ADHD-people; however, as Hallowell says, if you learn about your ADHD, it can become an ally. Our culture of sometimes wanting to be the victim needs to stop. For ADHD-people to thrive, they need to put the misguided idea of "victimhood" behind them. Knowing about our coming deaths, and why they are necessary also helped me put away this ADHD-victimhood mindset.

In contemplating this victimhood mindset though, all too often, people like to point the finger and blame others for their misfortunes instead of taking responsibility for their actions. However, when you point your finger at someone, three fingers are pointing back at you, as my grandmother Edna Davidson used to tell me. This type of mindset leads one to live a life devoid of passion, power and strength---almost a "living death" existence. Thinking that the world is against you is a narcissistic way of viewing life and prevents you from thinking about how to improve yourself. Such a person continues to find fault with others, creating a cycle of blame, anger and greed. And this cycle can create a dead-end life full of negativity.

Often, ADHD-people are down on themselves. If you tend to be a negative person, step back and think about your life and realize how fortunate you are to be living in the Western world. As a motivational speaker once pointed out, we should not forget that "two in 10 of the world's residents are chronically underfed. Ten million children work in fields, factories or brothels. In 2001, the world's 400 richest people earn[ed] more money than the world's 2.3 billion poorest. Fifteen percent of the world's people live in the 22 nations where the annual income is above $25,000. For everyone else, the average income is $600 a year."[780]

Most of us, especially ADHD-people, need to realize how lucky we are that anyone even cares enough to write or think about ADHD. For us, our biggest challenge is whether we see the glass as half-empty or half-full. It is in large part all about attitude. Seeing yourself and life as half-full is starting yourself on the path of greatness. It is a process, not an end state. As John Milton wrote in *Paradise Lost*, "The mind is its own place, and in itself can make a Heaven of Hell, a Hell of Heaven."[781] I would prefer all people to make a "Heaven of Hell," and when in "Heaven," to enjoy it and keep improving it throughout their lives. Of course, life is not always positive, but how one lives life with a positive attitude can make all the difference when making every day better than the previous one.

The philosophies in this book have followed the ancient Greek philosopher Socrates' statement that each one must "find what course of life is best." To do so, you have to also listen to Socrates' maxim that you must continue to examine your life.[782] Often people are swept along by events without ever influencing them. They take the path of least resistance instead of forging their own road. To live a productive ADHD-life, you have to follow the road less traveled, as poet Robert Frost so famously wrote in his poem *The Road Not Taken*. In other words, do not do what you think people expect of you. Instead, following what your creative ADHD-mind is telling you will bring you happiness. When you live with that goal in mind, especially if you have ADHD, then something wacky, creative, unique and impressive is about to happen.

Takeaways

- Defining problems to overcome and setting goals for ADHD-children are keys to success.

- The more you keep things in perspective, the better you can know yourself. By doing this, you will see which problems are worth overcoming and which goals are obtainable. And in keeping things in perspective, realize the importance of living in the now. Often an ADHD-person can be haunted by past mistakes. Instead of letting the past drag you down, take those experiences and grow from them.

- The more self-awareness you have, the stronger you can become, and the more focused you will be in knowing what you should be doing. By knowing what you are about (understanding ADHD), you free yourself of uncertainty and indecision.

- Do not do what you think people expect of you. Instead, following what your creative ADHD-mind is telling you will bring you happiness. When you live with that goal in mind, especially if you have ADHD, then something unique is about to happen.

Action Steps

- Realize life is short. Death is a certainty. As a result, seize the day and enjoy living. Do not live in the past—just learn from it.

- If you are a parent of an ADHD-child, see my 11 tips in the "Conclusion." It is my hope that if you follow them, you will enrich your life and the lives of your children.

Conclusion

"For we are all somehow dreadfully cracked about the head, and sadly need mending."

— Herman Melville, *Moby Dick*[783]

I AM DIFFERENT AND MANY people label me abnormal. Much of this difference comes from my ADHD which has helped me accomplish many things in life. Caring adults, a natural diet, frequent exercise and a positive mindset allowed me to adapt to my ADHD in a positive way. The process of how an ADHD-kid got to Yale and Cambridge was quite involved and there were many who helped me along the way, making my adventure unique. The very process of learning had been a challenge throughout my early life, but eventually I embarked on a journey that led me to write books, give lectures, and help produce television shows and radio interviews. How ironic that a boy with learning problems would teach people about history, the Holocaust, and the human condition. By dealing with this "learning problem," not only was I able to study at some of the greatest institutions in the world but I was also able to teach at some wonderful academic establishments. Moreover, there is no doubt in my mind that my ADHD also helped me as a financial advisor, a father and as a Marine Corps officer.

Even though I have been diagnosed with ADHD, I can state definitively that I do not have a disorder. I do not believe it is a handicap or that there is something wrong with me, and I do not like the term.[784] Using such a term or, more importantly, believing in it and focusing on the downside of the condition can "create additional pathology: a nasty set of avoidable, secondary problems, like shame, fear, and a sharply diminished sense of what's possible in life."[785] Some studies attribute the lower college attendance by males, in part, to the treatment of ADHD with drugs. The pathology that accompanies such treatment and the "disabled" label applied to kids with ADHD can, and often does, result in "low self-esteem and internalize[d] low expectations" and more males declining to attend university after high school.[786] Numerous studies have proven "that when we describe and define people, they will most often live up to that expectation."[787] Tell a kid often enough he is "'bad', and most likely he will become bad. Tell him he is 'brilliant,' and he will strive to achieve brilliance."[788]

However, ADHD can also cause problems. In my life, my divorce is a prime example. And both my grandfathers, my father and my paternal grandmother who I believe lived with ADHD, fell far short, in many respects, of living life well and were plagued by failures, addictions, divorces and premature death. So, you need to embrace the good ADHD can offer and guard against the harm it can cause as well.

I consider one of my biggest failures in life was not keeping my family together, and although it takes two, I feel I could have done so much more to have saved my marriage. Unfortunately, it is all academic now.

And after reviewing my grandfathers', father's and paternal grandmother's histories, I believe had they stayed away from the addictions that hurt them and the impulsive behavior that got them into trouble, they likely could have had more productive lives by harnessing the attributes of their ADHD.

One ADHD-trait that can be both positive and negative is called "hyper-focusing." I have it, and this helped me as an academic researcher, military officer, father, teacher and Certified Financial Planner. Once I get hooked onto a subject about which I feel passionate, I tend to not let go. As a result, I was able to focus on my schooling, writing my books, my children's activities and my current career. Once I started hyper-focusing on how to use ADHD to my advantage, it became a blessing and not a curse in most realms of my life. Conversely, though, I needed to do a better job of controlling it, especially when it took me away from focusing on things that mattered and needed attention, like my wife, or embracing my new life once I was separated and on the road of divorce. In these areas of my life, my hyper-focusing hurt me. Firstly, I did not see essential issues in my marriage that needed serious attention. And then lastly, once the breakup became a certainty, I was slow to move on to my new life. Therefore, be alert as to how and when you should hyper-focus.[789] I advise, therefore, that you avoid focusing too much on work, or trauma, or on a subject that will not help you in school, your marriage or your business. Find ways to get positive feedback that you can act on to make sure your hyper-focusing is helping you and not hindering you.

Moreover, learning is a lifelong process, not a goal. Ongoing learning helps us gain self-knowledge and a deeper understanding of how to live well. And when one knows the *why* of ADHD; namely, how it came into being historically and genetically, then answering the question of *how* to best use it in one's life becomes easier. Life is not something we initially choose. Two people come together, our parents, and do something humans (all animals) have been doing since we crawled out of the primordial soup. That act in itself is simple. Once the union of two people creates a life, guiding that child should be the focus of the parents and every educational system. Teaching human beings how to live well will benefit society as a whole. Working through it is not easy. It is a process, and that is all right.

We could not choose our parents, or time, or place of our birth or upbringing. What we can choose is what to do with our lives. Look at yourself and ask what you really want to do with your life. When you determine what that is, then go after it with passion. Don't be a passive recipient of whatever life throws at you. It is realistic to realize your life may be insignificant in the grand scheme of the universe. Also, it is all right to realize that you do not matter that much in affecting the trajectory of history. But each butterfly, each tree, each person, including you, makes a difference. And, even after you die, your legacy, the people you have touched and taught and influenced will carry on.[790] That will be your immortality.

As Samuel Beckett wrote in *Waiting for Godot*,

> Let us do something, while we have the chance! It is not every day that we are needed. Not indeed that we personally are needed. Others would meet the case equally well, if not better. To all mankind they were addressed, those cries for help still ringing in our ears! But at this place, at this moment of time, all mankind is us, whether we like it or not. Let us make the most of it, before it is too late! Let us represent worthily for once the foul brood to which a cruel fate consigned us![791]

Beckett is telling us that we must seize the moment to make our lives better than they were in the past. We only move above where we were yesterday by bettering ourselves educationally, morally and responsibility-wise today. Beckett encourages us to do the next right thing and to be stronger and wiser presently than in days gone by, and to do it all, without harming others.

What is essential in exploring all this knowledge, which should make the most arrogant man humble, is to understand, especially for those of us with ADHD/LD, that if we can live a life "true to thyself," we will have made a positive difference here. We give our lives value if we can make this place and the people we touch a little better than before we came. If we can leave this world, especially leave our LD-family, a bit stronger in perceiving themselves as unique instead of disabled, and leave mankind with all our brothers and sisters a little more tolerant and with a little more knowledge and stronger ideas, then we will not have lived in vain.

In the end, my experience taught me, that to control and best utilize LD/ADHD-traits, you, as the parent, and your LD/ADHD-children need to "live" these basic guidelines:

1. **Be consistent and have a regular program.** Children need to understand their boundaries and have structure. This is especially true for ADHD-kids as well as adults. Make a schedule and stick to it. ADHD-types always work best with routine.

2. **Give compliments.** When ADHD-kids start valuing their talents and abilities, they will learn how best to use their skills as Hunters.

3. **Never scold your children in public.** When you enforce discipline, do so in private. In general, correct or punish in private and praise in public.

4. **Get engaged in physical activity.** The best "drug" for ADHD is to be physically active. Many adults with the condition will be interested to know that one form of exercise, "sexual activity, is very good for [ADHD]."[792] Moreover, exercise also grows the brain in regions where ADHD-people need it.[793]

5. **Eat a healthy and all-natural diet.** I cannot emphasize enough how eating well saved my life. I am in much better shape than most men of my age, and this is partly due to my healthy diet. Stay away from artificial foods. They can harm you.

6. **Explore the possibility of past sexual abuse.** If it happened, tell the child that he or she is not guilty and help him or her to get counseling. Learn from your history and do not bury it.

7. **Teach ADHD-children they are different, not disabled.** Once ADHD is diagnosed, think of it as unique and special, rather than dysfunctional. Give children and adults diagnosed with ADHD the historical and evolutionary background of the condition to empower them with the knowledge of their genetics and legacies.

8. **Develop a support network.** The more you get the community involved in helping you with your ADHD-child, the more success you will have. Build a warm and loving community around your family. Don't hesitate to share with others your child's condition and what you think is most helpful for your child to thrive, like eating natural foods.

9. **Avoid using fear to motivate, especially if it is religious.** Religion should promote security, acceptance and love, not fear or sense of guilt. "In religion," British author Anna Jameson wrote, "what begins in fear usually ends in fanaticism. Fear, either as a principle or a motive, is the beginning of all evil."[794]

10. **Remember, not everyone will understand ADHD and, if some people leave you because of it, it is all right, even if that someone is a spouse.** Werner Goldberg, a dear friend and Holocaust survivor, declared, "Never run after those who do not want you."[795]

11. **Remember, life is short.** In a few decades, we all will be dead. Seize the moment and do not dwell on failures. Your

best can always be better. Try always to improve yourself. Remember, life is a passing shadow. Do all you can to make sure your life signifies something. Give it value. Being true to yourself should be your highest calling.

In the end, to overcome LD/ADHD is to realize the greatness within you. The body has a remarkable ability to adapt to situations and improvise. The more you learn what your skill sets are, the better off you will be as you learn how best to operate in a Farmer's world. If you have ADHD or dyslexia, remember that you are not defective, just different. Do not drag your selfhood around like a "ball and chain,"[796] but instead use your identity to make yourself more confident and stronger. Embrace it, and ignore negative feedback that says it's a disorder. As Joseph Campbell said, "The demon that you can swallow gives you its power, and the greater life's pain, the greater life's reply... You yourself are your creator."[797] Using the principles in this book of having a positive mindset, exercising regularly, eating a healthy, all-natural diet and having a supportive community will allow you to succeed. It took me to the halls of Yale and Cambridge and has helped me be a father, Marine, friend, professor, financial advisor, writer, historian and thinker. If I can be successful with ADHD and dyslexia, anybody can. Joseph Conrad truthfully wrote, "The mind of man is capable of anything."[798]

I envy no man who has more knowledge and abilities than I do, but I pity those who know less than I and could do more. ADHD-people can do much more than I have done. I am just an average person who achieved above average things because of the skills and habits presented in this book. I didn't write this book to toot my horn of egotism, and beat my drum of self-promotion even though I do know some of that is in here since the work is part autobiographical (if it seemed too much, I apologize). In doing so, though, I merely wanted to show that a person who has ADHD and LD as a child, or at any age, can overcome those difficulties and achieve whatever they put their mind and energy into. Everybody wants to achieve great things, but now it is up to you to put the effort into obtaining the goals you want for yourself. Do not be fearful. Go out there and do what you know is right. Knowledge without action is futile. You who have ADHD have greatness within you. Never forget it.

Afterword

ALL THREE OF MY CHILDREN have attended the excellent private school in Dallas, Parish Episcopal. Parish has a tradition that the seventh-graders all give a talk about the heroes in their lives who live according to the principles of the school which are: "Wisdom, Honor and Service." My daughter picked her paternal grandfather who is a world-renowned heart surgeon, caring doctor and good grandfather. I am honored that my boys, Justin and Ian, picked me. I wanted to share what they put together. One of the most honorable positions I hold is being a father, and I love all my children very much. My experiences with ADHD/dyslexia as a child made me very sensitive to how I was raising my children, and thus, I wanted to do my best to build a strong self-esteem in all of my progeny. ADHD taught me we should do all we can to make our kids feel confident with themselves and help them build strong foundations for success in school performance and athletic activities. Two of my proudest days ever happened when my sons read statements they wrote in front of their classes during Chapel about what they thought of me. I am honored to share them below.

Statement by Justin Bryan Rigg

Hello. My name is Justin Bryan Rigg, and tonight I will be talking about a very influential person in my life. I think that we all can agree that our parents play a big role in shaping the people we are. So, I'm here to talk about my dad, Bryan Mark Rigg and how he embodies the Parish tenant of "Honor" by aligning words with actions, helping others find their passion an continues to be courageous and resilient.

I think that one of the many qualities that makes my dad him is the fact that he will always align words with actions. If he says that he will do something for you, you can count on him to get it done. This quality has rubbed off on me as most parents tend to rub off on their kids. I try my best to keep my word and do it if I say I am going to do it. However, I am human and I do make mistakes.

Another great thing about my father is that he has been instrumental in helping others find their passion. Well, when I was little he introduced me to the military, specifically WWII, him being a historian and all. I now love this subject and cling to anything I can learn about it.

Finally, he is courageous and resilient. When he was a young boy, he was struggling with ADHD. Because of this the teachers couldn't control him. Despite this, he pushed on and now has his own business. He has taught me to never quit. When I was younger, he would always ask me, "What do Riggs do?" The answer he wanted and got was, "Never quit." Repeating this over and over for years and years has burned it into my mind and whenever I am about to quit, or stop early, I don't and I push through it and get it done.

So, I just want to thank him for all he has done for me. Love you Dad.

Justin Bryan Rigg, Spring 2017

Here I am with my sons Ian (14) and Justin (18) at the Phillips Exeter Academy and Phillips Andover Academy football game from 13 November 2021 taking place at Exeter Academy's stadium. I am happy to report that Exeter beat Andover 37-6 in this game. My son Justin is a Junior at Exeter and Ian was there to visit the school to ascertain whether or not he wanted to also attend this Pre-School.

Statement by Ian Mark Rigg

My father is one of the best men that I know.

Hello, my name is Ian Mark Rigg and today I am going to tell you how my dad represents the Parish tenant of "Service."

I would like to start off with the first part of the tenant, "Service" defined as "acting with empathy and compassion." My father rarely says any harsh words. In my whole life, I think I have seen him truly thrash something maybe three times. And although it is a little embarrassing for me, he somehow manages to make friends with anyone he meets. In addition to being very friendly, he also only offers constructive criticism, and to my knowledge, he has never criticized anyone without the intent of making them a better person.

Continuing on with making people the best versions of themselves, another part of the tenant of "Service" that he represents is "empowering the potential in others." My dad has never turned down a question from anyone, let alone myself. He also tries to answer to the best of his ability, never failing to explain any topic to the fullest. Going along with him being really friendly, he not only is good at making people better, he also loves it as well. Seeing people succeed and better themselves is one of his greatest pleasures.

He represents the last part of "Service" as he shares his talents without any expectation of reward. My dad has a PhD, played college football, and was a very avid basketball player, even playing in Europe for a little while [the International Sports Exchange for High School students]. My dad, like most, has volunteered as a coach for most of my sports' seasons leading up until this year, and he has tried his hardest to relay his years of knowledge and experience to all of my teammates and is happy to give me any advice at any time.

Although my dad could represent any tenant, "Service" stood out to me, as he is kind and loves to give aid to anyone and everyone who wants or needs it.

Ian Mark Rigg, Spring 2021

Bibliography

Books

Allen, J.G., *Traumatic Relationships and Serious Mental Disorders*, NY, 2001.

Alper, Matthew, *The God Part of the Brain: A Scientific Interpretation of Human Spirituality and God*, Naperville IL, 2008.

Audesirk, Teresa, Audesirk, Gerald and Byers, Bruce E. (eds.), *Biology: Life on Earth with Physiology*, Eleventh Edition, Hoboken, New Jersey, 2017.

Baker, Robin, *Sperm Wars: Infidelity, Sexual Conflict and Other Bedroom Battles*, NY, 2006.

Barkley, Russell, *Taking Charge of ADHD: The Complete Authoritative Guide for Parents*, NY, 1995.

Bauer, Yehuda, *A History of the Holocaust*, NY, 1982.

Bauer, Yehuda and Rotenstreich, Nathan, *The Holocaust as Historical Experience: Was the Holocaust Predictable? What Did They Know and When?*, NY, 1981.

Baum, Susan, and Owen, Steven V., *To Be Gifted & Learning Disabled: Strategies for Helping Bright Students with LD, ADHD, and More,* Waco, TX, 2004.

Beckett, Samuel, *Waiting for Godot*, NY, 1954.

Berenbaum, Michael, *The World Must Know: The History of the Holocaust as told in the United States Holocaust Memorial Museum*, Baltimore, 2007.

The Holy Bible: Old and New Testaments in the King James Version, Thomas Nelson Publishers, Nashville, 1976 (KJV (King James Version)).

The Student Bible: New International Version, Notes by Philip Yancey and Tim Stafford, Zondervan Bible Publishers, Grand Rapids, Michigan, 1987 (NIV (New International Version)).

Blanco, Walter & Roberts, Jennifer Tolbert (eds.), *Herodotus: The Histories*, NY, 1992.

Bradley, Renée, Danielson, Louis and Hallahan, Daniel P. (eds.), *Identification of Learning Disabilities: Research to Practice*, London, 2002.

Breggin, Peter R., *Toxic Psychiatry: Why Therapy, Empthay and Love Must Replace the Drugs, Electroshock, and Biochemical Theories of the 'New Psychiatry*, NY, 1994.

Burckhardt, Jacob, *The Greeks and Greek Civilization*, NY, 1998.

Burton, John, *Culture and the Human Body: An Anthropological Perspective*, Prospects Heights, Illinois, 2001.

Campbell, Joseph, *The Power of Myth with Bill Moyers*, NY, 1991.

Charny, Israel W. (ed.), *Encyclopedia of Genocide*, Volume I, Oxford, 1999.

Coon, Dennis, *Introduction to Psychology: Exploration and Application*, NY, 1980.

Crane, Laura Lee and Polk, Patricia, *Code 78: Teacher's Manual*, Fort Worth, 1975.

Dawkins, Richard, *The God Delusion*, NY, 2006.

--- *The Greatest Show on Earth: The Evidence for Evolution*, NY, 2009.

--- *The Selfish Gene*, Oxford, 2006.

Dawidowicz, Lucy, *The War Against the Jews 1933-1945*, NY, 1975.

Divine, Robert, Breen, T.H., Fredrickson, George, and Williams, R. Hal, *America: Past and Present*, 2nd Edition, London, 1987.

Donin, Hayim Halevy, *To Be a Jew: A Guide to Jewish Observance in Contemporary Life*, NY, 1971.

Dower, John W., *War Without Mercy: Race & Power in the Pacific War*, NY, 1986.

Ehrlich, Avrum M., *Leadership in the HaBaD Movement: A Critical Evaluation of HaBaD Leadership, History, and Succession*, Northvale, 2000.

Eliot, Charles W., (ed.), *The Complete Poems of Milton*, Danbury, CT., 1980.

Feingold, Ben F., *Why Your Child is Hyperactive*, NY, 1975.

Fishkoff, Sue, *The Rebbe's Army: Inside the World of Chabad-Lubavitch*, NY, 2003.

Fisher, Helen, *Anatomy of Love: A Natural History of Mating, Marriage, and Why We Stray*, NY, 2017.

--- *Why Him? Why Her?: How to Find and Keep Lasting Love*, NY, 2010.

Frank, Richard B., *Downfall: The End of the Imperial Japanese Empire*, NY, 1999.

Frankl, Victor, *Man's Search for Meaning: An Introduction to Logotherapy*, NY, 1963.

Gladwell, Malcolm, *David and Goliath: Underdogs, Misfits, and the Art of Battling Giants*, NY, 2015.

Goldstein, Michael and Goldstein, Sam, *Managing Attention Deficit Hyperactivity Disorder in Children: A Guide for Practitioners*, NY, 1998.

Green, Peter, *Alexander of Macedon 356-323 B.C.: A Historical Biography*, NY, 1991.

---*Ancient Greece: A Concise History*, NY, 1973.

Greenberg, Gary, *101 Myths of the Bible: How Ancient Scribes Invented Biblical History*, Naperville, Illinois, 2002.

Gregor, Michael & Stone, Gene, *How Not to Die: Discover the Foods Scientifically Proven to Prevent and Reverse Disease*, NY, 2015.

Grinker, Roy Richard, *Nobody's Normal: How Culture Created the Stigma of Mental Illness*, NY, 2021.

Grossman, David, *On Killing: The Psychological Cost of Learning to Kill in War and Society*, NY, 1996.

Hallowell, Edward, *Connect: 12 Vital Ties that Open Your Heart, Lengthen Your Life, and Deepen Your Soul*, NY, 1999.

Hallowell, Edward M., and Ratey, John J., *ADHD 2.0: New Science and Essential Strategies for Thriving with Distraction—from Childhood Through Adulthood*, NY, 2021.

---*Delivered from Distraction: Getting the Most out of Life with Attention Deficit Disorder*, NY, 2005.

---*Driven to Distraction: Recognizing and Coping with Attention Deficit Disorder from Childhood through Adulthood*, NY, 1994.

Harris, Sam, *The End of Faith: Religion, Terror, and the Future of Reason*, NY, 2004.

Hartman, Geoffrey (ed.), *Holocaust Remembrance: The Shapes of Memory*, NY, 1994.

Hartmann, Thom, *ADD Success Stories: A Guide to Fulfillment for Families with Attention Deficit Disorder*, Grass Valley, 1995.

--- *Attention Deficit Disorder: A Different Perception*, Grass Valley CA, 1997.

Hegel, G.W.F., *Reason in History: A General Introduction to the Philosophy of History*, Engelwood Cliffs NJ, 1953.

Hemingway, Ernest, *For Whom the Bell Tolls*, NY, 1968.

Herczeg, Yisrael Isser Zvi (ed.), *The Torah: With Rashi's Commentary, Genesis*, Brooklyn, 1995.

Hersey, Jane, *Why Can't My Child Behave?: Why Can't She Cope? Why Can't He Learn?*, Williamsburg, VA, 2014.

Hitchens, Christopher, *god is not Great: How Religion Poisons Everything*, NY, 2007.

Horowitz, Elliott, *Reckless Rites: Purim and the Legacy of Jewish Violence*, Princeton, 2006.

Hughes, Robert, *The Fatal Shore: The History of the Transportation of Convicts to Australia 1787-1868*, Suffolk, 1987.

Isaacson, Walter, *Benjamin Franklin: An American Life*, NY, 2003.

Johnson, Paul, *A History of the American People*, NY, 1997.

Kaufmann, Walter (trans. & ed.), *The Portable Nietzsche*, NY, 1969.

Keegan, John, *War and Our World*, NY, 1998.

Kershaw, Ian, *The Nazi Dictatorship: Problems and Perspectives of Interpretation*, NY, 1993.

Kipnis, Laura, *Against Love: A Polemic*, NY, 2003.

Kozloff, Martin A., *A Program for Families of Children with Learning and Behavior Problems*, NY, 1979.

Krutch, Joseph Wood (ed.), *Walden and Other Writings by Henry David Thoreau*, NY, 1989.

Lagassé, Paul (ed.), *The Columbia Encyclopedia*, NY, 2000.

Lessing, Gotthold Ephraim, *Nathan The Wise, Minna von Barnhelm, and Other Plays and Writings*, edited by Peter Demetz, NY, 1991.

Levin, Harry (ed.), *The Portable James Joyce*, NY, 1967.

Light, Jr., Donald, and Keller, Suzanne, *Sociology*, NY, 1982.

Lorayne, Harry, *Super Power Memory*, NY, 2008.

Melville, Herman, *Moby Dick*, Oxford, 2008.

Meyer, Winfried, *Unternehmen Sieben. Eine Rettungsaktion für vom Holocaust Bedrohte aus dem Amt Ausland-Abwehr im Oberkommando der Wehrmacht*, Frankfurt, 1993.

Mueller, Carl Richard (trans. & ed.), *Georg Büchner Complete Plays and Prose*, NY, 1963.

Myers, Albert Cook, *Quaker Arrivals at Philadelphia 1682-1750: Part 1-1682-1705*, Baltimore, 1957.

Nestor, James, *Breath: The New Science of a Lost Art*, NY, 2020.

Orlov, Melissa, *The ADHD Effect on Marriage: Understand and Rebuild Your Relationship in Six Steps*, Plantation, FL, 2010.

Perel, Sally, *Ich war Hitlerjunge Salomon*. Berlin, 1992.

Pirsig, Robert, *Zen and the Art of Motorcycle Maintenance*, NY, 1984.

Plato, *The Republic*, Franklin Center PA, 1975.

--- *The Trial and Death of Socrates: Apology*, Cambridge, 1975.

Poe, Edgar Allan, *Poetry and Tales*, Library of America, NY 1984.

Popper, Karl R., *Auf der Suche nach einer besseren Welt: Vorträge und Aufsätze aus dreißig Jahren*, München, 1984.

Porter, Roy, *The Greatest Benefit to Mankind: A Medical History of Humanity*, NY, 1997.

Price, Ken, *Separated Together: The Incredible WWII Story of Soulmates Stranded an Ocean Apart*, London, 2020.

Quillin, Patrick, *Healing Nutrients*, NY, 1989.

Redlich, Fritz, *Hitler: Diagnosis of a Destructive Prophet*, Oxford, 1998.

Rigg, Bryan Mark, *Flamethrower: Iwo Jima Medal of Honor Recipient and U.S. Marine Woody Williams and His Controversial Award, Japan's Holocaust and the Pacific War*, Dallas, 2020.

---*Hitler's Jewish Soldiers: The Untold Story of Nazi Racial Laws and Men of Jewish Descent in the German Military*, Kansas, 2002.

---*Lives of Hitler's Jewish Soldiers: Untold Tales of Men of Jewish Descent Who Fought for the Third Reich*, Kansas, 2009.

--- *The Rabbi Saved by Hitler's Soldiers: Rebbe Joseph Isaac Schneersohn and His Astonishing Rescue*, Kansas, 2016.

Robertson, Charles H., *Relationships, Love, Marriage, Hate, Divorce & Kinky Sex: Trials, Tribulations and Fascinating Stories of a Texas Divorce Lawyer*, Dallas, 2014.

Rose, Reginald, *Twelve Angry Men*, NY, 1955.

Rosenbaum, Ron, *Explaining Hitler: The Search for the Origins of His Evil*, NY, 1998.

Rousseau, Jean-Jacques, *The Social Contract and Discourses*, London, 1991.

Rowland, Beryl (ed.), *Companion to Chaucer Studies*, Oxford, 1979.

Rubenstein, Richard E., *When Jesus Became God: The Struggle to Define Christianity During the Last Days of Rome*, NY, 1999.

Russell, Bertrand, *Why I Am Not a Christian: And Other Essays on Religion and Related Subjects*, ed. by Paul Edwards, NY, 1957.

Schapiro, Jane, *Inside a Class Action: The Holocaust and the Swiss Banks,* Madison, 2003.

Shakespeare, William, *Hamlet.*

---*Macbeth.*

Shermer, Michael, *How We Believe: Science, Skepticism, and the Search for God,* NY, 2003.

The Complete Artscroll Siddur, eds. Rabbi Nosson Scherman & Rabbi Meir Zlotowitz, Brooklyn, 1984.

Sizer, Frances and Whitney, Eleanor, *Nutrition: Concepts and Controversies,* Belmont CA, 2003.

Smith, Seven B., *Spinoza, Liberalism, and the Question of Jewish Identity,* New Haven, 1997.

---*Spinoza's Book of Life: Freedom and Redemption in the Ethics,* New Haven, 2003.

Spong, John Shelby, *Rescuing the Bible from Fundamentalism: A Bishop Rethinks the Meaning of Scripture,* NY, 1991.

Stahlberg, Alexander, *Die verdammte Pflicht,* Berlin, 1987.

Stewart, Mark A., and Wendkos Olds, Sally, *Raising a Hyperactive Child,* NY, 1973.

Stringer, Chris, *Lone Survivors: How We Came to Be the Only Humans on Earth,* NY, 2012.

Tanaka, Yuki, *Hidden Horrors: Japanese War Crimes in World War II,* Lanham, MD, 2018.

Templeton, Charles, *Farewell to God: My Reasons for Rejecting the Christian Faith,* Toronto, Ontario, 1996.

Thucydides, *The Peloponnesian War,* Introduction done by T.E. Wick, NY, 1982.

Tiede, Tom, *Self-Help Nation,* NY, 2001.

Tolstoy, Leo, *War and Peace,* NY, 1968.

Van Creveld, Martin, *Technology and War: From 2000 B.C. to the Present,* NY, 1991.

Van der Kolk, Bessel A., McFarlane, Alexander C., and Weisath, Lars (eds.), *Traumatic Stress: The Effects of Overwhelming Experience on Mind, Body, and Society,* NY, 1996.

Von Clausewitz, Carol, *On War,* (eds.) Howard, Michael & Paret, Peter, Princeton, NJ, 1976.

Weinberg, Gerhard, *A World at Arms: A Global History of World War II,* NY, 1994.

Weiner, Michael (ed.), *Race, Ethnicity and Migration in Modern Japan,* NY, 2004.

Weiss, Lynn, *A.D.D. and Creativity: Tapping Your Inner Muse,* NY, 1997.

Wright, Lawrence, *Going Clear: Scientology, Hollywood, & the Prison of Belief,* NY, 2013.

Zabel, Mortan Dauwen (ed.), *The Portable Conrad,* NY, 1976.

Articles

"9 Strengths of Dyslexia," Nessy, 27 Dec. 2020.

Akutagava-Martins, Glaucia Chiyoko, Rohde, Luis Augusto, and Hutz, Mara Helena, "Genetics of Attention-Deficit/Hyperactivity Disorder: An Update," *The National Library of Medicine*, 11 Jan. 2016.

Allen, Jr., John L., "Second UN Panel Criticizes Vatican on Sex Abuse," *Boston Globe*, 23 May 2014.

Allen, Matthew, "Ten Years After Swiss Banks agreed to Pay Back Assets to Holocaust Victims, One of the Deal's Chief Architects Said it Helped Lift a Cloud Over the Country," *Swiss News*, 11 August 2008.

Arcos-Burgos, Mauricio, and Acosta, Maria Teresa, "Tuning Major Gene Variants Conditioning Human Behavior: The Anachronism of ADHD," *Current Opinion in Genetics and Development*, 17, 2007.

Asbury, Kyla, "Author files motion to dismiss lawsuit filed by World War II veteran," *West Virginia Record*, 18 Oct. 2019.

---"Well-known World War II vet Woody Williams sues author, publisher over book," *West Virginia Record*, 5 June 2019.

"Attention-deficit/hyperactivity Disorder (ADHD) in Children," *Mayo Clinic*, 25 June 2019.

Bloomfield, Douglas, "Credit Suisse Scandal is Nothing New for Bank that Helped Nazis—Opinion," *The Jerusalem Post*, 23 Feb. 2022.

Braithwaite, Tom, "Credit Suisse Pleads Guilty to Tax Evasion," *Financial Times*, 19 May 2014.

California's Office of Environmental Health Hazard Assessment, Health Effects Assessment, "Potential Neurobehavioral Effects of Synthetic Food Dyes in Children," April 2021.

Callaway, Ewen, "Did Hyperactivity Evolve as a Survival Aid for Nomads?," *New Scientist*, 10 June 2008.

"The Causes & Prevalence of Suicide Explained by Two Videos from Alain de Botton's School of Life," *Life, Philosophy*, 13 June 2018.

Chayka, Doug, "Revealed: Credit Suisse Leak Unmasks Criminals, Fraudsters and Corrupt Politicians," *The Guardian*, 20 Feb. 2022.

Chen, Chuansheng, Burton, Michael, Greenberger, Ellen, and Dmitrieva, Julia, "Population Migration and the Variation of Dopamine D4 Receptor (DRD4) Allele Frequencies Around the Globe," *Evolution of Human Behavior*, Vol. 20, Issue 5, September 2019, pp. 309-324.

Crowley, Jennifer, Ball, Lauren and Hiddink, Gerrit Jan, "Nutrition in Medical Education: A Systematic Review," *The Lancet Planetary Health*, Vol. 3, Issue 9, E379-E389, 1 Sept. 2019.

Denney, Justin T., Wadsworth, Tim, Rogers, Richard G. and Pampel, Fred C., "Suicide in the City: Do Characteristics of Place Really Influence Risk?," *Social Science Quarterly*, 96 (2), 1 June 2015.

Dey, Ronit, "What Do Baboons Eat? Do Baboons Eat Meat?" *Zoology Only*, 10 Oct. 2021.

The Economists, "Banks and the Holocaust; Unsettling," 17 August 2000.

Ehart, K., "Dyslexia, not Disorder," *Dyslexia: An International Journal of Research and Practice*, 17 Dec. 2008.

Eligon, John and Gatti, Claudio, "Iranian Dealings Lead to a Fine for Credit Suisse" *New York Times,* 15 Dec. 2009.

Emanuel, Janet Rettig, "Frederick Redlich, Former Dean of Yale Medical School, Dies," *Yale School of Medicine*, 12 Jan. 2004.

Esteller-Cucala, Paula, Maceda, Iago, Bøglum, Anders D., Demontis, Ditte, Faraone, Stephen V., Cormand, Bru, and Lao, Oscar, "Genomic Analysis of the Natural History of Attention-Deficit/Hyperactivity Disorder Using Neanderthal and Ancient Homo Sapiens Samples," *National Library of Medicine*, 25 May 2020.

Faiola Anthony and Boorstein, Michelle, "U.N. Panel Blasts Vatican Handling of Clergy Sex Abuse, Church Teachings on Gays, Abortion," *The Washington Post*, 5 Feb. 2014.

"Famous People with ADD/ADHD," *ADHD Center for Success*, 3 Oct. 2011.

Faraone Stephen V., and Larsson, Henrik, "Genetics of Attention Deficit Hyperactivity Disorder," *National Library of Medicine*, 11 June 2018.

"Female Infanticide," *BBC*, 22 March 2021.

Fox, Maggie, "Overdoes Deaths Hit Highest Number Ever Recorded, CDC Data Shows," *CNN*, 14 July 2021.

Freedland, Jonathan, "Pope Benedict Has to Answer for His Failure on Child Abuse," *The Guardian*, 15 February 2013.

Galway-Witham, Julia, Cole, James, and Stringer, Chris, "Aspects of Human Physical and Behavioural Evolution During the Last 1 Million Years," *Journal of Quaternary Science*, 2019.

Gokhman, David, Malul, Anat and Carmel, Liran, "Inferring Past Environments from Ancient Epigenomes," *Molecular Biology and Evolution*, Vol. 34, Issue 10, October 2017.

Goldstein, Joseph, "U.S. Soldiers Told to Ignore Sexual Abuse of Boys by Afghan Allies," *The New York Times*, 20 Sept. 2015.

Goodman, Lisl, "Insidious Omissions on Jews in War," *Sarasota Herald-Tribune*, 7 Jan. 1997.

Goodstein, Laurie, Cumming-Bruce, Nick and Yardley, Jim, "U.N. Panel Criticizes the Vatican Over Sexual Abuse," *New York Times*, 5 Feb. 2014.

Green, Kathleen, "ADHD: The Drug vs Diet Controversy," *Dallas Child,* March 2005.

Greiner, Jack, "Strictly Legal: War hero at war with book author," *The Enquirer* (Cincinnati.com), 5 Nov. 2019.

Grimm, Oliver, Kranz, Thorsten M., and Reif, Andreas, "Genetics of ADHD: What Should the Clinician Know?," *The National Library of Medicine*, 27 Feb. 2020.

Hauck, Grace, "Add Falling Sperm Counts to the List of Threats to Human Survival, Epidemiologist Wars," *USA Today*, 27 Feb. 2021.

"History of the Individualized Education Program (IEP)," Education Alternatives, 22 Oct. 2020.

Hoffman, Jon, "Flamethrower," *Marine Corps Gazette: Professional Journal of U.S. Marines*, Vol. 104 No. 10, October 2020, 94-5.

"Human Chromosome 2," *Evolution Library*, PBS, 2007.

Jaksa, Peter, "Good Stuff About ADHD!," *ADHD Center*, 7 March 2021.

"Japanese Minister Yoshitaka Shindo Visits Yasukuni Shrine Provoking China's Ire," *South China Morning Post*, 1 Jan. 2014.

Jitsuhara, Takashi, "Guarantee of the Right to Freedom of Speech in Japan—A Comparison with Doctrines in Germany," *Contemporary Issues in Human Rights Law*, Oct. 2017, 169-91.

Kimberlin, Madison, "Stephen King: Alcoholism, Drug Addiction and Fame," *Detox to Rehab*, 30 March 2020.

Ko, Kwang Hyun, "Origin of Human Language in an Evolutionary Context: Evolution-Progression Model," *Advances in Anthropology*, Vol. 5, No. 2, 2015.

Kobylewski, Sarah and Jacobson, Michael F., "Toxicology of Food Dyes," *National Library of Medicine*, July-Sept. 2012, 18(3), 220-46.

King, Tim, "Secret of Hitler's Jewish Soldiers Uncovered," *The London Telegraph*, 3 Dec. 1996.

Knowles, Harvard V., "A Need to Love," *The Independent School Bulletin: Environmental Education*, May 1971.

Knowles, Harvard and Weber, David, "The School Community as a Moral Environment," *Independent School*, Dec. 1978.

LaScala, Marisa, "The 3 Most Common Reasons Why Women Cheat, According to Relationship Experts," *Yahoo Life*, 3 March 2022.

Lucchetti, Aaron and Solomon, Jay, "Credit Suisse's Secret Deals," *The Wall Street Journal*, 17 Dec. 2009.

McKay, Brett, and McKay, Kate, "Shepherd Manhood vs. Farmer Manhood," *Character, Featured, Manly Lessons (Art of Manliness)*, 6 Oct. 2020.

Merikangas, James R., "Hitler: Diagnosis of a Destructive Prophet," *AM J Psychiatry*, 159:6, June 2002.

Milburn, Andrew, "Flamethrower," *Marine Corps History*, Vol. 7. No. 1, Summer 2021, 126.

Moyn, Samuel, "History's Revenge: What Happened to Jewish Faith When a New Attitude Toward the Past Emerged?," *Forward*, 9 Jan. 2004.

"Nationalist 'Japan Conference' Building Its Clout: Ten Days after the Meeting, Abe Officially Addressed the Issue of Revising the Pacifist Constitution," *Korea JoongAng Daily*, 3 May 2013.

"New Government Report Finds 'Toxic Heavy Metals' like Arsenic and Mercury in Popular Baby Foods," *CBS News*, 5 Feb. 2021.

New York Times, "New York Sues Credit Suisse Over Mortgages," 29 Nov. 2012.

Nichols, Michelle, "U.N. Chief Urges Equality Fight, U.S. Slams China for 'Murder' of Baby Girls," *Reuters*, 20 Sept. 2020.

Noakes, Jeremy, "The Development of Nazi Policy towards the German-Jewish 'Mischlinge' 1933–1945." *Leo Baeck Yearbook* 34, (1989): 291–354.

Patterson, Amanda, "Literary Birthday—17 May—Anna Brownell Jameson," *Writers Write*, 17 May 2016.

Peiper, Brian J., Ogden, Christy L., Simoyan, Olapeju M., Chung, Daniel T., Caggiano, James F., Nichols, Stephanie D., and McCall, Kenneth L., "Trends in Use of Prescription Stimulants in the United States and Territories, 2006 to 2016," *US National Library of Medicine National Institutes of Health*, 28 Nov. 2018.

Petrova, Jillian, "The Many Strengths of Dyslexics," *University of Michigan Dyslexia Help*, 27 Dec. 2020.

Pierce, Shanley, "Food for Thought: Medical Schools Lack Adequate Nutrition Education," *Texas Medical Center*, 25 Sept. 2019.

Pizzorno, Joseph, "Can We Say "Cure?," *U.S. National Library of Medicine Nation Institutes of Health*, Oct. 2016, 15(5), 8-12.

Qobil, Rustam, "The Sexually Abused Dancing Boys of Afghanistan," *BBC*, 8 Sept. 2010.

"Reye's Syndrome," *Mayo Clinic*, 15 Aug. 2020.

Rigg, Bryan Mark, "*Gefreiter* Werner Goldberg," 23 July 2020, Author Bryan Mark Rigg's Facebook page (https://www.facebook.com/bryanmarkrigg/posts/4124008054307982).

Rejón, Manuel Ruiz, "The Origin of the Human Species: A Chromosome Fusion?," *OpenMind BBVA*, 17 January 2017.

"Ritalin Abuse: Statistics," *PBS*, Frontline, 2001.

Roach, John, "Chimps Use 'Spears' to Hunt Mammals, Study Says: For the First Time, Great Apes Have Been Observed Making and Using Tools to Hunt Mammals, According to a New Study," *National Geographic*, 27 Feb. 2007.

Rojas, Neal and Chan, Eugenia, "Old and New Controversies in the Alternative Treatment of Attention-Deficit Hyperactivity Disorder," in *Mental Retardation and Developmental Disabilities Research Reviews*, 11: 116-130, 2005.

Sales, Nancy Jo, "Mr. Weber's Confession," *Vanity Fair*, Oct. 2021.

Saletan, William, "Was ADHD an Evolutionary Asset?," *Human Nature/New World Disorder*, 12 June 2008.

Sample, Ian, "Why Don't Humans Have a Penis Bone? Scientists May Now Know: Speed of Human Mating Might be Behind the Lack of a Baculum in Humans, Suggest Study Tracing Bone's Evolution," *The Guardian*, 13 Dec. 2016.

Schneps, Matthew H., "The Advantages of Dyslexia: With Reading Difficulties Can Come Other Cognitive Strengths," *Scientific American*, 19 Aug. 2014.

Schnoll, Roseanne, Burshteyn, Dmitry, and Cea-Aravena, Juan, "Nutrition in the Treatment of Attention-Deficit Hyperactivity Disorder: A Neglected but Important Aspect," *Applied Psychophysiology and Biofeedback*, Vol. 28, No. 1, pp. 63-75, March 2003.

Sherman, Natalie, "Purdue Pharma to Plead Guilty in $8bn Opioid Settlement," *BBC*, 21 Oct. 2020.

Smith, Aaron, "Robin Williams: Exploring Impulsivity and Suicide," *Potential Within Reach*, 25 Aug. 2014.

"The Social and Economic Costs of ADHD in Australia: Report Prepared for the Australian ADHD Professional Association," *Deloitte Access Economics,* July 2019.

Sapountzis, I., "From Jackson Pollock to Psychic Blades: Climbing the Semiotic Ladder in Working with Children with Attention-Deficit/Hyperactivity Disorder," *Psychoanalytic Psychology*, 37 (4), 2020, 305-312.

Schuster, Ruth, "Archaeologists Find Grim Proof of Man's Earliest War: Yet Some Believe Prehistoric Man was Largely Amiable: Hunter-Gatherers Could Simply Move On," *Haaretz*, 29 July 2014.

Stockdale, Steve, "Yearning to Know," *ETC: A Review of General Semantics*, Vol 63, No. 4, Oct. 2006.

Stockman, Farah, "Monticello Is Done Avoiding Jefferson's Relationship with Sally Hemings: A New Exhibit Grapples with the Reality of Slavery and Deals a Final Blow to Two Centuries of Ignoring or Covering Up What Amounted to an Open Secret," *New York Times*, 16 June 2018.

"Student with Disabilities," *National Center for Education Statistics*, May 2020.

Swanepoel, Annie, Music, Graham, Launer, John, and Reiss, Michael J., "How Evolutionary Thinking Can Help Us to Understand ADHD," *Cambridge University Press*, 2 Jan. 2018.

Varcoe, Fred, "Is Japan Becoming an Enemy of Press Freedom?" Number 1 *Shimbun*, 11 Sept. 2017.

Vierich, Helga, "Anthro-Ecology," *Anthroecology.com*, 10 March 2017.

Volokh, Eugene, "The Medal of Honor Recipient vs. The Historian, and the Right of Publicity," *The Volokh Conspiracy* (found at reason.com), 25 Oct. 2019.

"What Does it Mean to be Human?: Interbreeding," *Smithsonian, National Museum of Natural History*, 11 December 2020.

"What is IARC?," *Food Insight*, 19 Oct. 2020.

Wiesenthal Center Uncovers List of 12,000 Nazis in Argentina with Accounts Transferred to Credit Suisse, *Jewish News Syndicate*, 4 March 2022

Zeidner, Daniel, "Early ADHD Diagnoses and the Decline of Men in College: Boys Develop Low Self-Esteem and Internalize Low Expectations," *Wall Street Journal*, 24 Sept. 2021.

Interviews and Conversations

Interview with David Alkek, 10 Dec. 2020, 2 Jan. 2021, 26 March 2021.

Discussion with Laurie Bodine, 23 March 2005.

Discussion with Michael Berenbaum, 24 May 2014, 15 Feb. 2022.

Interview with Jerry Boswell, 5 April 2021, 10 Feb. 2022

Conversation with Detective Bradford, 25 Aug. 2021.

Interview Clint Bruce, 4 Jan. 2022.

Interview with Robert E. Corley, 6 Sept. 2021.

Discussion with Dr. Creedon, April 2004.

Interview Patty Crowley Brown, 23 March 2021, 2 Aug. 2021.

Interview with Mary Dalbey-Rigg, 20 Aug. 1995.

Interview with Werner Goldberg, 17 Oct. 1994.

Interview with Herschel Greenberg, 23 Feb. 2004.

Conversation with Ned Hallowell, 11 Sept. 2021.

Interview with Jack Herney, 4 April 2020.

Interview with Phoebe Hunt, 3 March 2012.

Conversation Harvard Knowles, 1 April 2015

Interview with Harvard Knowles, 21 Oct. 2018.

Conversation with Stephanie Lang, 22 April 2021, 20 July 2021.

Interview with Dwight Leonard, 8 March 1997.

Interview with Bud Littlefield, April 2008.

Conversation with Catherine Nolan, 19 March 2021.

Conversation with Melissa Orlov, 14 July 2021, 6 Aug. 2021.

Conversation with Andrew Polychronis, 1 June 1991.

Conversation with Fritz Redlich, 9 Sept. 2000.

Conversation with Donna Reynolds, 12 March 2021.

Conversation with Marilee Rigg, 3 Jan. 2005, 11 March 2021, 18 March 2021, 4 April 2021.

Interview with Mark Rigg, 18 Aug. 1996.

Discussion with Stephanie Rigg, 25, 27, 31 March 2015, 15 May 2015, 15 June 2015, 5 Oct. 2015.

Interview with Celeste Culver Rogers, 3 Aug. 2021.

Conversations with Jim Rose, 17 Jan. 2005, 23 Feb. 2005.

Conversations with Mary-Delle S., 22, 23, 24 April 2015, 9 May 2015.

Conversations with Paul S., 25 March 2015, 28 March 2015, 5 June 2015.

Discussion with Dr. Roseanne Schnoll, Associate Professor of Health and Nutrition Sciences at Brooklyn College, 17 Jan. 2005, 23 Dec. 2020.

Conversation with Hank Schuler, 30 Aug. 2001.

Conversation with Patricia Semprez, 20 Oct. 2021.

Conversation with Mrs. Sherilyn at the Child Protective Services of Tarrant County, 28 March 2005.

Interview with Yoshitaka Shindo, 9 April 2018.

Discussion with Mary Stewart, 31 Jan. 2005.

Interview with Madeline Teague, 24 May 2005, 15 Nov. 2006.

Interview with Rabbi Dr. Edgar Weinsberg, 7 March 2021, 18 Oct. 2021.

Conversation with Laurie Zuspic, 27 Jan. 2005.

Primary Sources

Arlington Police Dept., Report given to Clerk Shelly Lester, Case #2021-02150271, Case Against Sexual Predator Kevin W.

Case No. DF-15-11173, In the Matter of the Marriage of Stephanie Dawn Rigg and Bryan Mark Rigg, In the district court, 301st Judicial District, 18 March 2016.

Case No. 197676-2016 (Dallas Police Dept.—Stephanie Rigg Violence)

Case No. 285582-2016 (Dallas Police Dept.—Stephanie Rigg Violence)

Case No. 83-12594-R, In the District Court, 254th Judicial District, Dallas County, Texas, In the Matter of the Marriage of Linton Mark Rigg and Marilee Gladys Rigg, and in the interest of Bryan Mark Rigg, a child, 15 May 1984.

Letter Richard Brodhead to Yale Univ. School of Management, 5 Jan. 2001.

Ft. Worth, Texas Child Study Center Medical Records (FWT-CSCMR), Chart 158-75 MF, Bryan Mark Rigg.

The Founding Era Collection, Thomas Jefferson Papers, Docs. Jan. 1819- 4 July 1836, Jefferson to Henry Lee, 15 May 1826.

Letters Kathleen Brooks to Bryan Mark Rigg, 28-29 March 2005.

Wilburn Arnold Davidson Diary, 1967.

Letter Lisl Goodman to Jonathan Steinberg, 30 Jan. 1997.

Letter Harvard Knowles to Bryan Rigg, 6 Aug. 2005.

Loughmiller/Higgins Rigg Divorce File. 2015-2021

Mansfield Police Department, Report #20510433, Report given to Dectective Bell, Case Against Sexual Predator Kevin W.

Public Law, 88-352, 78 Statutes at Large 241 (Civil Rights Act of 1964).

Letter Jonathan Steinberg to Lisl Goodman, 8 Feb. 1997.

Talmud, Tractate of Shabbat (the Sabbath), page 31a.

Tarrant County Sherrif's Department, Case File #200503700, Report given to Officer Coursey, Case Against Sexual Predator Kevin W.

U.S. Marine Corps Medical File on Bryan Mark Rigg, Oct. 1999, Aug. 2001.

U.S. District Court for the Southern District of WV, Hershel Woodrow "Woody" Williams verse Bryan Mark Rigg, Case 3:19-cv-00423, Doc. 1, Filed 31 May 2019.

U.S. District Court for the Southern District of West Virginia Huntington Div., Hershel Woodrow "Woody" Williams v. Bryan Mark Rigg and John Doe Publishing Company, Civil Action No. 3:19-CV-00423, "Bryan Rigg's Motion to Dismiss Original Verified Complaint, Doc. #9, 18 Oct. 2019.

42 U.S.C. 12112(b)(5), 12182-84 (American with Disabilities Act of 1990)

J. Tanner Watkins, Dinsmore & Shohl, LLP, to Rigg, Hershel Woodrow "Woody" Williams Book Agreement: Cease and Desist, 3 May 2018.

J. Tanner Watkins, Dinsmore & Shohl, LLP, to Rigg, Hershel Woodrow "Woody" Williams Book Agreement: Cease and Desist, 18 June 2018.

Web Pages:

www.feingold.org

http://www.adhd.com/family/resources/fastfacts/whatisadhd.jsp?reqNavId=3.3.2

http://www.darkness2light.org/.

http://www.medterms.com/script/main/art.asp?articlekey=5351.

www.monticello.org/sallyhemings/

http://www.soulselfhelp.on.ca/afteff.html.

https://www.facebook.com/bryanmarkrigg/posts/4124008054307982

https://www.exeter.edu/about-us/academy-mission

https://www.freedomforuminstitute.org/

https://www.revolvy.com/page/Yoshitaka-Shind%C5%8D;

Acknowledgments

*"The work of the world is often performed brilliantly by those who
step up to it from out of idleness as well as out of toil."*
— Harvard V. Knowles, Phillips Exeter Academy
Graduation Talk, 2003[799]

A GOOD BOOK IS NEVER written alone. Numerous people have helped
me with this work throughout the years. Of course, I cannot thank
my mother enough, Marilee Rigg, née Davidson. She fought for me
and got me help during a time when there was little understanding of
and support for children with "learning disabilities." She was tireless
in her search for help. She also took the time at 84 years of age to
proofread the book and make sure my facts are correct. Often, she
would exclaim in giving me feedback, "Bryan, you cannot say that!"
To say the least, we had some fun and interesting conversations re-
hashing the past.

I also would like to thank my dear friend Dr. Roseanne Schnoll,
associate professor of health and nutrition sciences at Brooklyn
College, New York. She is an expert on nutrition and has provided
incredible support throughout the years and especially as I began to
write this book. Her constructive criticism, proofreading and suggested source material have helped me make this work stronger.
She believes that the positive changes I experienced while on The
Feingold Diet are remarkable and has invited me to speak about my

experiences at her school. Dr. Schnoll believes such a diet is the answer for most kids with ADHD.

My saintly teacher at Starpoint, Mary Stewart, took the time to read this book and give me invaluable feedback. Throughout the years, she has spent time with my family on trips (I wanted my children to get to know her) and we have discussed the possibility of writing such a work. She often would tell me, "I hope I had such an influence on my other students as well. You're rare in getting in touch with people to tell them how grateful you are about what they did for you in everything." On her last proofread, she wrote "Wow. You made me feel good about me! Actually, we did it together...you had all the right ingredients." As one can see, she still is encouraging and empowering me. When I went through my divorce, one of the first people I called was Mary and she talked to me often. She even called Stephanie a few times since she knew her well, and tried to help where she could. She became more to me than just a teacher in so many ways and I wrote this book, in many respects, for her.

The daughters of Laura Lee Crane (the head of Starpoint when I was there), Allen Walker and Lee Wood, provided detailed feedback and support for this work. Dr. Crane was unfortunately murdered in 2004 and unable to go through this work with me. Her spirit lives in the pages herein because she created the environment and school where Mary could help me most and I am forever grateful to her for her vision and leadership. Also, Robin Neely Davis, a teacher at Starpoint for 40 years, proofread my work and gave me insightful information about Dr. Crane, especially finding her manuscript called *Code 78* which was a teacher guide on how one should instruct LD-children to read and write when I was at Starpoint. This document gave me invaluable insights into the pedagogic techniques Dr. Crane implemented at Starpoint.

My drama teacher at Fort Worth Christian, Donna Reynolds (or Donna Drama as we good naturedly referred to her), also read this manuscript twice and gave me interesting feedback and context related to what she was doing in our classroom. Having one teacher mentor you for five years is unique for any child in and of itself, but to have one who was as creative, wacky, fun and ADHD as Donna, was a breath of fresh air. She became like a mother to me in many respects and although her own children had graduated from FWC by my senior year, she decided to stay on as my teacher during my last year there at school. The plays, dramatic duets and monologues that we students performed and she directed won many competitions. I will never forget her unwavering commitment to me and how it impacted the course of my life. She, along with Mary, made me strong and confident and I am eternally in their debt.

I must thank my former Yale mentor, Dean Susan Hauser, who helped me tremendously to navigate which classes to take and how to apply for graduate school. Without her help and guidance, I would not have received the Henry Fellowship to conduct my studies at Cambridge University. She also gave me excellent feedback on this manuscript. I am honored to have her as a wonderful mentor and friend.

For incredible words of support and editorial improvements, I like to thank Corrine Casanova, owner of the company *Daily House*. She read the book twice and gave me useful feedback on how to make the book stronger and more readable.

I am thankful to others who have helped me along the way by reading the work and offering constructive feedback: fellow author and University of Texas Southwestern Medical School professor Dr. David Alkek (USAF); mothers of ADHD-children Gina Gottlich and Kathianne Williams; excellent editor Shannon Christine; famous paleontologist of the London Natural History Museum, Chris Stinger; my fellow Exonian Annie Davidson; relationship expert and therapist Beth Johnson; dear friend Michael Scholten; Head of Upper Elementary at The Shelton School Amy Cushner (formerly known as Kelton); Executive Director Emeritus at The Shelton School Joyce Pickering; Heather McGehearty, co-founder of Stand Up LD; my friends Grant Farmer, Susan Fritz, Lee Mandel and Vajra Vogel; and my wonderful son, Justin Rigg. I am especially appreciative for Vajra's detailed suggestions about word usage and phraseology. I'd also like to recognize Bruno Nechamkin, a successful McDonald's operator and ADHD-person, for his excellent feedback. And my wonderful English teacher from Exeter, Harvard K. Knowles, looked over the manuscript and offered me constructive criticism. My first, first-grade teacher, Jim Rose, spent four hours at my office discussing my manuscript after proof-reading it. His verification of the facts within the manuscript and his general insights and feedback were greatly appreciated. Also, my seventh-grade history teacher, Patty Crowley Brown, provided helpful feedback and constructive criticism which, as always, I was grateful to receive. Catherine Nolan, a certified mediator, provided helpful advice and feedback on how best to structure this narrative, especially my divorce chapter. Reid Heller, a long-time family friend, lawyer and adjunct professor at the University of North Texas has provided helpful legal advice, historical insights and support to make this book stronger—thanks, Reid. My family law lawyer, Charles Robertson, has also provided helpful feedback and advice during the writing process. Thanks also go to my stepsister, Lori Mayfield, for her careful reading and feedback—she is also a fellow author and it is nice to have her help.

Once again, my beloved teacher from Exeter David Weber helped me tremendously to sharpen my arguments and maintain my focus on ADHD. He has remained a wonderful teacher throughout the years, and a dear friend.

I am grateful to another dear friend, who is like a sister to me, Gracie Golonka (USAF). She spent countless hours with me on the phone helping me with the text and the content. She knew Stephanie and me during our happy times, like many people mentioned here in this book, and has helped me not only put this book together, but also heal from the painful divorce. Friends like her help one get through the traumas of life---thank you Gracie.

National Director of the Feingold Association Jane Hersey has been a wonderful cheerleader throughout the years and an incredible resource for information as I wrote this book. Her detailed reading of the work helped me with my semantics and terminology, as well as with my source material. Her help and friendship are greatly appreciated.

Special thanks go to sexuality counselor Rabbi Dr. Edgar Weinsberg for his suggestions and incredible close reading of this text, helping me sharpen my arguments and think about my words, especially in exploring my divorce. Moreover, Weinsberg was a patient of Dr. Ned Hallowell for ADHD, and consequently, he offered unique insights into both ADHD and Dr. Hallowell's leadership in treating ADHD. (I cite Dr. Hallowell frequently throughout this book to support my arguments.) For all his help, I cannot thank Rabbi Weinsberg enough—he was a real *Mensch* and *Tzaddik*.

Psychologist Stephanie Lang spent many hours with me exploring the ideas I discuss in this book and giving me clinical feedback to assure the psychological terms and concepts I discuss are accurate and clear. Moreover, she has shared with me how this book has helped her help her clients as she has recommended it to them. I am honored that she has done so and I am grateful for her support and friendship. Melissa Orlov, author of *The ADHD Effect on Marriage* and fellow Exonian, also provided excellent guidance on selecting key topics to address and how to present supporting research.

For his support and friendship, I especially like to thank the world-renowned expert on ADHD/dyslexia, Dr. Edward "Ned" Hallowell. He has spent quality time with me discussing ADHD-issues and reading this manuscript. I am so humbled that Ned took the time out of his incredibly busy schedule to read my work and give me his approval of what I have written. This work has based many of its theories and conclusions on the numerous books penned by Hallowell as my bibliography and footnotes will attest. I am very blessed to call him friend and mentor.

For their incredible editorial feedback, suggestions and corrections, I like to thank Scott Drescher and Tom Berger. They both made this book more polished and easier to read through their editorial corrections and suggestions.

Nothing worthwhile is ever really done alone. We all have so many to thank for the good we have experienced in life. With the love and support of many people, named and unnamed, I was able to write this book. I thank you all.

Additional Advance Praise for
Conquering Learning Disabilities

"There's a lot of strength in this book. The childhood memories are very striking. [Rigg's] confident claim that 'disability' is the wrong language [for ADHD] is interesting and becomes increasingly persuasive as the book goes along."

David Weber, English teacher, Phillips Exeter Academy, 1970-2008

"This book has a lot of power in it for people and families dealing with ADHD and LD issues. If one takes the time to digest the information here, especially if he or she has some form of LD, then that person will come away with tools to help him or her live a more productive and stronger life."

Harvard V. Knowles, English teacher, Phillips Exeter Academy, 1974-2007

"This is the story of one child's struggle with LD, those who believed in and supported him, the trials he faced, and the successes he achieved. It contains valuable information for all who have this concern...For too long, we have looked on LD as a disease to be medicated, and ignored what a difference good diet, exercise, encouragement, proper support and perceptive teaching can make in the lives of children who are not disabled but only learn differently. The book advocates a new term, 'Unusual, with Full of Potential' or UFP rather than learning disabled, which so often causes such agony for children. This autobiographical book presents a chronological picture of everything the author experienced. I highly recommend it to all who have an interest in this subject. The recommendations at the end could change the way our country deals with LD and save so many lives which are now lost because of improper teaching. This book takes an important step in leading the way to a better education for our children."

Eugene Bonelli, PhD, former Dean (1979-1993),
Meadows School of the Arts, Southern Methodist University,
and former President, Dallas Symphony Orchestra

"Dr. [Benjamin] Feingold would have been so glad to claim you as one of 'our kids,' and so am I. Your book is amazing and will give so much hope to the countless families struggling with these Learning Disabilities."

Jane Hersey, national director of the Feingold Association and author of
Why Can't My Child Behave? Why Can't She Cope? Why Can't He Learn?

"This book can be so helpful to parents and teachers of ADHD-children."

James Rose, elementary school teacher at
Pantego Christian Academy for 28 years (1977-2004) and director of
Camp Thurman Christian Summer Camp for 35 years (1977-2014).

"Dr. Rigg is a distinguished historian, acclaimed writer, and successful businessman. It will surprise many to learn that this Yale graduate, who also has a PhD from Cambridge University, struggled with learning disabilities... In his new memoir, Rigg describes his struggles... to battle a predetermined life of academic and social failure, the life pattern many with ADHD seem to be fated. Examining literature on ADHD, Rigg outlines a program that proved highly beneficial for him that included the somewhat controversial effect of diet (he presents a balanced approach to the topic), the avoidance or discontinuance of the use of medicines, the benefits of aerobic exercise, and specialized attention for students with ADHD so that they can focus on achieving their high learning potential. Rigg's story about overcoming ADHD will inspire all students with learning disabilities and their families, showing them that their 'disability' can be overcome and their innate learning potential can flourish. As Rigg points out, 'It's not that you can't learn. You just learn differently.'"

Lee R. Mandel, MD, MPH, FACP, captain, Medical Corps,
U.S. Navy (Ret.), and author of *Unlikely Warrior:*
A Pacifist Rabbi's Journey from the Pulpit to Iwo Jima

"Bryan Rigg takes us on an incredible journey beginning with his difficult and painful childhood when he was diagnosed with learning disabilities. After failing first-grade twice and not expected to complete elementary school, he defied the odds and went on to receive his doctoral degree from Cambridge University. Rigg describes in beautiful detail how he not only overcame these challenges but was able to transform his chaotic energy into positive and focused behaviors. With the help of his devoted mother and dedicated teachers and utilizing nutritional interventions and self-regulatory behavioral strategies, Rigg was able to channel his learning differences to his advantage to accomplish extraordinary achievements. He conducted groundbreaking historical research, became a successful author, historian, professor and financial advisor. His insight, self-reflection and honesty make his story all the more compelling. This book serves as an inspiration to all who struggle with challenges that prevent them from realizing their dreams."

Roseanne Schnoll, associate professor of health
and nutrition sciences at Brooklyn College, New York

"Read this book. It is an invaluable guide for caregivers and people with ADHD and other Learning 'Disabilities.' This book offers concrete steps toward overcoming an often-maligned set of personal traits which, as the author writes, can transform perceived liabilities into successful patterns of living. Dr. Rigg delineates a host of strategies to help people of all ages cope more effectively as they adapt to personal and professional learning challenges. I particularly enjoyed Rigg's call for more compassion on the part of religious educators and clergy. I only wish I could have read this book earlier in my life to broaden my arsenal of coping mechanisms (since I also have ADHD). That's because the author offers multiple paths for living more readily with ADHD, based on his personal and academic struggles and successes, coupled with his access to an array of outstanding documented resources. Add to this the author's riveting writing style, and you will find this book can be instrumental in helping you clear the way toward resolving your own learning and coping concerns."

Rabbi Dr. Edgar Weinsberg, sexuality counselor and author of *Conquer Prostate Cancer: How Medicine, Faith, Love and Sex Can Renew Your Life*

"Dr. Rigg shows from his personal experience how he overcame a terrible handicap of ADHD. With diligent and unswerving drive, he not only finished at top schools, but also earned a PhD from Cambridge University. He is the author of six books, but this one will prove to be a life-changing experience for persons and their families who struggle with this problem."

David Alkek, MD, University of Texas Southwestern Medical School professor and author of *The Self-Creating Universe*

"This book tells the life story of Dr. Rigg, specifically through the lens of his struggles with ADHD. It is incredibly inspirational and motivational, and full of life lessons for everyone, but especially for those with ADHD and their family members, friends, teachers, and therapists. I am a therapist. When I was only half-way through reading this book, I already had a handful of clients I was recommending it to. I was also sharing with them key insights already gained. Many (especially therapist types) will especially appreciate how vulnerable Dr. Rigg is in sharing about the pain and struggles he experienced in his relationships, such as his 'failed' marriage, and the role of ADHD in these, and tips to do it differently. I also thought that Dr. Rigg was brave and right on to talk about the negative impact of religions using guilt, shame and threats of hell to motivate behavior, especially for those with ADHD. My very favorite part was when he wrote about death—and the value of staying aware of one's upcoming death. And how this helps you to find and follow your passion while helping others. I found that this book will help you develop a positive mindset about ADHD and that positive mindset will generalize to other things as well. I couldn't put this book down for long before I was eager to pick it up and finish reading the compelling and inspiring story of Dr. Rigg's life. It inspired me personally as well to do more things that I want to do. May you find it similarly pleasurable."

Stephanie Lang, PhD, LPC, LMFT, LSOTP, NCC, director of Lang Consulting International and The Fulfilling Place, LLC. She is the author of the upcoming book, *Inside the Earliest Stages of Relationships That Turn Violent (Compared to Those That Don't): How to Choose the Right Partner and How TO BE the Right Partner.*

"Bryan has made this scholarly, comprehensive work on ADHD a fascinating read, which I've rarely seen in my work or personal reading experience. I must say, despite the seriousness of Bryan's subject, I read much of his book with a grin on my face, sometimes because of his beyond-belief achievements that keep popping up (how happy this makes me as his former teacher!), but sometimes because of the way he turned a painful, horrifying story into one where I suddenly gave out a full, out-loud laugh. I'm grateful he gives ADHD families hope and practical direction and at the same time helps us all understand ADHD better. This is a must-read for every teacher."

Patty Crowley Brown, CEO of *The Write Word* **and former junior high history teacher at Fort Worth Christian School (1981-1987).**

"I enjoyed reading Bryan's book very much. I especially loved his chapters about Starpoint School, Laura Lee Crane, and the women of Starpoint who changed his life. Maybe not for the same reasons, but they changed my life as well. I am forever grateful for those who loved Starpoint so very much. Thank you, Bryan, for telling your remarkable story!"

Robin Neely Davis, teacher at Starpoint School,

Texas Christian University, for 40 years.

"I have practiced family law for over 50 years. Bryan Rigg's book is a helpful guide to how one with ADHD/LD can live a more productive life with both relationships and learning. Moreover, his chapter on his divorce is really a message of hope for people thinking about marriage or who are married (and even those who are contemplating divorce). Good communication is one of the most important factors in having a good marriage. People who do not have ADHD/LD often have a difficult time with communicating with a spouse who suffers from those disabilities. In other words, his chapter about divorce can help people strengthen their relationships and prevent some of the pitfalls Bryan experienced, and which, quite frankly, I have seen others suffer from too when they dissolve their unions. This book will help many in making their marriages, partnerships and unions stronger and that is why Bryan wrote it and he should be applauded for it."

Charles H. Robertson, author of *Relationships, Love,*

Marriage, Hate, Divorce & Kinky Sex: Trials, Tribulations

and Fascinating Stories of a Texas Divorce Lawyer

"This book illustrates powerfully how therapeutic and special needs schools play a significant role in healing and helping children with various forms of LD. Bryan Rigg's journey to learn how to learn should be read by every person, therapist, parent and teacher affected by ADHD/dyslexic/LD-issues. It is a powerful work of literature and compelling memoir of hope."

Peter Chorney, Executive Director of the Therapeutic Grove School

in Madison, Connecticut (1996-present).

"A captivating story of courage and commitment *2 Never Give Up* no matter what your age!!! The theme of WHAT WE DO WITH THE LIVES WE HAVE BEEN GIVEN MATTERS is compelling. For five years, I was privileged to teach Bryan in Junior High and High School theatre. Every part he was ever given REEKED of excellence!!! If you want to be encouraged in your life, *read this book.*"

Donna Reynolds, head of the Drama Department,
Fort Worth Christian (1983-1990).

"As a clinician in the brain science field for almost 20 years, I found Bryan's deep dives into difficult topics and experiences with his subsequent insights extraordinarily comprehensive and elucidating. At parts of his narrative, I was riveted and immersed in the story line, and also giggled at his often self-deprecating humor at times. Some key points worth highlighting are how labels, both self-assigned but also by others in ones life, can be not only unhelpful but closer to damaging.

The idea that ADHD is a natural human condition and should be consider a normal variant of temperament, especially in today's overstimulated and distractible environments would be nicely applied to all education. Taking the "disorder" component out of such diagnoses might be a good first step. Bryan's story demonstrates how PTSD could more appropriately be described as Post Traumatic Growth (PTG), the theory developed by psychologists Richard Tedeschi, PhD, and Lawrence Calhoun, PhD. PTG is a concept describing positive psychological change experienced as a result of struggling with highly challenging, stressful life circumstances. As he discusses, the successes in Bryan's life may largely be attributable to the grit and perseverance fostered through the adversities he faced and overcame, even used as motivation.

The final idea that continued to come to mind as I read the book especially during mentions of Joseph Campbell, was *The Hero's*

Journey, a template that involves going from the known to the un-known adventures in life, making victorious choices, and returning changed or transformed. Bryan's decision to document and share the details of his story is a clear depiction of such a journey.

Dee O'Neill, Licensed Professional Counselor, Board Certified Fellow in Neurofeedback, Cogmed Working Memory Qualified Coach, Licensed HeartMath Certified Trainer

"I love the light for it shows me the way, yet I will endure the darkness for it shows me the stars." The family of **Dr. Laura Lee Crane, former Director of Texas Christian University's Starpoint School (1974-1990)** suggested this phrase by Og Mandeo to be used as a guiding principle while reading Bryan Rigg's book *Conquering Learning Disabilities*. The phrase was read at Dr. Laura Lee's robing during her PhD ceremony.

As a dyslexic myself I know all too well the trials and tribula-tions that LD children face especially 30 plus years ago. In this book, Bryan Rigg presents a surprisingly vulnerable look at his own experi-ences as a person with learning differences. Bryan's life today is a tes-tament to the success of his diet and exercise approach to overcoming his own struggles with ADHD. Bryan is one of the most well-spoken and highly educated people I have ever met which is a direct result of his disciplined approach to overcoming his own challenges and leaning into his strengths. I highly recommend this book especially to parents of children with learning differences."

Eric McGehearty, Entrepreneur, Artist, Dyslexic, and CEO of Globe Runner

Endnotes

1   Talmud, Tractate of *Shabbat* (the Sabbath), 31a.

2   Charles W. Eliot (ed.), *The Complete Poems of Milton*, Danbury, CT., 1980, John Milton, "Paradise Lost," 94.

3   Slowly, but surely, Learning Disabilities is being replaced with the term Learning Differences. I will explore this throughout the book, but since for the longest time, Learning Disabilities has been used to describe people with ADHD and dyslexia, the two conditions I struggled with the most as a child, I have used Learning Disabilities throughout the work. I do not like the word usage of Learning Disabilities, but since it has been used by the medical community to define me and others with similar issues, it will be used as such throughout the book for simplicity's sake.

4   Dyslexia is an LD-issue, but I highlight it and separate it from ADHD since it was something I struggled with and is a condition unique unto itself.

5   Richard Dawkins, *The God Delusion*, NY, 2006, 318.

6   Edward M. Hallowell and John J. Ratey, *Delivered from Distraction: Getting the Most Out of Life with Attention Deficit Disorder*, NY, 2005, 4, 22; Edward M. Hallowell and John J. Ratey, *Driven to Distraction: Recognizing and Coping with Attention Deficit Disorder from Childhood through Adulthood*, NY, 1994, 43-4.

7   Edgar Allan Poe, *Poetry and Tales*, Library of America, NY 1984, "The Raven," 83.

8   Ibid.

9   Thom Hartmann, *Attention Deficit Disorder: A Different Perception*, Grass Valley CA, 1997, ix; Brian J. Peiper, Christy L. Ogden, Olapeju M. Simoyan, Daniel T. Chung, James F. Caggiano, Stephanie D. Nichols, and Kenneth L. McCall, "Trends in Use of Prescription Stimulants in the United States and Territories, 2006 to 2016," *US National Library of Medicine National Institutes of Health*, 28 Nov. 2018; Roy Richard Grinker, *Nobody's Normal: How Culture Created the Stigma of Mental Illness*, NY, 2021, xix.

10   Thom Hartmann, *Attention Deficit Disorder: A Different Perception*, Grass Valley CA, 1997, xi, 10.

11   Hallowell and Ratey, *Delivered from Distraction*, xxx; Conversation Ned Hallowell, 11 Sept. 2021; Hallowell and Ratey, *ADHD 2.0*, xv.

12   Hallowell and Ratey, *Delivered from Distraction*, 25; Malcolm Gladwell, *David and Goliath: Underdogs, Misfits, and the Art of Battling Giants*, NY, 2015, 102.

13   See Russell Barkley, *Taking Charge of ADHD: The Complete Authoritative Guide for Parents*, NY, 1995, 73; Interview with Bud Littlefield, April 2008; Conversation with Marilee Rigg, 3 Jan. 2005; Thom Hartmann, *ADD Success Stories: A Guide to Fulfillment for Families with Attention Deficit Disorder*, Grass Valley, 1995, 6.

14   Conversation Marilee Rigg, 2 Feb. 2002.

15   Conversation Marilee Rigg, 31 March 2021.

16   Dr. Hallowell believes this Hunter/Farmer dichotomy to describe ADHD-types and non-ADHD-types is very accurate. Conversation Ned Hallowell, 11 Sept. 2021.

17   Herman Melville, *Moby Dick*, Oxford, 2008, 32-3, 73. Melville's life was full of many LD-issues. He had a difficult time with his relationships, bounced around with his jobs, and was extremely creative and could become hyper-focused. He was hyper-focused when he was a duties warden at harbors paying close attention to ships' inventories and he became hyper-focused when he wrote his books, especially *Moby Dick* (which he did in one year!). But he had many of the classic ADHD-symptoms having struggled in school, in his marriage, with jobs and with poverty.

18   Walter Kaufmann (trans. & ed.), *The Portable Nietzsche*, NY, 1969, "On Truth and Lie," 44. Nietzsche's life had many ADHD-traits. He was impulsive, brilliant in thinking out of the box, sexually destructive (he died of syphilis) and was a tormented soul. These are typical ADHD-traits.

19   Conversation Ned Hallowell, 11 Sept.2021.

20   This citation comes from: https://sites.google.com/a/ccpsnet.net/english-10-survival-site/home/essay-prompt-pages/quote-based-essay-prompts/michelangelo-quote-prompt#:~:text=Original%3A,themselves%2C%20they%20will%20never%20improve.

21   Barkley, 27.

22   Joseph Wood Krutch (ed.), *Walden and Other Writings by Henry David Thoreau*, NY, 1989, 107.

23   Tom Tiede, *Self-Help Nation*, NY, 2001, 3, 28. One of the biggest false teachers is Tony Robbins. He is full of platitudes and does not really have the pedigree or education to help people achieve great things by adhering to reason and logic. He behaves like a modern-day evangelical preacher without the religion, promising wealth and happiness to those who follow only his message of being "great" and "being positive" etc.

24   Although the U.S. population in 2020 was 331,449,281, I add 20 million due to the undocumented residents living here. See Hallowell and Ratey, *ADHD*

2.0, xv, 13; Interview Dr. Hallowell, 11 Sept. 2021. See also Glaucia Chiyoko Akutagava-Martins, Luis Augusto Rohde and Mara Helena Hutz, "Genetics of Attention-Deficit/Hyperactivity Disorder: An Update," *The National Library of Medicine*, 11 Jan. 2016. In this medical article, the authors put the numbers of children at 5% to 7% with ADHD and adults with ADHD at 2.5% to 5%.

25   Hallowell and Ratey, ADHD 2.0, xv.

26   Kathleen Green, "ADHD: The Drug vs Diet Controversy," *Dallas Child* March 2005, 26. This is a dramatic increase from the estimate of 1995 that there were 2 million children with ADHD in the US (Barkley, 3). Renée Bradley, Louis Danielson, and Daniel P. Hallahan (eds.), *Identification of Learning Disabilities: Research to Practice*, London, 2002, "Introduction," xxv; Hartmann, *Attention Deficit Disorder*, ix; Patrick Quillin, *Healing Nutrients*, NY, 1989, 185; Hallowell and Ratey, *Driven to Distraction*, 6; Peiper, Ogden, Simoyan, Chung, Caggiano, Nichols, and McCall, "Trends in Use of Prescription Stimulants in the United States and Territories, 2006 to 2016," *US National Library of Medicine National Institutes of Health*, 28 Nov. 2018; "Students with Disabilities," National Center for Education Statistics, May 2020. Since several sources give different ADHD-numbers in the U.S., the percentage spread has a large gap of between 10% to 20%. This is because professionals use different definitions to define ADHD.

27   Stephen V. Faraone and Henrik Larsson, "Genetics of Attention Deficit Hyperactivity Disorder," *National Library of Medicine*, 11 June 2018. In this article, the authors claim that ADHD has a 74% heritability rate. See also Oliver Grimm, Thorsten M. Kranz and Andreas Reif, "Genetics of ADHD: What Should the Clinician Know?," *The National Library of Medicine*, 27 Feb. 2020. These authors claim ADHD has almost an 80% heritability rate.

28   Bradley, Danielson, and Hallahan (eds.), *Identification of Learning Disabilities*, Daniel P. Hallahan and Cecil D. Mercer, "Chapter 1: Learning Disabilities: Historical Perspectives," 50.

29   Dr. Hallowell cites research though, that when an ADHD-child starts early with medication, it actually helps prevent addiction later when he or she is an adult. So, although avoiding medication is something I encourage people to explore if they can, taking medication early on does not necessarily promote drug use later after the person is conditioned to rely on pills to manage their "problem." See Hallowell and Ratey, *ADHD 2.0*, 117.

30   Hartmann, *ADD Success Stories*, 2.

31   Ibid.

32   Peter Green, *Ancient Greece: A Concise History*, NY, 1973, 56; Smith, *Spinoza's Book of Life*, 93.

33   *Portable Nietzsche*, "Thus Spoke Zarathustra: Third Part," 306.

34 Hallowell and Ratey, *Delivered from Distraction*, 37. Since Hallowell did most of the writing for this book, and others where Ratey is cited as co-author, when such sources are cited, they will often just mention Hallowell although Ratey was an advisor to the works.

35 Hallowell and Ratey, *Driven to Distraction*, 70.

36 Ibid.

37 Ibid.

38 Hallowell and Ratey, *Delivered from Distraction*, 23.

39 Renowned allergist, Dr. Benjamin Feingold, said the "experts" were wrong in "saying that hyperactivity goes away at puberty." It stays with one for their entire lives. Email Jane Hersey to Bryan Rigg, 17 Jan. 2021.

40 Barkley, 17, 19, 53-4. Barkley also describes ADHD as a "developmental disorder of self-control (DDSC)." He further believes the research that shows ADHD-people's orbital-frontal cortex, which deals with behavior, is not as active as in non-ADHD-people. Barkley, 53.

41 Interview Jane Hersey, 28 Nov. 2020. National Director of the Feingold Association Jane Hersey says that there are many problems with Barkley and his methods. According to her, his claims are not backed up by any serious research he has completed involving ADHD-children and should be used with caution. She stated, "he's one of an army of 'experts' who make a good living not helping children and their families! You don't go to the baker who burns the bread." Email Hersey to Rigg, 17 Jan. 2021.

42 Rosenanne Schnoll, Dmitry Burshteyn, and Juan Cea-Aravena, "Nutrition in the Treatment of Attention-Deficit Hyperactivity Disorder: A Neglected but Important Aspect," in *Applied Psychophysiology and Biofeedback*, Vol. 28, No. 1, March 2003, 63; http://www.adhd.com/family/resources/fastfacts/whatisadhd.jsp?reqNavId=3.3.2; Hartmann, *Attention Deficit Disorder*, 2-3.

43 Hartmann, *Attention Deficit Disorder*, 144.

44 Grimm, Kranz and Reif, "Genetics of ADHD: What Should the Clinician Know?," *The National Library of Medicine*, 27 Feb. 2020.

45 Hallowell and Ratey, *Delivered from Distraction*, 55.

46 Schnoll, Burshteyn and Cea-Aravena, "Nutrition in the Treatment of Attention-Deficit Hyperactivity Disorder: A Neglected but Important Aspect," *Applied Psychophysiology and Biofeedback*, Vol. 28, No. 1, March 2003, 63; http://www.adhd.com/family/resources/fastfacts/whatisadhd.jsp?reqNavId=3.3.2; Hallowell and Ratey, *Delivered from Distraction*, 26, 55; Hartmann, *Attention Deficit Disorder*, 2-3. See also Daniel Zeidner, "Early ADHD Diagnoses and the Decline of Men in College: Boys Develop Low Self-Esteem and Internalize Low Expectations," *Wall Street Journal*, 24 Sept. 2021.

47 Bradley, Danielson, and Hallahan (eds.), *Identification of Learning Disabilities*, Daniel P. Hallahan and Cecil D. Mercer, "Chapter 1: Learning Disabilities: Historical Perspectives," 22.

48 Ibid.

49 Bradley, Danielson, and Hallahan (eds.), *Identification of Learning Disabilities*, Daniel P. Hallahan and Cecil D. Mercer, "Chapter 1: Learning Disabilities: Historical Perspectives," 51; Bradley, Danielson, and Hallahan (eds.), *Identification of Learning Disabilities*, Jim Ysseldyke, "Response to "Learning Disabilities: Historical Perspectives," 90.

50 Ibid.

51 Stewart and Olds, 25.

52 Richard Dawkins, *The Selfish Gene*, Oxford, 2006, 28.

53 Dawkins, *The Selfish Gene*, 60; Chris Stringer, Lone Survivors: *How We Came to Be the Only Humans on Earth*, NY, 2012, 117.

54 Stringer, 117. See also Baker, 3.

55 Barkley feels that ADHD has a strong genetic component. Barkley, 76; Hartmann, *Attention Deficit Disorder*, 21; Sizer and Whitney, 482; Melissa Orlov, *The ADHD Effect on Marriage: Understand and Rebuild Your Relationship in Six Steps*, Plantation, FL, 2010, 7.

56 One study found ADHD-genes were more prevalent with nomadic, hunting cultures, than with sedentary societies. See Chuansheng Chen, Michael Burton, Ellen Greenberger and Julia Dmitrieva, "Population Migration and the Variation of Dopamine D4 Receptor (DRD4) Allele Frequencies Around the Globe," *Evolution of Human Behavior* 20, 1999, 309-324. Another, more recent study claimed, "[G]iven the lack of genomic data available for ADHD, these theories [about ADHD-genes] have not been empirically tested...Our analysis indicates that ADHD-associated alleles are enriched in loss of function intolerant genes, supporting the role of selective pressures in this early-onset phenotype." Paula Esteller-Cucala, Iago Maceda, Anders D. Bøglum, Ditte Demontis, Stephen V. Faraone, Bru Cormand and Oscar Lao, "Genomic Analysis of the Natural History of Attention-Deficit/Hyperactivity Disorder Using Neanderthal and Ancient Homo Sapiens Samples," *National Library of Medicine*, 25 May 2020. Another study claimed, "Decades of research show that genes play a vital role in the etiology of attention deficit hyperactivity disorder (ADHD) and its comorbidity with other disorders. Family, twin, and adoption studies show that ADHD runs in families. ADHD's high heritability of 74% motivated the search for ADHD susceptibility genes." Faraone and Larsson, "Genetics of Attention Deficit Hyperactivity Disorder," *National Library of Medicine*, 11 June 2018. See also William Saletan, "Was ADHD an Evolutionary Asset?," *Human Nature/New World Disorder*, 12 June 2008. This ADHD-gene might be the DRD4 7R genetic variant.

57 Stringer, 118.

58 Hartmann, *ADD Success Stories*, Introduction by John J. Ratey, xiii; Kozloff, 1; Hallowell and Ratey, *Delivered from Distraction*, 7.

59 National Director of the Feingold Association Jane Hersey claimed that Dr. William Walsh, PhD, has conducted research on how "lead and other toxins can damage the brain and lead to criminal behavior." Email Hersey to Rigg, 17 Jan. 2021. Toxins also cause obesity, and salmon, unfortunely, is listed among the most toxic foods. One study found 12 pesticides in salmon fillets from grocery stories. It can take your body 50-75 years to get the toxins out of your body. Michael Gregor & Gene Stone, *How Not to Die: Discover the Foods Scientifically Proven to Prevent and Reverse Disease*, NY, 2015, 112-3.

60 Michael & Stone, 82.

61 <u>Ibid</u>.

62 Ibid.

63 Email Hersey to Rigg, 17 Jan. 2021.

64 Hallowell and Ratey, *Driven to Distraction*, x.

65 Hallowell and Ratey, *Delivered from Distraction*, 4; Hartmann, *ADD Success Stories*, 3; Goldstein and Goldstein, *Managing Attention Deficit Hyperactivity Disorder in Children*, NY, 1998, 6, 10; Hallowell and Ratey, Driven to Distraction, x; Orlov, viii; Hallowell and Ratey, *ADHD 2.0*, xiv.

66 Hallowell and Ratey, *ADHD 2.0*, xiv.

67 *The Student Bible: New International Version*, Notes by Philip Yancey and Tim Stafford, Zondervan Bible Publishers, Grand Rapids, Michigan, 1987 (NIV (New International Version)), 25.

68 Even though Genesis or *Bereishees* (בראשית – Hebrew for "in a beginning") says the universe came into being in six days, astrophysicists, including my former Yale Professor Lawrence Kraus, will tell you that all the scientific evidence shows it took place around 13.7 billion years for everything to be like it is now after the Big Bang. Our earth, by studying the spectrometry of the sun, has been around for around 4.5 billion years. Charles Templeton, *Farewell to God: My Reasons for Rejecting the Christian Faith*, Toronto, Ontario, 1996, 29.

69 Christopher Hitchens, *god is not Great: How Religion Poisons Everything*, NY, 2007, 57-8, 260; Michael Shermer, *How We Believe: Science, Skepticism, and the Search for God*, NY, 2003, 134, 198. Religious literalists place the start of mankind at 4004 B.C. (B.C.E). Gary Greenberg, 101 *Myths of the Bible: How Ancient Scribes Invented Biblical History*, Naperville, Illinois, 2002, 81; John Shelby Spong, *Rescuing the Bible from Fundamentalism: A Bishop Rethinks the Meaning of Scripture*, NY, 1991, 38. This date was calculated by Bishop of Armagh, James Ussher, who counted the generations noted in the Bible and came up with this date. Hitchens (ed.), *The Portable Atheist*, Carl Sagan, "The God Hypothesis," 228. Some creationists try to use geology to say the earth is only 10,000 years old when the science shows it is billions of years old. Shermer, xiv.

70 Conversation with Andrew Polychronis, 1 June 1991.

71 The Founding Era Collection, Thomas Jefferson Papers, Docs. Jan. 1819- 4 July 1836, Jefferson to Henry Lee, 15 May 1826.

72 Hartmann, *ADD Success Stories*, xviii-xix. Melissa Orlov, an expert on ADHD, disagrees with Hartmann's use of the Farmer/Hunter dynamic. I feel it is a useful way to help ADHD-types understand their condition and why it is a genetic reality for many. As a result, as a historian, I find Hartmann's use of the Hunter/Farmer metaphor useful in helping ADHD-types understand their condition and non-ADHD-types to understand why ADHD-people are the way they are. Conversation with Melissa Orlov, 6 Aug. 2021. Dr. Hallowell agrees with Hartmann and me that the Farmer/Hunter dynamic is a useful way to view ADHD- and non-ADHD-types. Conversation with Dr. Hallowell, 11 Sept. 2021.

73 Conversation Dr. Hallowell, 11 Sept. 2021.

74 Hartmann, *ADD Success Stories*, xviii-xix. See also Stringer, 272, 275.

75 Hartmann, *ADD Success Stories*, xviii-xix.

76 Hartmann, *ADD Success Stories*, xviii-xix; Hartmann, Attention Deficit Disorder, xxiv.

77 Annie Swanepoel, Graham Music, John Launer and Michael J. Reiss, "How Evolutionary Thinking Can Help Us to Understand ADHD," *Cambridge Univ. Press*, 2 Jan. 2018.

78 Donald Light, Jr. and Suzanne Keller, *Sociology*, NY, 1982, 500.

79 Feedback on manuscript by psychologist Stephanie Lang, 22 May 2021. See also Gladwell, 101-2.

80 Joseph Campbell, *The Power of Myth with Bill Moyers*, NY, 1991, 66.

81 Barkley, 65. See also Orlov, 18.

82 Light & Keller, 68. See also Dawkins, *The Selfish Gene*, viii, x.

83 Light & Keller, 69; Jacob Burckhardt, *The Greeks and Greek Civilization*, NY, 1998, 40-62.

84 Baker, 124.

85 Helga Vierich, "Anthro-Ecology," *Anthroecology.com*, 10 March 2017; Ewen Callaway, "Did Hyperactivity Evolve as a Survival Aid for Nomads?," *New Scientist*, 10 June 2008.

86 Poe, "William Wilson," 338.

87 Hartmann, *ADD Success Stories*, 3-4. See also Hallowell and Ratey, *ADHD 2.0*, 5.

88 Hartmann, *ADD Success Stories*, 3-4.

89 Hallowell and Ratey, *ADHD 2.0*, 6.

90 Hartmann, *ADD Success Stories*, 3-4. See also Hallowell and Ratey, *Delivered from Distraction*, xxxiii

91 Dawkins, *The Selfish Gene*, 48.

92 Ibid., 86.

93 Dawkins, *The Selfish Gene*, 48; Teresa Audesirk, Gerald Audesirk, and Bruce E. Byers (eds.), *Biology: Life on Earth with Physiology*, Eleventh Edition, Hoboken, New Jersey, 2017, 330.

94 Poe, "The Tell-Tale Heart," 555.

95 Hartmann, *ADD Success Stories*, 5. See also McKay and McKay, "Shepherd Manhood vs. Farmer Manhood," 6 Oct. 2020.

96 Hallowell and Ratey, *Delivered from Distraction*, 6.

97 Ibid.

98 Hartmann, *ADD Success Stories*, 5.

99 Ibid.

100 Hartmann, *Attention Deficit Disorder*, 26.

101 McKay and McKay, "Shepherd Manhood vs. Farmer Manhood," 6 Oct. 2020.

102 Hartmann, *Attention Deficit Disorder*, xxvii; John Keegan, *War and Our World*, NY, 1998, xii.

103 Stringer, 270-1; Baker, 124, 127-8.

104 Dawkins, *The Selfish Gene*, 66.

105 Richard B. Frank, *Downfall: The End of the Imperial Japanese Empire*, NY, 1999, 135.

106 Hartmann, *Attention Deficit Disorder*, xxvii.

107 Frank, 135.

108 Stringer, 159.

109 NIV (New International Version), 28; Yisrael Isser Zvi Herczeg (ed.), *The Torah: With Rashi's Commentary, Genesis*, Brooklyn, 1995, 42 fn 4. The Torah calls Cain a "city-builder." Herczeg (ed.), *The Torah: With Rashi's Commentary, Genesis*, 47.

110 NIV (New International Version), 28. It appears Cain only offered God fruits of the "poorest" of quality whereas Abel offered God the highest quality of his flock. Herczeg (ed.), *The Torah: With Rashi's Commentary, Genesis*, 42 fn 5. The ancient Jewish historian, Josephus, explored the concept that the different ways of procuring their food created a different "set of virtues" for each of the brothers. Abel's virtues embraced "simplicity," moving around throughout the wild "where he pleased," and being satisfied with "what grew naturally on its own accord." As a result, Josephus believed Abel was a "lover of righteousness [and] excelled in virtue" compared to his brother Cain, who was a "covetous man" whose very name means "possession." As a result, Cain wanted more and more and was never satisfied, thereby creating the negative character traits of greed and lust. Brett McKay and Kate McKay, *Art of Manliness,* 6 Oct. 2020.

111 NIV (New International Version), 28.

112 James Nestor, Breath: *The New Science of a Lost Art*, NY, 2020, 12.

113 Nestor, 12. Evolutionary biologist Richard Dawkins also notes that snoring in Hunter-cultures was dangerous and probably got the snorer in trouble with predators, and thus, this trait within a Hunter-community probably got

weeded out by the fact that snoring Hunters got eaten themselves, and thus, were less likely to pass on their genes. Dawkins, *The Selfish Gene*, 308.

114 Nestor, 12.

115 Ibid.

116 "The Causes & Prevalence of Suicide Explained by Two Videos from Alain de Botton's School of Life," *Life, Philosophy*, 13 June 2018; Justin T. Denney, Tim Wadsworth, Richard G. Rogers and Fred C. Pampel, "Suicide in the City: Do Characteristics of Place Really Influence Risk?," *Social Science Quarterly*, 96 (2), 1 June 2015.

117 Baker, 369-70.

118 Porter, 18, 45. See Stringer, 270; Paul Johnson, *A History of the American People*, NY, 1997, 33 and Gregor & Stone, 79.

119 Porter, 21, 26, 165-6.

120 Stringer, 273.

121 Robert Divine, T.H. Breen, George Fredrickson, and R. Hal Williams, *America: Past and Present*, 2nd Ed., London, 1987, 10. Roy Porter, *The Greatest Benefit to Mankind: A Medical History of Humanity*, NY, 1997, 21, 26, 165-6; John Burton, *Culture and the Human Body: An Anthropological Perspective*, Prospects Heights, Illinois, 2001, 21; Hartmann, *Attention Deficit Disorder*, xxvii; http://www.nativeweb.org/pages/legal/amherst/lord_jeff.html; Hartmann, *ADD Success Stories*, 7; Light & Keller, 344-5. See Johnson, *The American People*, 33.

122 Light & Keller, 343; Burckhardt, 40-62; McKay and McKay, "Shepherd vs. Farmer," 6 Oct. 2020; Stringer, 116.

123 Steven B. Smith, *Spinoza's Book of Life: Freedom and Redemption in the Ethics*, New Haven, 2003, 94.

124 Stringer, 140.

125 Hartmann, *Attention Deficit Disorder*, xxiv; Stringer, 24, 206; Nestor, 12, 14; Audesirk, Audesirk, and Byers (eds.), *Biology: Life on Earth with Physiology*, 330-7. Chimpanzees and baboons are known to be hunters/gatherers and we all stem from the same ancestor. In fact, humans and chimpanzees share together about 99.5% of their evolutionary history together. Knowing that our primitive ancestors had to be hunters/gatherers in order to survive gives further proof that the ADHD-Hunter ensured survival. Since the Hunter/Gatherer-gene insured survival, then it continued to get passed on into subsequent generations and into subsequent species through a process known as natural selection. Dawkins, *The Selfish Gene*, xix; John Roach, "Chimps Use 'Spears' to Hunt Mammals, Study Says: For the First Time, Great Apes Have Been Observed Making and Using Tools to Hunt Mammals, According to a New Study," *National Geographic*, 27 February 2007; Ronit Dey, "What Do Baboons Eat? Do Baboons Eat Meat?" *Zoology Only*, 10 Oct. 2021; Baker, 127-8.

126 Stringer, 274.

127 Dawkins, *The Selfish Gene*, 34.

128 Stringer, 270.

129 Dawkins, *The Selfish Gene*, 20, 35.

130 Julia Galway-Witham, James Cole, and Chris Stringer, "Aspects of Human Physical and Behavioural Evolution During the Last 1 Million Years," *Journal of Quaternary Science*, 2019, 16.

131 Hitchens, 93.

132 Manuel Ruiz Rejón, "The Origin of the Human Species: A Chromosome Fusion?," OpenMind BBVA, 17 January 2017: "Human Chromosome 2," *Evolution Library, PBS*, 2007; Audesirk, Audesirk, and Byers (eds.), *Biology: Life on Earth with Physiology*, 330, 332.

133 Ibid.

134 Dawkins, *The Selfish Gene*, 262.

135 Stringer, 29-30, 173.

136 Ibid., 206.

137 Richard Dawkins, *The Greatest Show on Earth: The Evidence for Evolution*, NY, 2009, 367.

138 Conversation with Dr. Brian Mason, 1 Aug. 2000.

139 Hitchens, 82.

140 Ian Sample, "Why Don't Humans Have a Penis Bone? Scientists May Now Know: Speed of Human Mating Might be Behind the Lack of a Baculum in Humans, Suggest Study Tracing Bone's Evolution," *The Guardian*, 13 December 2016; Dawkins, *The Selfish Gene*, 307.

141 Dawkins, *The Selfish Gene*, 307-8.

142 Ibid, 308.

143 Sample, "Why Don't Humans Have a Penis Bone?"

144 Stringer, 70, 109, 147. See also Galway-Witham, Cole, and Stringer, "Aspects of Human Physical and Behavioural Evolution During the Last 1 Million Years," 1-2, 16.

145 Stringer, 71.

146 Ibid., 106, 109.

147 "What are the World's Deadliest Animals?," *BBC News*, 15 June 2016; Stringer, 106.

148 Stringer, 147.

149 Ibid., 147.

150 Ibid., 148.

151 Ibid., 110.

152 Ibid., 106.

153 Ibid., 106.

154 Ibid., 270.

155 Dawkins, *The Selfish Gene*, 45.

156 Ibid., 46.

157 Stringer, 116.

158 Hartmann, *Attention Deficit Disorder*, xxvii.

159 Stringer, 57, 79.

160 Ibid., 54.

161 "What Does it Mean to be Human?: Interbreeding," *Smithsonian, National Museum of Natural History,* 11 Dec. 2020.

162 David Gokhman, Anat Malul, and Liran Carmel, "Inferring Past Environments from Ancient Epigenomes," *Molecular Biology and Evolution*, Vol. 34, Issue 10, Oct. 2017, 2430.

163 Mauricio Arcos-Burgos and Maria Teresa Acosta, "Tuning Major Gene Variants Conditioning Human Behavior: The Anachronism of ADHD," *Current Opinion in Genetics and Development*, 17, 2007, 234-238.

164 Stringer, 278.

165 Stringer, 117, 270; Light & Keller, 500; Gokhman, Malul, and Carmel, "Inferring Past Environments from Ancient Epigenomes," 2429-2438; Baker, 127-8. Of course, some populations did both farming and hunting and others just fished.

166 Hartmann, *Attention Deficit Disorder*, xxiv.

167 Stringer, 270; Light & Keller, 500.

168 Gokhman, Malul, and Carmel, "Inferring Past Environments from Ancient Epigenomes," 2429.

169 Hallowell and Ratey, *ADHD 2.0*, 6.

170 Burckhardt, 40-62; McKay and McKay, "Shepherd vs. Farmer," 6 Oct. 2020.

171 Keegan, *War and Our World*, 27. There is evidence that when resources became scarce, then war became a byproduct between different Hunter-tribes. Fred Wendorf discovered the oldest battlefield of mankind being as ancient as 13,000 years at Jebel Sahaba in the Sudan. Here, it appears that two groups, one African and the other Semitic, clashed over fresh water. Ruth Schuster, "Archaeologists Find Grim Proof of Man's Earliest War: Yet Some Believe Prehistoric Man was Largely Amiable: Hunter-Gatherers Could Simply Move On," *Haaretz*, 29 July 2014.

172 Hartmann, *ADD Success Stories*, 7, 9; Martin Van Creveld, *Technology and War: From 2000 B.C. to the Present*, NY, 1991, 11-2; Hartmann, *Attention Deficit Disorder*, xxvii; Porter, 17, 44; Burton, 19; Matthew Alper, *The God Part of the Brain: A Scientific Interpretation of Human Spirituality and God*, Naperville, 2008, 43-44.

173 Jean-Jacques Rousseau, *The Social Contract and Discourses*, London, 1991, 84.

174 Burton, 91. How does one come to this number of 180 million? In short, here are the deaths per some of the major events: Russo-Japanese War, 40,000;

WWI, 9 million; Armenian Genocide, 1 million; Russian Civil War, 13.5 million; WWII, 60 million; Nazi Holocaust and Mass-Murder, 11.7 million; Japan's Holocaust, 22-40 million; Chinese Civil War, 2 million; Moa's mass-murder, 70 million; Korean War, 5 million; Vietnam War, 2 million; Iran-Iraq War, 500,000; Yugoslavia civil war in the 1990s, 140,000; Rwanda Genocide, 1 million.

175 Hartmann, *ADD Success Stories*, 7, 9; Hartmann, *Attention Deficit Disorder*, xxvii. The ancient historian Josephus, although not using a term like genocide, also promoted the idea that cities cause conflict and warfare because they are based on greed and vice, causing harm to their neighbors. He was basing his theory on his analysis of the Cain and Abel story and how cities arose in history. McKay and McKay, "Shepherd vs. Farmer," 6 Oct. 2020.

176 Keegan, *War and Our World*, 27.

177 Burckhardt, 40-62.

178 Hartmann, *Attention Deficit Disorder*, xxvii-xxviii.

179 Elliott Horowitz, *Reckless Rites: Purim and the Legacy of Jewish Violence*, Princeton, 2006, 121.

180 Bryan Mark Rigg, *Flamethrower: Iwo Jima Medal of Honor Recipient and U.S. Marine Woody Williams and His Controversial Award, Japan's Holocaust and the Pacific War*, Dallas, 2020, chapter 5.

181 Bryan Mark Rigg, *The Rabbi Saved by Hitler's Soldiers: Rebbe Joseph Isaac Schneersohn and His Astonishing Rescue*, Kansas, 2016, 36-44.

182 Hartmann, *Attention Deficit Disorder*, xxvii-xxviii, 171. Ironically, although one might think farming communities are healthier, they actually are worse for the population from a medical point of view. Anthropologist John Burton wrote, "The popular view that domesticated plants and animals improved the human condition is fundamentally incorrect." Burton, 21.

183 Hartmann, *ADD Success Stories*, 11. See also Hartmann, *Attention Deficit Disorder*, 30-1.

184 Hartmann, *ADD Success Stories*, 11; Hartmann, *Attention Deficit Disorder*, 30-1; *America: Past and Present*, 32; Goldstein & Goldstein, *Managing Attention Deficit Hyperactivity Disorder in Children*, xii.

185 Ibid.

186 Walter Isaacson, *Benjamin Franklin: An American Life*, NY, 2003, 151; Johnson, *The American People*, 95-6.

187 Isaacson, 151.

188 Ibid.

189 Ibid.

190 William A. Hotchkiss, *A Codification of the Statute Law of Georgia, Including the English Statutes of Force*, Savannah, 1845, 20. This source about Georgia

was found at http://www.sodomylaws.org/sensibilities/georgia.htm#fn1. See also *America: Past and Present*, 109-10.

191 Hartmann, *Attention Deficit Disorder*, 31; Grinker, 16.

192 Grinker, 15.

193 Albert Cook Myers, *Quaker Arrivals at Philadelphia 1682-1750: Part 1-1682-1705*, Baltimore, 1957; http://www.heritagepursuit.com/Clinton/ClintonBVernon.htm; https://www.ancestry.com/family-tree/person/tree/152494213/person/412125520928/hints?usePUBJs=true; http://linton-research-fund-inc.com/John_LINTON_1662_1709.html; http://linton-re-search-fund-inc.com/CANTERBURY_the_ship.html See also Isaacson, 8-9.

194 "The Social and Economic Costs of ADHD in Australia: Report Prepared for the Australian ADHD Professional Association," Deloitte Access Economics, July 2019; Robert Hughes, *The Fatal Shore: The History of the Transportation of Convicts to Australia 1787-1868*, Suffolk, 1987, 1-2, 39-42, 62-4, 371-80.

195 Johnson, *The American People*, 53.

196 "Student with Disabilities," *National Center for Education Statistics*, May 2020.

197 *America: Past and Present*, 17.

198 David Baker, "The Origin of Agriculture in Africa: First Farmers in the Cradle of Humanity," *Khan Academy*, 22 March 2021.

199 Johnson, *The American People*, 242-4, 429; Farah Stockman, "Monticello Is Done Avoiding Jefferson's Relationship with Sally Hemings: A New Exhibit Grapples with the Reality of Slavery and Deals a Final Blow to Two Centuries of Ignoring or Covering Up What Amounted to an Open Secret," *New York Times*, 16 June 2018; www.monticello.org/sallyhemings/

200 K. Ehart, "Dyslexia, not Disorder," *Dyslexia: An International Journal of Research and Practice*," 17 Dec. 2008; Matthew H. Schneps, "The Advantages of Dyslexia: With Reading Difficulties Can Come Other Cognitive Strengths," *Scientific American*, 19 Aug. 2014; Jillian Petrova, "The Many Strengths of Dyslexics," *Univ. of Michigan Dyslexia Help*, 27 Dec. 2020.

201 Dawkins, *The Selfish Gene*, 50.

202 "9 Strengths of Dyslexia," Nessy, 27 Dec. 2020.

203 Schneps, "The Advantages of Dyslexia," *Scientific American*, 19 Aug. 2014.

204 Gladwell, 105.

205 Smith, *Spinoza's Book of Life*, 84.

206 Hartmann, *Attention Deficit Disorder*, ix.

207 Baker, 285. Baker documents that when a gene is seen at least at a 6% rate in a population, then it has an advantage to those who have it.

208 This quote comes from Elie Wiesel's essay "Why I Write" in his book *From the Kingdom of Memory*.

209 Interview Phoebe Hunt, 3 March 2012.

210 Interview Marilee Rigg, 3 Jan. 2005.

211 See http://www.medterms.com/script/main/art.asp?articlekey=5351.

212 National Director of the Feingold Association Jane Hersey writes that many mothers they have documented anecdotally, "connect stress during pregnancy to a child's later problems." Email Hersey to Rigg, 17 Jan. 2021.

213 For an interesting book on "normalcy," see Grinker's *Nobody's Normal*.

214 Ben F. Feingold, *Why Your Child is Hyperactive*, NY, 1975, 49.

215 Hallowell and Ratey, *Delivered from Distraction*, 87; Neal Rojas and Eugenia Chan, "Old and New Controversies in the Alternative Treatment of Attention-Deficit Hyperactivity Disorder," 128, in *Mental Retardation and Developmental Disabilities Research Reviews*, 11: 116-130 (2005).

216 Ibid.

217 Ibid.

218 Quillin, 9, 54.

219 Ft. Worth, Texas Child Study Center Medical Records (FWT-CSCMR), Chart 158-75 MF, 19 Feb. 1975, 1. It seems that this was a common form of punishment when I was growing up. See Hallowell and Ratey, *Delivered from Distraction*, 99.

220 Mark A. Stewart and Sally Wendkos Olds, *Raising a Hyperactive Child*, NY, 1973, 78. Since Ms. Sally Wendkos Olds only helped Dr. Mark A. Stewart write this book, when the scientific claims are cited in the text, only his name will be used.

221 Stewart and Wendkos Olds, 265.

222 Stewart and Wendkos Olds, 6; Barkley, 40.

223 Stewart and Wendkos Olds, 156.

224 William Sheridan Allen, *The Nazi Seizure of Power: The Experience of a Single German Town 1922-1945*, NY, 1984, I.

225 Interview Clint Bruce, 4 January 2022.

226 Hallowell and Ratey, *Delivered from Distraction*, 111.

227 Bessel A. van der Kolk, Alexander C. McFarlane, and Lars Weisath (eds.), Traumatic Stress: *The Effects of Overwhelming Experience on Mind, Body, and Society*, NY, 1996, 31. See also Price, 228-9.

228 Laurie Goodstein, Nick Cumming-Bruce and Jim Yardley, "U.N. Panel Criticizes the Vatican Over Sexual Abuse," *New York Times*, 5 Feb. 2014; Faiola and Michelle Boorstein, "U.N. Panel Blasts Vatican Handling of Clergy Sex Abuse, Church Teachings on Gays, Abortion," *The Washington Post*, 5 Feb. 2014; John L. Allen, Jr., "Second UN Panel Criticizes Vatican on Sex Abuse," *The Boston Globe*, 23 May 2014; Jonathan Freedland, "Pope Benedict Has to Answer for His Failure on Child Abuse," *The Guardian*, 15 Feb. 2013.

229 Mansfield Police Dept., Report #20510433, Report given in 2005 to Officer Bell concerning sexual assault by Kevin W.; Tarrant County Sherrif's Dept., Case File #200503700, Report given in 2005 to Officer Coursey concern-

ing sexual assault by Kevin W.; Arlington Police Department, Report given to Clerk Shelly Lester, Case #2021-02150271, 8 August 2021, Case Against Sexual Predator Kevin W.; Stewart and Wendkos Olds, 156.

230 Arlington Police Dept., Report given to Clerk Shelly Lester, Case #2021-02150271, 8 Aug. 2021, Case Against Sexual Predator Kevin W.

231 http://www.geocities.com/HotSprings/2656/parent.html. Letters Kathleen Brooks to Bryan Mark Rigg, 28-29 March 2005; http://www.darkness2light.org/; Baker, 324.

232 Interview with Celeste Culver Rogers, 3 Aug.2021.

233 Interview with Patty Crowley Brown, 2 Aug. 2021.

234 Interview with Patty Crowley Brown, 23 March 2021; Interview with Celeste Culver Rogers, 3 Aug. 2021.

235 Arlington Police Department, Report given to Clerk Shelly Lester, Case #2021-02150271, 8 Aug. 2021, Case Against Sexual Predator Kevin W. During Detective Bradford's investigation, she found that Kevin's ex-wife divorced him, in part, because he was addicted to porn. He was estranged from his daughter. And during the interview with his half-brother, Stephen, although he claimed he was not attacked by him, Stephen claimed he would not be surprised to find out Kevin was a pedophile since he thought of him as a sick individual. As of the writing of this book, the investigation is ongoing about Kevin. Conversation with Detective Bradford, 25 Aug. 2021.

236 Rigg, *The Rabbi Saved by Hitler's Soldiers*, vi.

237 Peter Green, *Alexander of Macedon 356-323 B.C.: A Historical Biography*, NY, 1991, 11, 26.

238 Joseph Goldstein, "U.S. Soldiers Told to Ignore Sexual Abuse of Boys by Afghan Allies," *The New York Times*, 20 Sept. 2015; Rustam Qobil, "The Sexually Abused Dancing Boys of Afghanistan," *BBC*, 8 Sept. 2010.

239 Discussion with Dr. Kevin Creedon, April 2004.

240 J.G. Allen, *Traumatic Relationships and Serious Mental Disorders*, NY, 2001, 144-7. See Ken Price, *Separated Together: The Incredible WWII Story of Soulmates Stranded an Ocean Apart*, London, 2020, 84, 226, 228-9.

241 Allen, 144-7.

242 http://www.soulselfhelp.on.ca/afteff.html; J.G. Allen, *Traumatic Relationships and Serious Mental Disorders*, NY, 2001, 144-7.

243 Bessel A. van der Kolk, Alexander C. McFarlane, and Lars Weisath (eds.), *Traumatic Stress: The Effects of Overwhelming Experience on Mind, Body, and Society*, NY, 1996, 31. See also Price, 228-9.

244 Edward Hallowell, *Connect: 12 Vital Ties that Open Your Heart, Lengthen Your Life, and Deepen Your Soul*, NY, 1999, 148-9.

245 Victor Frankl, *Man's Search for Meaning: An Introduction to Logotherapy*, NY, 1963, 104.

246 <u>Ibid</u>., 115.

247 77 Robin Williams Quotes on Life (2021 Update) (quoteambition.com)

248 Stewart and Wendkos Olds, 4.

249 <u>Ibid</u>., 63.

250 Barkley, vii, 21; Stewart and Wendkos Olds, 8, 63.

251 Mortan Dauwen Zabel (ed.), *The Portable Conrad*, "Prince Roman," NY, 1976, 79.

252 Barkley, 18.

253 Interview with Marilee Rigg, 16 Feb. 2005.

254 Barkley, 70-71; Hallowell and Ratey, *Driven to Distraction*, 51.

255 Tiede, 179.

256 Jane Hersey, *Why Can't My Child Behave?: Why Can't She Cope? Why Can't He Learn?*, Williamsburg, VA, 2014, 2, 6.

257 <u>Ibid</u>.

258 NIV (New International Version), 571.

259 Feingold, 99.

260 FWT, CSCMRC, 158-75 MF, 19 Feb. 1975, 1-2.

261 Hallowell and Ratey, *Delivered from Distraction*, 121; Stewart and Wendkos Olds, 254; Martin A. Kozloff, *A Program for Families of Children with Learning and Behavior Problems*, NY, 1979, 16.

262 FWT, CSCMRC, 158-75 MF, 19 Feb. 1975, 1-2.

263 <u>Ibid</u>.

264 For a history of this term, see Klaus W. Lange, Susanne Reichl, Katharina M. Lange, Lara Tucha and Oliver Tucha, "The History of Attention Deficit Hyperactivity Disorder," *US National Library of Medicine National Institutes of Health*, 30 Nov. 2010 & Sam D. Clements, "Minimal Brain Dysfunction in Children: Terminology and Identification Phase One of Three-Phase Project," *U.S. Department of Health, Education and Welfare*, 1966.

265 Dennis Coon, *Introduction to Psychology: Exploration and Application*, NY, 1980, 360-1.

266 Stewart and Wendkos Olds, 15.

267 Hallowell and Ratey, *Driven to Distraction*, 13.

268 FWT, CSCMRC, 158-75 MF, 22 April 1975, 1-2. The MBD condition has also been called brain-injury syndrome (Barkley, 24); Feingold, 18; Hartmann, *Attention Deficit Disorder*, xi. Sometimes this was also called minimal brain injury. Bradley, Danielson, and Hallahan (eds.), *Identification of Learning Disabilities*, Jack Fletcher, Marcia Barnes, David Francis, and Sally Shaywitz, "Chapter III: Classification of Learning Disabilities: An Evidence-Based Evaluation," 187; Bradley, Danielson, and Hallahan (eds.), *Identification of Learning Disabilities*, Daniel P. Hallahan and Cecil D. Mercer, "Chapter 1: Learning Disabilities:

Historical Perspectives," 17; Stewart and Wendkos Olds, 13, 15; Michael Goldstein and Sam Goldstein, *Managing Attention Deficit Hyperactivity Disorder in Children: A Guide for Practitioners*, NY, 1998, xi, 5; Coon, 360-1; Laura Lee Crane and Patricia Polk, Code 78: *Teacher's Manual*, Fort Worth, 1975, 1. Although there are two authors on the manuscript, the bulk of the research and writing was done by Dr. Crane. Hence, when this source is referenced, it will use only her name.

269 Ibid.
270 Poe, "William Wilson," 347.
271 Conrad, "Amy Foster," 156.
272 No. 83-12594-R, In the District Court, 254th Judicial District, Dallas County, TX, In the Matter of the Marriage of Linton Mark Rigg and Marilee Gladys Rigg, and in the interest of Bryan Mark Rigg, a child, 15 May 1984.
273 Interview with Mark Rigg, 18 Aug. 1996.
274 Napoleon Bonaparte (essaydocs.org)
275 Conversation with Hank Schuler, 30 Aug. 2001; Interview with Mark Rigg, 18 Aug. 1996.
276 Interview with Marilee Rigg, 4 April 2021; Interview with Dwight Leonard, 8 March 1997.
277 Interview with Mary Dalbey-Rigg, 20 Aug. 1995.
278 Wilburn Arnold Davidson Diary, 8 March 1967.
279 Interview with Dwight Leonard, 8 March 1997.
280 Conversation with Hank Schuler, 30 Aug. 2001.
281 Bradley, Danielson, and Hallahan (eds.), *Identification of Learning Disabilities*, Daniel P. Hallahan and Cecil D. Mercer, "Chapter 1: Learning Disabilities: Historical Perspectives," 24.
282 Feingold, 3, 16; Hartmann, *Attention Deficit Disorder*, 68. According to Dr. Russell Barkley, up to 35% of all ADHD-kids "may fail to complete high school"(Barkley, 18). He also quotes a figure that 25% "are expelled from high school" (Barkley, 19); Barkley, 18; Hallowell and Ratey, *Driven to Distraction*, 16, 44.
283 Stewart and Wendkos Olds, 77; Conversation with Marilee Rigg, 3 Jan. 2005; Hartmann, *ADD Success Stories*, xix; Hartmann, *Attention Deficit Disorder*, 10, 58; Hallowell and Ratey, *Delivered from Distraction* 25, 101, 121; Barkley, 73; Goldstein & Goldstein, *Managing Attention Deficit Hyperactivity Disorder in Children*, xiv; Hallowell and Ratey, *Delivered from Distraction*, xxx.
284 Hersey, 353.
285 Ibid., 356.
286 Stewart and Wendkos Olds, 77; Conversation with Marilee Rigg, 3 Jan. 2005; Hartmann, *ADD Success Stories*, xix; Hartmann, *Attention Deficit Disorder*, 10, 58; Hallowell and Ratey, *Delivered from Distraction* 25, 101, 121; Barkley, 73; Goldstein & Goldstein, *Managing Attention Deficit Hyperactivity Disorder in Children*, xiv.

287 ADHD-people do also have problems with foreign languages. Hallowell and Ratey, *Delivered from Distraction*, 77.

288 Bradley, Danielson, and Hallahan (eds.), *Identification of Learning Disabilities*: Daniel P. Hallahan and Cecil D. Mercer, "Chapter 1: Learning Disabilities: Historical Perspectives," 43 & Barbara Foorman, "Classroom Prevention Through Differentiated Instruction: Response to Jenkins and O'Connor," 154; and Phyllis Raynor, "Early Identification and Intervention for Young Children with Reading/Learning Disabilities," 173.

289 Susan Baum and Steven V. Owen, *To Be Gifted & Learning Disabled: Strategies for Helping Bright Students with LD, ADHD, and More*, Waco, TX, 2004, xiii.

290 FWT, CSCMRC, 158-75 MF, 7 March 1979, 2-3.

291 Bradley, Danielson, and Hallahan (eds.), *Identification of Learning Disabilities*: Daniel P. Hallahan and Cecil D. Mercer, "Chapter 1: Learning Disabilities: Historical Perspectives," 43 & Barbara Foorman, "Classroom Prevention Through Differentiated Instruction: Response to Jenkins and O'Connor," 154; and Phyllis Raynor, "Early Identification and Intervention for Young Children with Reading/Learning Disabilities," 173.

292 Ibid.

293 Bradley, Danielson, and Hallahan (eds.), *Identification of Learning Disabilities*, Joseph Jenkins and Rollanda O'Connor, "Chapter II: Early Identification and Intervention for Young Children with Reading/Learning Disabilities," 127, 135.

294 FWT, CSCMRC, 158-75 MF, 7 March 1979, 2-3.

295 Ibid., 3.

296 Conversation with Marilee Rigg, 3 Jan. 2005.

297 Fidgetting and rocking in chairs often falling over is something that happens to some hyperactive children. Stewart and Wendkos Olds, 5. Also, breaking of pencils seems to be a response ADHD-kids may have when they cannot understand an assignment during grade school. See Hallowell and Ratey, *Driven to Distraction*, x.

298 Conversations with Jim Rose, 17 Jan. 2005, 23 Feb. 2005.

299 Conversations with Jim Rose, 17 Jan. 2005, 23 Feb. 2005. In reviewing the manuscript, Jim Rose notes, "I never doubted how intelligent you were and your desire to learn." However, in saying this, he noted that the frustration I had at not being able to learn like others was apparent for all to see and this worried him. Review by James Rose of *Overcoming Learning Disabilities*, 22 Jan. 2021.

300 Conversations with Jim Rose, 17 Jan. 2005, 23 Feb. 2005.

301 Kozloff, 15; Stewart and Wendkos Olds, xi, 35; Hersey, 123.

302 Hersey, 123.

303 Kozloff, 15; Stewart and Wendkos Olds, xi, 35.

304 Hallowell and Ratey, *Driven to Distraction*, 43.
305 Conversation Ned Hallowell, 11 September 2021.
306 Jim Rose feels bad about this today and wished he had not performed spankings. When reading this section, he wrote, "Yep, too tough—please forgive me." Administrating spankings at schools was just how things were done back in the 1970s. Review by James Rose of *Overcoming Learning Disabilities*, 22 Jan. 2021.
307 Stewart and Wendkos Olds, xi-xii.
308 Goldstein & Goldstein, *Managing Attention Deficit Hyperactivity Disorder in Children*, 18.
309 Conversations with Jim Rose, 17 Jan. 2005, 23 Feb. 2005.
310 Stewart and Wendkos Olds, 264.
311 Conversations with Jim Rose, 17 Jan. 2005, 23 Feb. 2005.
312 Interview Madeline Teague, 24 May 2005.
313 Interview with Marilee Rigg, 3 Jan. 2005.
314 Bradley, Danielson, and Hallahan (eds.), *Identification of Learning Disabilities*: Joseph Jenkins and Rollanda O'Connor, "Chapter II: Early Identification and Intervention for Young Children with Reading/Learning Disabilities," 99, 101; Phyllis Raynor, "Early Identification and Intervention for Young Children with Reading/Learning Disabilities," 173.
315 Ibid.
316 Hersey, 13. ADHD-children often have problems with motor coordination. I especially did with tying my shoes or writing out letters.
317 Hersey, 13; Barkley, 88.
318 Feingold, 57; U.S. Marine Corps Medical File on Bryan Mark Rigg, Oct. 1999, Aug. 2001; Medical Exams with Dr. Michelle Brochner, 2013.
319 FWT, CSCMRC, 158-75 MF, 7 March 1979, 2-3.
320 Bradley, Danielson, and Hallahan (eds.), *Identification of Learning Disabilities*, Daniel P. Hallahan and Cecil D. Mercer, "Chapter 1: Learning Disabilities: Historical Perspectives," 32.
321 Ibid.
322 "History of the Individualized Education Program (IEP)," Education Alternatives, 22 Oct. 2020.
323 42 U.S.C. 12112(b)(5), 12182-84 (Americans with Disabilities Act of 1990); Barkley, 107.
324 Public Law, 88-352, 78 Statutes at Large 241 (Civil Rights Act of 1964). For an interesting essay on how Special Education is and should be implimented in public schools, see "Parents' and Educators' Perspectives on Inclusion of Students with Disabilities," by James M. Kauffman, Bernd Ahrbeck, Dimitris Anastasiou, Jeanmarie Badar, Jean B. Crockett, Marion Felder, Daniel P. Hallahan, Garry Hornby, Joao Lopes, Paige C. Pullen and Carl R. Smith in the

book *New Directions in Inclusive Education: Perspectives, Realities, and Research,* edited by C. Byle & K. Allen and James M. Kauffman, Bernd Ahrbeck, Dimitris Anastasiou, Jeanmarie Badar, Marion Felder and Betty A. Hallenbeck, "Exceptionality," Vol. 29, No. 1, 2021, 16-28.

325 Barkley, 18, 96-7; Stewart and Wendkos Olds, 73.

326 Ibid.

327 Barkley, 18.

328 Barkley, 70-71; Hallowell and Ratey, *Driven to Distraction,* 51.

329 Russell, 40.

330 Methylphenidate hydrochloride.

331 FWT, CSCMRC, 158-75 MF, 26 March 1979, 2; Conversation with Marilee Rigg, 3 Jan. 2005.

332 As dictionary.com defines rickets: "A deficiency disease resulting from a lack of vitamin D or calcium and from insufficient exposure to sunlight, characterized by defective bone growth, occurring chiefly in children. Also called rachitis (*aka* rickets).

333 Interview Jerry Boswell, 5 April 2021.

334 Stewart and Wendkos Olds, 239.

335 Ibid., 241.

336 Stewart and Wendkos Olds, 233, 241, 255-8; Feingold, 62. Although Barkley thinks drugs like Ritalin can be helpful, he also lists several side effects that can occur. Barkley, 255-8. Stephen Boyd, Kathryn Dykman, Candace McDaniel, Bill McAnalley, Bob Ward and Reg McDaniel, "The Science of Glyconutritional Supplementation: A Rediscovery of Primal Components in Human Nutrition," *Fisher Institute of Medical Research,* December 1998.

337 Quillin, ix, 8, 23, 185, 208; Feingold, 36, 103. Many medications for ADHD are not taken during pregnancy due to side effects. Orlov, 93.

338 Feingold, 36, 103.

339 "Ritalin Abuse: Statistics," PBS, Frontline, 2001.

340 Quillin, ix, 8, 23, 185, 208; Feingold, 36, 103. Ritalin is often overused and has negative effects for many. See also Hersey, 40.

341 My next-door neighbor, Jerry Boswell, also had a long talk with my parents about drugs which may have also had an influence on them taking me off of drugs to treat ADHD. Jerry is head of CCHR here in Texas, an advocate for choosing natural solutions for hyperactive children instead of drugs. Interview with Jerry Boswell, 5 April 2021.

342 Hersey, 224.

343 Ibid., 226.

344 Ibid., 358.

345 Hartmann, *Attention Deficit Disorder,* 67. Although Hallowell supports the use of drugs, he does admit that cocaine and Ritalin have similar effects on

the ADHD-mind. Since we know cocaine is bad for you, one might also argue that Ritalin, since it has the similar effect and is a drug, is also bad for you. Hallowell does concede that for those who drugs help, they should know that it only ameliorates the syndrome but does not cure it. Hallowell and Ratey, *Driven to Distraction*, 173, 235.

346 Quillin, 23-4.

347 Ibid. See also Gregor & Stone, 10-11.

348 Hallowell and Ratey, *Delivered from Distraction*, 245-7. Discussion with Dr. Halowell's patient Rabbi Ed Weinsberg, 7 March 2021; Conversation with Ned Hallowell, 11 Sept. 2021.

349 Hallowell and Ratey, *Delivered from Distraction*, 245-7; Conversation with Ned Hallowell, 11 Sept. 2021. See aso Orlov, 16, 75-6. I also disagree with Orlov's heavy focus on medications instead of diet and exercise.

350 Feingold, 63-4. See also Gregor & Stone, 10-11.

351 Hallowell and Ratey, *Driven to Distraction*, 235.

352 Quillin, 30.

353 Stewart and Wendkos Olds, 233.

354 Hartmann, *ADD Success Stories*, 149.

355 Ibid.

356 Stewart and Wendkos Olds, 245.

357 Hartmann, *Attention Deficit Disorder*, 92.

358 Ibid., 83.

359 Interview with David Alkek, 10 Dec. 2020. See also Joseph Pizzormo, "Can We Say "Cure?", *U.S. National Library of Medicine Nation Institutes of Health*, Oct. 2016, 15(5), 8-12.

360 Quillin, 30-31. See also Gregor & Stone, x-xi, 1.

361 Dr. Roseanne Schnoll, an expert nutritional scientist, says that medical schools are sorely lacking in offering nutritional science as a part of their curriculums. She writes, "Most medical schools offer less than 30 hours of nutrition education and this may only include the direct role of nutrients in cellular energy production." Dr. David Alkek, M.D., disagrees based on his own experience.

362 Quillin, 44. National Director of the Feingold Association, Jane Hersey wrote that even training for dietitians is not very good today. She wrote, "The American Dietetics Assocaition (their old name) has been a foe for years [of the Feingold diet]. It gets lots of money from Big Food [companies]." Letter Jane Hersey to Bryan Rigg, 17 Jan. 2021. For some recent research on this topic, see Shanley Pierce, "Food for Thought: Medical Schools Lack Adequate Nutrition Education," Texas Medical Center, 25 Sept. 2019; Jennifer Crowley, Lauren Ball, and Gerrit Jan Hiddink, "Nutrition in Medical Education: A Systematic Review," *The Lancet Planetary Health*, Vol. 3, Issue 9, E379-E389, 1 Sept. 2019.

363 Quillin, 35; Gregor & Stone, 119.

364 Gregor & Stone, 2.

365 Hartmann, *Attention Deficit Disorder*, 82-6.

366 Hartmann, *Attention Deficit Disorder*, 103, 105-7. See also Barkley, 55-6; Gregor & Stone, 8.

367 Dina Gusovsky, "Americans Consume Vast Majority of the World's Opioids," *CNBC*, 27 April 2016.

368 Natalie Sherman, "Purdue Pharma to Plead Guilty in $8bn Opioid Settlement," BBC, 21 Oct. 2020.

369 Maggie Fox, "Drug Overdoes Deaths Hit Highest Number Ever Recorded, CDC Data Shows," *CNN*, 14 July 2021.

370 Gregor & Stone, 239.

371 Ibid., 244.

372 Hartmann, *Attention Deficit Disorder*, 44, 77, 160-2.

373 Ibid. See also Zeidner, "Early ADHD Diagnoses and the Decline of Men in College," *Wall Street Journal*, 24 Sept. 2021.

374 Campbell, 110.

375 Feingold, 63-4.

376 "Attention-deficit/hyperactivity Disorder (ADHD) in Children," *Mayo Clinic*, 25 June 2019; Feingold, 63-4; Goldstein & Goldstein, *Managing Attention Deficit Hyperactivity Disorder in Children*, xiii.

377 Schnoll, 64; Green, "AHDH," 28; Barkley, viii, 66-8; Quillin, 184; Feingold, 12, 16.

378 Hersey, 82, 207, 210, 214.

379 Ibid.

380 Peiper, Ogden, Simoyan, Chung, Caggiano, Nichols, and McCall, "Trends in Use of Prescription Stimulants in the United States and Territories, 2006 to 2016," *US National Library of Medicine National Institutes of Health*, 28 Nov. 2018.

381 Quillin, 2.

382 Ibid., 8-9.

383 Ibid., 9.

384 Hartmann, *Attention Deficit Disorder*, 49; Hallowell and Ratey, *Delivered from Distraction*, 110; Quillin, 38, 210; Hallowell and Ratey, *Driven to Distraction*, 261

385 Green, "ADHD," 29. And sometimes, medications quite simply don't work. See Orlov, 94-5.

386 Hallowell and Ratey, *Delivered from Distraction*, 17.

387 Hartmann, *Attention Deficit Disorder*, 64; Hallowell and Ratey, *Driven to Distraction*, 238.

388 Acetylsalicylic acid.

389 "Reye's Syndrome," *Mayo Clinic*, 15 Aug. 2020; Hersey, 8, 221.

390 Hersey, 8, 221.

391 Hartmann, *Attention Deficit Disorder*, 68, 91. Interestingly, it seems ADHD-people have less dopamine than non-ADHD-people, and a key problem with Parkinson's patients is that they don't produce enough dopamine. Barkley, 60.

392 Hallowell and Ratey, *Delivered from Distraction*, 63.

393 Although Feingold's findings have helped thousands of children, his conclusions are controversial. People have questioned the validity of his claims since his conclusions "were based on his own clinical observations rather than on rigorous experimental evidence" (Schnoll, 64). Yet, the countless cases he documented showing how people's health improved by eating healthier, all-natural foods cannot be disputed. He wrote in 1968 that there was ample evidence to see that there is a direct correlation with hypersensitivity to eating artificial flavors and colors (Feingold, 12). Numerous studies have been conducted that have tried to disprove Feingold's theory, but these studies have yielded "mixed and inconsistent results" (Green, "AHDH," 28). According to Barkley, diet does not play any role in ADHD (Barkley, viii, 66-8). I strongly disagree, because my life and the lives of others have been profoundly affected by Feingold's principles. However, anecdotal evidence is not respected in academics. In general, the jury is still out about diet, but there seems to be more and more evidence that the healthier you eat, the better you will behave and live, especially if you are ADHD. Quillin, 184; Feingold, 16. National Director of the Feingold Association Jane Hersey wrote, "Feingold told us that as a clinician, his role was to help the patient get well, even if he did not understand how the therapy worked…he cited the example of aspirin which was used even though its mechanism was not understood. It was the job of the researchers to understand WHY something worked and he called on the government and his colleagues to begin doing this research." Email Hersey to Rigg, 17 Jan. 2021.

394 Hartmann, *Attention Deficit Disorder*, xiii; Rojas and Chan, 117-21; Quillin, 6, 13.

395 Feingold, 3, 6; Quillin, 20.

396 Quillin, 181.

397 Feingold, 21, 110.

398 Hersey, 22, 26, 255.

399 Feingold, 25-48.

400 Sarah Kobylewski and Michael F. Jacobson, "Toxicology of Food Dyes," *National Library of Medicine*, July-Sept. 2012, 18(3), 220-46; "What is IARC?," *Food Insight*, 19 Oct. 2020.

401 Hersey, 25, 143, 195, 254, 286; Quillin, 125.

402 California's Office of Environmental Health Hazard Assessment, Health Effects Assessment, "Potential Neurobehavioral Effects of Synthetic Food Dyes in Children," April 2021, 23.

403 Discussion with Dr. Roseanne Schnoll, 17 Jan. 2005; Quillin, 125, 182; Hersey, 75, 78, 104.

404 Hersey, 78.

405 Discussion with Dr. Roseanne Schnoll, 17 Jan. 2005; Quillin, 125, 182.

406 Gregor & Stone, 206.

407 Hersey, 196-8. See also Orlov, 13.

408 Hersey, 196-8; Paul Lagassé (ed.), *The Columbia Encyclopedia*, NY, 2000, 1989. See also Gregor & Stone, 203.

409 Quillin, 7, 9, 18.

410 Ibid.

411 Peiper, Ogden, Simoyan, Chung, Caggiano, Nichols, and McCall, "Trends in Use of Prescription Stimulants in the United States and Territories, 2006 to 2016," *US National Library of Medicine National Institutes of Health*, 28 Nov. 2018.

412 Schnoll, 71; Hersey, 79. Frances Sizer and Eleanor Whitney, *Nutrition: Concepts and Controversies*, Belmont CA, 2003, 482.

413 Quoted in Hersey, 1. Feingold, 74.

414 Feingold, 73-4.

415 Ibid.

416 Feingold, 73-4; Hersey, 119.

417 Feingold, 36, 79.

418 Stewart and Wendkos Olds, 68.

419 Hersey, 114.

420 Ibid., 114, 131, 141.

421 Quillin, 58, 185; Hersey, 141.

422 Ibid.

423 Quote from Green, "ADHD," 28. See also Roseanne Schnoll, Dmitry Burshteyn, and Juan Cea-Aravena, "Nutrition in the Treatment of Attention-Deficit Hyperactivity Disorder: A Neglected but Important Aspect," *Applied Psychophysiology and Biofeedback*, Vol. 28, No. 1, March 2003.

424 Schnoll, 63; Green, "ADHD," 28; Hersey, 123.

425 Hersey, 130.

426 Green, "ADHD," 27.

427 Quote from Green, "ADHD," 27. See also Schnoll, 67; Hersey, 90.

428 Green, "ADHD," 28. See Frank Lawlis, *The ADD Answer: How to Help Your Child Now*; Hersey, 104. In my opinion, do away with all sugar. The CDC estimates that 37% of U.S. adults have prediabetes. That is 86 million people, "most of who will become full-blown diabetics." Gregor & Stone, 120.

429 Hartmann, *ADD Success Stories*, 43. Processed sugar is sugar that has been extracted from the sugar cane or beets without the other elements of the plants being there.

430 Feingold, 78.

431 Feingold, 14, 132, 135; Hersey, 25.

432 Gregor & Stone, 6.

433 FWT-CSCMR, Case Summary, 22 April, 3 and Chart 1-58-75, 26 March 1979.

434 Hersey, 122.

435 Gregor & Stone, 200-4.

436 Hersey, 12.

437 Ibid., 128.

438 Hallowell and Ratey, *Delivered from Distraction*, 121; Hersey, 34, 42, 109, 134. Many chemicals used to clean swimming pools are harmful to kids, especially ADHD-children. Email Hersey to Rigg, 17 Jan. 2021.

439 Grace Hauck, "Add Falling Sperm Counts to the List of Threats to Human Survival, Epidemiologist Wars," *USA Today*, 27 Feb. 2021.

440 Ibid.

441 Ibid.

442 Ibid.

443 Hersey, 24; Hartmann, *Attention Deficit Disorder*, xii.

444 Hersey, 211.

445 Hartmann, *Attention Deficit Disorder*, 49; Hallowell and Ratey, *Delivered from Distraction*, 110; Quillin, 38, 210; Hallowell and Ratey, *Driven to Distraction*, 261

446 Quillin, 7, 9, 18.

447 Sarah Kobylewski and Michael F. Jacobson, "Toxicology of Food Dyes," *National Library of Medicine*, July-Sept. 2012, 18(3), 220-46; "What is IARC?," *Food Insight*, 19 Oct. 2020.

448 *Portable Nietzsche*, "Thus Spoke Zarathustra: Second Part," 208.

449 Bradley, Danielson, and Hallahan (eds.), *Identification of Learning Disabilities*, Daniel P. Hallahan and Cecil D. Mercer, "Chapter 1: Learning Disabilities: Historical Perspectives," 46.

450 Orlov, 86. ADHD-expert Melissa Orlov believes that learning one has ADHD as an adult is much harder to deal with than finding out as a child and beginning to deal with the condition early in life.

451 Hallowell and Ratey, *Delivered from Distraction*, 80.

452 Conversation with Mary Stewart, 29 Jan. 2005.

453 Hallowell and Ratey, *Delivered from Distraction*, xxvii; Hartmann, *Attention Deficit Disorder*, 41; Hallowell and Ratey, *Driven to Distraction*, 52.

454 Hallowell and Ratey, *Driven to Distraction*, 12; Gerhard Weinberg, *A World at Arms: A Global History of World War II*, NY, 1994, 894; John W. Dower, *War Without Mercy: Race & Power in the Pacific War*, NY, 1986, 47; Israel W. Charny (ed.), *Encyclopedia of Genocide*, Vol. I, Oxford, 1999, 150; Rigg, *Flamethrower*, chapter 5.

455 "Female Infanticide," *BBC*, 22 March 2021; Michelle Nichols, "U.N. Chief Urges Equality Fight, U.S. Slams China for 'Murder' of Baby Girls," *Reuters*, 20 Sept. 2020; Baker, 375.

456 Kozloff, 1, 10, 12, 15.

457 Ibid.

458 Ibid.

459 Interview Marilee Rigg, 16 Feb. 2005.

460 Being called dumb, stupid or lazy is a common experience ADHD-kids often endure. It is an uneducated response of people who may interact with ADHD-children. Hallowell and Ratey, *Driven to Distraction*, 16-7.

461 Obviously then, at the age of eight, I could not now understand verbally what Mary had told me. However, this is how I remembered our meeting and it made a huge impression.

462 Conversation with Mary Stewart, 29 Jan. 2005.

463 Ibid.

464 Bertrand Russell, *Why I am Not a Christian: And Other Essays on Religion and Related Subjects*, ed. by Paul Edwards, NY, 1957, 46-7.

465 Ibid.

466 Bradley, Danielson, and Hallahan (eds.), *Identification of Learning Disabilities*, Joseph Jenkins and Rollanda O'Connor, "Chapter II: Early Identification and Intervention for Young Children with Reading/Learning Disabilities," 134. See also Hartmann, *Attention Deficit Disorder*, 67.

467 Conversation with Mary Stewart, 29 Jan. 2005.

468 Hallowell, *Connect*, 190.

469 Harvard Knowles, "A Need to Love," *The Independent School Bulletin: Environmental Education*, May 1971, 5.

470 Hallowell, *Connect*, 169.

471 Hartmann, *Attention Deficit Disorder*, 35.

472 Ibid., 38.

473 For an interesting case study proving this claim above, see Orlov, 86-8.

474 Barkley, 82, 86-7.

475 Stewart and Wendkos Olds, 59.

476 Ibid., 60.

477 Ibid.

478 Smith, *Spinoza's Book of Life*, 148-9.

479 Knowles, 5.

480 Hallowell and Ratey, *Driven to Distraction*, 37.

481 Crane, 3-4.

482 Ibid., 4-5.

483 Ibid., 5.

484 Ibid., 6.

485 Ibid., 7.

486 Ibid., 12.

487 Kozloff, 2.

488 Ibid., 10.

489 Berlin, liv.

490 Kozloff, 17-20.

491 Ibid., 20.

492 Conrad, "Editor's Introduction," 28. See also Hallowell and Ratey, *ADHD 2.0*, 53

493 Hallowell and Ratey, *ADHD 2.0*, 53

494 Hallowell, *Connect*, xvi-xvii.

495 Barkley, 83.

496 Https://afsp.org/suicide-statistics/. See also Gregor & Stone, 199.

497 Hallowell and Ratey, *ADHD 2.0*, xv.

498 Ibid., xv-xvi.

499 See Grinker, 155--70, 177-80; Hallowell and Ratey, *ADHD 2.0*, 53.

500 Hartmann, *ADD Success Stories*, 59.

501 Conversation with Jim Rose, 23 Feb. 2005.

502 Allen, 6.

503 Ibid. See also Grinker, 164-5.

504 Hartmann, *ADD Success Stories*, 15, 52.

505 Orlov, 152.

506 Hartmann, *Attention Deficit Disorder*, xxxiv-xxxv.

507 Hartmann, *ADD Success Stories*, 15, 52; Hartmann, *Attention Deficit Disorder*, xxxiv-xxxv; Kozloff, 1.

508 Hallowell and Ratey, *ADHD 2.0*, xiv.

509 In 1966, M.J.Neeley and his wife Alice founded Starpoint to develop a school that could help teach children like their severely learning disabled grandson who had been refused admission by other schools. The Neeleys endowed Starpoint through Texas Christian University and it became one of the first laboratory schools in the country for children with learning disabilities. When Alice Neely died in 1986, Mr. Neeley and his daughters decided to honor Alice for her support for Starpoint. They commissioned an artist to turn a family picture into a bronze sculpture to put in front of the school depicting Alice's mother, Mary Brazelton Snead, reading to her granddaughters. The bronze sculpture has this motto, created by Mr. Neeley, inscribed on it: "Yearning to Know." Steve Stockdale, "Yearning to Know," *ETC: A Review of General Semantics*, Vol 63, No. 4, Oct. 2006.

510 Hartmann, *ADD Success Stories*, 15, 52; Hartmann, *Attention Deficit Disorder*, xxxiv-xxxv; Kozloff, 1.

511 Plato, *The Trial and Death of Socrates: Apology*, Cambridge, 1975, 39. See also Campbell, 65.

512 Kozloff, 2.

513 Leo Tolstoy, *War and Peace*, NY, 1968, 565.

514 Hallowell and Ratey, *Delivered from Distraction*, 15-6.

515 Ibid.

516 Hallowell and Ratey, *Delivered from Distraction*, 15-6.

517 Hartmann, *ADD Success Stories*, 30; Hallowell and Ratey, *Delivered from Distraction*, 15-6; Barkley, 83; Sizer and Whitney, 482.

518 Gregor & Stone, 87.

519 Hallowell and Ratey, *ADHD 2.0*, 39-40.

520 Ibid.

521 Discussion with Laurie Bodine, 23 March 2005; Discussion with Laurie Zuspic, 27 Jan. 2005.

522 Discussion with Mary Stewart, 31 Jan. 2005.

523 This phrase comes from Juvenal, the Roman poet who lived in the late 1st and early 2nd century C.E. His full name was Decimus Junius Juvenalis.

524 Hartmann, *ADD Success Stories*, 15-6; Hartmann, *Attention Deficit Disorder*, 43, 68, 154-5.

525 Ibid.

526 Barkley, 73, 75.

527 Conversation with Laurie Zuspic, 27 Jan. 2005. Although I was not the cause of my parent's breakup, ADHD-kids often cause problems adding to marital discord. See Hallowell and Ratey, *Driven to Distraction*, 53.

528 According to Barkley, "[M]ore than 20% of children engage in theft, more than 40% drift into early tobacco and alcohol use, and more than 25% are expelled from high school because of serious misconduct" (Barkley, 19).

529 Hartmann, *Attention Deficit Disorder*, 65.

530 Harry Lorayne has developed this type of memory technique into an art form. See Harry Lorayne, *Super Power Memory*, NY, 2008.

531 Conversation with Donna Reynolds, 12 March 2021.

532 The offensive line at my school averaged around 250 pounds each, which for our small private school in 1989 was quite considerable.

533 My offensive linemen were Ryan Williamson, Traes Howard, Eric Greear, Nelson Mitchell, Tray Johnson and Chris Turner.

534 Hartmann, *Attention Deficit Disorder*, 8.

535 Albert Cook Myers, *Quaker Arrivals at Philadelphia 1682-1750: Part 1-1682-1705*, Baltimore, 1957; http://www.heritagepursuit.com/Clinton/ClintonBVernon.htm; https://www.ancestry.com/family-tree/person/tree/152494213/person/412125520928/hints?usePUBJs=true; http://linton-research-fund-inc.com/John_LINTON_1662_1709.html; http://linton-research-fund-inc.com/CANTERBURY_the_ship.html

536 https://www.exeter.edu/about-us/academy-mission

537 Recently, David Weber has fallen from grace for misconduct he committed with one of his students. According to him, he "only" hugged and kissed the

student, but also claims there was nothing sexual about it (the woman in question doesn't even remember the event). He openly has admitted to this transgression. However, the woman he supposedly kissed has no memory of it. Nonetheless, Exeter Academy has punished him by publicizing his behavior and banning him from campus. Most students of his have found the way Exeter has treated him unfair, but he, nonetheless, admits he did something he should not have. Although this event is troublesome, he still was a wonderful teacher and had a stellar career—even the woman he supposedly kissed, admits to this about him. For an article about this event, see Nancy Jo Sales, "Mr. Weber's Confession," *Vanity Fair*, Oct. 2021.

538 *Walden and Other Writings by Henry David Thoreau*, 7.
539 Knowles gave us all this mandate to think about at the beginning of reading this book, and I wrote it down in the front of my book when our class began in March 1991.
540 Knowles, 6.
541 Letter from Knowles to Rigg, 6 Aug. 2005.
542 Melville, 18.
543 Ibid., 45.
544 Ibid., 303.
545 Shakespeare, *Hamlet*, Act 3, Scent 1.
546 NIV (New International Version), 532.
547 Stephen King, *Christine*, NY, 1983.
548 Melville, 437.
549 Conversation with Stephanie Lang, 22 April 2021.
550 Interview with Jack Herney, 4 April 2020.
551 Knowles & Weber, 13.
552 Ibid.
553 Ibid., 15.
554 Ibid.
555 Ibid., 16.
556 Ibid.
557 Ibid.
558 Knowles, 6.
559 Campbell, 46.
560 Hersey, 14.
561 Hallowell and Ratey, *Driven to Distraction*, 12.
562 Ibid., 48.
563 NIV (New International Version), 857.
564 Harry Levin (ed.), *The Portable James Joyce*, NY, 1967, "A Portrait of the Artist," 373-5.
565 NIV (New International Version), 38, modern commentary entitled "A Catastrophe Sent from God—Sodom: A City that Earned Destruction," 38.

566 Melville, 70.

567 Ibid., 76.

568 Dawkins, *The God Delusion*, 311-44; Hitchens, 2007, 217-28.

569 Poe, "Arthur Gordon Pym," 1170.

570 *Portable Nietzsche*, "The Antichrist," 589.

571 NIV (New International Version), 855.

572 Richard E. Rubenstein, *When Jesus Became God: The Struggle to Define Christianity During the Last Days of Rome*, NY, 1999, 70-76, 97, 180-1.

573 Notes by psychologist Stephanie Lang, 22 May 2021.

574 Russell, 17-8.

575 The Book of Life is mentioned seven times in the book of Revelation. (See Revelation 3:5, 13:8, 17:8, 20:12, 20:15, 21:27, 22:19).

576 Knowles and Weber, "The School Community as a Moral Environment," Independent School, Dec. 1978, 13.

577 Russell, 47.

578 Knowles & Weber, 13.

579 Robert Pirsig, *Zen and the Art of Motorcycle Maintenance*, NY, 1984, 135.

580 Sam Harris, *The End of Faith: Religion, Terror, and the Future of Reason*, NY, 2004, 44.

581 Pirsig, 280, 283.

582 Tolstoy, 425.

583 Dawkins, *The God Delusion*, 318.

584 Hallowell, *Connect*, 166.

585 Russell, 46.

586 Campbell, 147.

587 Hartmann, *ADD Success Stories*, 6. See also, Sizer and Whitney, 482.

588 *The Portable James Joyce*, "The Dead," 221.

589 Conrad, "Editor's Introduction," 19.

590 Ibid., 38.

591 Gotthold Ephraim Lessing, *Nathan The Wise, Minna von Barnhelm, and Other Plays and Writings*, ed. Peter Demetz, NY, 1991, 198.

592 Hartmann, *ADD Success Stories*, 15.

593 Conversation with Melissa Orlov, 14 July 2021.

594 My most notable published student, Anthony Newpower, wrote *Iron Men and Tin Fish: The Race to Build a Better Torpedo During World War II* (Praeger, 2006).

595 Samuel Beckett, *Waiting for Godot*, NY, 1954, Act II, 52.

596 Aaron Smith, "Robin Williams: Exploring Impulsivity and Suicide," Potential Within Reach, 25 Aug. 2014: I. Sapountzis, "From Jackson Pollock to Psychic Blades: Climbing the Semiotic Ladder in Working with Children with Attention-Deficit/Hyperactivity Disorder," *Psychoanalytic Psychology*, 37 (4), 2020, 305-312; Madison Kimberlin, "Stephen King: Alchoholism, Drug

Addiction and Fame," *Detox to Rehab*, 30 March 2020; Peter Jaksa, "Good Stuff About ADHD!," *ADHD Center*, 7 March 2021; "Famous People with ADD/ADHD," *ADHD Center for Success*, 3 Oct. 2011.

597 Hersey, 358.

598 Poe, "Chronology," 1369.

599 Hartmann, *Attention Deficit Disorder*, 72, 141-4; Hallowell and Ratey, *Delivered from Distraction*, 108; Barkley, 83; Hallowell and Ratey, *Driven to Distraction*, 52.

600 Paul Lagassé (ed.), *The Columbia Encyclopedia*, NY, 2000, 2253.

601 Hartmann, *ADD Success Stories*, 12. .

602 Bradley, Danielson, and Hallahan (eds.), *Identification of Learning Disabilities*, Jim Ysseldyke, "Response to "Learning Disabilities: Historical Perspectives," 92.

603 Special thanks to psychologist Stephanie Lang for help with this phraseology. Notes by psychologist Lang, 22 May 2021. To explore the power of being positive, see Carol Dweck's *Mindset: The New Psychology of Success*.

604 In discussions with Jerry Boswell, who is a Scientologist and had some interaction with L. Ron Hubbard, he feels that Hubbard was anything but ADHD. He said he could concentrate on many things and was very well-organized. Interview Jerry Boswell, 10 Feb. 2022. However, after reading Lawrence Wright's book *Going Clear* about L. Ron Hubbard, it seems logical that he was very ADHD-like in that he had unbelievable creativity (wrote numerous science fiction books), problems with impulse control, a zany-imagination, two failed marriages, incredible energy and a religious awakening. Lawrence Wright, *Going Clear: Scientology, Hollywood, & the Prison of Belief*, NY, 2013, x, 42, 43, 44, 47, 48, 49, 58, 59, 62, 72.

605 Karl R. Popper, *Auf der Suche nach einer besseren Welt Vorträge und Aufsätze aus dreißig Jahren*, München, 1984, 79-98.

606 Russell, 162.

607 Hallowell and Ratey, *Delivered from Distraction*, 9.

608 Hallowell and Ratey, *Delivered from Distraction*, 9; Hartmann, *ADD Success Stories*, xviii.

609 Seven B. Smith, *Spinoza, Liberalism, and the Question of Jewish Identity*, New Haven, 1997, 124-5.

610 Hallowell and Ratey, *ADHD 2.0*, xvii.

611 Hallowell and Ratey, *Delivered from Distraction*, 4, 22; Hallowell and Ratey, *Driven to Distraction*, 43-4.

612 Interview Robert E. Corley, 6 Sept. 2021.

613 https://chadd.org/adhd-in-the-news/adhd-can-be-a-ceos-secret-superpower/#:~:text=Bill%20Gates%2C%20Walt%20Disney%2C%20Richard,complete%20order%20in%20their%20disorder; Gladwell, 106, 117-9.

614 Steven B. Smith, *Spinoza's Book of Life: Freedom and Redemption in the Ethics*, New Haven, 2003, 80.

615 Barkley, 43.

616 Campbell, 66.

617 Ibid., 238.

618 Carl Richard Mueller (Trans. & ed.), *Georg Büchner Complete Plays and Prose*, NY, 1963, "Danton's Death, Act I, Scene I," 3.

619 Charles H. Robertson, *Relationships, Love, Marriage, Hate, Divorce & Kinky Sex: Trials, Tribulations and Fascinating Stories of a Texas Divorce Lawyer*, Dallas, 2014, 187.

620 Conversation with Dr. Stephanie Lang, 20 July 2021.

621 Email from Rabbi Edgar Weinsberg to Bryan Rigg, 28 Oct. 2021.

622 Conversation with Rabbi Edgar Weinsberg, 18 Oct. 2021.

623 Ibid.

624 Orlov, 188.

625 Ibid.

626 Ibid.

627 To explore some of the issues academically I was experiencing with Steph, and which are sometimes common in relationships, see Baker, 194, 206-7.

628 Orlov, 207.

629 Ibid., 207-8.

630 Of course, I would not want to eliminate the three outcomes of our marriage; namely, our three wonderful children. So although I wish Steph and I never had married, I am still thankful she gave me three incredible kids.

631 Stephanie admitted to her lover, Charlie B., that she was bisexual and wanted to explore that part of her sexuality, something I had never known about her. Email from Charlie B., to Stephanie Rigg 31 March 2015, Loughmiller/ Higgins Rigg Divorce File. Charles wrote, "Stephanie, Lunch was such a wonderful surprise! Thank you. It picked me up. I have to get my head around you with a woman. More off-limits discussions about your sexual preferences. I guess I will need to become more open minded." Well, I, like Charlie, would have had a difficult time bringing another woman into my bedroom with Stephanie and maybe this was another reason why Stephanie was ready to divorce. Sexual awakenings nowadays have created stress in many relationships. I feel sorry for Stephanie if she was struggling with her sexuality because this must have been difficult for her to deal with during our marriage and would explain, to some degree, some of our problems. See also Baker, 203, 300, 304.

632 Plato, *The Trial and Death of Socrates: Apology*, Cambridge, 1975, 39. See also Campbell, 65.

633 In *The ADHD Effect on Marriage*, Melissa Orlov discusses this reality. See Orlov, 67. See also Baker, 154.

634 Melissa Orlov in her book *The ADHD Effect on Marriage* discusses how non-ADHD-people of ADHD-spouses often feel exhausted. See Orlov, 112, 122.

635 Cause No. DF-15-11173, In the Matter of the Marriage of Stephanie Dawn Rigg and Bryan Mark Rigg, In the district court, 301st Judicial District, 18 March 2016, 48.

636 Discussion with Stephanie Rigg, 25 March 2015.

637 Stephanie explored this with her lover Charlie in a biography she wrote for him about her "sad" life. Stephanie Rigg to Charlie B., Feb. 2015, Loughmiller/Higgins Rigg Divorce File.

638 Discussion with Stephanie Rigg, 25, 27, 31 March 2015. ADHD-relationship therapist Melissa Orlov says that this can often happen to couples where sex starts to feel like a chore. If this happens, Orlov strongly recommends counseling. Orlov, 207.

639 Discussion with Stephanie Rigg, 25, 27, 31 March 2015.

640 Ibid.

641 Ibid.

642 In legal depositions, although the files are full of this exchange, Stephanie has denied what she said. Soon after I had this conversation with her on 25 March 2015, I called her father about it. He in turn called Stephanie and discussed this with her. He then called me back on 28 March 2015 and said, "Bryan, Stephanie is angry. You cannot let Justin know she said this." He never denied she said this and told me he reprimanded her for saying such a thing. Conversation with Paul S., 28 March 2015. Weeks later, Stephanie's mother, Stephanie and I had a long discussion. During the conversation, Stephanie's claims about me and Justin came up. Stephanie never denied what she had said and my mother-in-law, Mary Delle S., said, "Bryan, I understand what Stephanie said is hurtful. I even remember wishing [my son] would die when he was suffering from cancer as a baby, so I know how she feels. So, this isn't something to hold against her." Conversation Mary Delle S., 9 May 2015.

643 Discussion with Stephanie Rigg, 25 March 2015.

644 See Orlov, 97, 112 for a similar case studies.

645 Orlov, 119.

646 Lovers who are having affairs often do take "pleasure" in discussing the faults of each other's partner. See Baker, 131.

647 Orlov, 101.

648 Ibid., 101-3.

649 This moral truth has also been explored by such great writers as Aesop and Mark Twain, so Chaucer is not unique in exploring this concept and phraseology. See Beryl Rowland (ed.), *Companion to Chaucer Studies*, Oxford, 1979.

650 Smith, *Spinoza's Book of Life*, 75.

651 Ibid.

652 Ibid.

653 Ibid.

654 Discussion with Stephanie Rigg, 15 June 2015.

655 <u>Ibid</u>.

656 Ibid.

657 Something that I now find strange and that some therapists have told me is a telltale sign that a partner is having an affair is when frequency of sexual intercourse increases. Well, a few months before the divorce, Steph wanted to have sex much more than usual. I thought that was great at the time, but have since learned that was a sign that her hormones were getting an extra kick-start with all the oxytocin she was receiving from her new relationship on the side. For an interesting review of this phenomenon, see Laura Kipnis's book *Against Love: A Polemic.*

658 Marisa LaScala, "The 3 Most Common Reasons Why Women Cheat, According to Relationship Experts," Yahoo Life, 3 March 2022.

659 Ibid.

660 Discussion with Stephanie Rigg, 26 April 2015.

661 Email Lori Mayfield to Bryan Rigg, 11 May 2021.

662 Discussion with Mary-Delle S., 22, 23, 24 April 2015.

663 Discussion with Paul S., 5 June 2015.

664 <u>Ibid</u>.

665 Ibid.

666 Discussion with Marilee Rigg, 11 March 2021.

667 This German medieval phrase noted that the marriage certificates, using ink and water, did not create more loyalty than blood lines of families when the certificate was violated, like adultery often does. As a result, the phrase "Blood is thicker than water," means the ink and water used to make such legal documents never can trump family relationships once a divorce starts in earnest.

668 Orlov, 5.

669 Five things shook me. One, Stephanie had been using Charlie for months to vet potential lawyers for her divorce. Email Charlie B. to Stephanie Rigg, 15 April 2015, Loughmiller/Higgins Rigg Divorce File. Secondly, she and he had reviewed each other's financial statements in order to ascertain how much they each would receive in a divorce so they would know what they would have once together. I was shocked that what Steph and I had built up from nothing had been paraded in front of her lover in order to find out how to divide it up. Since both families had similar estates, both Charlie and Stephanie were excited that when they got together, they would once again have the sizeable estates they currently had, leaving Charlie's wife and me with half of what we at that time had. Third, she was plotting with Charlie to remain married to me for one to two more years so she could use the money I was earning to get

an MBA and, then launch her career and marry Charlie. This would give him time to get a divorce and be free by the time she finished her degree. Email Stephanie Rigg to Charlie B., 18 April 2015, Loughmiller/Higgins Rigg Divorce File; Text Stephanie Rigg to Charlie B. 3 April 2015, Loughiller/ Higgins Rigg Divorce File; Charlie B. to Stephanie, 3 April 2015, Loughmiller/ Higgins Divorce File. Fourth, she sent some erotic pictures to Charlie she had sent to me only months before asking him if he would "set the neighborhood on fire" with them. Email Stephanie Rigg to Charlie B., 18 April 2015, Loughmiller/Higgins Rigg Divorce File. Loughmiller/Higgins Rigg Divorce File. Last of all, in playful banter with Charles, Stephanie talked about the possibility of doing bodily harm to me. Email Charlie B. to Stephanie Rigg, 3 April 2015; 12 April 2015. Loughmiller/Higgins Rigg Divorce File; Case No. 197676-2016 (Dallas Police Department—Stephanie Rigg Violence); Case No. 285582-2016 (Dallas Police Department—Stephanie Rigg Violence). I acknowledge now that many of the issues raised here are common to divorcing couples and that when people take their affection elsewhere, they do not necessarily behave the best. But even now, my ADHD-brain does not forget things easily that it once had hyper-focused on. I hope this chapter above helps ADHD-people prevent divorce. In short, be careful what you say about those you once loved.

670 Discussion with Stephanie Rigg, 25 March 2015. Often, women do latch themselves onto men who show promise to be successful and have the "potential of, wealth, status, stability and durability," and not for love. Baker, 144.

671 77 Robin Williams Quotes on Life (2021 Update) (quoteambition.com)

672 Poe, "Bernice," 225.

673 Poe, "The Assassination," 202.

674 Mary Stewart, who often talked to me during this time and even spoke with Stephanie on several occasions trying to put us back together, offers this insight: "I feel she was too insecure to talk about her own vulnerabilities. They grew and grew until they took over." Email Mary Stewart to Bryan Rigg, 29 Nov. 2020.

675 Orlov, 188.

676 Conversation with Stephanie Rigg, 5 Oct. 2015.

677 Faraone and Larsson, "Genetics of Attention Deficit Hyperactivity Disorder," National Library of Medicine, 11 June 2018. In this article, the authors claim that ADHD has a 74% heritability rate. See also Grimm, Kranz and Reif, "Genetics of ADHD: What Should the Clinician Know?," *The National Library of Medicine*, 27 Feb. 2020. These authors claim ADHD has almost an 80% heritability rate.

678 Special thanks to Dr. Alkek for the help with the phraseology of the above sentence.

679 Helen Fisher, *Why Him? Why Her?: How to Find and Keep Lasting Love*, NY, 2010; Helen Fisher, *Anatomy of Love: A Natural History of Mating, Marriage, and Why We Stray*, NY, 2017.

680 Frankl, x-xi.

681 Robertson, 221.

682 Ibid., 60.

683 Orlov, 196.

684 Robertson, 59.

685 See Orlov's section entitled, "The Energy and Speed of ADHD," 19-21.

686 Hemingway, 305.

687 Frankl, 58-9.

688 Walter Blanco & Jennifer Tolbert Roberts (eds.), *Herodotus: The Histories*, NY, 1992, 285, Thomas Babington MacAulay, "The Purpose and Method of History."

689 Ian Kershaw, *The Nazi Dictatorship: Problems and Perspectives of Interpretation*, NY, 1993, 217.

690 Bryan Mark Rigg, *Hitler's Jewish Soldiers: The Untold Story of Nazi Racial Laws and Men of Jewish Descent in the German Military*, Kansas, 2002, xi.

691 Rigg, *Hitler's Jewish Soldiers*, 72; Yehuda Bauer, *A History of the Holocaust*, NY, 1982, 54.

692 See Perel's book, Sally Perel, *Ich war Hitlerjunge Salomon*. Berlin, 1992.

693 Diary entry after my meeting with Dean Brodhead, 22 April 1994.

694 Professor Jeremy Noakes of Exeter University in England wrote an excellent essay in 1989 about the *Mischlinge* that helped me find archival sources. See Jeremy Noakes, "The Development of Nazi Policy towards the German-Jewish 'Mischlinge' 1933–1945." *Leo Baeck Yearbook* 34, (1989): 291–354.

695 To learn more about Stahlberg, see his memoir, Alexander Stahlberg, *Die verdammte Pflicht*, Berlin, 1987.

696 Bryan Mark Rigg, *Lives of Hitler's Jewish Soldiers: Untold Tales of Men of Jewish Descent Who Fought for the Third Reich*, Kansas,2009, 172-83; Rigg, *Hitler's Jewish Soldiers*, 29-30, 139-40, 177-8, 193, 201, 231, 257-9, 288.

697 Rigg, *Lives of Hitler's Jewish Soldiers*, 205-28.

698 Ibid., 183-92.

699 To learn about Berenbaum's work, see Michael Berenbaum, *The World Must Know: The History of the Holocaust as told in the United States Holocaust Memorial Museum*, Baltimore, 2007.

700 This number for Jewish *Mischlinge* is probably on the lower end. See Rigg, *Hitler's Jewish Soldiers*, 63-5.

701 Wiesenthal sometimes held on to strange theories about history. He was obsessed, for example, about the story that Hitler hated Jews because he had come down with syphilis by having sex with a Jewish prostitute, something

that has never been proven. Ron Rosenbaum, *Explaining Hitler: The Search for the Origins of His Evil*, NY, 1998, xxxv, 197.

702 Hallowell and Ratey, *Delivered from Distraction*, 37.

703 Tim King, "Secret of Hitler's Jewish Soldiers Uncovered," *The London Telegraph*, 3 Dec. 1996.

704 Lisl Goodman, "Insidious Omissions on Jews in War," *Sarasota Herald-Tribune*, 7 Jan. 1997; Letter Lisl Goodman to Jonathan Steinberg, 30 Jan. 1997.

705 Letter Jonathan Steinberg to Lisl Goodman, 8 Feb. 1997.

706 Ibid.

707 See Winfried Meyer, *Unternehmen Sieben. Eine Rettungsaktion für vom Holocaust Bedrohte aus dem Amt Ausland-Abwehr im Oberkommando der Wehrmacht*, Frankfurt, 1993. In Meyer's footnotes #197 and #203 (referring to passages on pages 136 and 138 respectively), Meyer thanks Rabbi Avraham Laber for translating the passages in question from Hebrew to English. When Laber directed me to the same passages, he showed me the book documenting the report given by Chaim Liebermann. Meyer failed to cite this book as the original source of Liebermann's statement. Meyer should have credited *Shumuos Vsipurim* by Rabbi Raphael N. Cohen, and published in Israel in 1977 by Kfar Chabad Publishers.

708 The phraseology above comes from a mandate called Sayre's law, named after Wallace Stanley Sayre (1905–1972), a political scientist and professor at Columbia University, NY City.

709 Clemens Heni, "Why Prof. Wolfgang Benz is Headed in the Wrong Direction," *Wissenschaft und Publizistik als Kritk*, 1 May 2009. Dr. Heni wrote this article while he was a researcher at the Yale Initiative for the Interdisciplinary Study of Anti-Semitism (YIISA), Yale University. See also Benjamin Weinthal, "Berlin Professor Slammed for Defending Nazi," *The Jerusalem Post*, 31 Jan. 2010; Interview Deidra Berger, 20 June 2014.

710 Letter from Richard Brodhead to Yale University School of Management, 5 Jan. 2001.

711 Sue Fishkoff, *The Rebbe's Army: Inside the World of Chabad-Lubavitch*, NY, 2003, 7.

712 Avrum M. Ehrlich, *Leadership in the HaBaD Movement: A Critical Evaluation of HaBaD Leadership, History, and Succession*, Northvale, 2000, 5-6, 292-5; Interview Herschel Greenberg, 23 Feb. 2004.

713 Samuel Moyn, "History's Revenge: What Happened to Jewish Faith When a New Attitude Toward the Past Emerged?", *Forward*, 9 January 2004. Moyn writes a review about David N. Myers' *"Resisting History: Historicism and Its Discontents in German-Jewish Thought."*

714 Hallowell and Ratey, *Delivered from Distraction*, 4, 22; Hallowell and Ratey, *Driven to Distraction*, 43-4.

715 Reginald Rose, *Twelve Angry Men*, NY, 1955, Act II.

716 Yehuda Bauer & Nathan Rotenstreich, *The Holocaust as Historical Experience: Was the Holocaust Predictable? What Did They Know and When?*, NY, 1981, Henry L. Feingold & Isaiah Trunk, "Discussion: *The Judenrat* and the Jewish Response," 252.

717 Two board members did defend my research and pushed against those who sided with Shindo over me. They were Laura Leppert, IJAA member and founder of *Daughters of World War II* (her father fought on Iwo) and Bonnie Haynes, IJAA member and widow of famous USMC Major General and Iwo veteran Fred Haynes. Laura Leppert, 24 May 2019; Conversation between Rigg and Iba Takamasa, 18 Nov. 2018; Conversation between Rigg and Shayne Jarosz, 26 Feb. 2019; Conversation between Rigg and Jarosz, 21 May 2019.

718 Telephone conversation with Lt. Gen. Norm Smith, 16 Jan. 2019; Letter 5 April 1968 Takeo Miki of the MOFA to U.S. Ambassador U. Alexis Johnson (National Archives Diplomatic Correspondence concerning Treaties with the U.S. and Japan); Letter Shindo to IJAA, DD Dec. 2018.

719 Conversation with VP of Military History Tours & IJAA Staff Member, Lt. Col. Raul "Art" Sifuentes, 28 Feb. 2019; Conversation with Lt. Gen. Norm Smith, IJAA President and CEO, 16 Jan. 2019; Conversation with Shayne Jarosz, VP, Educational Programs Military History Tours & Former IJAA Board Member, 22 Feb. 2019; Conversation with Bonnie Haynes, IJAA Board Member, 27 Feb. 2019; "Nationalist 'Japan Conference' Building Its Clout: Ten Days after the Meeting, Abe Officially Addressed the Issue of Revising the Pacifist Constitution," Korea JoongAng Daily, 3 May 2013; "Japanese Minister Yoshitaka Shindo Visits Yasukuni Shrine Provoking China's Ire," South China Morning Post, 1 Jan. 2014; https://www.revolvy.com/page/Yoshitaka-Shind%C5%8D; Yuki Tanaka, *Hidden Horrors: Japanese War Crimes in World War II*, Lanham, MD, 2018, xxvii, 112, 259.

720 Interview Shindo, 9 April 2018.

721 Orlov, 182; Hallowell and Ratey, *ADHD 2.0*, 12.

722 J. Tanner Watkins, Dinsmore & Shohl, LLP, to Rigg, Hershel Woodrow "Woody" Williams Book Agreement: Cease and Desist, 3 May 2018; J. Tanner Watkins, Dinsmore & Shohl, LLP, to Rigg, Hershel Woodrow "Woody" Williams Book Agreement: Cease and Desist, 18 June 2018.

723 U.S. District Court for the Southern District of WV, Hershel Woodrow "Woody" Williams verse Bryan Mark Rigg, Case 3:19-cv-00423, Doc. 1, Filed 31 May 2019, 1-20.

724 Geoffrey Harper, Winston & Strawn, LLP to J. Tanner Watkins, Dinsmore & Shohl, LLP, 9 July 2018. See also United States District Court for the Southern District of West Virginia Huntington Division, Hershel Woodrow "Woody" Williams v. Bryan Mark Rigg and John Doe Publishing Company,

Civil Action No. 3:19-CV-00423, "Bryan Rigg's Motion to Dismiss Original Verified Complaint, Doc. #9, 18 Oct. 2019 (See Appendix 1). Legal scholar and lawyer Mark Weitz wrote that Woody's "publicity claim is just not supportable" and the "state claims regarding contract are likewise weak, if not totally unsupportable." Email Mike Briggs to Rigg, 25 Dec. 2019.

725 https://www.freedomforuminstitute.org/

726 Book Agreement proposal approved by Woody for Rigg, 6 March 2018, p. 1, Sec. 7. Book Content and Publication. Draft of legal agreement drawn up by Dale Egan, VP Hershel Woody Williams Medal of Honor Foundation (HWWMHF).

727 Telephone conversation with Alex Novak, 18 June 2018.

728 Kyla Asbury, "Well-known World War II vet Woody Williams sues author, publisher over book," *West Virginia Record*, 5 June 2019; Kyla Asbury, "Author files motion to dismiss lawsuit filed by World War II veteran," *West Virginia Record*, 18 Oct. 2019; Eugene Volokh, "The Medal of Honor Recipient vs. The Historian, and the Right of Publicity," *The Volokh Conspiracy* (found at reason.com) 25 Oct. 2019; Jack Greiner, "Strictly Legal: War hero at war with book author," *The Enquirer* (Cincinnati.com), 5 Nov. 2019.

729 Telephone conversation with Judith Schnell, 12 Dec. 2019; Email Rigg to Schnell, 12 Dec. 2019.

730 Telephone conversation with Joe Skaggs, 10 Jan. 2020; Telephone conversation with Heather Carter,10 Jan. 2020.

731 Johnson, *The American People*, 205-7.

732 Philip A. Crowl and Jetek A. Isely, *The U.S. Marines and Amphibious War Its Theory and Its Practice in the Pacific*, Princeton, 1951, vi.

733 The Founding Era Collection, Thomas Jefferson Papers, Docs. Jan. 1819- 4 July 1836, Jefferson to Henry Lee, 15 May 1826.

734 Jon Hoffman, "Flamethrower," *Marine Corps Gazette: Professional Journal of U.S. Marines*, Vol. 104 No. 10, October 2020, 94-5; Andrew Milburn, "Flamethrower," *Marine Corps History*, Vol. 7. No. 1, Summer 2021, 126.

735 Speech given to Phillips Exeter Academy's graduating class of 2003 by Harvard V. Knowles.

736 *New York Times*, "New York Sues Credit Suisse Over Mortgages," 29 Nov. 2012.

737 Douglas Bloomfield, "Credit Suisse Scandal is Nothing New for Bank that Helped Nazis—Opinion," *The Jerusalem Post*, 23 February 2022; Wiesenthal Center Uncovers List of 12,000 Nazis in Argentina with Accounts Transferred to Credit Suisse, *Jewish News Syndicate*, 4 March 2022; Jane Schapiro, *Inside a Class Action: The Holocaust and the Swiss Banks*, Madison, 2003, 47, 114, 129, 131, 137, 157-9; Doug Chayka, "Revealed: Credit Suisse Leak Unmasks Criminals, Fraudsters and Corrupt Politicians," *The Guardian*, 20 Feb. 2022.

738 Discussion with Michael Berenbaum, 24 May 2014.

739 Chayka, "Revealed: Credit Suisse Leak Unmasks Criminals, Fraudsters and Corrupt Politicians," *The Guardian*, 20 Feb. 2022

740 Matthew Allen, "Ten Years After Swiss Banks agreed to Pay Back Assets to Holocaust Victims, One of the Deal's Chief Architects Said it Helped Lift a Cloud Over the Country," *Swiss News*, 11 August 2008; *The Economists*, "Banks and the Holocaust; Unsettling," 17 August 2000.

741 See Jane Schapiro's *Inside a Class Action: The Holocaust and the Swiss Banks* and Tom Boker's *Nazi Gold: The Full Story of the Fifty-Year Swiss-Nazi Conspiracy to Steal Billions from Europe's Jews and Holocaust Survivors*. The books helped start follow on research about the bank and its past. Discussion with Michael Berenbaum, 24 May 2014.

742 Rosenbaum, vii.

743 Hartmann, *Attention Deficit Disorder*, xi, 10; Hallowell and Ratey, *Delivered from Distraction*, xxx.

744 James R. Merikangas, "Hitler: Diagnosis of a Destructive Prophet," *AM J Psychiatry*, 159:6, June 2002, 1066.

745 Janet Rettig Emanuel, "Frederick Redlich, Former Dean of Yale Medical School, Dies," *Yale School of Medicine*, 12 Jan. 2004.

746 Fritz Redlich, *Hitler: Diagnosis of a Destructive Prophet*, Oxford, 1998.

747 Redlich, 266-7. See also Grinker, 142.

748 See Redlich, 266-7, 332, for information about Hitler's Hyperactivity and possible ADHD.

749 Redlich, 300.

750 Ibid., 281

751 Ibid., 223.

752 Merikangas, 1067; Redlich, xv, 232, 237, 239-44, 254, 279, 333, 338-9, 341.

753 Merikangas, 1067; Redlich, 200, 215, 219, 232-7, 253, 265, 270, 275, 293, 337, 349, 360.

754 Hallowell and Ratey, *Delivered from Distraction*, 4, 22; Hallowell and Ratey, *Driven to Distraction*, 43-4.

755 Rosenbaum, 40, 69, 87, 224, 282, 389; Redlich, 73, 103, 313.

756 Redlich, 316.

757 *The Holy Bible: Old and New Testaments in the King James Version*, Thomas Nelson Publishers, Nashville, 1976.

758 Smith, *Spinoza's Book of Life*, 80.

759 Ibid., 84.

760 Conversation Patricia Semprez, 20 Oct. 2021.

761 Best Jobs for People with ADHD (healthline.com) (www.healthline.com/health/adhd/best-jobs#lightning-pace); Jobs for People with ADHD: 16 Creative ADD Career Options (additudemag.com); The 20 Best Jobs for

People for ADHD | Fairygodboss. See also Orlov, 26; Swanepoel, Music, Launer and Reiss, "How Evolutionary Thinking Can Help Us to Understand ADHD," *Cambridge Univ. Press*, 2 Jan. 2018.

762 *Portable Nietzsche*, "Twilight of the Idols," 467.

763 Ernest Hemingway, *For Whom the Bell Tolls*, NY, 1968, 14.

764 Plato, *The Republic*, Franklin Center PA, 1975, 263-7.

765 Breaking the rules is a hallmark of being ADHD (Barkley, 29). Hopefully, one learns how to do so, not illegally, but in ways that are advantageous to his or her condition.

766 Ethics of the Fathers, Mishnah, Tractate Avot, Chapter 3: 1. See Rabbis N. Scherman and M. Zlotowitz (eds.), *The Complete Artscroll Siddur*, Brooklyn, 1984, 557.

767 Tiede, 6.

768 Hemingway, 169.

769 *Walden and Other Writings by Henry David Thoreau*, 7.

770 Stephen King, *Dark Tower Set*, NY, 2016.

771 G.W.F. Hegel, *Reason in History: A General Introduction to the Philosophy of History*, Engelwood Cliffs NJ, 1953, 23.

772 David Grossman, O*n Killing: The Psychological Cost of Learning to Kill in War and Society*, NY, 1996, 33.

773 Special thanks to Dr. David Alkek for the help with the phraseology of the above sentence.

774 Hartmann, *ADD Success Stories*, 38.

775 Ibid.

776 Dallas Philosophers Forum lecture by Dr. Paul Tobolowsky entitled "Life, Mortality and Evolution," 26 Oct. 2021.

777 Lucy Dawidowicz, *The War Against the Jews* 1933-1945, NY, 1975, 306.

778 Hegel, *Reason in History*, 29.

779 Hallowell and Ratey, *Delivered from Distraction*, xxi. Although Hallowell uses the acronym ADD, I have changed it in this book to the clinically correct acronym ADHD to prevent confusion. See Hallowell and Ratey, *Delivered from Distraction*, xxxiii, 4.

780 Tiede, 127-8.

781 Charles W. Eliot (ed.), *The Complete Poems of Milton*, Danbury, CT., 1980, John Milton, "Paradise Lost," 94.

782 Plato, *The Trial and Death of Socrates: Apology*, 39.

783 Melville, 73.

784 Bradley, Danielson, and Hallahan (eds.), *Identification of Learning Disabilities*, Sandra Britt "Response to "Learning Disabilities: Historical Perspectives," 71.

785 Hallowell and Ratey, *Delivered from Distraction*, 4. See also Zeidner, "Early ADHD Diagnoses and the Decline of Men in College," *Wall Street Journal*, 24 Sept. 2021.

786 Zeidner, "Early ADHD Diagnoses and the Decline of Men in College," *Wall Street Journal*, 24 Sept. 2021.

787 Hartmann, *Attention Deficit Disorder*, xxxi-xxxii.

788 Ibid.

789 Hartmann, *ADD Success Stories*, 4.

790 Special thanks to Dr. David Alkek for the help with the phraseology of the above sentence.

791 Samuel Beckett, *Waiting for Godot*, NY, 1954, Act II, 51.

792 Hallowell and Ratey, *Driven to Distraction*, 252.

793 Hallowell and Ratey, *ADHD 2.0*, 39-40.

794 Amanda Patterson, "Literary Birthday—17 May—Anna Brownell Jameson," Writers Write, 17 May 2016.

795 Interview with Werner Goldberg, 17 Oct. 1994; Bryan Mark Rigg, "Gefreiter Werner Goldberg," 23 July 2020, Author's Bryan Mark Rigg Facebook page (https://www.facebook.com/bryanmarkrigg/posts/4124008054307982).

796 Conrad, "Editor's Introduction," 46.

797 Campbell, 202.

798 Conrad, "Heart of Darkness," 540.

799 Speech given to Phillips Exeter Academy's graduating class of 2003 by Harvard V. Knowles.

Index

Biography:

BRYAN MARK RIGG, PhD, CFP° was born in Arlington Texas in 1971. He attended Yale University and graduated with honors in 1996 majoring in History, German Studies and English. Yale awarded him the Henry Fellowship to attend Cambridge University where he received his MA in 1997 and his PhD in 2002. He has written five books on World War II and the Holocaust: *Hitler's Jewish Soldiers* (2002), *Rescued from the Reich* (2004), *Lives of Hitler's Jewish Soldier* (2009), *The Rabbi Saved by Hitler's Soldiers* (2016) and *Flamethrower* (2020). He is currently working on a definitive historical work on the mass-murder committed by the Japanese during WWII entitled *Japan's Holocaust*. His first book *Hitler's Jewish Soldiers* won the prestigious William E. Coby Award in 2003 for the best military history book of 2002. His work has been featured in the *London Telegraph*, *New York Times* and the *Los Angeles Times*. Moreover, his work has been the subject of many TV shows and movies; namely, NBC Dateline in the US, WDR Docudrama in Germany and Channel One in Israel. He has also served as a volunteer in the Israel Army and as an officer in the United States Marine Corps. Currently, he runs his own Financial Advisory firm, Rigg Wealth Management, LLC, and is the proud, single father of three wonderful children.